T0326930

"*Introducing Medieval Biblical Interpretati* problem of explaining the methods that mediev .... to their reading of the Scriptures. Simultaneously a work of rigorous intellectual history and a handbook for recovering a lost way of reading, this book offers close readings of selected interpretive examples from across both the monastic and scholastic tradition, paying special attention to the interpretation of the letters of Paul. Those new to the tradition will find a book packed with insight into the way medieval exegetes read according to both the letter and the spirit. Scholars of medieval exegesis will find a concise introduction to a complex and still underused repertoire of well-chosen texts."

—**Rachel Fulton Brown**, author of *Mary and the Art of Prayer: The Hours of the Virgin in Medieval Christian Life and Thought*

"Levy takes the reader through the fascinating world of eight centuries of medieval exegesis. His masterful selection of texts and authors allows the story to be told by the original voices. Paraphrasing important parts of medieval commentaries, Levy navigates us securely through a wealth of texts, figures, and information. He shows exegetical methods, explains hermeneutical concepts, and grants access to the workshops of medieval exegetes. The book is a welcome guide not only for students but also for any advanced reader with an interest in biblical exegesis. Last but not least, it supports the new awareness in contemporary exegesis of tradition, intertextuality, and the manifold dynamics of biblical texts."

—**Thomas Prügl**, University of Vienna

"With crisp writing and clear organization, Levy walks readers through the ancient and medieval centuries of biblical interpretation. He lets the medieval voices speak for themselves through ample selections from primary source material, which makes this volume especially suited for classroom use. Pointing out that biblical scholars married faith and reason—though not always in balance—Levy displays how the Bible has been interpreted and reinterpreted in different cultural, intellectual, and chronological contexts. It is the proverbial 'one book' you'd place in someone's hand."

—**Christopher M. Bellitto**, Kean University

"Levy writes of the Venerable Bede, 'Bede admits that while it is true that many before him have commented on [the book of Genesis], such works might prove too difficult for most readers and complete editions too expensive. He would summarize them, therefore, taking what could be most useful to non-experts.' What Bede did for eighth-century readers Levy has done for twenty-first-century readers—taken a vast amount of information that is often available only to the specialist and made it easily and enjoyably accessible to nonexperts. For those unfamiliar with medieval biblical interpretation, this volume is a readable yet rich introduction to the topic. It lays out the broad trajectory of medieval biblical interpretation and demonstrates its relevance for the Christian church today."

—**Greg Peters**, Torrey Honors Institute, Biola University

"With discriminating erudition as deep as it is wide and unfailing clarity of exposition, Levy covers the sweep of Western Christian biblical exegesis from the church fathers to the fifteenth century. As he shows, whether as monks, pastors, or masters in the schools, medieval exegetes had more in common than has sometimes been imagined. To one degree or another, they all drew on multilevel and intertextual exegesis as well as on the secular learning at their command. And while they all accepted the divine inspiration of the text and the authority of earlier commentators, they also took seriously their right and duty to draw selectively on scriptural texts and traditions along with their personal insights in applying the Bible to their own situational, devotional, pedagogical, and polemical agendas. Levy's book provides a rich banquet for both specialist and nonspecialist readers interested in the history of biblical exegesis and offers food for thought for scholars currently engaged in biblical study."

—**Marcia L. Colish**, Oberlin College; visiting fellow
in history, Yale University

INTRODUCING
Medieval Biblical
Interpretation

INTRODUCING
Medieval Biblical Interpretation

The Senses of Scripture in Premodern Exegesis

Ian Christopher Levy

Baker Academic

a division of Baker Publishing Group
Grand Rapids, Michigan

© 2018 by Ian Christopher Levy

Published by Baker Academic
a division of Baker Publishing Group
PO Box 6287, Grand Rapids, MI 49516-6287
www.bakeracademic.com

Printed in the United States of America

Library of Congress Cataloging-in-Publication Data
Names: Levy, Ian Christopher, author.
Title: Introducing medieval biblical interpretation : the senses of scripture in premodern exegesis / Ian Christopher Levy.
Description: Grand Rapids : Baker Academic, 2018. | Includes index.
Identifiers: LCCN 2017040939 | ISBN 9780801048807 (pbk. : alk. paper)
Subjects: LCSH: Bible—Criticism, interpretation, etc.—History—Middle Ages, 600–1500.
Classification: LCC BS500 .L48 2018 | DDC 220.609/02—dc23
LC record available at https://lccn.loc.gov/2017040939

Unless otherwise indicated, all translations of primary source material are the author's.

18 19 20 21 22 23 24   7 6 5 4 3 2 1

In memory of my father,
Alan M. Levy

Contents

Preface

A great deal of work has been done in the field of medieval biblical hermeneutics over the past eighty years since Beryl Smalley first published her path-
breaking *Study of the Bible in the Middle Ages*. There is, of course, Henri
de Lubac's multivolume *Exégèse médiévale* to consider, and more recently
the prodigious scholarship of Gilbert Dahan, principally exemplified by his
L'exégèse chrétienne de la Bible en Occident médiéval. This is only the tip
of the iceberg, though, as one could go on for pages recounting the work of
many eminent scholars. Thus when I agreed to take on the task of writing
this volume for Baker Academic Press, it all seemed a bit overwhelming. It
was not clear to me at first how I could get a handle on the vast amounts of
primary and secondary material so as to produce a coherent account. My fears
were gradually allayed, however, as I found that the durable threads that run
through the centuries would lead me along from one exegete to another and
from one theme to the next. The continuity inherent in this sacred tradition
proved to be an internal guide.

In many ways I have followed a conventional path in structuring the book,
which moves in orderly fashion across the centuries, with some periods given
more attention than others. For the most part, I devote sections within chapters
to particular exegetes who best exemplify some period or genre of exegesis.
An attempt, moreover, has been made to display the active work of the medieval exegetes, to let them speak for themselves with minimal interference.
If I have succeeded, the diligent reader of this volume will have ingested a
good deal of medieval biblical exegesis. This is a modest book, perhaps, but
it is thick with primary material, the translations of which are my own unless
otherwise indicated.

It would have been impossible to begin, let alone complete, the present
volume if one did not also rely on the efforts of modern scholars whose facility

with the sources is both staggering and inspiring. Like Bernard of Chartres, I too was able to stand on the shoulders of giants even if I could not do full justice to all that I have learned from them. I remain grateful for the assistance of these scholars, some of whom I have been able to consult personally and to work with in other projects over the years. To name just a few: Marcia Colish, Boyd Coolman, Franklin Harkins, Philip Krey, Frans van Liere, Thomas Prügl, and Thomas Ryan. When this book had reached the stage of near-final draft, I sent it to David Nelson, the editor at Baker Academic who has been overseeing the project. He took the time to read it all very carefully and offer valuable comments. I am thankful to him for all of his encouragement, guidance, and dedication. Warm thanks are owed also to Wells Turner and the entire team at Baker for their excellent work in bringing this volume to press. Last, I want to express my gratitude to my wife, Michelle, for her consistent support throughout this and so many other endeavors.

Abbreviations

General and Bibliographic

CCCM   Corpus Christianorum: Continuatio Mediaevalis. Turnhout: Brepols, 1966–.
CCSL   Corpus Christianorum: Series Latina. Turnhout: Brepols, 1953–.
CSEL   Corpus Scriptorum Ecclesiasticorum Latinorum. Vienna, 1866–.
DRA   Douay-Rheims, 1899 American edition
Eng.   English Bible versification
FC   Fathers of the Church. Washington, DC: Catholic University of America Press, 1947–.
fol(s).   folio(s)
LCL   Loeb Classical Library. Cambridge, MA: Harvard University Press, 1912–.
MS   manuscript
MT   Masoretic Text
PL   Patrologia Latina [= *Patrologiae Cursus Completus*. Series Latina]. Edited by Jacques-Paul Migne. 217 vols. Paris, 1844–55.
SC   Sources chrétiennes. Paris: Cerf, 1943–.
ST   Thomas Aquinas, *Summa theologiae*
Vulg.   Vulgate versification

Old Testament

Gen.	Genesis	1 Sam.	1 Samuel
Exod.	Exodus	2 Sam.	2 Samuel
Lev.	Leviticus	1 Kings	1 Kings
Num.	Numbers	2 Kings	2 Kings
Deut.	Deuteronomy	1 Chron.	1 Chronicles
Josh.	Joshua	2 Chron.	2 Chronicles
Judg.	Judges	Ezra	Ezra
Ruth	Ruth	Neh.	Nehemiah

Esther	Esther	Joel	Joel
Job	Job	Amos	Amos
Ps(s).	Psalm(s)	Obad.	Obadiah
Prov.	Proverbs	Jon.	Jonah
Eccles.	Ecclesiastes	Mic.	Micah
Song	Song of Songs	Nah.	Nahum
Isa.	Isaiah	Hab.	Habakkuk
Jer.	Jeremiah	Zeph.	Zephaniah
Lam.	Lamentations	Hag.	Haggai
Ezek.	Ezekiel	Zech.	Zechariah
Dan.	Daniel	Mal.	Malachi
Hosea	Hosea		

New Testament

Matt.	Matthew	1 Tim.	1 Timothy
Mark	Mark	2 Tim.	2 Timothy
Luke	Luke	Titus	Titus
John	John	Philem.	Philemon
Acts	Acts	Heb.	Hebrews
Rom.	Romans	James	James
1 Cor.	1 Corinthians	1 Pet.	1 Peter
2 Cor.	2 Corinthians	2 Pet.	2 Peter
Gal.	Galatians	1 John	1 John
Eph.	Ephesians	2 John	2 John
Phil.	Philippians	3 John	3 John
Col.	Colossians	Jude	Jude
1 Thess.	1 Thessalonians	Rev.	Revelation
2 Thess.	2 Thessalonians		

Old Testament Apocrypha / Deuterocanonical Books

Sir./Ecclus.	Sirach/Ecclesiasticus
Wis.	Wisdom of Solomon

Introduction

Saint Jerome provided the medieval exegetical tradition with an evocative image of peeling back the outer leaves of the letter to get at the rich marrow of meaning beneath the text's surface. Repeated in one form or another across the centuries, this organic depiction of Scripture with its rough husk and sweet fruit succinctly captures the spirit of medieval biblical hermeneutics. It is premised upon the conviction that Holy Scripture is a sacred text replete with mysteries to be quarried by faithful readers in their quest for an ever deeper understanding of the Triune God. The exegetes whom we will encounter in this volume were committed to the principle that Scripture was composed under the direction of a divine author in the person of the Holy Spirit, and they believed that any attempt to comprehend this sacred text was possible only under this same Spirit's guidance.

Yet we may still be left to ask whether medieval hermeneutics has any continuing relevance in an age dominated by the historical-critical method. Even were we to grant that the medieval quest for deeper spiritual senses beneath the text yielded beautiful and stirring theological insights, can we honestly endorse its presuppositions and methods? Has not more than a century of higher criticism put paid to all those allegorical readings of the biblical text, lovely as they might have been? By way of an answer, we ought first to offer some basic definition of the historical-critical method. As defined by the Pontifical Biblical Commission in its comprehensive review of scriptural interpretation issued in 1993, it is "historical" insofar as "it seeks to shed light upon the historical processes which gave rise to biblical texts," and critical in that "it operates with the help of scientific criteria that seek to be as objective as possible."[1] Yet even as the commission affirmed the significant contributions that historical criticism has made to biblical studies, that method's limitations

---

1. Pontifical Biblical Commission, *The Interpretation of the Bible in the Church* (Boston: St. Paul Books and Media, 1993), 38.

were also acknowledged. For by restricting itself to the text's meaning within its own historical circumstances, historical criticism ignores other possible meanings that may have been revealed to later generations of faithful interpreters throughout the church's history.[2]

Clearly, then, a balance must be struck that at once acknowledges the irreversible advances made by the historical-critical method even as one affirms the church's lasting commitment to the deeper spiritual senses beyond the immediate historical circumstances of the text. In this vein, the Pontifical Biblical Commission asserted that "one must reject as unauthentic every interpretation alien to the meaning expressed by the human authors in their written text. To admit the possibility of such alien meanings would be equivalent to cutting off the biblical message from its root, which is the Word of God in its historical communication." Nevertheless, the commission also cautioned that "there are reasons . . . for not taking 'alien' in so strict a sense as to exclude all possibility of higher fulfillment. The paschal event, the death and resurrection of Jesus, has established a radically new historical context, which sheds fresh light upon the ancient texts and causes them to undergo a change in meaning." For the faithful, a sense of continuity between the Old and the New Testaments emerges when one trusts that "the Holy Spirit, principal author of the Bible, can guide human authors in the choice of expressions in such a way that the latter will express a truth the fullest depths of which the authors themselves do not perceive." Here, then, we have what the commission calls the "fuller sense" (*sensus plenior*), "defined as a deeper meaning of the text, intended by God but not clearly expressed by the human author."[3] We ought to point out here that such hermeneutical principles are not the sole province of Roman Catholicism. The renowned Protestant biblical scholar Brevard Childs has also argued that "allegory or typology, when properly understood and practiced, remains an essential part of Christian interpretation."[4]

At the conclusion of this volume, we will revisit questions of medieval and modern hermeneutical strategies to see if there may not be a good deal of common ground after all. In the remainder of the introduction, though, I will say a few words about what to expect in this volume. The material covered spans some one thousand years from late antiquity up until the eve of the Reformation. Perhaps the very first issue to be clarified is that, when discussing premodern exegesis, we are by no means reverting to a period lacking in scholarly sophistication. Origen of Alexandria and then Jerome, just to name

2. Ibid., 41.
3. Ibid., 84–87.
4. Brevard Childs, *Biblical Theology: A Proposal* (Philadelphia: Fortress, 2002), 71.

two especially astute commentators, were extremely adept at working through the many philological and lexical challenges that their texts presented. These men, along with Augustine of Hippo and the Venerable Bede, set the course for the centuries that followed. The establishment of a reliable Latin text, well grounded in the Hebrew and Greek originals, was considered essential from the Carolingian period straight through into the fifteenth century. This concern was itself grounded in the bedrock hermeneutical principle that the search for meaning begins with a solid grasp of the text's literal-historical sense. Perhaps no two medieval exegetes will better exemplify this commitment than the twelfth-century Augustinian canon Hugh of St. Victor and the fourteenth-century Franciscan friar Nicholas of Lyra.

So it was that the medieval exegetes, like modern practitioners of the historical-critical method, were attuned to the nuances of ancient languages, textual variations, and cultural contexts in which these books were produced. As we have seen, though, the medieval exegete then goes further, since his analysis does not end with the establishment of the literal-historical sense of the text. That sense is not an end but rather a foundation on which a greater edifice of meaning is constructed. Presupposing as they did the divine authorship of Holy Scripture (*sacra scriptura*), medieval exegetes maintained that the God of history had imbued events, places, and people with spiritual significance such that they could point beyond themselves to deeper salvific realities. In fact, the more one knew about everything from geography to botany, the better equipped one was to plumb the depths of the biblical text and unveil its mysteries. The sacred page (*sacra pagina*) and the created order depicted therein came to serve as a mirror (*speculum*) reflecting the saving work of the divine author across the plane of human history.

The points sketched above regarding the fecundity of meaning to be discovered through the techniques of medieval hermeneutics form the subject matter of our book. The opening chapter will be devoted to the patristic era, skimming the surface as we must, but still setting out the principles that guided the exegetes of later centuries. Here we will encounter not only Origen of Alexandria but also Diodore and Theodore of the Antiochene tradition. From there our attention turns to the West: Augustine of Hippo, Gregory the Great, John Cassian (who had himself learned from the Eastern monks), and finally Jerome. So great was the influence of these writers, not only evinced in the consistent citation of their work across the ages but more fundamentally in the adoption of their greater hermeneutical vision, that one could scarcely make sense of medieval exegesis apart from them.

At this point we move into the earlier Middle Ages (chap. 2), beginning with the eighth-century Anglo-Saxon monk and scholar Bede, whom later generations actually counted among the fathers. We will then cross the English Channel and look at the scholarship produced on the Continent during the Carolingian Renaissance, really an ambitious reform program that placed classical erudition at the service of biblical exegesis. These efforts cemented in the consciousness of northern European Christendom the need for rigorous training in the liberal arts as a prerequisite for the study of Scripture and theological analysis.

The seeds sown in the ninth century were steadily blooming in the cathedral schools of the eleventh century (chap. 3), notably evinced in the commentaries on the Psalms and Pauline epistles produced by Bruno of Cologne. The letters of the apostle Paul, which were already receiving sustained attention among Carolingians such as Haimo of Auxerre, increasingly assumed a position of importance in the French schools because of their rich theological content. Paul's works were carefully analyzed so as to uncover the inherent logical structure of their arguments, dealing with central questions of ecclesiology, sacraments, and soteriology.

Three chapters in this volume are devoted to exegesis in the twelfth century (chaps. 4–6). We will look first at the monastic tradition, beginning with the Benedictines and concluding with two giants of the Cistercian tradition. The monastics were men and women whose lives were formed by the rule they lived by in the monastery, this "school of Christ" (*schola Christi*) marked by prayerful reading (*lectio divina*), through which the exegete entered meditatively into the world of the biblical text. Along with the men we will be reading in this chapter—Rupert of Deutz, Bernard of Clairvaux, and William of Saint Thierry—we will also examine the works of the brilliant abbess Hildegard of Bingen. All of these monastic exegetes, although perhaps especially Bernard and William, exhibit an intimacy with the person of Christ that is both remarkable and encouraging.

Of the chapters devoted to twelfth-century exegesis, chapter 5 focuses exclusively on the school of Augustinian canons working in the Abbey of St. Victor, on the outskirts of Paris. The leader of this school, Hugh of St. Victor, insisted on the careful analysis owed to the literal-historical sense of the text as the foundation laid for the spiritual senses. Contemplation of these spiritual senses would then facilitate the spiritual re-formation of the reader that was the goal of the canons' sacred studies. Even though most of our attention is given to Hugh in this chapter, we will also look at Richard and Andrew, who made major exegetical contributions in their own right, the latter exhibiting a keen interest in the work of the Jewish biblical scholars flourishing in France at this time.

The final chapter on the twelfth century (chap. 6) takes us back to the cathedral schools of northern France, first Laon and then Paris. It was the

Laon school that produced the *Glossa Ordinaria*, the standard commentary on Scripture that henceforth became a staple of the medieval classroom. Now the entire Bible could be read with the commentary tradition quite literally at one's fingertips, for in the margins and even between the lines were embedded snippets of patristic exegesis on a given passage, the raw material for which was often culled from earlier Carolingian collections. The schools were also the place of increasingly sophisticated and substantial theological analysis as difficult questions that arose from the morning's exegetical sessions were given sustained attention in the afternoon. It was here in the twelfth-century schools that theology began to come into its own as a science; now doctrinal questions could be treated separately from exegesis. Nevertheless, the scriptural basis for all church teaching was never lost sight of; the sacred page remained the font of divine revelation.

The longest single chapter in this volume (chap. 7) discusses the late medieval universities, running from the thirteenth to the fifteenth centuries. Here we enter the age of the licensed master of theology, whose very title testifies to his commitment to lecturing on Holy Scripture: "*magister sacrae paginae.*" It is now the mendicant orders that take center stage, principally the Dominicans and Franciscans who began to arrive at the University of Paris in the first half of the thirteenth century. We will not only read the likes of Thomas Aquinas, Bonaventure, Peter John Olivi, and Nicholas of Lyra; we will also turn to leading secular masters such as Henry of Ghent, John Wyclif, and Jean Gerson, in addition to Paul of Sainte-Marie, a convert from Judaism who responded to the work of Nicholas of Lyra. Of principal interest to us in this chapter will be the exegetical theories that these masters constructed, especially with regard to matters of authorship, authorial intention, and the multivalence of a text's literal sense.

That we may not be confined to theory and thus detached from the practical application of biblical hermeneutics to the life of the late medieval church, a brief chapter (chap. 8) traces the ways in which some of these same commentators analyzed biblical texts central to defining the role of the papacy. Most noteworthy in this section will be the ways in which exegetes offered nuanced positions that carefully balanced different New Testament texts, permitting one passage to aid in the interpretation of another, so as to render determinations on the controversial contemporary issue of the scope of papal authority.

The conclusion will bring us back to some of the questions addressed here in the introduction as we ask, "Can medieval biblical exegesis speak to us today?" This will allow us to delve ever so slightly into some principles of modern hermeneutical theory and maybe even to conclude that the medieval exegetes could actually be quite up to date!

1

The Age of the Fathers

"The Gospel is not located in the bare words [*verbis*] of the Scriptures but in their deeper meaning [*in sensu*], not in outward appearances but in the marrow, and not in the leaves of the sayings but in the root of their reason [*non in sermonum foliis, sed in radice rationis*]."[1] So said Jerome in his commentary on the Epistle to the Galatians. Although there are many passages that one might draw from the fathers to this effect, none would convey any more concisely the patristic conception of Holy Scripture's multifarious layers of meaning. If this saint wanted authorization for seeking mystical designations beneath the letter of the biblical text, he needed to look no further than the apostle Paul's own momentous appeal to allegory when addressing the Galatians:

> For it is written that Abraham had two sons, one by a slave woman and the other by a free woman. One, the child of the slave, was born according to the flesh; the other, the child of the free woman, was born through the promise. Now this is an allegory [*allēgoroumena*]: these women are two covenants. One woman, in fact, is Hagar, from Mount Sinai, bearing children for slavery. Now Hagar is Mount Sinai in Arabia and corresponds to the present Jerusalem, for she is in slavery with her children. But the other woman corresponds to the Jerusalem above; she is free, and she is our mother. (4:22–26)

So it was that when Jerome reviewed this passage in his commentary, he observed that allegory properly belongs to the art of grammar and differs from metaphors and other tropes. Noting that allegory is an instance of one

1. *Comm. in Epistolam ad Galatas* (PL 26:322c–d).

thing being signified in the words and another in the meaning, Jerome proceeded to point out that while allegories are to be found among the orators and poets, they are also employed in Holy Scripture.[2] Trained in classical grammar by the esteemed master Donatus, Jerome recognized, as did so many of his contemporaries, that Scripture could be mined for its grammatical, rhetorical, and dialectical riches. Yet Scripture possesses a quality that none of the great texts of antiquity could boast; it has a divine author whose limitless gift for subtle discourse renders it an inexhaustible trove of sacred mystery. It is in this vein that our opening chapter on the patristic period seeks, however modestly, to establish the exegetical modus operandi that formed the foundation for centuries of biblical interpretation across the Middle Ages. To be sure, medieval scholars made great and original advances in the study of Scripture; there were brilliant thinkers among their ranks. Nevertheless, the church fathers remained their authorities; they showed the way and provided the warrant for the progress made in the monasteries and the schools of medieval Europe.

Writing in the final decades of the second century, Irenaeus of Lyons established an abiding exegetical principle: Scripture in its totality will be rendered coherent only when Christ the Word is understood to stand at the center of salvation history as it has been recorded across the Old and New Testaments. Both Testaments, in seamless continuity, relate the action of the divine Word throughout sacred time, culminating in the Word's incarnation. Old Testament prophecies are to be adduced as proof of history's fulfillment in the incarnate Word, who thereby confirms the unified work of the Triune God, and the revelation of his will, across both Testaments.[3] Thus, as Irenaeus combated both gnostics and Marcionites, he insisted that there is only one God, whom the prophets proclaimed and Christ himself confessed to be his Father. Rather than severing the relationship between the God of the Old Testament and the Christ of the New, therefore, we ought to recognize that the Father and Son bear testimony to each other.[4] For Christ the Word was already active in the law and the prophets, proclaiming the Father, and through the incarnation, the Father was thereby manifested in the visible Son.[5] The principle of unity

2. *Comm. in Epistolam ad Galatas* (PL 26:389c).

3. See Bernard Sesboüé, "La preuve par les Écritures chez saint Irénée," *Nouvelle Revue Théologique* 103 (1981): 872–87; D. Farkasfalvy, "Theology of Scripture in St. Irenaeus," *Revue Bénédictine* 78 (1968): 319–33; and Dennis Minns, "Truth and Tradition: Irenaeus," in *The Cambridge History of Christianity*, ed. Margaret M. Mitchell and Frances M. Young (Cambridge: Cambridge University Press, 2006), 1:261–73.

4. *Adversus haereses* 4.2.1–5, ed. Adelin Rousseau and Louis Doutreleau, 5 vols., SC 211 (Paris: Cerf, 1965–82), 4:397–406.

5. *Adversus haereses* 4.6.6 (SC 211, 4:448–50).

proves to be a divine person, the one author who is the eternal Word of God.[6] As the final cause of the law (Rom. 10:4), Christ brought to culmination what he himself had brought into being in the first place.[7]

If a person stands at the center of salvation history and proves to be the axis on whom this history turns, then the authoritative interpretation of that history could be located in what Irenaeus designated the "rule of truth" (*regula veritatis*), that standard against which every reading of Scripture must be measured.[8] It was in this same vein that Tertullian appealed to the "rule of faith" (*regula fidei*), which he ultimately traced back to Christ himself. This *regula fidei* was not a fixed formula, but rather a basic outline of orthodox doctrine.[9] It came to serve as a hermeneutical key to Scripture that provided a coherent story line (*hypothesis*) reflecting the arrangement (*oikonomia*) of its divine author. So it was that Irenaeus could accuse the gnostics of substituting their own story for that of Scripture and thus distorting the meaning of the text in the process.[10] Such appeals to a unifying theme were not unique to Irenaeus and Tertullian or even to Christian authors generally. The Neoplatonists also employed this hermeneutic when they determined that the dialogues of Plato must, like a living organism, have one purpose (*telos*), a single perspective (*skopos*).[11] In the fourth century, for example, Athanasius argued against the Arians that his reading of Scripture was correct with regard to the divine status of the Son because it accorded with the rule of faith, which provided access to the mind (*dianoia*) of Scripture. Recent interpretations might therefore take precedence over older readings if they are found to cohere with this overarching *dianoia*.[12]

The Literal and the Allegorical

As we touched on above, to allegorize means most basically "to speak so as to imply other than what is said."[13] The Stoics allegorized many myths about

6. *Adversus haereses* 4.9.1 (SC 211, 4:480).
7. *Adversus haereses* 4.12.4 (SC 211, 4:518).
8. *Adversus haereses* 1.9.4 (SC 211, 1/2:150).
9. *De praescriptione haereticorum* 13 (CCSL 1:197–98). See also L. W. Countryman, "Tertullian and the Regula Fidei," *The Second Century* 2 (1982): 208–27.
10. Joseph Trigg, "The Apostolic Fathers and Apologists," in *The History of Biblical Interpretation*, ed. A. Hauser and D. Watson (Grand Rapids: Eerdmans, 2003), 1:328–29.
11. Frances Young, *Biblical Exegesis and the Formation of Christian Culture* (Grand Rapids: Baker Academic, 2002), 25.
12. Ibid., 44–45.
13. H. G. Liddell and Robert Scott, *Greek-English Lexicon*, abridged ed. (Oxford: Clarendon, 1986), 35.

the gods so as to make them suitable to their own sensibilities and philo-sophical system. Classical authors applied the method of *allēgorēsis* to their great ancient texts; the Neoplatonist Porphyry, for instance, provided an al-legorical reading of Homer. Moreover, these Greek practitioners of *allēgorēsis* maintained that the deeper meaning was, in fact, the intended meaning of the myth and that mythical texts may indeed have more than one sense, such that there exists a hierarchy of meanings. Jewish exegetes also adopted this method as the philosopher Philo of Alexandria argued that the Torah was rich in philosophy beneath the surface of its various legal prescriptions. Philo did not discount the literal meaning of the Hebrew Bible, but it was for him of secondary importance. Elite readers searched out the hidden meanings, which revealed spiritual truths. The story of creation in Genesis, for instance, could be read as a meditation on the different aspects of human nature so that Adam represents the intelligence, Eve human sensitive faculties, and the beasts of the garden the passions.[14] It was within this wider intellectual climate that Christians of the second and third centuries developed sophisticated allegori-cal approaches to their own sacred texts. Clement of Alexandria sought out what he called the "*epopteia*," which is the hidden meaning of the biblical text there to be plumbed by the experienced exegete.[15] Central to this entire enterprise, however, was a basic principle that the Christians of late antiquity had inherited from their pagan forebears: texts were to be studied for the sake of moral improvement, for advancing in virtue.[16] Thus for the patristic commentators, as Frances Young writes, "the purpose of biblical exegesis, implicit and explicit, was to form the practice and belief of Christian people, individually and collectively."[17]

Origen of Alexandria

Origen of Alexandria, who flourished in the middle of the third century, was a foundational figure in the history of Western exegesis. Although generally known for his sometimes elaborate allegorical readings of Scripture, Origen was nevertheless a very careful scholar fully attuned to the complexities of the biblical text and biblical history. He believed that text criticism must be

14. Manlio Simonetti, *Biblical Interpretation in the Early Church: An Historical Introduc-tion to Patristic Exegesis*, trans. John Hughes (Edinburgh: T&T Clark, 1994), 5–7; and Mark Edwards, "Figurative Readings: Their Scope and Justification," in *The New Cambridge History of the Bible*, 4 vols. (Cambridge: Cambridge University Press, 2013), 1:714–33, esp. 716–20.
    15. Simonetti, *Biblical Interpretation*, 34–37.
    16. Young, *Biblical Exegesis*, 248–63.
    17. Ibid., 299.

the first step of the exegetical process. One then launched into the explanation (*exēgētikon*), which entails determining the meaning of the usage of words (*glōssēmatikon*). From there one proceeded to historical analysis (*historikon*), followed by grammatical analysis (*technikon*), and then the work of discerning figures of speech. Having finally arrived at the foundation of the narrative, one then sought out the deeper meaning, or intention (*skopos*), of the text.[18] That is why Origen insisted that to understand the biblical authors, one must read them possessed of the same Holy Spirit as indwelt the authors themselves as they wrote. To grasp the full import of the gospels, one should have the mind (*nous*) of Christ, which itself is a gift of the Spirit.[19]

Even as Origen sought the spiritual meaning of the text, that which would facilitate the soul's deeper union with God, the history recorded in Scripture always remained profoundly meaningful for him. As Henri de Lubac has shown, Origen grounded his exegesis in the incarnate Christ: word was united to flesh just as spirit to letter. In Origen's view, many events in the Old Testament are recounted in Scripture precisely for their greater christological meaning. More specifically, Origen looked to the centrality of the sacrifice of Christ on the cross as being at the heart of the mystery of salvation.[20] As Scripture turns on the axis of the cross, the study of Scripture must be the highest expression of the Christian life. As Origen saw it, to immerse oneself in biblical exegesis was a lofty and demanding vocation that could be likened to the call of the Old Testament priests and Levites. Those engaged in scriptural studies have raised themselves above the world of flesh and blood to contemplate things of the spirit; they have set aside the pleasures of the flesh for contemplation.[21] For all of the controversy that surrounded Origen in the centuries after his death, his exegetical works had a profound influence throughout the West. This was in no small part facilitated by the Latin translations of those works made by Rufinus and Jerome, thereby extending his readership. It seems safe to say that it was really Alexandrian exegesis, rather than Antiochene, that ultimately carried the day in the Western church deep into the Middle Ages.[22]

In the fourth book of his massive *On First Principles*, Origen succinctly laid out his own exegetical method. First he affirmed that the Old Testament

---

18. Mark W. Elliot, "Exegetical Genres in the Patristic Era," in *New Cambridge History of the Bible*, 1:775–97.

19. Henri Crouzel, *Origen: The Life and Thought of the First Great Theologian*, trans. A. S. Worrall (San Francisco: Harper & Row, 1989), 74–75.

20. Henri de Lubac, *History and Spirit: The Understanding of Scripture according to Origen* (1950; San Francisco: Ignatius, 2007), 103–204.

21. Peter W. Martens, *Origen and Scripture: The Contours of an Exegetical Life* (Oxford: Oxford University Press, 2012), 89–106.

22. Simonetti, *Biblical Interpretation*, 88–90.

Scriptures, which prophesy about Christ and demonstrate his divinity, are each divinely inspired (*divinitus inspirata/theopneustos*). Hence those writings that announced Christ's coming and his teaching speak with full power and authority.[23] The advent of Jesus Christ has, in turn, opened the eyes of readers who might have otherwise been skeptical about the divinity of the law and the prophets, showing them that these writings were indeed composed with the help of divine grace. The light present in the law of Moses, but previously hidden under a veil, has begun to shine forth with Christ's advent. The veil had been finally removed, and the good things, whose shadow the letter (*littera/ gramma*) displayed, gradually came to be fully known.[24] That people may miss the greater import of such things is certainly not the fault of Scripture itself. The divinity of Scripture, which pertains to all of its parts, is in no way undermined by human weakness. It is owing to our own frailty, Origen says, that we cannot discern the hidden splendor of its teaching concealed within what might otherwise be regarded as the lowly and contemptible literal sense.[25]

It is for lack of a proper reading strategy that the salvific import of the Scriptures is so often missed. Countless errors arise, Origen says, because so many people have failed to find the path that governs the exploration of these holy books. First, there are Jews who were bound to the strict literal sense of the prophecies that foretold Christ's coming. When the promises of the prophets were not explicitly fulfilled according to the letter at Christ's advent, they refused to receive him.[26] Then there are the Marcionites, who also read Old Testament passages too literally and have thus developed the notion of an imperfect creator-god who is a source of malevolent action in the cosmos.[27] Finally, there are the simpler Christian people, who, in their naïveté, attribute to God all sorts of unfitting features.[28] As Origen sees it, all of these false opinions can be traced back to a failure to understand Scripture in the spiritual sense (*secundum spiritalem sensum / kata pneumatika*); it must always be remembered that we are dealing not with the writings of human authors but rather with works that have been inspired by the Holy Spirit, by the will of the Father through Jesus Christ.[29] Thus, as exegetes work through various

---

23. *De principiis* 4.1.6, in *Origenes Vier Bücher von den Prinzipien*, ed. Herwig Görgemanns and Heinrich Karpp (Darmstadt: Wissenschaftliche Buchgesellschaft, 1976), 686–88. See the English translation in *Biblical Interpretation in the Early Church*, trans. and ed. Karlfried Froehlich (Philadelphia: Fortress, 1984), 52.

24. *De principiis* 4.1.6 (Görgemanns and Karpp, 686–88; Froehlich, 53).

25. *De principiis* 4.1.7 (Görgemanns and Karpp, 690–92; Froehlich, 53).

26. *De principiis* 4.2.1 (Görgemanns and Karpp, 694–96; Froehlich, 54–55).

27. *De principiis* 4.2.1 (Görgemanns and Karpp, 698–700; Froehlich, 55).

28. *De principiis* 4.2.1 (Görgemanns and Karpp, 698–700; Froehlich, 55–56).

29. *De principiis* 4.2.2 (Görgemanns and Karpp, 700–702; Froehlich, 56).

passages in Scripture, many of which are rich in spiritual meanings, they must always keep in mind the greater purpose, or perspective (*skopos*), of the Holy Spirit. It is the Spirit, with the grand sweep of salvation history in his sights, who has enlightened the prophets and apostles regarding these great mysteries.[30]

That one might not accuse him of generating his methods out of whole cloth, Origen was quick to see that Scripture itself provides warrant for the exegetical techniques that he proposes. The three levels of scriptural meaning that Origen located in Scripture had already been set forth by Solomon: "And you, write down those things threefold in your counsel and wisdom that you may reply with the words of truth to those who ask of you" (Prov. 22:20–21). The three levels of Scripture correspond to a basic anthropological model whereby each human being is composed of flesh, soul, and spirit in ascending order. It was along these lines that different readers, depending on their exegetical sophistication, could find something valuable in the text. The simple person may be edified by the flesh of Scripture, its obvious historical meaning; the somewhat more advanced by its soul, or moral sense; but the perfect by the spiritual sense of the contemplative.[31] Thus, while not discounting the first two levels, Origen insisted that this last and highest level is reserved for those readers equipped to identify heavenly realities.[32] Origen was not, however, attempting to classify, or rank, believers according to some inherent capacity to grasp the truth. Rather, as Young observes, Origen envisioned the work of the biblical exegete as assisting fellow Christians to make their way. Each level was suitable for people at different stages of their journey: purification, knowledge, and finally union with God. Holy Scripture's three levels could thus provide each person, at whatever stage in life, with a meaning befitting their present state.[33]

The actual practice of biblical interpretation that facilitated spiritual ascent could be arduous; in fact, it was not intended to be easy. Some of the dilemmas induced by the bare letter of Scripture, according to Origen, were placed in the text on purpose precisely to counteract our tendency to complacency. If the usefulness of legal prescriptions and the theological coherence of historical narratives were automatically evident in every instance, it would not occur to us that there might be some other meaning beside the obvious one. It is for this reason that the Word of God arranged for the insertion of certain offensive features, of stumbling blocks and impossibilities amid the law and historical narratives. He did not want us to be carried away by the unspoiled charm of the plain text such that we would refuse to move beyond the letter.

---

30. *De principiis* 4.2.7 (Görgemanns and Karpp, 720–22; Froehlich, 61).
31. *De principiis* 4.2.4 (Görgemanns and Karpp, 708–12; Froehlich, 57–58).
32. *De principiis* 4.2.6 (Görgemanns and Karpp, 714–16; Froehlich, 59).
33. Young, *Biblical Exegesis*, 241–42.

What is more, the Word used actual historical events wherever they could be accommodated to these mystical meanings, hiding the deeper sense from the multitude. Hence there can be woven into the historical narrative some feature that did not actually happen, perhaps because it was impossible or simply because it did not occur.[34] Nevertheless, we ought to remember that there are also some scriptural passages that have no bodily, or literal, sense at all. That is when we must search straightaway for the soul and spirit of the passage.[35]

We need to be clear, however, about what Origen meant by the "literal sense." It was, as Henri Crouzel notes, the "raw matter of what is said" apart from any consideration of the biblical author's further intention. That is why Origen might dismiss the literal sense as impossible when found in a trope or parable. In that case he would reckon the spiritual sense to be the intended meaning of the parable.[36] No one, Origen said, could be expected to believe that God actually went about planting a garden to the east in Eden. Thus when the Lord is depicted as walking through the garden, and Adam hiding behind a tree, no one will doubt that these details point figuratively to greater mysteries. There are innumerable examples of things that are represented as having happened according to a literal reading of the text but did not actually happen on that level. Both the Old and New Testaments are full of such passages. Consider, for instance, the devil leading Jesus up on a high mountain to show him the kingdoms of the world (Matt. 4:8). Only a superficial reader, according to Origen, would think that one could see with the eyes of the flesh the kingdoms of the Persians and the Indians.[37]

Having said all of this, Origen nevertheless insisted that he had no intention of discounting out of hand the literal sense itself or the historical value of Scripture. Just because one particular story did not happen does not mean that none of the narrated events actually occurred. Nor because a particular law is unreasonable or impossible in its plain reading ought we to conclude that no law should be observed literally. In fact, Origen says, the actual historical accounts recorded in Scripture far outnumber the purely spiritual texts that have been woven into them. After all, "Honor your father and mother that it may be well with you" (Exod. 20:12) is useful without any anagogy and ought to be kept; even the apostle Paul cites it verbatim (Eph. 6:2).[38]

With these basic exegetical parameters in mind, we can look briefly at how Origen interpreted the Scriptures for his fellow Christians. In his homilies

---

34. *De principiis* 4.2.9 (Görgemanns and Karpp, 726–30; Froehlich, 62–63).
35. *De principiis* 4.2.5 (Görgemanns and Karpp, 712–14; Froehlich, 58).
36. Crouzel, *Origen*, 62.
37. *De principiis* 4.3.1 (Görgemanns and Karpp, 730–34; Froehlich, 63–64).
38. *De principiis* 4.3.4 (Görgemanns and Karpp, 740–44; Froehlich, 66).

on Exodus, Origen remarked on the wonderful fecundity of the sacred text; each word of divine Scripture is like a seed whose nature it is to multiply diffusely.[39] Indeed, there is nothing in the law and the prophets that is devoid of mysteries.[40] So many things in the divine law (*lex divina*) have been submerged in deep mysteries (*profundis demersa mysteriis*) before which we ought to pray, "From the depths I have cried to you, Lord" (Ps. 129:1 Vulg. [130:1 Eng.]).[41] Origen's immediate task in this work, so he tells us, is to see whether a spiritual reading of the text will unlock the mystery of the descent of the patriarchs into Egypt.[42] Far from seeing himself as engaged in some novel enterprise, Origen wishes only to cultivate the seeds of the spiritual understanding (*semina spiritualis intelligentiae*) that the church has already received from the apostle Paul.[43] Origen observes that it was Paul who pressed beyond the literal meaning of Exodus when, in 1 Corinthians, he likened the crossing of the Red Sea to baptism and the cloud that followed the Israelites to the Holy Spirit (1 Cor. 10:1–4).[44]

It was preeminently the moral part (*locus moralis*) of the text that Origen wished to highlight so that he might edify the souls of the hearers.[45] Depicted in the Exodus account is a struggle for the moral life of believers, who must beware lest they find themselves enlisted as soldiers of Pharaoh led by the spirit of this world (*spiritus mundi*).[46] The faithful instead have been called by Christ to leave behind the works of Pharaoh, to depart from the land of Egypt, and to cast aside barbarian customs.[47] Origen was not calling into question the history of Israel's liberation recounted in the book of Exodus, which formed the foundation of his allegorical readings. Yet beneath that history—recounted, he says, in such minute detail that would otherwise seem pointless—he found enduring spiritual lessons that could be applied by his fellow Christians to their own lives. Thus Origen called on his congregation to pray that by his mercy the Lord would snatch them up from the land of Egypt and thus from the power of darkness in their own lives.[48]

39. *In Exodum* 1.1, in *Homilien zum Hextaeuch in Rufins Übersetzung*, ed. W. A. Baehrens, 2 vols. (Leipzig: Hinrichs, 1920), 1:145. See the English translation in *Origen on Exodus*, trans. Ronald Heine, FC (Washington, DC: Catholic University of America Press, 1982), 227.

40. *In Exodum* 1.4 (Baehrens, 149; Heine, 231).

41. *In Exodum* 4.2 (Baehrens, 173; Heine, 263).

42. *In Exodum* 1.2 (Baehrens, 147; Heine, 228).

43. *In Exodum* 5.1 (Baehrens, 184–85; Heine, 277).

44. *In Exodum* 5.1 (Baehrens, 184; Heine, 276).

45. *In Exodum* 1.4 (Baehrens, 149; Heine, 232).

46. *In Exodum* 1.5 (Baehrens, 151; Heine, 234).

47. *In Exodum* 1.5 (Baehrens, 153–54; Heine, 237–38).

48. *In Exodum* 4.9 (Baehrens, 183; Heine, 274).

The inner moral struggle within each Christian played out here in Exodus has been placed within the greater drama of salvation history as it unfolds across the Old and New Testaments. Even as Pharaoh represents the devil and Egypt the sinful world, so the two midwives who nursed Moses are figures of the two Testaments. Souls born in the church are thus attended by these Testaments as if by midwives, Origen says, inasmuch as the antidote of instruction is conferred from the reading of the Scriptures. Pharaoh, however, attempts to kill the male children (who represent the human rational faculty) by means of these same Testaments when he suggests heretical readings of Scripture.[49] Then Pharaoh's daughter may be regarded as the church, which is gathered from the gentiles, finding Moses in the marsh, cast off by his own people. The law was lying helpless, enclosed in offensive interpretations, until the church of the gentiles would appropriate the law to itself within the courts of wisdom.[50]

For Origen, it was precisely the full realization of the Old Testament in the New that made possible the moral perfection of believers, that is, their liberation from the darkness of Egyptian servitude. Thus as Moses ascended Mount Sinai, so the Christian must ascend to the lofty understanding of the law, to the peak of spiritual understanding (*spiritualis intelligentia*), rather than remaining in the lowly place of the letter (*in humili loco litterae*).[51] Now we go forth from Egypt, leaving behind the world to serve the Lord in faith.[52] We withdraw from the Egypt of vices and pass over the floods of the world as on a sure pathway through Jesus Christ.[53]

Last, we will say a short word about Origen's commentary on the Song of Songs. Although incomplete, this work set the tone for a thousand years of Western commentary. Origen identified the book as a marriage song that Solomon wrote in the form of a drama and sang under the figure (*instar*) of a bride about to wed, who is burning with heavenly love for her bridegroom, who is the Word of God (*sermo Dei*). Reading the text allegorically, Origen opened up two complementary strands of interpretation. On one level the bride can be taken as the individual human soul made in Christ's image; she also represents the whole church, which is yearning for Christ, the spouse to whom she has been joined.[54] This love song is therefore both personal and

49. *In Exodum* 2.2 (Baehrens, 157; Heine, 242).
50. *In Exodum* 2.4 (Baehrens, 160; Heine, 246).
51. *In Exodum* 3.2 (Baehrens, 165; Heine, 252).
52. *In Exodum* 3.3 (Baehrens, 165; Heine, 253).
53. *In Exodum* 3.3 (Baehrens, 171; Heine, 259).
54. *Comm. in Cant. Canticorum*, prologue 1.1, in *Commentaire sur le Cantique des Cantiques*, ed. Luc Brésard and Henri Crouzel, SC 375 (Paris: Cerf, 1991), 1:80–81. See the translation in *Commentary on Song of Songs*, trans. R. P. Lawson, Ancient Christian Writers 26 (New York: Newman, 1956), 21.

corporate, denoting either the church (*ecclesia*) in relation to Christ or the soul (*anima*) in her union with the Word of God (*Verbum Dei*).[55] Aflame with longing for her spouse and vexed by the inward wound of love, the bride pours out her prayer to God. Here, then, is the church, which longs for union with Christ.[56] Yet this is also the individual soul whose only desire is to be united to the Word and to enter into the mysteries of his wisdom as into the chambers of her heavenly bridegroom. Finally, when her mind is filled with divine perception and understanding, she will come to believe that she has received the kisses of the Word of God himself.[57]

Either way one reads it—and the two are certainly not mutually exclusive—this is a love song. Origen was aware that the Greeks had also composed such works in dialogue form to reveal the power of love that leads the soul from earth to the lofty heights of heaven. They knew that the highest beatitude can be attained only under the stimulus of love's desire.[58] And now, by God's power, Origen hopes that he too can address the nature of love, a wholesome love that will thereby build up chastity.[59] It makes no difference whether Scripture speaks of love (*amor*) or of charity (*caritas*) or of affection (*dilectio*), except that the word "charity" is so highly exalted that even God himself is called charity (1 John 4:7–8). Because God the Father is charity, and the Son likewise, he requires in us something akin to himself.[60] Called to participate in the divine nature of love by way of God the Son, we are to be conformed to God through charity itself. So it is then that, in the Song of Songs, the figures of the bride and bridegroom are employed by Solomon to teach us that communion with God is to be attained through the paths of charity and love.[61]

The Antiochene Exegetes

While not constituting a school of exegesis as such, a collection of like-minded exegetes linked to Antioch were concerned that excessive allegorization of the Scriptures might undermine the very foundations of biblical history. This is not to say that the Antiochene exegetes were wedded to the literal meaning of the text to the exclusion of all mystical interpretations, but they did proceed more cautiously than their Alexandrian counterparts. Thus in his commentary

---

55. *Comm. in Cant. Canticorum* 1.2 (SC 375:176–77; Lawson, 58).
56. *Comm. in Cant. Canticorum* 1.3–5 (SC 375:178–79; Lawson, 59).
57. *Comm. in Cant. Canticorum* 1.8–12 (SC 375:182–85; Lawson, 60–61).
58. *Comm. in Cant. Canticorum*, prologue 2.1 (SC 375:90–91; Lawson, 23–24).
59. *Comm. in Cant. Canticorum*, prologue 2.3 (SC 375:90–91; Lawson, 24).
60. *Comm. in Cant. Canticorum*, prologue 2.25–27 (SC 375:108–12; Lawson, 32–33).
61. *Comm. in Cant. Canticorum*, prologue 3.47 (SC 375:130–32; Lawson, 40–41).

on the Psalter, Diodore of Tarsus assigned a christological reading only to Psalms 2, 8, and 44, which the Jews themselves also regarded as messianic. Theodore of Mopsuestia, for his part, was willing to allow for a typological reading of Old Testament texts provided that they bear some similarity to their New Testament counterparts, such that Jonah could serve as a proleptic symbol, or foreshadowing (*typos*), of Christ. Like Diodore, Theodore was very cautious in dealing with the Psalms; hence he looked for explicit New Testament applications of the messianic psalms. Theodore was also attuned to the subtleties of metaphorical speech, and so where Alexandrians may spin these figurative expressions into allegories, Theodore determined that metaphorical language belongs to the literal sense.[62]

Diodore, for his part, had actually developed multiple categories of discourse that went beyond the plain literal sense. In addition to the deeper spiritual meaning that he called *theōria*, Diodore listed figuration (*tropologia*), parable (*parabolē*), and enigma (*ainigmata*), all of which are acceptable as allegory precisely because they all—in one form or another—remain true to their historical context.[63] In the prologue to his Psalms commentary, he divided the Psalter broadly into ethical and doctrinal categories, and from there he went on to make further subdivisions. Diodore certainly regarded the book of Psalms as a spiritual guide to which the faithful could turn in times of trial, noting that the Holy Spirit has foreseen all manner of situations in which believers may find themselves. Diodore thus held that, although the Psalms address David's own life, they also speak to the whole of Israel and then, even beyond, to Christians today. In that vein he tells his readers that "we will not shrink from the truth but will expound it according to the historical substance [*historia*] and the plain literal sense [*lexis*]; . . . we will not disparage anagogy and the higher *theōria*. For history is not opposed to *theōria*. On the contrary, it proves to be the foundation of the higher senses." What Diodore warned against, however, was the lapse into allegory, which (according to him) does away with the historical foundation, thereby opening the door to flights of fancy on the part of reckless readers. Yet having indicated his aversion to allegory, Diodore had to meet the potent challenge of Paul's own words in Galatians 4:24, where he explicitly invoked the term "allegory" (*allēgoroumena*). To this Diodore answers that the apostle had

62. Frances Young, "Traditions of Exegesis," in *New Cambridge History of the Bible*, 1:734–51; Simonetti, *Biblical Interpretation*, 67–74.
63. *Preface to the Commentary on Psalm 118*, in Froehlich, *Biblical Interpretation in the Early Church*, 87–94. See also John Behr, "Diodore of Tarsus and His Exegesis," in *Handbuch der Bibel-Hermeneutiken: Von Origenes bis zur Gegenwart*, ed. Oda Wischmeyer (Berlin: de Gruyter, 2016), 35–46.

actually adopted the way of *theōria* even though he did so under the name of allegory, for he never sacrificed the historical content of the Genesis narrative even as he expanded its application.[64]

Theodore of Mopsuestia also grappled with Paul's allegorization of the Genesis account, taking to task irresponsible exegetes who cannot grasp the subtleties of the apostle's method. "There are people who take great pains to twist the senses of the divine Scriptures and make everything written therein serve their own ends. They dream up silly fables in their own heads and give their folly the name of allegory. They (mis)use the Apostle's term as a blank authorization to abolish all meanings of divine Scripture." What these allegorists miss, according to Theodore, is that Paul was not discarding the history in this case, but instead established similarities between those ancient events and the contemporary situation; allegory for Paul is thus a comparison or juxtaposition of past and present. Yet if the allegorists had their way, Theodore cautions, "Adam is not Adam, paradise is not paradise, the serpent not the serpent," with the result that there will be no historical foundation remaining, thereby compromising the integrity of salvation history itself.[65] This attempt to achieve a reasonable balance of the historical and the spiritual senses remained integral to biblical exegesis throughout the patristic and medieval periods.

Augustine of Hippo

Among the church fathers, Augustine of Hippo had perhaps the deepest and most enduring effect on the Western theological tradition as a whole, from soteriology to ecclesiology and certainly biblical exegesis. Although Augustine produced a staggering array of works that, in some form, addressed scriptural interpretation, it was his *De doctrina christiana* that stood as the principal interpretative paradigm throughout the Middle Ages. This was no mere handbook of exegesis; it belonged to a great and ambitious project of reformation. As Peter Brown has observed, in an age when great texts were the basis of culture, Augustine was determined that the Bible would form the foundation of a new "Christian culture." This would not, however, entail the wholesale rejection of pagan learning (as we shall see) but rather its incorporation into the grand endeavor.[66]

---

64. *Prologue to the Psalms*, in Froehlich, *Biblical Interpretation in the Early Church*, 82–86.
65. *Commentary on Galatians*, in Froehlich, *Biblical Interpretation in the Early Church*, 95–103.
66. Peter Brown, *Augustine of Hippo* (Berkeley: University of California Press, 2000), 256–66.

For Augustine, the fundamental integrity of Holy Scripture, its coherence and comprehensiveness, had to be grounded in a hermeneutical system capable of dealing with the myriad exigencies of the text. It was not only a matter of meeting the challenges of pagans or heretics but, more important, sustaining believers along their own journeys. The reliability, the trustworthiness, of Scripture as a guide for Christian life must not only be asserted but also supported if the pilgrims are to make their way to their homeland. Augustine made this point succinctly: "Faith will stagger if the authority of the Divine Scriptures wavers. Indeed, if faith staggers, charity itself languishes."[67]

At the outset of *De doctrina christiana*, Augustine explains to his readers that he wants to lay out for them certain precepts necessary for meaningful discussion, or investigation, of the Scriptures (*tractandarum scripturarum*).[68] This education in divine things is not intended to stifle the inspired creativity of the reader or to exalt the magisterial status of the teacher. Rather, Augustine says, that human beings should offer one another such instruction belongs to the realm of charity; it is the "knot" that holds people together.[69] Precisely because love rests at the center of Scripture, for Augustine, all genuine interpretation and instruction will by definition proceed on that basis. Looking to the First Epistle to Timothy, "But the aim of such instruction is love that comes from a pure heart, a good conscience, and a sincere faith" (1 Tim. 1:5), Augustine insists that faith, hope, and charity will be the foremost prerequisites for any investigation (*ad tractionem*) of the Scriptures.[70] Faithful exegetes, therefore, never exult in their own skills as though sheer erudition will unveil the mystery of the text; rather, they submit themselves to the Scriptures in a state of humble receptivity: "We must become meek through piety so that we do not contradict Divine Scripture."[71] For Augustine, therefore, biblical exegesis is an existential enterprise that takes hold of the whole person. Scripture claims the utmost reverence on the part of the believer. Affective devotion (*pietas*) will believe in, and accede to, the authority of the sacred books.[72] This is a theme that runs throughout the entire work and, it may be safely said, throughout all of Augustine's writings.

As Augustine begins to construct his hermeneutical system from the ground up, he establishes a fundamental distinction between signs (*signa*) and things

67. *De doctrina christiana* 1.37.41, ed. Joseph Martin, CCSL 32 (Turnhout: Brepols, 1962), 30; English translation by D. W. Robertson (Upper Saddle River, NJ: Prentice Hall, 1958), 31.
68. *De doctrina christiana*, prooemium 1 (CCSL 32:1; Robertson, 3).
69. *De doctrina christiana*, prooemium 6 (CCSL 32:4; Robertson, 6).
70. *De doctrina christiana* 1.40.44 (CCSL 32:32; Robertson, 33).
71. *De doctrina christiana* 2.7.9 (CCSL 32:36–37; Robertson, 38).
72. *De doctrina christiana* 2.7.10 (CCSL 32:37; Robertson, 39).

(*res*) that proves absolutely vital to the entire process. Here he explains that while every sign is a thing (or it would be nothing at all), not all things are signs. Human authors use signs in the form of words (*verba*) to signify some actual thing in the world. Yet God, the divine author of Scripture, not only can signify things with words, but can also employ things themselves as signs of still greater things.[73] It is precisely because God can employ physical things as signs of greater spiritual realities that exegetes must learn all they can about the natural sciences, so as to pick up on the divine cues. The more one knows about the properties of some plant or animal, the better prepared one is to grasp its deeper spiritual significance.[74] Augustine therefore encourages Christians to draw on the best of pagan learning and place it in the service of the gospel, as he himself had learned from the Platonists. Such forays into the classical tradition were famously likened by Augustine to the Israelite despoiling of the Egyptians upon the flight from Egypt, thereby reclaiming the treasures of God. Indeed, Augustine says, the exodus account was surely intended as a figure (*figuratum est*) meant to foreshadow (*praesignaret*) such a reclamation of knowledge. As all truth is from God, so whatever the great pagan scholars had learned they received from God; now this knowledge will serve the highest good.[75]

In keeping with the wider patristic tradition, Augustine maintained that the biblical text was finally unlocked only with the advent of Christ, whose passion and resurrection shed light on the whole of salvation history. Consequently, failure to recognize Jesus as the Christ leaves the reader at a grave disadvantage, consigned to the mundane and unable to ascend to the spiritual heights. So it was, according to Augustine, that Jews had mistaken signs for things. They were lost in the letter (*littera*) and therefore missed the spiritual import of the things that were functioning as signs. Hence they remained on the level of merely carnal sacrifice when they should have seen such rites as pointing to the greater reality of Christ's perfect sacrifice on the cross.[76] That the biblical text may be misunderstood is largely due to the fact that meanings are hidden under unknown or ambiguous signs. Linguistic signs, in turn, vary between the proper and the metaphorical, the latter of which expands the range of a word's signification in a given context.[77]

If ignorance of metaphorical signs leaves readers perplexed, this is a cue that they must devote themselves to studying not only words but also the

73. *De doctrina christiana* 1.2.2 (CCSL 32:7; Robertson, 8–9).
74. *De doctrina christiana* 2.16.23–24 (CCSL 32:48–50; Robertson, 50–51).
75. *De doctrina christiana* 2.40.60–61 (CCSL 32:73–75; Robertson, 75–76).
76. *De doctrina christiana* 3.5.9–6.10 (CCSL 32:82–83; Robertson, 83–85).
77. *De doctrina christiana* 2.10.15 (CCSL 32:41; Robertson, 43).

very things that are signified. Therefore it is crucial that biblical exegetes possess more than grammatical aptitude; they must be well acquainted with the natural sciences too if they hope to understand what is meant by Scripture's use of figurative sayings (*figuratae locutiones*).[78] As mentioned above, all the liberal arts will be pressed into service. For beyond the trivium, there remains the study of the quadrivium, learning the ways of the natural world, those phenomena represented by linguistic terms. Of course, the question will arise as to precisely how the reader can discern whether something should be taken properly or metaphorically, whether its meaning had been transferred or not. There must be some means of investigation (*modus inveniendae*), some method to determine whether to take an expression literally or figuratively. It can be summed up this way, Augustine says: whatever in Scripture does not pertain to virtuous behavior or the truth of the faith should be taken figuratively. For all scriptural instruction must ultimately promote the love of God and neighbor.[79]

We noted earlier that the affective piety of the reader was an essential component of the hermeneutical process. To this observation should be added the specifically christological dimension that orients the exegete. Genuine comprehension of the sacred text comes only to the reader who is humble of heart, rooted in charity, and easily subjected to Christ.[80] Christ is the true teacher who must illuminate our minds if we are to grasp the truth.[81] The Christ of the gospels is not only the exemplar of charity and humility, but he is also the eternal Word of God through whom the cosmos was brought into being and can be comprehended. As Mark Jordan has shown, Augustine recognized it was the divine Word who ultimately and decisively explicated the words of Scripture.[82] Brenda Schildgen has likewise noted that Augustine, while fully aware of language's limitations and provisional quality, could nevertheless find meaning anchored in the one source of all meaning, the divine Word.[83] Holy Scripture, grounded as it is in the Word of God, serves as our guide: the *verba* all lead us to our final goal of resting within the *Verbum*. We must beware lest we become entangled in the material things of this world and with a clouded mind begin to enjoy some inferior thing in place of God. All the things of this world are to be used for assistance during our sojourn here on earth as we make our way to the homeland, where we will at last enjoy the

---

78. *De doctrina christiana* 2.16.23 (CCSL 32:48–49; Robertson, 50).
79. *De doctrina christiana* 3.10.14 (CCSL 32:86; Robertson, 87–88).
80. *De doctrina christiana* 2.42.63 (CCSL 32:76–77; Robertson, 78).
81. *De magistro* 11.38, ed. K.-D. Daur, CCSL 29 (Turnhout: Brepols, 1970), 196.
82. Mark Jordan, "Words and Word: Incarnation and Signification in Augustine's *De Doctrina Christiana*," *Augustinian Studies* 11 (1980): 177–96.
83. Brenda Deen Schildgen, "Augustine's Answer to Jacques Derrida in the *De Doctrina Christiana*," *New Literary History* 25 (1994): 383–97.

Trinity. To that end the wayfarers must purge their minds of inferior loves, ordering their affections, so that with clear minds, illuminated by grace, they will successfully navigate their voyage home.[84]

Wending our way back to the Trinity, we will place our trust in the divine author of Scripture, who discloses a seemingly endless series of mysteries that draw us closer to our ultimate goal. We are constantly reading signs that point us farther down the road to ever greater realities, which means that we must ask what these signs are intended to mean. This, in turn, raises the question of authorial intention—both human and divine. How many meanings might there be in a given text? How would we know which are legitimate (intended by the author) and which are only the product of our own imagination? Augustine was confident that the Spirit of God, who is at work through the human authors, has foreseen the various meanings that we may find in a single passage, all of which may be accepted provided that they agree with the truth conveyed in other passages of Scripture.[85] It was along these lines that, in his *Confessions*, Augustine addresses the possibility of multiple true meanings within a single passage. Two people may disagree about what Moses had meant by some statement recorded in Scripture, each claiming to know the mind of Moses. And yet, according to Augustine, Moses may well have intended many meanings, all of which are true and thus discerned by different people. Ultimately, Moses is speaking under the inspiration of the Holy Spirit, the font and guarantor of all truth. There within the words of the inspired human author rest all the true meanings that have been found and many more besides that we have yet to find.[86] Carol Harrison puts it well: "The meanings and truths which the text of Scripture contain remain eschatologically open, provisional and inconclusive; always capable of further, future, different interpretations so long as they too resonate with the single unifying rule of the double commandment."[87] That being said, the interpretation of Scripture is never a purely individualistic exercise in which the pious believer sets out alone in search of the divine meaning. Augustine counsels that when the literal reading generates ambiguous meanings, one should have recourse to the rule of faith (*regula fidei*) as it is found not only in the clearer passages (*plenioribus locis*) of Scripture but also as established by the authority of the church.[88]

84. *De doctrina christiana* 1.3.3–10 (CCSL 32:8–12; Robertson, 9–13).
85. *De doctrina christiana* 3.27.38 (CCSL 32:100; Robertson, 101–2).
86. *Confessiones* 12.42, ed. Martin Skutella and Luc Verheijen, CCSL 27 (Turnhout: Brepols, 1990), 240–41.
87. Carol Harrison, "Augustine," in *New Cambridge History of the Bible*, 1:676–96.
88. *De doctrina christiana* 3.2.2 (CCSL 32:77–78; Robertson, 79).

Toward the end of *De doctrina christiana*, Augustine commends to his readers some exegetical advice from an unlikely, or at least unexpected, source: the late fourth-century Donatist theologian Tyconius. In his *Book of Rules* Tyconius locates "certain mystical rules [*regulae mysticae*] which reveal what is hidden in the whole Law and make visible the treasures of truth which are invisible to some."[89] Endorsed as they were by Augustine, these guidelines subsequently passed into the Western medieval exegetical tradition. The first two rules were perhaps the most impactful, bearing as they do a direct connection to larger (and potentially controversial) questions of ecclesiology. The first concerns the Lord and his body, which is to say, Christ and the church. Discussions in Scripture, it is noted, can move from head to body, or body to head, while still on the subject of one and the same person (*una eademque persona*). So it is, for example, that we find one person speaking in the Song of Songs: "As a bridegroom [Christ] decked out with a crown and as a bride [church] adorned with her jewels" (Isa. 61:10).[90] The second rule extends this to the bipartite body of the Lord, or better still, the true and mixed body (*verum atque permixtum*) of the Lord, or even the true and simulated (*verum atque simulatum*). As we are told, hypocrites are not really part of the Lord's body in eternity, or even now, despite the fact that they seem to be members of his church. Here then is the "mixed church" (*ecclesia permixta*) in which good and bad fish are presently caught up within a single net. Both parts may be addressed in a single passage, although they nevertheless remain distinct. For instance, we read in Isaiah 42:16–17, "I will lead the blind," while he speaks to the other part, "They are turned back."[91] The third rule addresses promises and the law, or the spirit and the letter, or yet still grace and commandment. To miss these crucial distinctions, Augustine says, is to open the door to the Pelagian heresy.[92] The fourth rule covers species and genus, or part and whole. Thus something might be spoken in Scripture to the city of Jerusalem, for example, which actually has a much wider application intended for all people.[93] The fifth rule addresses times, in which intervals of time hidden in the Scriptures can be discovered either by synecdoche (a part for the whole or the whole for a part) or numbers such as seven, ten, or twelve, which convey completeness. Thus "Seven times a day I will praise you" (Ps. 118:164 Vulg. [119:164 Eng.]) means all the time.[94] The sixth rule is that of recapitulation

89. *De doctrina christiana* 3.30.43 (CCSL 32:103; Robertson, 102–3).
90. *De doctrina christiana* 3.31.44 (CCSL 32:104; Robertson, 106).
91. *De doctrina christiana* 3.32.45 (CCSL 32:104–5; Robertson, 106).
92. *De doctrina christiana* 3.33.46 (CCSL 32:105–6; Robertson, 107–8).
93. *De doctrina christiana* 3.34.47 (CCSL 32:106–7; Robertson, 108–9).
94. *De doctrina christiana* 3.35.50 (CCSL 32:110–11; Robertson, 112).

whereby some things in Scripture are described as though they follow each other in the order of time, or narrate a continuous sequence of events, when the narrative covertly refers to previous events that have been omitted.[95] Finally, the seventh rule speaks to the devil and his body. It is basically the converse of the first rule. The devil is the head of the wicked, who are in some sense his body, just as the faithful are members of Christ's body. Sometimes Scripture says things of the devil that actually refer to his body, which comprises not only those people manifestly outside the church but also some of those presently mingled within it.[96]

We have seen, therefore, that Tyconius's rules facilitated christological readings of the Old Testament that could, in turn, also be ecclesiological. Augustine interpreted Psalms in a christological vein that might not have pleased the likes of Theodore of Mopsuestia but certainly won the day in the medieval West. Commenting on Psalm 1, "Blessed is the person who does not follow the advice of the wicked," Augustine immediately asserts that these words apply to Jesus Christ, the God-man.[97] That "He will be a tree planted by streams of water" (Ps. 1:3) may in turn refer to Wisdom itself, who deigned to assume humanity for our salvation such that it is the human Christ who is planted like this tree. Appealing to other psalms that invoke similar images can then serve to bolster this christological reading: "The river of God is brimming with water" (Ps. 64:9).[98] The words of the second psalm, "Yet I have been established by him a king over Zion" (Ps. 2:6), clearly proceed from the mouth (*ex persona*) of our Lord Jesus Christ himself.[99] And because such words can be spoken of or by Christ, they may refer to Christ's humanity, or his divinity, or both. Augustine was always alert to multiple possible meanings. Thus "the Lord said to me, 'You are my son; today I have begotten you'" (Ps. 2:7) could be a prophetic statement regarding Christ's human birth, Augustine says, although it more likely refers to the eternal birth of the Word. In this case "today" may indeed signify the present, since in eternity there is neither past nor future, only the eternal now. Hence this psalm proclaims, according to Augustine, the true and catholic faith of the eternal generation of the power and wisdom of God.[100]

If both the divine and human natures of Christ may be the subject of any given psalm, so the psalms may be speaking of Christ in his singular or

95. *De doctrina christiana* 3.36.52 (CCSL 32:111–12; Robertson, 113).

96. *De doctrina christiana* 3.37.55 (CCSL 32:114–15; Robertson, 115–16).

97. *Enarrationes in Psalmos* 1.1, ed. J. Fraipont and Eligius Dekkers, CCSL 38 (Turnhout: Brepols, 1956), 1. See the English translation in *Augustine on the Psalms*, trans. Maria Boulding (Hyde Park, NY: New City, 2000), 67.

98. *In Psalmos* 1.2 (CCSL 38:2; Boulding, 68).

99. *In Psalmos* 2.5 (CCSL 38:4–5; Boulding, 72).

100. *In Psalmos* 2.6 (CCSL 38:5; Boulding, 72–73).

corporate person, thus with respect to head or members. "I rested and fell asleep and I arose" (Ps. 3:5) is spoken in the person of Jesus Christ (*ex persona Christi*) with regard to his passion and resurrection.[101] Likewise, "You Lord are my support" (Ps. 3:3) is spoken by Christ to God in keeping with his humanity (*secundum hominem*), as the Word assumed human nature.[102] Yet this same psalm, according to Augustine, can also be understood of the whole Christ (*totus Christus*), that is to say, Christ as both head and body; Christ's body the church is beset by persecutions throughout the whole earth and therefore can say, "You are my support, my glory." The church, after all, does not attribute preeminence to herself since she understands by whose grace and mercy she exists.[103] In this vein, "she who receives the inheritance" refers to the church, who receives eternal life as her inheritance through Christ and thereby possesses God himself.[104] And when she calls out to God, "Hear my words," she seeks the Lord's assistance so that she may pass through the vileness of this world and finally reach him.[105] The church's prayers to God are often voiced in the Psalter, which makes them no less christological, since she is the very body of Christ. Thus she prays that God might "make my steps perfect in your pathways" so that her love may grow to perfection through those narrow paths by which she attains God's rest. "And that my footprints may not be obliterated" is her request that the signs of her journey would not be removed. These are the signs, Augustine says, that have been impressed like footprints (*vestigia*) on the sacraments and apostolic writings.[106] Augustine's christological reading of the Psalter is indicative of the way in which patristic exegetes, and their medieval successors, found Christ throughout the Old and New Testaments and in this way unified the Scriptures around not merely a theological theme but an eternal person.

Gregory the Great

Gregory the Great, one of the four great Latin fathers of the church (along with Ambrose, Augustine, and Jerome), was a Benedictine monk elevated to the papacy. He had received a solid classical education, wrote good Latin, and was well acquainted with the works of the other fathers. As an exegete,

---

101. *In Psalmos* 3.1 (CCSL 38:7; Boulding, 76).
102. *In Psalmos* 3.3 (CCSL 38:8; Boulding, 77).
103. *In Psalmos* 3.9 (CCSL 38:11–2; Boulding, 81–82).
104. *In Psalmos* 5.1 (CCSL 38:19; Boulding, 93).
105. *In Psalmos* 5.2 (CCSL 38:19; Boulding, 93).
106. *In Psalmos* 16.5 (CCSL 38:92; Boulding, 185).

Gregory was above all else interested, as R. A. Markus observes, in moral questions. The old divide between the Christian and the pagan world that marked the times of Augustine had, by the late sixth century, given way to a divide within the church itself: those who lived a good Christian life and those who did not.[107] Although a pope and statesman, Gregory remained at his core a Benedictine monk seeking union with God in prayer. As Jean Leclercq remarked, for Gregory, "The Christian life is conceived of as, above all, a life of detachment and desire: detachment from the world and from sin, and intense desire for God. This attitude is already a prayer in itself, a life of prayer."[108] Holy Scripture would then be at the center of such contemplation, a sustained process of deep meditation wherein the readers immersed themselves in, and thereby absorbed, the wisdom of the Scriptures. Gregory thus presented the evocative image of ruminating (*ruminamus*) on the green leaves of Scripture, chewing them over again as a cow with its cud.[109] In this vein he could say that, when reading Scripture, "We are being fed with the fodder of truth" (*veritatis pabulo pascimur*).[110]

Gregory's exegetical masterpiece was his commentary on the book of Job, appended to which was a letter to the Christian scholar Leander, wherein Gregory offered a concise overview of his approach to the entire enterprise of biblical exegesis. Here he tells Leander that, at the request of fellow monks who had asked for this work, he would search out not only the literal-historical sense of words (*verba historiae*) for the allegorical sense (*per allegoriarum sensus*) but then also press beyond to the exercise of moral action (*exercitium moralitatis*), which presents an even more serious obligation. He would accompany what he found with other texts of Scripture and finally tie together all of these expositions for the clarification of difficult sections.[111] The exegetical process could not proceed in the case of Scripture, however, as it might when reading the classical authors. Hence in words that echoed down through the Middle Ages, Gregory declared that he would not make himself a slave to

107. R. A. Markus, *Gregory the Great and His World* (Cambridge: Cambridge University Press, 1997), 34–50.

108. Jean Leclercq, *The Love of Learning and the Desire for God: A Study of Monastic Culture*, trans. C. Misrahi (New York: Fordham, 1988), 29.

109. *Homiliae in Hiezechihelem Prophetam* 1.5.1, ed. Marcus Adriaen, CCSL 142 (Turnhout: Brepols, 1971), 57. See also G. R. Evans, *The Thought of Gregory the Great* (Cambridge: Cambridge University Press, 1986), 87–95; and John Moorhead, *Gregory the Great* (London: Routledge, 2005), 49–67.

110. *Homiliae in Hiezechihelem Prophetam* 1.9.30 (CCSL 142:139–40).

111. *Ad Leandrum* 1, in *Moralia in Iob*, ed. M. Adriaen, CCSL 143 (Turnhout: Brepols, 1979), 2; English translation in *Moral Reflections on the Book of Job*, vol. 1, *Preface and Books 1–5*, trans. Brian Kerns (Collegeville, MN: Cistercian Publications, 2014), 49.

the art of rhetoric; by no means was he going to subject the words of divine revelation to the rules of Donatus (*ut verba caelestis oraculi restringam sub regulis Donati*).[112] Precisely because Holy Scripture has its own eloquence, Gregory need make no apologies on its behalf.

As the volumes grew larger, Gregory admitted that he sometimes had to set aside the literal sense so that he could pursue the senses that lead to contemplation and moral action.[113] Admittedly, there are times when a literal reading of the text (*iuxta litteram*) leads to error; indeed, sometimes the words themselves militate against their own literal exposition. Thus when the words on the page appear to be inconsistent, that is the cue that there is a deeper meaning to be sought.[114] Along these lines, within his homilies on the prophet Ezekiel, Gregory stated that the book of sacred eloquence (cf. Ezek. 2:9) is written inwardly (*intus*) through allegory and outwardly (*foris*) through history. The inward amounts to the spiritual understanding, while the outward is the simple sense of the letter. The first promises invisible things, whereas the second functions on a moral level as it disposes visible things through the rectitude of its precepts. And yet even as the inward sense does speak of "heavenly secrets" revealed to us by the Spirit, there are still some things that remain hidden to us now, known only by the angels.[115]

Gregory's search for the spiritual, or inner, meaning ought not to be taken as a repudiation of the literal, or outward, sense of the text. He insisted that exegetes must first find their bearings on the foundations of history (*fundamenta historiae*). Only when this groundwork has been laid does one elevate the mind's construction into an edifice of faith through the symbolized spiritual meaning, and finally adorn the building with exterior color through the charm of moral action.[116] Gregory even warned of those who fail to take the words of sacred history literally (*verba historiae iuxta litteram*). They may actually be covering up the light of the truth that is offered as they force an allegorical reading on the text and thereby lose its edifying meaning.[117] At one point Gregory beseeches the monks that, while raising their minds to a spiritual understanding (*spiritalem intellegentiam*), they not abandon their respect for history (*a veneratione historiae non recedat*).[118] Thus as he led his fellow monks through the book of Job, Gregory insisted that they first plant

112. *Ad Leandrum* 5 (CCSL 143:7; Kerns, 1:55).
113. *Ad Leandrum* 2 (CCSL 143:3; Kerns, 1:50).
114. *Ad Leandrum* 3 (CCSL 143:5; Kerns, 1:52).
115. *Homiliae in Hiezechihelem Prophetam* 1.9.30 (CCSL 142:139–40).
116. *Ad Leandrum* 3 (CCSL 143:4–5; Kerns, 1:51).
117. *Ad Leandrum* 3–4 (CCSL 143:5; Kerns, 1:53).
118. *Moralia in Iob* 1.37.57 (CCSL 143:58; Kerns, 116).

the roots of the story so that they might then be able to satisfy their minds with the fruits of allegory (*de allegoriarum fructu satiare*).[119]

Finally, and most poignantly, Gregory spoke to Leander of his own suffering, the constant stomach pains that left him exhausted for lack of appetite. Here the fully human dimensions of this contemplative exegete emerge; here we see the man existentially engaged with the living text. Gregory told his friend that the more depressed he found himself by present suffering, the more consoled he was by the certain promises of eternal life. Perhaps it is divine providence, he opined, that he would comment on stricken Job after having been so stricken himself and thus better understand the soul of the one scourged through the lashes that he himself has received.[120] Addressing Gregory's confession, Jean Leclercq commented with typical insight that "Gregory's poor health is one of the great events in the history of spirituality, since to some degree it determines his doctrine. . . . For him, man's suffering is by no means a theoretical notion; he knew it from the inside at the cost of sensitivity that was sharpened and increased by the difficulties of each day."[121]

It was in the preface to his Job commentary that Gregory reflected on the question of biblical authorship. He confidently assured the monks that the true author of Scripture is the Holy Spirit (*auctor libri Spiritus sanctus*). It is the Spirit who dictated what was to be written and inspired it. Consider, Gregory says, if we received a letter from some great person, how absurd it would be to wonder by whose pen it was written. The scribe is of no importance when we know who sent the letter and what it is about.[122] None of this is to discount the role of human authors, but only to highlight their unique role as inspired agents of the divine author. Thus, when the human authors give information about themselves as though speaking of others, this is because they are writing under the inspiration of the Spirit. These human writers were placed above themselves, having been inspired by the Holy Spirit. Blessed Job, filled with the Spirit, could therefore write of his own deeds as though they were not his, just as Moses had also done.[123]

What, then, is the book of Job all about? According to Gregory, the man Job embodies great mysteries regarding the incarnation. In fact, Job's own suffering was itself a form of prophecy pointing to the mystery of Christ's passion. Because Christ is the head of the body, which is the church, Job may

119. *Praefatio* 10.21 (CCSL 143:24; Kerns, 1:75).
120. *Ad Leandrum* 5 (CCSL 143:6; Kerns, 1:54).
121. Leclercq, *Love of Learning*, 28.
122. *Praefatio* 1.2 (CCSL 143:8–9; Kerns, 1:57–58).
123. *Praefatio* 1.3 (CCSL 143:9–10; Kerns, 1:58–59).

at times symbolize either the head or the body.[124] Drawing on Jerome's *Book of Hebrew Names*, Gregory explained that Job means "one who suffers," thereby symbolizing Christ by his very name. Thus we read of both the passion of the mediator himself and the trials of the church, which is crucified by the many troubles she bears in this present life.[125] It is fitting, moreover, that we are not told how long Job's trials lasted, for the church will likewise face trials in this world, the duration of which we cannot determine.[126] Other actors in this narrative also bear symbolic value. Job's wife, who tempted him to curse God, typifies those who live according to the flesh, behave wickedly in the church, and oppress the faithful, while Job's friends prefigure the heretics, who pretend to offer sound advice but in reality lead believers astray through their false teachings.[127] Such correlations belong to the very construction of Holy Scripture, as Gregory declared when commenting on the wheels of Ezekiel's vision (Ezek. 1:16). He found that the wheel within the wheel is the New Testament: what the Old Testament pointed to (*designavit*), the New Testament showed forth (*exhibuit*). For example, Eve having been produced from the side of sleeping Adam foreshadows the church formed from Christ as he was dying. Isaac carrying the wood to the altar of his own sacrifice looks forward to Christ carrying the wood of his own cross to his passion.[128]

Gregory begins his exposition of the book of Job by reflecting on the holiness of Job the man, who, despite his many concerns, offered himself up in constant attentiveness to God. Even though the evangelical counsel to leave all things behind had not yet been revealed, Job already abided by it in his heart.[129] Having brought the monks through an overview of Job's story, Gregory then returns to the beginning to point out the secret of the allegories (*allegoriarum secreta*).[130] We believe what happened in this story, Gregory says, but now it is time to see its fulfillment through the allegorical sense. In the case of Job the man, an allegorical reading is ultimately christological. Gregory observes that, just as Job means "one who suffers," so Uz means "counselor." Surely this must be Jesus Christ, of whom Isaiah says, "He took on himself our sufferings" (Isa. 53:4), and Wisdom herself speaking though Solomon says: "I,

124. *Praefatio* 6.14 (CCSL 143:19–20; Kerns, 1:70).
125. *Praefatio* 7.16 (CCSL 143:20–21; Kerns, 1:71–72). See Jerome, *Liber interpretationis hebraicorum nominum*, in *Opera exegetica* 1, ed. Marcus Adriaen et al., CCSL 72 (Turnhout: Brepols, 1959), 133.
126. *Praefatio* 8.17 (CCSL 143:21–22; Kerns, 1:73).
127. *Praefatio* 6.15 (CCSL 143:20; Kerns, 1:71).
128. *Homiliae in Hiezechihelem Prophetam* 1.6.15 (CCSL 142:75).
129. *Moralia in Iob* 1.5.7 (CCSL 143:28; Kerns, 1:81–82).
130. *Moralia in Iob* 1.10.14 (CCSL 143:31; Kerns, 1:85).

Wisdom, dwell in counsel, and I am to be found among learned thoughts" (Prov. 8:12). That Job dwells in the land of Uz points therefore to Wisdom, who bore the sufferings of the passion for our sake and made the hearts of those dedicated to his counsels his own habitation.[131]

From the symbolic value of names to numbers, Gregory hits upon the seven sons and three daughters of Job. Noting that Scripture employs the number seven to symbolize perfection, the seven sons can be reckoned the apostles, who put the counsels of perfection into practice. That there were twelve apostles symbolizes the perfection implied in the seven gifts of grace. And the number seven itself grows into twelve when we multiply its parts: three times four. So it was that the apostles went to the four regions of the earth to preach the Trinity.[132] The moral aspect is revealed as the birth of the seven sons symbolizes the seven virtues of the Holy Spirit born within us. These seven sons of ours need the three sisters of faith, hope, and charity that they may be perfected and reach the number ten.[133] Job's early rising to offer a holocaust for each son can then be manifested in our own lives when we are radiant with the light of compunction and leave behind the night of our humanity by opening our minds to the rays of the true light. As a holocaust is a sacrifice totally consumed, so the offering of a holocaust is to burn the mind completely with the fire of compunction, while its heat burns on the altar of love and consumes our impure thoughts.[134]

Such forays into etymology and numerology might leave the modern reader a bit exasperated. But Gregory never lost sight of the narrative sweep of Scripture, its characters and their lives, the totality of which was designed to bring us to a greater knowledge of ourselves and lead us in our journey. Sacred Scripture, Gregory says, is presented like a kind of mirror (*quasi quoddam speculum*) to the eyes of our mind so that we might see our interior face within it. There we recognize both our ugliness and our beauty; there we measure our progress and see how far we are from our goal. In Scripture we can see how Job is described as strengthened by temptation while David is beaten down by it, so that the virtues of our great leaders may at once encourage our hope, and their failures counsel caution and humility. Even as we must bear the weight of fear sometimes, we will not despair, strengthened as we are by the example of virtuous living, which promotes confidence and hope.[135]

131. *Moralia in Iob* 1.11.15 (CCSL 143:31–32; Kerns, 1:85).
132. *Moralia in Iob* 1.14.19 (CCSL 143:33–34; Kerns, 1:87).
133. *Moralia in Iob* 1.27.38 (CCSL 143:45–46; Kerns, 1:100–101).
134. *Moralia in Iob* 1.35.49 (CCSL 143:50–51; Kerns, 1:107).
135. *Moralia in Iob* 2.1.1 (CCSL 143:59; Kerns, 1:117).

John Cassian

The monk and spiritual writer John Cassian spent much of his career in fifth-century Gaul following a sojourn in Egypt. His classic work *The Conferences* recounts his conversations with various holy men of the Eastern desert. Cassian no doubt rearranged these sources to suit his own purposes and likely added a fair amount of his own material. Still, the final text is what concerns us, and it is a wonderful guide not only to the spiritual life but also to the place of Scripture within that life.

In the eleventh conference, Cassian recounts how he and his companions left Syria for Egypt in their quest for a "greater grace of perfection," seeking the counsel of holy men "whose reputation for sanctity had made them glorious everywhere."[136] There he met monks "whose old age and holiness, in bodies now bent over, shines so brightly in their faces that the mere sight of them is able to teach a great deal to those who gaze upon them." In fact, one would learn from them not so much through words (*verbis*) but rather by the example of their holy life (*sanctae vitae exemplo*).[137] The lives of these men had been formed by immersion in the Scriptures; they were actualizing all that they had meditated on for decades. Thus, as the father Chaemeron explained to Cassian and his companions, divine Scripture (*scriptura divina*) arouses the will to ascend the ladder of perfection, as "the divine word [*sermo divinus*] has in some way established different ranks and different measures of perfection itself."[138] Chaemeron concluded with a word from the psalmist on the way to blessedness: "Continually to learn and to teach the disposition by which we may cling to the Lord" (Ps. 1:2). So it is, the father says, that we ought to meditate on this disposition (*affectus*) day and night, "always chewing on this heavenly food." Such constant rumination (*perpetua ruminatio*) is the life of the monk who seeks the grace of perfection.[139] As Douglas Burton-Christie observes, for the desert fathers "to ruminate on Scripture was to embark upon a deeply personal drama that the monks referred to as the quest for purity of heart."[140]

In the fourteenth conference, Cassian sought the instruction of Abba Nesteros, who, upon learning that these monks had committed parts of Scripture to memory, proceeded to offer them a lesson in hermeneutics. Nesteros noted

136. *Collationes* 11.1, CSEL 13:314; *The Conferences*, trans. and annotated by Boniface Ramsey, Ancient Christian Writers 57 (New York: Paulist Press, 1997), 409.

137. *Collationes* 11.2 (CSEL 13:315; Ramsey, 409–10).

138. *Collationes* 11.12 (CSEL 13:326; Ramsey, 417–18).

139. *Collationes* 11.15 (CSEL 13:332; Ramsey, 422).

140. Douglas Burton-Christie, *The Word in the Desert: Scripture and the Quest for Holiness in Early Christian Monasticism* (Oxford: Oxford University Press, 1993), 299.

first that knowledge (*scientia*) can be divided between the practical (*practike*) and the theoretical (*theoretike*). The first "reaches its fulfillment in correction of behavior and in cleansing of vice." The second "consists in the contemplation of divine things and in the understanding of most sacred meanings."[141] Nesteros observes that, while the practical can be pursued apart from the theoretical, it is not so the other way around, precisely because a pure moral disposition is essential for embarking on the path to contemplation: "In vain, therefore, does someone who does not reject the contagion of vice strive for the vision of God."[142]

It was the theoretical sort of knowledge that could then be subsequently divided into historical interpretation and spiritual understanding, and it is here that Cassian hands down what became the classic medieval paradigm of the four scriptural senses. Galatians 4:22–31 was employed as a starting point to explain the process. According to Nesteros, as recounted by Cassian, history embraces knowledge of past and visible things and thus corresponds to Paul's recounting of the fact that Abraham had two sons born of the free and slave women. What follows, however, belongs to allegory. For the events that took place (*in veritate gesta sunt*) prefigured the form of another mystery (*sacramentum*), namely, the two covenants. Anagogy proceeds from here, mounting from spiritual mysteries (*mysteria*) to even more sublime and sacred secrets, as Paul goes on to speak of the heavenly Jerusalem. And finally there is tropology, the moral explanation, which pertains to correction of life and practical instruction as though these two covenants referred to practical and theoretical discipline. At this point Nesteros explains that the aforementioned four levels may apply to one biblical event or place, in this case Jerusalem, which can be read in a fourfold manner. Historically it is the city of the Jews; allegorically it is the church; anagogically the heavenly city of God; and tropologically the human soul that is either commended or castigated by God. Thus allegory is a sort of revelation, a spiritual understanding that lays bare what had been concealed by the historical narrative. Tropology allows for the prudent examination of whatever pertains to practical direction, to order the useful and the good. Anagogy directs us to what lies in the future, exhorting us to our final end.[143]

By the late Middle Ages a mnemonic refrain had emerged that was frequently rehearsed by exegetes as they tipped their hats to the four senses before presenting more complex variations on this basic theme: *Littera gesta docet,*

---

141. *Collationes* 14.1 (CSEL 13:398–99; Ramsey, 505).
142. *Collationes* 14.2 (CSEL 13:399; Ramsey, 505).
143. *Collationes* 14.8 (CSEL 13:404–7; Ramsey, 509–11).

quid credas allegoria, moralis quid agas, quo tendas anagogia. That is, the letter teaches you about the historical events, the allegorical sense what you ought to believe, the moral sense how you ought to behave, and the anagogical sense what you should strive to attain.

For Nesteros, however, all biblical interpretation is ultimately a matter of spiritual growth. And we may surely assume that Cassian approved of this father's words, which he recounted: "If you wish to attain to a true knowledge of Scripture, then, you must first hasten to acquire a steadfast humility of heart which will, by the perfection of love, bring you not to the knowledge that puffs up (1 Cor. 8:1) but to that which enlightens. For it is impossible for the impure mind to receive the gift of spiritual knowledge [*scientia spiritualis*]." The proper spiritual discipline is thus the sine qua non of all biblical study. And the study of Scripture, for Nesteros, means nothing less than immersion in the texts. He insists that "the successive books of Holy Scripture must be diligently committed to memory and ceaselessly reviewed." The result is a "double fruit" that at once preserves the mind from harmful thoughts and prepares it through meditation for clearer understanding of its mysteries.[144] "As our mind is increasingly renewed by this study, the face of Scripture will also begin to be renewed [*innovari*], and the beauty of a more sacred understanding will somehow grow with the person who is making progress."[145]

Entering deeply into the sacred text clearly transcends a merely intellectual endeavor. Purity of heart will be required for anyone attempting to comprehend the Scriptures. Memorization of texts and clever interpretations devised by even the most erudite do not count as genuine understanding. For the arrogant and the vain cannot possibly attain a genuine spiritual knowledge of the text.[146] Such people are simply incapable of plumbing the spiritual depths of Scripture. "True knowledge [*vera scientia*] is possessed only by true worshippers of God." One can hardly expect someone who has "stained the Catholic faith with unclean works" to have acquired it. The way to genuine comprehension, therefore, is by increasing our practical perfection through righteous works. "No one can properly arrive at searching into the testimonies of God unless he first enters undefiled upon the way of Christ by his practical way of life." So it is that one will often find genuine spiritual knowledge (*vera et spiritualis scientia*) flourishing among the otherwise uncultured and barely literate.[147] Only by living out the text, and not merely "filling the air

---

144. *Collationes* 14.10 (CSEL 13:410–11; Ramsey, 513–15).
145. *Collationes* 14.11 (CSEL 13:411–13; Ramsey, 515).
146. *Collationes* 14.14 (CSEL 13:416–17; Ramsey, 519).
147. *Collationes* 14.16 (CSEL 13:418–21; Ramsey, 520–21).

with words," as one father chastised his disciple, did the monk come to greater understanding of the divine Scriptures.[148]

Jerome

The last of the fathers that we will look at in this chapter, Jerome, hailed from Stridon in present-day Croatia. We noted that as a young man Jerome had studied with the renowned grammarian Donatus before going on to study Greek in Antioch and later learning Hebrew with the help of a Jewish convert. Jerome continued his Hebrew studies in Rome, where he consulted with Jews in their synagogues. All of this language work would eventually be brought to bear when, at the request of Pope Damasus, Jerome undertook a revision of the Latin Bible, which came to be known as the Vulgate and was read throughout the Middle Ages. Jerome's work on the New Testament consisted mainly of revising the Old Latin (*Vetus Latina*). In fact, much of the New Testament Vulgate edition was not even his own work but rather that of Rufinus the Syrian. The work that Jerome did on the Old Testament, however, was quite substantial. He produced the so-called Gallican Psalter by correcting the Latin with the aid of Origen's *Hexapla* edition, which lined up the Hebrew text and various Greek translations side by side. Jerome later undertook a revised translation of the Psalms based on the Hebrew, hence the *Hebraica Veritas*. He believed this to be imperative, having seen how the Greek translations provided in the *Hexapla*—those of Aquila, Symmachus, and Theodotion—exposed how the classic Septuagint (LXX) version differed from the Hebrew text. For Jerome to depart from the Septuagint and thus begin a new translation from the Hebrew was a bold move. Hilary of Poitiers, for instance, had claimed that the seventy translators who produced the Septuagint had access to a secret oral tradition that later translators did not possess. Augustine believed that the Septuagint was a divinely inspired translation designed to lead the gentiles to the Messiah.[149]

Jerome's allegiance to the Hebrew text of the Old Testament was not born simply of a desire for scholarly precision. Like his contemporaries, Jerome believed that Hebrew was the original human language; the multiplicity of languages was therefore God's punishment for the presumptuous tower of Babel (Gen. 11:1–9). Jerome had long been motivated to incorporate into his studies the wisdom inherent in Hebrew. In his *Hebrew Questions*, he appealed

---

148. Burton-Christie, *Word in the Desert*, 160–66.
149. Adam Kamesar, "Jerome," in *New Cambridge History of the Bible*, 1:653–75.

to rabbinic sources and gathered material from Josephus's *Antiquities*. In fact, it was during his work on the *Questions* that he came to recognize the urgent need to recover the *Hebraica Veritas*. What he could not have known, however, was that the Septuagint actually preserved some more ancient readings than the Hebrew texts on which he was basing his new translation. Jerome was also moved by apologetic reasons to jettison the Septuagint. Jews of his own day, now relying on the Hebrew canon, did not accept the Septuagint as an authentic Old Testament text, which meant, in turn, that any Christian arguments made from the Septuagint regarding Christ's divinity and his fulfillment of Old Testament prophecies would be dismissed out of hand. Among the problems with Jerome's Latin translation of the Hebrew, however, is that he edited the text in the process. He therefore introduced explanations into the text, condensed prolix passages, and even reconfigured some to smooth out inconsistencies. This is because Jerome was after readability: he wanted to present the Christian public with a comprehensible and edifying text. In the process, as Kelly observes, Jerome set aside the strict dictates of his classical Latin education so as to create a new "Christian Latin," the impact of which was felt for centuries to come in the Western church.[150]

Jerome was a prolific author, with numerous commentaries and letters to his name in addition to his work on the Bible. His many prologues to various biblical books open a window into his thinking about the canon, the process of translation, and the nature of Scripture as a sacred text. In his prologue to the Pentateuch, for instance, Jerome points out that the gospel writers and Paul offer many quotations of the Old Testament that are not found as such in the Septuagint. Which version of the text should one adopt? For Jerome, the best course of action is to stick with the apostles, since they were filled with the Holy Spirit. We follow the apostles, he says, for it is through their mouth that Christ himself speaks. This great translation project is obviously a daunting task, and so Jerome prays that he will be guided by the same Spirit through which the books themselves were written.[151] In his prologue to the gospels, addressed to Pope Damasus, Jerome also laments the precarious and awesome assignment he has undertaken. Who would dare add to, change, or correct these ancient books?[152] And when he set out to translate the Psalms anew from the Hebrew text, rather than the Greek, Jerome was clearly on the defensive. We see this in his prologue to the Hebrew Psalter, where he

150. J. N. D. Kelly, *Jerome: His Life, Writings, and Controversies* (London: Duckworth, 1975), 153–67.

151. *Biblia Sacra iuxta Vulgatum Versionem*, ed. Robert Weber (Stuttgart: Deutsche Bibelgesellschaft, 1969), 3–4.

152. *Biblia Sacra iuxta Vulgatum Versionem*, 1515–16.

complains of those who prize novelty in all things except when it comes to the study of the Scriptures; then they are content with the old flavor.[153]

Translation is, of course, a subtle operation that demands flexibility on the part of the translator. In his prologue to the book of Job, Jerome stated that he sometimes offers a very literal translation, at other times tries to capture the larger sense of the passage, and then sometimes employs a mix of both approaches (*nunc verba, nunc sensus, nunc simul utrumque resonabit*). Here Jerome also makes clear that he has no wish to condemn the old translation, even as he recognizes that some parts of it are obscure, omitted, or have suffered scribal corruption. He hopes only to make such passages clearer in his own translation.[154]

The Vulgate Bible does not reflect Jerome's ideal canon, since it includes books belonging to the Septuagint that were too popular to be omitted. Jerome made his own views on the canon known in his prologue to the books of Kings, also known as the *Prologus Galeatus*. Here he divided the Old Testament into three sections, comprising twenty-two books in all: the five books of Moses; eight books of the prophets; and nine books of the sacred writings. It was in this prologue that Jerome specifically denied full canonical status to the Wisdom of Solomon, Sirach, 1 and 2 Maccabees, Judith, and Tobit. These he deemed the apocryphal books (*inter apocrifa seponendum . . . non sunt in canone*), which is not to say that he found no value in them. They could be read for edification but were not so authoritative that they could form the basis of Christian doctrine. However, Jerome later spoke of Judith along with Ruth and Esther as "sacred volumes" and referred to Sirach as "Holy Scripture" in his Isaiah commentary, while Wisdom is cited as Scripture (*dicente Scriptura*) in his Jeremiah commentary.[155]

The *Prologus Galeatus* was widely known in the Middle Ages and accepted by some, but it did not command universal adherence. Despite Jerome's authoritative status in the area of biblical studies, there was another ancient source to which medieval exegetes also looked. This was the *Decretum Damasi*, or *De explanatione fidei catholicae*, which was established at a Roman council in 382. Proclaiming the divine Scriptures to be "the foundation upon which the catholic church throughout the world has been founded," this decree provided a list of the Scriptures that have been accepted by the universal catholic church. The list included the very books that Jerome had

153. *Biblia Sacra iuxta Vulgatum Versionem*, 768–69.
154. *Biblia Sacra iuxta Vulgatum Versionem*, 731–32.
155. *Biblia Sacra iuxta Vulgatum Versionem*, 364–66. See also E. F. Sutcliffe, "Jerome," in *The Cambridge History of the Bible*, ed. G. W. H. Lampe (Cambridge: Cambridge University Press, 1969), 2:83–93.

left out of his canon: Wisdom of Solomon, Sirach, 1 and 2 Maccabees, Judith, and Tobit.[156] This document was later incorporated into the *Decretum Gelasianum,* compiled in about 495, perhaps in southern Gaul. It seems that the first three parts of the *Decretum Gelasianum* constitute the earlier *Decretum Damasi,* to which two parts were later added during the pontificate of Gelasius I (492–96).[157] The document as a whole later circulated under the name of Gelasius and eventually entered into the canon law collections attributed to him.[158]

By the seventh century, Isidore of Seville points out that the Jewish canon of the Old Testament accepts twenty-two books, which are then divided into the three categories of law, prophets, and sacred writings. Yet, Isidore says, Christians accept a fourth category not found in the Hebrew canon, which includes the books of Sirach, Judith, Tobit, and others: "For although the Jews put them separately into the apocrypha, the Church of Christ nevertheless honors and proclaims them among the divine books."[159] As for the New Testament, Isidore contends that there are two orders: the evangelical and the apostolic, that is, the four gospels and all the rest of the books from the epistles to the Apocalypse.[160] The writers of these sacred books speak to us through the Holy Spirit for our instruction, since they wrote down precepts for living and the rule of belief (*praecepta vivendi et credendi regulam conscripserunt*).[161]

Isidore also addressed the very concept of an apocryphal book. Books, he says, are considered apocryphal because they have come into doubt. Their origin is unknown even to the fathers, from whom authority and certainty regarding the veracity of the Scriptures come down to the church in later generations. Although there may be some truth within these books, the falsity that they also possess excludes them from holding canonical authority.[162] Isidore was furthermore concerned to defend the textual integrity of the Old Testament books that the church does accept. Thus he contended that Ezra, under the inspiration of the Holy Spirit (*divino afflatus Spiritu*), had corrected the volumes that were corrupted during the Babylonian captivity.[163]

---

156. *De explanatione fidei catholicae* (PL 19:787–93).
157. *Decretum Gelasianum* (PL 59:157–64). See D. J. Chapman, "On the Decretum Gelasianum: De Libris Recipiendis et non Recipiendis," *Revue Bénédictine* 30 (1913): 187–207, 315–33.
158. Gilbert Dahan, *L'exégèse chrétienne de la Bible en Occident médiéval* (Paris: Cerf, 1999), 57–61.
159. *Etymologiarum* 6.1 (PL 82:229d–30a).
160. *Etymologiarum* 6.1 (PL 82:230a).
161. *Etymologiarum* 6.2 (PL 82:235b).
162. *Etymologiarum* 6.2 (PL 82:235b).
163. *Etymologiarum* 6.3 (PL 82:235c).

As we shall see in later chapters, the state of the biblical canon and the relative authority of various authors were still open questions. Beyond those issues, the status of the biblical text itself, after centuries of recopying and attempts at emendation, could be quite a contentious issue. One thing that was not in doubt throughout the Middle Ages, however, was the status of the church fathers; their exegetical authority exceeded that of even the most ingenious medieval master.

2

The Early Middle Ages

This chapter marks a transition from the patristic age, which flourished largely in the Mediterranean world of the Roman Empire, to the medieval era as it unfolded in western and northern Europe. We begin with a polymathic historian and exegete hailing from the outermost reaches of Western Christendom in the eighth century. Although he lived centuries after Jerome and Augustine, the Anglo-Saxon monk and scholar Bede the Venerable (672–735) was ranked among the great Latin fathers by future generations. A child oblate, Bede spent his life from age seven at the Northumbrian monastery of Wearmouth-Jarrow, which had been founded by Benedict Biscop in 674–81. A native speaker of Old English, Bede received a solid education, reading the Greek and Latin Christian writers as well as the classical authors and learning Gregorian chant. While Bede himself never left England, his reputation for both scholarship and sanctity stretched to the Continent; in fact, some of his relics made it all the way to the monastery at Fulda in Germany.[1]

Bede's first-rate education owes much to the remarkable library at Wearmouth-Jarrow, which, despite its remote location, managed to amass some two hundred volumes, thanks to the industry of its abbot Ceolfrith. This collection contained not only writings of the church fathers but also works such as Virgil's *Aeneid* and *Georgics* and Pliny the Elder's *Natural History*, among others.[2] This monk living at the northern edge of Christian

---

1. Michelle Brown, "Bede's Life in Context," in *The Cambridge Companion to Bede*, ed. Scott DeGregorio (Cambridge: Cambridge University Press, 2010), 3–24.

2. Rosalind Love, "The World of Latin Learning," in *Cambridge Companion to Bede*, 40–53.

Europe was therefore able to immerse himself in the classical age that Jerome and Augustine knew so well and thus to extend their epoch into his own. To its lasting credit, moreover, Wearmouth-Jarrow produced three complete one-volume Vulgate Bibles (i.e., pandects), one of which survives intact: the Codex Amiatinus, a deluxe edition that the abbot Ceolfrith, having made the long and arduous journey to the center of Latin Christendom, presented to the pope in 716.

Near the end of his most celebrated work, the *Ecclesiastical History* (5.24), Bede recounted a life immersed in the Scriptures: "And from that time [age seven] spending all the days of my life in the mansion of the same monastery, I have applied all my diligence to the study of the Scriptures [*meditandis Scripturis operam dedi*]; and observing the regular discipline and keeping the daily service of singing in the church. I have delighted always either to learn, or to teach, or to write."[3] Bede's output in scriptural studies alone was prodigious. The audience for his biblical commentaries comprised laymen as well as bishops and monks, most of whom would have been of aristocratic status. These were people sufficiently educated to follow and appreciate his erudite Latin prose and his subtle theological exposition. Bede always wrote, however, with pastoral goals foremost in mind: biblical exegesis must find practical application in the life of his fellow Anglo-Saxon Christians. Part of this larger effort meant rendering the vast and unwieldy patristic corpus manageable for his readers. Thus in the preface to his work on Genesis, Bede admits that while it is true that many before him have commented on this book, such works might prove too difficult for most readers and complete editions too expensive. He would summarize them, therefore, taking what could be most useful to nonexperts. Bede was not only a compiler and arranger of patristic exegesis; he also tackled biblical books for which there was little or no patristic precedent, such as Tobit and Ezra-Nehemiah, among others. With respect to exegetical methodology, Bede was certainly conversant with the fourfold exegesis laid out by John Cassian, but he did not rigidly apply all four levels to every text. Thus he would very often speak in terms of a basic twofold distinction between the literal-historical on the one hand, and the figurative, mystical, or hidden sense on the other. In the case of the Song of Songs, however, he maintained that that there was no literal meaning, such that it had to be read purely on the level of the spiritual or typical sense.[4]

3. *Ecclesiastical History*, trans. J. E. King, LCL 248, 2 vols. (Cambridge, MA: Harvard University Press, 1930), 2:382–83.

4. Scott DeGregorio, "Bede and the Old Testament," in *Cambridge Companion to Bede*, 127–41.

With respect to the New Testament, Bede wrote substantial commentaries on the Gospels of Mark and Luke, as well the Acts of the Apostles, and the catholic epistles. Here too Bede undertook his exegetical work with pastoral aspirations. Thus even as he located all manner of spiritual readings, it was their moral application that he wanted to draw out for his readers.[5]

Putting his classical education to work in the service of Holy Scripture, much as the fathers had done, Bede took it upon himself early in his career to compose a short grammatical-rhetorical textbook, *De schematibus et tropis*, which later became a staple of Carolingian education. While it was not a work of originality, it was a masterful compendium, ideal for teaching young clerics the essential facets of the trivium and drawing on such esteemed sources as Augustine, Cassiodorus, Isidore of Seville, and the grammarian Donatus.[6] At the outset, Bede offers brief definitions of his subject matter, noting that what the Greek grammarians had called a "schema," he and his sources refer to as a habit, form, or figure, because through it speech is in a certain manner clothed or adorned. As for tropic discourse (*tropica locutio*), it was customarily defined as an instance of linguistic transference (*translata dictione*) whereby a phrase is employed not according to its proper signification, but improperly, in order to highlight some likeness and also for the sake of adornment. Beyond these broad definitions there will be many species, all of which the diligent exegete will need to be aware when reading Scripture. Having thus defined his subject matter, Bede then draws the reader's attention to the unique status of Holy Scripture. Scripture exceeds all other writings by virtue of its divine authority and its usefulness in leading to eternal life but also by its antiquity.[7] Thus, in the first part of the work, from the wide array of extant verbal arrangements (*schemata*), Bede has taken it upon himself to gather up from Scripture eighteen of the most prominent: *prolepsis*, *zeugma*, *hypozeuxis*, and so forth. What made this list especially valuable to his readers is that Bede's examples are drawn directly from Scripture. For each entry, Bede begins with a short definition of the schema before providing the biblical example. In this way beginners can cement the principle in their mind and then on their own search for similar instances across the Scriptures.[8]

5. Arthur Holder, "Bede and the New Testament," in *Cambridge Companion to Bede*, 142–55; and Paul Meyvaert, "Bede the Scholar," in *Essays in Commemoration of the Thirteenth Centenary of the Birth of the Venerable Bede*, ed. Christi Famulus and Gerald Bonner (London: SPCK, 1976), 150.

6. *De schematibus et tropis*, ed. C. B. King, CCSL 123a (Turnhout: Brepols, 1975), 142–71.

7. *De schematibus et tropis* 1 (CCSL 123a:142–43).

8. *De schematibus et tropis* 1 (CCSL 123a:142–51).

In the second part, Bede turns to tropes, or transferred signification, which also come in many varieties, from metaphor to synecdoche, to hyperbole, and allegory, among others.[9] For our purposes we will look at Bede's treatment of allegory (of which, he states, there are many sorts). Here, though, Bede follows the traditional definition that Jerome had given: allegory is a trope by which something is signified other than what is said. For example, "Lift up your eyes and see the countries, for they are white already to harvest" (John 4:35) means "Understand that the people have already been prepared to believe."[10] As Bede continues, he explains that an allegory sometimes occurs by means of historical facts (*factis*) and sometimes only by words (*verbis*). An example of the former can be found in the apostle Paul's invocation of the Genesis account, "It is written that Abraham had two sons, one from the slave woman and one from the free woman," which are "the two testaments" (Gal. 4:22–24). However, it is an allegory in words alone when we read "A rod from the root of Jesse, and a flower from his root will ascend" (Isa. 11:1), by which is signified, according to Bede, that from the lineage of David, the Lord and Savior would be born through the Virgin Mary. And yet there are still other instances when by facts and words one and the same reality (*res*) is allegorically signified. Thus the selling of Joseph to the Ishmaelites for twenty pieces of silver (Gen. 37:28) is a factual occurrence that refers allegorically to Christ, just as the words of the prophet Zechariah also apply to Christ when he said "They weighed for my wages thirty pieces of silver" (Zech. 11:12). And again, it is related as historical fact that David was "ruddy and beautiful to behold" as he was anointed by Samuel (1 Sam. 16:11–12), while one reads in the Song of Songs "My beloved is white and ruddy, chosen out of thousands" (Song 5:10 DRA). According to Bede, both the 1 Samuel passage and the Song of Songs verse mystically signify (*mystice significat*) Christ, the mediator who is adorned with wisdom and virtue but is also red with the effusion of blood and anointed by God the Father "with the oil of gladness above all of your companions" (Ps. 44:8 Vulg. [45:7 Eng.]).[11]

Bede then expands on the genre of allegory, whether by deeds or words, noting that an allegory may point to a historical reality (*res*); be a type; be tropological, thus denoting a moral principle; or be anagogical, figuratively denoting some meaning that leads to higher things. Bede maintains that through one historical event some other historical reality can be signified. For example, when the patriarch Jacob said "Judah is a lion's whelp; to the

9. *De schematibus et tropis* 2 (CCSL 123a:152–71).
10. *De schematibus et tropis* 2 (CCSL 123a:161–62).
11. *De schematibus et tropis* 2 (CCSL 123a:165–66).

prey my son, you have gone up" (Gen. 49:9), this can be understood to refer to the actual kingdom and the victories of David. Yet on a spiritual, or typological, level Jacob's words can refer to Christ or the church, since the very same discourse of Jacob can be faithfully received (*fideliter accipitur*) regarding the Lord's passion and resurrection. Bede pursues further variations, but he wishes to impress upon the reader the range of meanings that one passage may possess. There are times when, through one and the same thing or word (*in uno eodemque re vel verbo*), history, along with the mystical sense regarding Christ and the church, and tropology, along with anagogy, might be figuratively intimated (*figuraliter intimatur*). Bede uses the temple of the Lord as an example: historically (*iuxta historiam*) it was the house built by Solomon; allegorically it was the Lord's body as he said, "Destroy this temple and I will raise it up in three days" (John 2:19), or the church as Paul says, "The temple of the Lord is holy, which you are" (1 Cor. 3:17); tropologically it is any of the faithful: "Do you not know that your body is a temple of the Holy Spirit who is within you" (1 Cor. 6:19); and anagogically it is the joy of the heavenly dwelling to which he aspired when he said, "Blessed are those who dwell in your house" (Ps. 83:5 Vulg. [84:4 Eng.]).[12]

Such, then, was the sort of preparatory training designed to equip English, and later Carolingian, biblical scholars as they set about their work. In this vein, before turning to Bede's exegetical works, we can briefly consider his comments on a verse from the Song of Songs wherein he addresses the mysteries of Scripture and the task of the exegete: "Your lips, my spouse, are dripping honeycomb" (Song 4:11). Bede writes,

> A honeycomb is honey in the comb, and honey in the comb is the spiritual sense of the divine scriptures in the letter that is rightly called a dripping honeycomb; for a honeycomb drips when it has more honey than its wax chambers can hold, doubtless because the fecundity of the holy scriptures is such that a verse that was written in a short line fills many pages if one squeezes it by careful examination to see how much sweetness of spiritual understanding it contains inside. . . . Therefore the honeycomb is not only full of honey but it is also dripping from the lips of the bride when the church's teachers show that it contains the manifold abundance of inner sweetness, whether in figures of the law, or in the prophetic sayings, or in the mystical words and deeds of the Lord himself, and then prepare from them the sumptuous dishes that are most pleasing to her faithful members (that is, to worthy listeners) and most salutary for their souls.[13]

12. *De schematibus et tropis* 2 (CCSL 123a:166–69).
13. *Expositio in Canticum Canticorum* 3.4.10, ed. David Hurst, CCSL 119b (Turnhout: Brepols, 1983), 260. Translation given in George Hardin Brown, *A Companion to Bede* (Woodbridge, UK: Boydell, 2010), 37–38.

Although there are surely hundreds of such paeans to Scripture written across the Middle Ages, Bede's evocative and sensual portrayal of the sacred page and its interpretation—the sweetness of God's Word—is especially stirring.

Adept in the application of the four senses of Scripture, and certainly willing to pursue the deeper spiritual meaning of the text where appropriate, Bede never lost sight of the importance of the underlying literal-historical level. So it is in his Genesis commentary that Bede cautions the reader, "But it must be carefully observed, as each one devotes his attention to the allegorical senses [*sensibus allegoricis*], how far he may have forsaken the manifest truth of history [*apertam historiae fidem*] by allegorical interpretation [*allegorizando*]."[14] Hence when Bede addresses the creation accounts in Genesis, he does not question their historical veracity as Origen had done some five hundred years earlier. Yet when he comes to the (second) account of humanity's beginnings, Bede declares that it was "for the sake of a deeper mystery" (*altioris mysterii*) that the bone was removed from Adam while he was asleep. "For it signified that the sacraments of salvation were to come from the side of Christ on the cross by the death of the sleeping one, namely the blood and water, from which his bride, the Church, would be founded." Indeed, there would have been no reason for Adam to have slept, Bede says, except that this great mystery, or sacrament (*tanti sacramenti*), might be symbolized (*esset figura*) in this divine action. Bede continues that Scripture employs a figurative word (*typico verbo*) here to again signify this great mystery, noting that rather than using words such as "made" (*fecit*), "formed" (*formavit*), or "created" (*creavit*), it is said that the Lord "built" (*aedificavit*) the rib that he took from Adam, "as if it were a house [*tamquam domum*]," thereby linking this account to Hebrews 3:6, "which house [*domum*] we are if we hold fast the confidence and glory of hope unto the end." And so, Bede concludes, it was fitting that the human race might begin in this manner, thereby offering a prophetic prefiguration of the redemption that this same Creator would establish at the end time.[15] Nothing is done without a reason; no word is out of place when read in the context of the whole Bible. Here, then, the Epistle to the Hebrews provides the explanation—indeed the christological significance—necessary for fully grasping the meaning of this Genesis account.

14. *Expositio in Genesim* 1.1, ed. C. W. Jones, CCSL 118a (Turnhout: Brepols, 1967), 3. *On Genesis*, trans. Calvin Kendall (Liverpool: Liverpool University Press, 2008), 69. For further discussion, see Kendall, "The Responsibility of *Auctoritas*: Method and Meaning in Bede's Commentary on Genesis," in *Innovation and Tradition in the Writings of the Venerable Bede*, ed. Scott DeGregorio (Morgantown: West Virginia University Press, 2006), 101–19.
15. *Expositio in Genesim* 1.2.20–22 (CCSL 118a:56–57; Kendall, 122).

Bede continued to trace the christological and ecclesiological dimensions of this creation account as he turned to the Latin, as well as the underlying Hebrew, significance of the designations "man" and "woman." Whether his etymology is accurate is beside the point. What is important is that Bede, here dependent upon Jerome (*Heb. quaest.* 2.23), was willing to employ whatever linguistic information was available to him in order more fully to engage the letter of the text and thus unlock its deeper mysteries. To that end he observes that just as the Latin word for woman (*virago*) is derived from the word for man (*vir*), so in Hebrew "woman" (*ishah*) is derived from "man" (*ish*). None of this is without significance as Bede links it to the mysteries of Christ and his church. As Adam gave a share of his name to his partner created from his flesh, so "our Lord Jesus Christ also gave a share in his name to his church, which he redeemed at the price of his own body and blood and chose as a bride for himself, so that it was called 'Christian' from Christ."[16]

Pursuing this line of typology, Bede traces the significance for the incarnation in the verse, "Wherefore a man shall leave his father and mother and shall cleave to his wife, and they shall be two in one flesh" (Gen. 2:24). Bede has already established that the creation of woman from man speaks to the church's procession from Christ, but what are we to make of this man having left behind father and mother? This mystery can be unlocked first of all by turning to the New Testament, specifically the apostle Paul's declaration that "when he [Christ] was in the form of God, he thought it not robbery to be equal with God, but emptied himself, taking on the form of a servant" (Phil. 2:6–7). And so, Bede says, Christ had thus left his Father, not that he forsook his Father, but that he relinquished the glorious form of equality with the Father when he lived among humankind. As for his mother, this symbolizes his having left the synagogue of the Jews when he cleaved to the church that had been gathered from all the nations, such that they would now be one flesh in the blessing of the new covenant. Christ, therefore, "was made our partner through the flesh, so that we can be the body of his head" (cf. Eph. 1:22–23).[17]

In a letter addressed to Bishop Acca of Hexam at the opening of his commentary on the Gospel of Luke, Bede offers us a valuable glimpse of his quotidian modus operandi. First, there was the sheer physical labor of producing an exegetical text, as Bede himself had served simultaneously as author (*dictator*), scribe (*notarius*), and copyist (*librarius*). He therefore did not follow the usual procedure of a master dictating his work to a scribe taking notes upon a wax tablet, before committing it to parchment. Rather, Bede personally

---

16. *Expositio in Genesim* 1.2.22–23 (CCSL 118a:57; Kendall, 123).
17. *Expositio in Genesim* 1.2.24 (CCSL 118a:58; Kendall, 124).

took upon himself the painstaking work of the monastic scriptorium. Here he also informs Acca of his method of citing the different church fathers that he quotes throughout the commentary. Bede will use letters placed in the margins of the text to designate the author, whether Augustine, Gregory, or Jerome, diligently marking where their words begin and end, lest he appear to be plagiarizing their work.[18]

One recalls that in the opening verses of his gospel, Luke had explained to his patron Theophilus his purpose and methods employed in composing this work. Bede immediately latched on to Luke's pastoral concerns; his reason (*causa*) for writing this gospel, Bede says, was to counter the preaching of false evangelists, those leaders of sects who disseminate their heresy under apostolic identities. Bede reports that their writings have appeared under the names of Thomas and Bartholomew, among others of the Twelve. Luke therefore offers his patron an authentic account as opposed to those heretical tracts that are devoid of the inspiration of the Holy Spirit. Thus while heretics such as Basilides present works that have covered over the truth of history (*veritatem historiae*), Luke is handing down what others have actually witnessed of the incarnate Lord. Luke, in other words, has taken it upon himself not merely to recount the ministry of Jesus but also to defend Christian orthodoxy. Here as well there is a sense of immediacy, as Bede assures all readers of Luke that they too can share in that first-century address to Theophilus. As his very name means "lover of God" or "one loved by God," so all who love God and desire to be loved by him may also read this work as addressed to them.[19] Across the centuries, Luke is speaking to the monks, priests, and laypeople of the monasteries, villages, and castles by the Rivers Tyne and Wear.

Bede's pastoral orientation should not obscure the fact that his Luke commentary is replete with spiritual interpretations of one sort or another. There is, for instance, the typological reading of the angel's appearance before Zechariah at the right hand of the altar (Luke 1:11). Bede finds it fitting that the angel would come in this way, thereby signifying the advent of Christ the true priest and the mystery of his universal sacrifice.[20] That the name "Jesus" proclaimed to Mary (1:31) means "savior" leads Bede to cite the angel's words to Joseph in the Gospel of Matthew: "He will save his people from their sins" (Matt. 1:21). Bede points out that the angel did not say "the people of Israel" but rather "his own people," thereby designating the universal scope

18. *Expositio in Lucae Evangelium*, prologue, ed. David Hurst, CCSL 120 (Turnhout: Brepols, 1960), 7.
19. *Expositio in Lucae Evangelium* 1.1–4 (CCSL 120:19–20).
20. *Expositio in Lucae Evangelium* 1.11 (CCSL 120:24).

of Christ's salvific activity. The words of the angel recorded by Luke, here brought into sharper focus with a turn to Matthew's Gospel, speak therefore to the unity of faith among the circumcised and uncircumcised; two peoples called from different backgrounds have become a single congregation, one sheepfold with one shepherd.[21]

And in the next verse a sophisticated christological point is made: "He will be great and called Son of the Most High" (Luke 1:32). Christ therefore is at once Son of the Most High, who was conceived in his mother's womb and born as a man within time, created from his mother, and yet also God, born before all time from the Father. If it is this very same man who is God, Bede says, this must refute Nestorius, who held that the man alone, but not the Word, was born of the Virgin Mary, thus resulting not in a genuine unity of person but merely an inseparable fellowship. By Bede's analysis, however, this would be to say that there is not one Christ, who is true God and true man, but rather two, which is blasphemous (*nefas*) to assert. It would lead, furthermore, to positing not a Trinity but a quaternity. Yet the "catholic faith" maintains, according to Bede, that just as any single human being is a union of body and soul, so the one Christ is rightly confessed to be both Word and man.[22] Such a battle with Nestorianism was typical of Bede's persistent concern to secure his fellow Englishmen in the true faith and to shore up the solidly catholic credentials of the English church itself.

Moving deeper into Luke's Gospel, we come to Bede's comments on the parables of the good Samaritan and prodigal son, which are illustrative of his pastoral exegesis. Filled as these treatments are with mystical expositions, they nonetheless offer moral guidelines for living out the Christian life. Also interesting, although not unique to Bede, is the ease with which he provided spiritual interpretations of what were already parables—that is, stories told for the sake of moral instruction as opposed to historical narratives (*res gestae*). Bede begins his exposition of the good Samaritan (Luke 10:30–37) noting that, in his response to the lawyer, Christ wishes to teach us the way to heavenly life. Here we will find, Bede says, that steadfast mercy for one's neighbor demands of us that we outwardly demonstrate our love, not by a mere show of words (*non verbo tenus*), but by concrete action. Yet this parable of the good Samaritan, a moral exercise instituted "under the rules of allegory" (*sub allegoriae regulis*), actually has a dual purpose. For Christ, according to Bede, had tempered his response in such a way that he might instruct us not only in the mercy to be shown to our neighbor but also by the same parable

21. *Expositio in Lucae Evangelium* 1.31 (CCSL 120:31–32).
22. *Expositio in Lucae Evangelium* 1.32 (CCSL 120:32).

to demonstrate how the Son of God deigned to become a neighbor to us by taking on human nature.[23]

Bede's spiritual reading of the parable itself does follow Augustine closely,[24] although it is more than a simple repetition of his patristic forebear. What Bede has chosen from the fathers, how he has arranged it, and what he has added of his own serves the single end of edifying fellow members of the English church. Here the man who makes his way down from Jerusalem to Jericho is Adam and consequently is the human race itself, fallen from the celestial city of peace and into mortal misery. The robbers are the devil and his angels, who were able to prey on Adam in his fallen state; unless he had not already become swollen on the inside, he would not so easily have succumbed to their outward temptations. As it was, though, the demons stripped him of the garments of glory and immortality. This Bede likens to the fate of the prodigal son, who had also lost this original mantle, which he subsequently recouped in his repentance.[25]

Continuing along the trajectory of salvation history, having begun with the fall, we reach the giving of the law. Thus the priest and the Levite who happen upon the man (Luke 10:31–32) represent the old law, which could point to the wounds of a languishing world but was unable to cure them. Indeed, this would have been impossible, in keeping with the admonition that the blood of calves, sheep, and goats could not take away sin (Heb. 10:4).[26] Salvation therefore comes in the person of the Samaritan, who signifies the Lord himself, the one "who for us men and our salvation descended from heaven," as Bede cites the Nicene Creed. Christ has entered into this present life and taken his place alongside man wasting away from his wounds; here he quotes the apostle Paul: "He was made in the likeness of men" (Phil. 2:7). Finally, the inn to which the Samaritan takes the wounded man is the church, which refreshes the pilgrim on his return to his native land.[27]

At the conclusion of his parable, Jesus asks the lawyer who of the three was the neighbor to the man who had fallen among thieves, to which the lawyer correctly answers, "The one who had mercy on him" (Luke 10:36–37). At this point, Bede acknowledges that the Lord's meaning (*sententia*) is certainly clear according to the literal sense (*iuxta litteram manifesta*): no one is as close to us, and thus our neighbor (*proximum*), as the one who has mercy. Yet, Bede says, there is a still more sacred understanding to be found; for if no one is

23. *Expositio in Lucae Evangelium* 10.28–29 (CCSL 120:221–22).
24. *Quaestiones en. s. Luc.* (PL 35:1340).
25. *Expositio in Lucae Evangelium* 10.30 (CCSL 120:222).
26. *Expositio in Lucae Evangelium* 10.31–32 (CCSL 120:223).
27. *Expositio in Lucae Evangelium* 10.33–34 (CCSL 120:223).

more near (*proximus*) than the one who bound up our wounds, let us love that one as though loving the Lord our God. As nothing is as close as the head to the members, let us then also love the one who is an imitator of Christ.[28] Bede has thereby drawn his readers into the larger mystery of Christ's body, the church, so as to show them their neighbors not simply as proximate and even beneficent human beings but especially as participants in the divine life by virtue of their union with the Son of God.

Bede's reading of the prodigal son (Luke 15:11–32) also draws on Augustine as well as Ambrose, but here again there is original material. The man with two sons is understood to be God the Father, progenitor of two sorts of human beings: the first, represented by the older son, are those who have remained worshipers of the one God, while the younger signifies those who have deserted God for the worship of idols.[29] Addressing the younger son's eventual repentance and desire to return to his father (15:18–19), Bede extols the mercy of God. Confessing that he has sinned against heaven, thus in the sight of the angelic spirits and saints who are seated with God, the son also confesses his sin before the father, which signifies for Bede the interior locked room of conscience that only the eyes of God can penetrate. That he confesses his unworthiness even to be called his son thereby refutes the Pelagians, according to Bede, who trust that they can be saved by their own power. Such misplaced confidence runs "contrary to the most open meaning of the truth" (*contra apertissimam veritatis sententiam*) Bede says, for the Lord himself has said that "apart from me you can do nothing" (John 15:5).[30] Bede's concern that Pelagianism, an originally English heresy, be specifically rebutted may be indicative of its lasting attractiveness to Bede's fellow Anglo-Saxon Christians.

The son's return and investment with a new robe (Luke 15:22) speak not only to the reinstatement of one lost sinner but also to the restoration of the fallen human race. The first robe had been the garment of innocence that the first humans had received at their creation and then been persuaded to cast off. Following the guilt of their trespass, the man and woman then recognized themselves to be nude, having lost the mantle of glory and immortality. The servants summoned by the father in the parable to clothe the prodigal son are the preachers of reconciliation offering humankind the original robe whereby they might become coheirs with Christ. The ring that the son receives is the sign of sincere faith, given in the hand so that through works faith might be illustrated, and through faith works firmly grounded. And the shoes for his

---

28. *Expositio in Lucae Evangelium* 10.36–37 (CCSL 120:224).
29. *Expositio in Lucae Evangelium* 15.11–12 (CCSL 120:287).
30. *Expositio in Lucae Evangelium* 15.18–19 (CCSL 120:289–90).

feet signify the office of evangelization; running along its course, these feet will be preserved inviolate and fortified so as to tread safely over serpents and scorpions.[31]

We can conclude our section on the Venerable Bede with a look at his important commentary on the Old Testament books of Ezra and Nehemiah. Scott DeGregorio, following the line earlier established by Alan Thacker, has pointed to Bede's concern for the reform of the Northumbrian church, which is borne out not only in both his *Ecclesiastical History* and *Life of St. Cuthbert* but also in his exegetical works, notably the Ezra-Nehemiah commentary. Bede, as DeGregorio has pointed out, looked to the Old Testament accounts of reform and renewal in ancient Israel as a model for his own day. These biblical texts could speak directly, therefore, to contemporary churchmen who might need to be reminded of their pastoral obligations.[32] In the case of Ezra-Nehemiah, Bede clearly recognized the power and relevance of this work, which had never received a patristic commentary of its own. Bede, therefore, had to start from scratch. He turned to the fathers for guidance, principally Jerome, and could apply some of their wisdom, but in creating a stand-alone commentary, he was on his own. It is a testimony to Bede's pioneering work on Ezra-Nehemiah, as well as the reverence in which he was held by succeeding generations, that the twelfth-century *Glossa Ordinaria* produced at Laon relied solely on Bede to provide commentary for these books.[33]

In his prologue Bede informs Bishop Acca that, in keeping with the words of "the famous translator and interpreter of Holy Scripture Jerome," he too, with the gracious assistance of Jesus Christ, would attempt "to find, when the bark of the letter is peeled back [*retecto cortice litterae*], something deeper and more sacred in the marrow of the spiritual sense [*in medulla sensus spiritalis*], since by prophetic figures but in a clear way [this book] designates the Lord himself and his temple and city, which we are," for already, "the prophets . . . themselves had foretold that the same events which Ezra and Nehemiah wrote about, would be carried out under the figure of Christ and the Church [*sub figura Christi et ecclesiae*]."[34]

At the outset of the commentary, Bede reminds his readers that "in the Holy Scriptures each one of the elect and all the Church together [i.e., the whole

31. *Expositio in Lucae Evangelium* 15.22 (CCSL 120:291).
32. *On Ezra and Nehemiah*, trans. Scott DeGregorio (Liverpool: Liverpool University Press, 2006), xxxi–xxxviii. See Alan Thacker, "Bede's Ideal of Reform," in *Ideal and Reality in Frankish and Anglo-Saxon Society: Studies Presented to J. M. Wallace-Hadrill* (Oxford: Oxford University Press, 1983), 130–50.
33. DeGregorio, *On Ezra and Nehemiah*, xxxvi.
34. *Expositio in Ezram et Neemiam*, prologue, ed. D. Hurst, CCSL 119a (Turnhout: Brepols, 1969), 237; *On Ezra and Nehemiah*, trans. DeGregorio, 1–2.

body of the just] are customarily called God's house or temple, because God deigns to dwell in the hearts of those who believe and hope in him and love him." Hence Ezra-Nehemiah, recounting as it does the reconstruction of the temple, can be read as an ecclesiological text. Here Bede declares that the first temple, built by Solomon, already served as a symbol (*figura*) of the spiritual house or temple, and Solomon himself (whose name means "peaceful") fittingly symbolized Christ, whose "empire will be multiplied, and there will be no end of peace" (Isa. 9:7).[35] And yet this same temple, defiled by persistent evil and ultimately destroyed, "signifies [*significat*] the more weighty faults of those who, though they were united with the members of the Holy Church through the confession of the right faith and the sacrament of the washing of salvation, nonetheless were cast down once more from the foundation of the faith by the deception of evil spirits and were consumed in the flames of vices." During the subsequent seventy years in Babylon, the Israelites repented of their sins; that they finally returned to rebuild their temple and city is likewise not without symbolic value. For it "figuratively designates" (*figurate designat*) the restoration of all those who have been deceived by the devil but later, by grace and the illumination of the Holy Spirit, return to the church and so begin once more to keep the divine law.[36] Bede continues this theme of repentance and restoration, speaking of "those who were separated because of their sins from the communion and society of the Holy Church," once more taking up good works and joining again the ranks of the faithful. For, according to Bede, all that is recounted here "typologically denotes" (*typice denuntiant*) the return of penitents to the church. And now Bede wants to expound upon these events recounted by Ezra "according to the spiritual sense [*spiritali sensu*] so that it may be more clearly disclosed [*manifestius patefiat*] how those who have perished due to negligence and error should be brought back to repentance."[37]

As we observed above, Bede sought exemplars in the Old Testament who could serve the cause of reform within the Northumbrian church. The Persian king Darius fits the bill on this score, presenting a model of pious kingship as he orders the reconstruction of the temple (Ezra 6:6–7). Bede makes this very plain: "Let Darius designate the dutiful devotion of those kings who, recognizing the will of God, endeavored not only not to resist the Christian faith but also assist it with their decrees." That funds were provided out of the king's treasury speaks to "the Church throughout the world having been enriched by the generosity of royal gifts."[38] Darius's pledge of protection

---

35. *Expositio in Ezram et Neemiam* 1 (CCSL 119a:241; DeGregorio, 6).
36. *Expositio in Ezram et Neemiam* 1 (CCSL 119a:242; DeGregorio, 7–8).
37. *Expositio in Ezram et Neemiam* 1 (CCSL 119a:243; DeGregorio, 9).
38. *Expositio in Ezram et Neemiam* 2 (CCSL 119a:294–95; DeGregorio, 88–89).

(Ezra 6:12) is also read in contemporary terms, as Bede observes: "This occurs in the same way today in the Holy Church when terrestrial powers that have been converted to the faith issue public edicts for the establishment of the Church."[39]

Just as Darius exemplified the devout king who provided for God's people, so Ezra himself could serve as a type of Christ, leading his people out of captivity to freedom in Jerusalem. He is invested with "pontifical authority" (*pontificali auctoritate*) as he purges the people of their foreign wives, thereby providing an example to the contemporary church, a point that Bede reckons is already clear to the more erudite reader (*docto lectori*), but one he will further elucidate for the less learned (*simplicioribus*).[40] Here again kings are called on to assist holy men in their reforming tasks, just as Artaxerxes had thrown his weight behind the sacred work of Ezra (Ezra 7:21–22). "Christian rulers," Bede says in the clearest terms, "must also order all who are subjected to them to give whatever our Lord and *Pontifex* may ask of them without any hesitation."[41] Bede does not hesitate, therefore, to draw such a connection between the Persian king and the kings of his own day. In fact, he says that in drawing up this decree, Artaxerxes "clearly expresses what devotion Christian kings in later days would have and what they were to do with respect to the true faith." Thus when commenting on the verse, "Blessed be the Lord the God of our fathers, who has put it in the king's heart to glorify the house of the Lord which is in Jerusalem" (7:27), Bede writes: "And who would hesitate to confess that his words were holy and mystical [*sancta eius ac mystica dicta*]?"[42]

Finally, though, Bede also has words of warning for those churchmen who not only neglect their flocks but also burden them with excessive taxes. Commenting on Nehemiah 5:1–4, "Now there was a great outcry of the people," Bede writes in a tone reminiscent of a letter he sent to Bishop Ecgberht,

> For how many are there among God's people who willingly desire to obey the divine commands but are hindered from being able to fulfill what they desire not only by a lack of temporal means and by poverty, but also by the examples of those who seem to be endowed with the garb of religion but who exact an immense tax and weight of worldly goods from those they claim to be in charge of while giving nothing for their eternal salvation either by teaching them or by providing them with examples of good living or by devoting efforts to works

39. *Expositio in Ezram et Neemiam* 2 (CCSL 119a:296; DeGregorio, 91).
40. *Expositio in Ezram et Neemiam* 2 (CCSL 119a:309–10; DeGregorio, 113–14).
41. *Expositio in Ezram et Neemiam* 2 (CCSL 119a:316; DeGregorio, 123).
42. *Expositio in Ezram et Neemiam* 2 (CCSL 119a:318–19; DeGregorio, 126).

of piety for them? Would that some Nehemiah (i.e., "consoler from the Lord") might come in our own days and restrain our errors, kindle our breast to love of the divine, and strengthen our hands by turning them away from our own pleasures to establishing Christ's city.[43]

There is no need to resort to allegory in this case; the literal sense of the text gets the point across quite effectively. So it is that Bede calls on the reader to observe the "literal meaning" (*iuxta litteram*) of the cries of this afflicted people and in the just response (Neh. 5:7–8) not to seek the allegorical sense (*allegoriae sensum*) but again to observe the precise literal meaning (*ipsum litterae textum*). Let us actually carry out what this text demands, Bede exhorts his fellow churchmen, not only through daily almsgiving but also by caring for people in time of famine, and not merely giving to the poor when we can but also forgiving them the debts we are accustomed to exact, so that the Father might also forgive us our own debts.[44] Bede's practical application of biblical exegesis designed to guide the contemporary church was very much embraced on the continent by scholars in the age of Charlemagne.

The Carolingian Era

Within just a few decades of Bede's death a great project of cultural renewal was under way on the European continent within the kingdom of the Franks. At the heart of this Carolingian Renaissance, taken up during the reign of Charles the Great (Charlemagne), was the recovery of classical learning, most clearly manifested in the renewed attention paid to the trivium: dialectic, grammar, and rhetoric. It was well understood that the reformation of Frankish society would depend on education: to read, write, and pronounce Latin correctly. The liberal arts were essential to achieving this task. In fact, John Scotus believed that these arts were inherent to humankind and had been obscured only in the wake of the fall. To learn the liberal arts was itself an effort to recover the original human condition.[45] Matters of grammar and style were not merely the preoccupation of scholarly monks; they were also taken very seriously at the highest levels of Frankish society. So it was that Alcuin of York responded by letter to a set of grammatical questions that had been raised in the court of Charlemagne. He was asked, for instance, about the

43. *Expositio in Ezram et Neemiam* 3 (CCSL 119a:359–60; DeGregorio, 184).
44. *Expositio in Ezram et Neemiam* 3 (CCSL 119a:360; DeGregorio, 184–85).
45. John Contreni, "Learning in the Early Middle Ages," in *Carolingian Learning, Masters and Manuscripts* (Hampshire, UK: Ashgate, 1992), 1–21.

gender of certain nouns and the correct use of prefixes—questions that he answered on the basis of what he had read in the Latin grammarian Priscian, Jerome, and the Greek version of the Psalms.[46]

As we have seen, the road had been well paved for the Carolingians by the church fathers, who had themselves been heavily indebted to classical culture and knew well the works of Cicero and Priscian. Already in the sixth century, Cassiodorus cited the works of those he called the *introductores*, who provided general hermeneutical rules, and the *expositores*, namely, the patristic commentators on the different books of the Bible. This system was retained by the Carolingians, who placed in the first category such works as Augustine's *De doctrina christiana*, Isidore of Seville's *Etymologies*, and Jerome's *Book of Hebrew Names*. These were works that could readily help the reader grasp the language and style, as well as the names, places, and history of the biblical text. The commentators (*expositores*) principally relied on were the Latin doctors: Ambrose, Jerome, Augustine, and Gregory the Great, but not to the exclusion of Origen (in Latin translation) and the Venerable Bede. Although the Carolingian scholars were not slavish adherents to their patristic forebears, their deference to the authoritative texts (*auctoritates*) they had inherited was unmistakable.[47] Patristic exegesis not only formed the basis of Carolingian biblical study, therefore, but also supported the larger societal reforms undertaken during the reign of Charlemagne and beyond. A series of ecclesiastical councils (Frankfurt 794, Aachen 816, Meaux 845, and Pavia 850) made rules requiring bishops to study Scripture according to the wisdom of the fathers and to see to the education of their clergy.[48]

Carolingian biblical studies were generally undertaken with the pastoral goal of instructing the clergy as well as the educated laity. Although the Carolingians were not the first to pose a comprehensive study program— Cassiodorus had laid one out in the sixth century—they actually followed through on a consistent and comprehensive level throughout their lands: all bishops and abbots were obliged to establish schools. The bishops were constantly trying to add to their libraries volumes that would assist them in biblical studies. Commentaries were written with the needs of a specific patron in mind, whether a king, queen, bishop, or abbot. For instance, Emperor Lothair

46. John Contreni, "The Carolingian School: Letters from the Classroom," in *Carolingian Learning, Masters and Manuscripts*, 81–111.

47. Pierre Riché, "Instruments de travail et méthodes de l'exégète a l'époque carolingienne," in *Le Moyen Age et la Bible*, ed. Pierre Riché and Guy Lobrichon (Paris: Beauchesne, 1984), 147–61, esp. 152–54.

48. John J. Contreni, "The Patristic Legacy to c. 1000," in *The New Cambridge History of the Bible* (Cambridge: Cambridge University Press, 2013), 2:505–35.

had asked for a literal commentary on the book of Genesis, a spiritual commentary on the prophet Jeremiah, and an anagogical commentary on Ezekiel. Patrons wanted to see many of the church fathers represented within these works; the commentators obliged them by harmonizing their patristic sources. When the fathers were silent on a particular issue, some commentators dared not offer an opinion. Others, such as Rabanus Maurus and Claude of Turin, did venture an opinion with the assistance, they claimed, of divine grace. Yet even as these Carolingian commentators utilized patristic sources, they sought to impose a "plain style," editing them for the sake of brevity and simplification on behalf of the reader. Some commentators followed Bede's practice of placing the initials of the church father in the margin so as to distinguish the fathers' contributions from their own. Aware that even the best efforts of harmonization were no substitute for the original texts, the authors put readers on notice that any apparent contradictions in the commentary stemmed from the fact the patristic excerpts were taken out of context.[49] On one occasion, Rabanus Maurus mentions that, in his commentary on the Pauline epistles, he had excerpted those parts of earlier patristic works that he deemed necessary so that readers might thereby get at the meaning (*sensus*) of the various doctors. As for those readers who do not like his editorial choices, they were invited to take a look at the original sources for themselves.[50]

One will notice that, whether it is Holy Scripture or the writings of the fathers, it was to the written word that the Carolingians looked for guidance in the ordering of a Christian state. Rabanus could, therefore, regard the Old Testament principally as a lawbook, which contained the perfect *lex divina* to guide Carolingian kings and judges in the execution of their duties. Bishops were to read the book of Judges and monarchs the books of Kings and Chronicles. Holy Scripture presented the perfect model to inform their decisions. So it was that Rabanus the Benedictine monk served the needs of the Frankish state. The court accordingly looked to Rabanus as the *magister orthodox* who could be counted on to convey the wisdom of the fathers needed for proper governance.[51]

Along these lines Rosamond McKitterick has effectively argued that Carolingian reform was built on the principle of textual authority, most notably evinced in the correction of the Bible, which was the text par excellence. In

49. John J. Contreni, "Carolingian Biblical Studies," in *Carolingian Essays*, ed. Uta-Renate Blumenthal (Washington, DC: Catholic University of America Press, 1983), 71–98.

50. *Ad Lucam monachum et diaconum* (PL 111:1273d–75a).

51. Mayke De Jong, "Old Law and New-Found Power: Hrabanus Maurus and the Old Testament," in *Centres of Learning: Learning and Location in Pre-modern Europe*, ed. J. Drijvers and A. MacDonald (Leiden: Brill, 1995), 161–76.

the transmission of the written word, the emphasis was laid on ancient learning in the form of a text; texts and arguments based on texts therefore were the foundation of authority.[52] It is no coincidence that when the laity wished to demonstrate their religious devotion, they often did so through the gift of books to churches. Hence there emerged what McKitterick describes as a "literate piety: religious observance as much for the laity as for the clergy was defined and directed by the written word."[53] In this vein Celia Chazelle observes that, in the midst of the dispute with the Greek church over the use of images, the *Libri Carolini* emphasized that Scripture remained the source of Christian learning and culture. It was the written word, rather than the image, that the Carolingians principally relied on to promote the Christian faith. In this they took their cue from Augustine's *De doctrina christiana*: words functioning as signs excelled all other human means of communication.[54]

If Carolingian culture relied principally on the written word rather than on oral traditions and images, it stands to reason that a fair proportion of the population possessed at least basic reading skills. In fact, laypeople of both sexes did learn Latin in schools and attained different levels of proficiency, depending on their career paths. It can be assumed, for instance, that most nobles were proficient enough in Latin to be able to read laws and charters. Literacy, therefore, was not the unique province of the clergy. Very often the learning of Latin began in the home, where mothers served as the primary teachers. Consider the noblewoman Dhuoda, who composed a guide in manners and morals for her son William as he headed off for service in the court of Charles the Bald. In her work, Dhuoda clearly exhibits knowledge of the works of Augustine and Gregory as well as a solid grasp of certain New Testament books.[55]

We may be accustomed to think of Latin as a rarified language, an ancient tongue removed from everyday speech. This was not really the case, however, among the Carolingians. Latin grammar as a staple of reform was indicative of an effort to recover the proper use of a known rather than foreign language. In the western part of the Frankish empire, spoken and written

---

52. Rosamond McKitterick, *History and Memory in the Carolingian World* (Cambridge: Cambridge University Press, 2004), 218–44.

53. Rosamond McKitterick, *The Carolingians and the Written Word* (Cambridge: Cambridge University Press, 1989), 270.

54. Celia Chazelle, "'Not in Painting but in Writing': Augustine and the Supremacy of the Word in the *Libri Carolini*," in *Reading and Wisdom: The "De doctrina christiana" of Augustine in the Middle Ages*, ed. Edward English (Notre Dame, IN: University of Notre Dame Press, 1995), 1–22.

55. McKitterick, *Carolingians and the Written Word*, 211–27.

Latin were not two separate languages at this time, but rather two forms of the same language. And even in the eastern half of the empire, with its own Germanic dialects, Latin was not unknown, since it had long been the language of legal and ecclesiastical texts. Thus, whether one spoke a Romance language or Old High German, one would already be familiar with Latin at some level. For the Romance speakers, it was a matter of learning the higher form of one's own language; for the German speakers, it meant learning a new language that was nevertheless not alien to one's own culture. Literacy in the Carolingian period, in its highest form, was the ability both to read and to write formal Latin.[56]

This appraisal of literacy is worth bearing in mind as we move into later centuries. For even as we examine biblical commentaries composed by an erudite class of monks and schoolmen, we should not imagine that God's Word in written form (i.e., Holy Scripture) did not filter down to the rest of medieval society. Michael Clanchy has noted that a basic knowledge of Latin was common among the gentry after 1100. Public officials such as sheriffs would also have had some facility with Latin in order to carry out their duties. Even among the peasant classes, many were functionally literate. Peasants, moreover, would have been immersed in the Latin of the liturgy and were expected to recite the creed and Paternoster, presumably in Latin rather than the vernacular. These same people were likely able also to make out the Latin words on the parchment of a charter.[57] Sacred writing—Bible, fathers, liturgy, prayers—made its presence felt across medieval society.

Rabanus Maurus

As should have been gathered from the discussion above, training of the clerics who would staff the churches on every level would have to be a top priority if true reform was to reach all precincts of Carolingian society. For that reason Rabanus Maurus composed an instructional manual for clerics to ensure that they would have a proper foundation for the studies that would enable them to fulfill their ecclesiastical duties. In his *De clericorum institutione* Rabanus emphasizes the need for lectors to have a firm knowledge (*scientia*) of the meaning of the text and the very words that they are reading at Mass. For only when correctly educated in these things can the reader grasp the distinction of meanings and thereby tailor his speaking accordingly. Pronunciation,

56. Ibid., 1–22.
57. Michael Clanchy, *From Memory to Written Record: England, 1066–1307* (Oxford: Blackwell, 1993), 186–91.

cadence, and emphasis all play a role in making the text intelligible. Even noting where the accent falls on syllables points up the need for training in the art of grammar.[58]

As he moves on to discuss Holy Scripture, both its construction and interpretation, Rabanus begins by distinguishing the two Testaments. He speaks first of the old law (*vetus lex*) given to the Jews through Moses and the prophets, known as the Old Testament (*vetus testamentum*), the word "testament" itself referring to its worthy witnesses (*idoneis testibus*). As for the new law (*nova lex*), this is the gospel given through Jesus Christ and his apostles. If the old law might be reckoned the root, Rabanus says, so the new law is the fruit stemming from that root (*fructus ex radice*). In fact, not only was Christ predicted within the old law, but he also spoke through the prophets. And so the princes of the church have handed down the books of the Old Testament, which under love of doctrine and piety are to be read and received. Rabanus then presents a list of Old and New Testament books, the total number adding up to seventy-two canonical books (*libri canonici*). This is a fitting number, he says, since Moses chose seventy elders who prophesized, Jesus Christ commanded seventy-two disciples to preach the gospel, and there are seventy-two languages diffused throughout the world. The Holy Spirit fittingly foresaw that there should be a book for every nation so that all might be edified to the perfection of the grace of faith. And it should be observed that Rabanus unhesitatingly includes Tobit, Judith, Ecclesiasticus, and the others of that division without reference to Jerome's reservations about these so-called apocryphal books.[59]

In this vein, on the role of the Spirit in the making and transmission of Scripture, Rabanus speaks of Ezra being filled with the Holy Spirit (*divino afflatus Spiritu*) as he gathered up and corrected the texts. Rabanus proceeds to recount the creation of the Septuagint during the reign of Ptolemy and the legend of the seventy translators in their separate cells providing a translation unified not only in understanding (*intellectus*) but even in its words (*sermones*). Rabanus (like Augustine) took this seemingly miraculous homogeneity as proof that the books were translated under the direction of the Holy Spirit. Rabanus goes on to identify the translations included in Origen's *Hexapla*, the various Latin translations, and finally Jerome's culminating role in the process. As he concludes this chapter, Rabanus again emphasizes that the writers of the sacred books spoke under divine inspiration (*divina inspiratione*) for the sake of our edification. Yet he also declares that the author (*auctor*)

---

58. *De clericorum institutione* 2.52 (PL 107:263b–64d).
59. *De clericorum institutione* 2.53 (PL 107:364d–65d).

of the Scriptures, properly speaking, remains the Holy Spirit. For it is the Spirit himself who wrote (*ipse scripsit*), and so dictated, what must then be written down by the prophets.[60]

That Holy Scripture remained the foundation for all Christian doctrine is evinced in Rabanus's remarks on the creed (*symbolum*), which he regards as a compendium of what has been gathered up by the apostles from all the Scriptures. The creed was compiled, Rabanus says, for the sake of those who were unable to read the Scriptures, so that they too might keep in their hearts all the truths necessary for salvation.[61] And so, in no uncertain terms, Rabanus affirms that the foundation and perfection of prudence is the knowledge (*scientia*) of Holy Scripture, which pours forth from immutable and eternal wisdom and proceeds from the mouth of the Most High. The firstborn, before all created things to be distributed by the Holy Spirit, this unquenchable light shines through the vase of Scripture like a lantern illuminating the whole world. Thus Scripture may be reckoned not only the teacher (*doctrix*), but also the illuminator (*illuminatrix*) of all human beings, radiating the very truth and wisdom that Rabanus equates with Christ himself.[62]

This is not to say that Scripture is always easy to understand. Rabanus readily admits that the divine books contain many difficult passages filled with symbolic discourse. Yet the Holy Spirit has remedied the Holy Scriptures such that what is spoken openly in some passages might clear up what seems off-putting in those more obscure sections. Rabanus was thus following Augustine's line that there is nothing said obscurely that is not elsewhere said quite clearly (*plenissime*).[63] Much of Rabanus's advice here reads, not surprisingly, like Augustine's *De doctrina christiana*, including the assertion that there may be many senses within the same passage of Scripture. This poses no danger, however, so long as the different senses can be shown to be either congruous with the truth or taught in other places of Scripture. Hence the same words (*eadem verba*) may be understood in many ways (*pluribus modis*), inasmuch as the one Holy Spirit is working through the various human authors.[64]

All of this points to the need for instruction in the liberal arts, as Rabanus then describes grammar as the knowledge of interpreting (*scientia interpretandi*) the works of poets and historians and the principle (*ratio*) of writing and speaking correctly: "This is the origin and foundation of the liberal arts." It is fitting that one would study this discipline in the Lord's school, Rabanus

60. *De clericorum institutione* 2.54 (PL 107:365d–67d).
61. *De clericorum institutione* 2.56 (PL 107:369b).
62. *De clericorum institutione* 3.2 (PL 107:379b–d).
63. *De clericorum institutione* 3.3 (PL 107:380b–c).
64. *De clericorum institutione* 3.15 (PL 107:391d–92b).

says, for how else would one grasp the force of speech (*vim vocis*) and the power of letters and syllables? Rabanus proceeds to list the sorts of tropes found in the divine books: allegories, enigmas, and parables; hence the need for the art of grammar to help us work through the ambiguities of the text, as the proper meaning of the words (*ad proprietatem verborum*) sometimes leads to absurdities.[65] All seven liberal arts are discussed, including rhetoric for the preacher of the divine law, since this is the knowledge of speaking well. One must see that the word of God is fittingly proclaimed, and one must know how to both defend the truth and defeat falsity through coherent argumentation.[66] Dialectic is here described as the discipline of rational questioning; it is even reckoned the "discipline of disciplines" because it teaches one how to teach and how to learn. Dialectic is indispensable for investigating truth and revealing falsity. Clerics must learn this most noble art, Rabanus insists, that they might be prepared to defend the faith against the wiles of heretics.[67]

Rabanus Maurus was only one among a host of biblical scholars flourishing in the first half of the ninth century. We will look at just a few of them below, paying special attention to their commentaries on the Pauline epistles. It is noteworthy that there was a surge of interest in those texts, most likely because they proved to be a theological storehouse, laying the foundation for much of church doctrine. From sacramental theology to soteriology and ecclesiology, Paul laid out careful arguments that could then be pursued in greater detail by the Carolingian theologians. What is more, the apostle very often built his own theology on the basis of biblical exegesis as he explicated Old Testament texts, thereby providing a model for future exegetes. For our purposes, we can briefly survey the way that several of these Carolingian exegetes considered questions of faith and grace within the epistles.[68]

Claude of Turin and Sedulius Scottus

We begin with Claude of Turin (d. 827), a Spaniard who served as chaplain to Louis the Pious and master of the royal schools of Aquitaine. In about 818 Louis appointed Claude bishop of Turin. His lectures on the Bible formed the basis for his commentaries composed at the behest of the emperor. Claude had earlier studied with Leidrad, archbishop of Tours, who had written to

---

65. *De clericorum institutione* 3.18 (PL 107:395b–d).
66. *De clericorum institutione* 3.19 (PL 107:396c–d).
67. *De clericorum institutione* 3.20 (PL 107:397c–d).
68. Some of the following material has been adapted from my essay, "Commentaries on the Pauline Epistles in the Carolingian Era," in *A Companion to St. Paul in the Middle Ages*, ed. Steven Cartwright (Leiden: Brill, 2013), 145–74.

Charlemagne in 813 of how the schools were now successfully training men in biblical studies such that some had learned how to decipher the spiritual meaning of the texts and read them allegorically, from the prophets and gospels to the epistles. Claude often equipped his commentaries with an index at the front of the book listing the names of the chapters as well as a key to the names of sources whose initials he placed in the margins. His work marks a real advance on his predecessor Wigbod, for instance, as he offered a much greater variety of sources in short bites adapted specifically to the text at hand. Claude has even been reckoned the first among the Carolingian scholars to break free of the so-called catena mentality (i.e., stringing together a series of patristic texts). No doubt Claude was aided in his efforts by being able to make use of the best libraries of his time at Lyons, among other places. He even had access to Augustine's *Retractationes*, which helped him locate other Augustinian texts.[69]

Claude, for his part, never claimed to be offering new or original exegesis. In his Galatians commentary, he candidly acknowledges that he had largely drawn together passages from the commentaries of Augustine and Jerome, but he says that he has also made use of other works by Augustine that seemed pertinent to this exposition.[70] Yet this is not to deny that Claude had specific thoughts regarding the subject matter. In his general preface to the epistles, Claude tells his readers that Paul's central purpose throughout his writings is to abolish human merit and extol the grace of God.[71] When Claude defines the grace of God, it is in keeping with Augustine's dictum: grace is that by which sins are forgiven so that we might be reconciled to God. Claude thereby makes it clear that our sins are forgiven apart from the merit of works.[72] Hence Paul will not glory in "his own righteousness or teaching but only in the faith of the cross through which all sins are forgiven."[73]

The concise definition of grace as the remission of sins should not be read, however, so as to discount the genuine transformation that takes place in the life of the believer. In this vein, Claude turns to Jerome when discussing the new life in Christ. Paul's life has been completely transformed precisely

---

69. Michael Gorman, "The Commentary on Genesis of Claudius of Turin and Biblical Studies under Louis the Pious," *Speculum* 72 (1997): 279–329. See also P. Bellet, "Claudio de Turin, autor de los comentarios 'In genesim et regum' del Pseudo Euquerio," *Revue Biblique* 9 (1950): 209–23; and Mark Zier, "Claudius of Turin," in *Dictionary of the Middle Ages*, ed. Joseph R. Strayer (New York: Scribners, 1982), 3:436–47.

70. *Enarratio in epistolam D. Pauli ad Galatas, Auctoris epistola dedicatoria* (PL 104:841c–42c).

71. *Praefatio in commentarios suos ad epistolas Pauli Apostoli* (PL 104:840b).

72. *Enarratio in epistolam D. Pauli ad Galatas* 1 (PL 104:845a–b).

73. *Enarratio in epistolam D. Pauli ad Galatas* 5 (PL 104:909c).

because Christ now lives in him (Gal. 2:20), which means he is filled with all the virtues, including wisdom, strength, reason, and peace.[74] Again, in keeping with Jerome, Claude declares that to await the hope of righteousness (Gal. 5:5) is to place one's hope in Christ because "he is truth, patience, hope, and righteousness."[75] And then, following Augustine, Claude contends that the new life in Christ will be marked by the ability to love and freely serve one's neighbor. One will now serve in love (Gal. 5:13), rather than in fear, because love has liberated believers from the yoke of guilt and thereby freed them for mutual service.[76]

On matters of exegetical method, Claude appealed to Jerome's comment that allegory is a grammatical art whereby one thing is symbolized by another. The apostle Paul had laid down a twofold rule for allegory that preserves the truth of the history even as one comes to understand the symbolism of the figures. Hence we find in Galatians 4:24–31 that Paul first recounts that Abraham actually had two wives, and then later shows us what they symbolize.[77] Claude, moreover, follows Jerome's comments on Galatians 3:8, where the apostle Paul says that Scripture foresaw that God would justify the gentiles. Thus simplistic views of Scripture are dispelled and its fecundity extolled, for Paul's remark refers not to the mere parchment but rather to "the Holy Spirit and the meaning that remains hidden within the words of the text."[78]

Sedulius Scottus (d. 860) was an Irish monk who had emigrated to the Continent and worked for a time in Liège. In addition to being a biblical commentator, he was an accomplished poet and grammarian. Sedulius commented on all the Pauline epistles, drawing chiefly from Jerome, Augustine, and Pelagius (mistakenly cited at the time as Jerome). His exegesis is careful and literal as he pays close attention to the Hebrew and Greek for important words. The introduction to his Pauline commentaries reveals Sedulius's classical training in the liberal arts as he presents an *accessus ad auctorem*, noting the seven sorts of circumstances that need to be accounted for when reading a text: person, fact, cause, time, place, manner, and material. That is to say: who does it, what he does, why he does it, when he does it, where he does it, how he does it (e.g., whether well or wickedly, foolishly or wisely), and by what material or faculty he does it (e.g., whether he kills by sword or by poison).[79] Hence

---

74. *Enarratio in epistolam D. Pauli ad Galatas* 2 (PL 104:864c).
75. *Enarratio in epistolam D. Pauli ad Galatas* 5 (PL 104:892d).
76. *Enarratio in epistolam D. Pauli ad Galatas* 5 (PL 104:895d).
77. *Enarratio in epistolam D. Pauli ad Galatas* 4 (PL 104:888a–b).
78. *Enarratio in epistolam D. Pauli ad Galatas* 3 (PL 104:868a).
79. *Sedulii Scotti Collectaneum in Apostolum*, ed. Hermann Josef Frede and Herbert Stanjek (Freiburg: Herder, 1996), Praefatio 1. See also Denis G. Brearley, "Sedulius Scottus," in *Dictionary of the Middle Ages*, ed. Joseph Strayer (New York: Scribner's Sons, 1982), 11:141.

Sedulius pointed out that according to the logicians a person is an individual essence or substance of a rational nature. But he finds that there are actually all sorts of ways in which a person can be considered: race, citizenship, parents, education, profession, dignity, customs, and many more.[80]

In his Romans commentary Sedulius, attempting to organize the text for his readers, begins by observing a sevenfold division in Paul's opening remarks. First, the apostle speaks of himself; second, he extols the gospel of God; third, he extols the mediator of God and man in keeping with his divine and human natures; fourth, he shows the election of the apostolic flock; fifth, he declares the general call of the gentiles to faith in Christ; sixth, the special call to the Romans themselves; and finally he expresses his hope that the grace and peace that are gifts of the Holy Spirit be made present to the Roman church from God the Father and the Lord Jesus Christ. With this division in mind, Sedulius says, we can now proceed to elucidate each part individually.[81]

Commenting on Paul's greeting to the Romans (1:7), Sedulius states that "grace is to be equated with the forgiveness of sins, and peace the reconciliation of the impious to God the creator." Sedulius explains, furthermore, that the etymology of the word "grace" can be traced to fullness and in turn signifies charity, inasmuch as the fullness of the law is charity.[82] The righteousness of God now revealed had been hidden in the law (Rom. 1:17). It is revealed to those who, by their faith in the Old Testament, come to have the faith of the new gospel. Thus they are directed from the faith of the law to the faith of Christ. Appealing to Augustine here, Sedulius observes that we move from faith in the words by which we believe in what we do not see to the faith of things that we will obtain in eternity. And lest the apostle Paul seem to reprove works when commending faith and grace, it is made clear that the just person who lives by faith is the person who has good works.[83]

Sedulius connects exegetical method to salvation history when he observes in his Galatians commentary that the Galatians had reverted to the law only when they forsook the spiritual meaning of the text and began to follow the bare literal sense. Relying on Jerome, he finds that Paul has presented the church with an exegetical rule based on his treatment of Genesis 21 (Gal. 4:21–31). Here the apostle followed allegorical principles even as he maintained the truth of the history. In this way one can explain the figures of the Old Testament, since Abraham really did have two sons, and on that historical basis Paul demonstrates what they prefigure. This leads Sedulius to cite the standard four

80. *Sedulii Scotti Collectaneum in Apostolum*, ed. Frede and Stanjek, Praefatio 1–2.
81. *In epistolam ad Romanos* 1 (Frede and Stanjek, 17; PL 103:9b–c).
82. *In epistolam ad Romanos* 1 (Frede and Stanjek, 29; PL 103:15b).
83. *In epistolam ad Romanos* 1 (Frede and Stanjek, 39; PL 103:19b–c).

levels of Scripture: history, allegory, tropology, and anagogy. Unlike Rabanus Maurus, who quoted John Cassian's treatment of the four levels at length, Sedulius only briefly recounts how Jerusalem can be read as at once temporal city, church, soul, and heavenly city.[84] It should also be remembered that Sedulius did not think that Christians were the only ones capable of reading the biblical text spiritually. The patriarchs and prophets must have also done this since they too were justified by faith and not by works of the law.[85] For it is by faith alone (*sola fide*), as he says here in his Galatians commentary, that all believers across the ages are saved. By faith believers put on Christ in order to become children of God by grace, not by nature. Only Christ, the unique Wisdom of God, is the Son by nature (Gal. 3:22–27).[86] Note, however, that the righteousness of God entails both sanctification through faith and the remission of sins.[87] Salvation does indeed mean coming to Christ by faith alone. Yet, Sedulius says, the apostle Paul still believes in works of grace, for without these, faith is dead. Although it is true that a person can be justified by faith without works of the law (Rom. 3:28), since faith works through love in the heart, this must not be to the neglect of works. Those who act unjustly, following their initial justification, surely spurn the grace of justification.[88]

In fact, none of the saints, or indeed the Lord himself, destroyed the law, although the law's temporal glory has been surpassed when compared with the eternal glory to come in Christ. Sedulius thus found that Paul had addressed two sorts of law when recounting the justification of Abraham (Rom. 4:1–2), one of works and the other of faith; it is the latter that excludes self-glorification. The root of justice is not grounded in works, but rather it is from the root of justice that there grows the fruit of works.[89] This is what it means to serve in the newness of the spirit (Rom. 7:6). It entails freedom from the old spirit contained in the bare letter of the law. Believers are called instead to grasp the full content of the spiritual sense unveiled by the Holy Spirit.[90] Of course, one is also set free from sin, which is itself often equated directly with the devil. Although when Paul confesses that sin dwells within (Rom. 7:17), Sedulius takes this to be the custom of sinning that has been transfused from Adam. It dwells within as though it were a guest, as one thing abiding within another. Freedom and servitude can, however, be taken

84. *In epistolam ad Galatas* 4 (Frede and Stanjek, 538–89; PL 103:191a).
85. *In epistolam ad Galatas* 2 (Frede and Stanjek, 522; PL 103:185a).
86. *In epistolam ad Galatas* 3 (Frede and Stanjek, 530–31; PL 103:188a–b).
87. *In epistolam ad Romanos* 3 (Frede and Stanjek, 97; PL 103:42b).
88. *In epistolam ad Romanos* 3 (Frede and Stanjek, 103–4; PL 103:45a–b).
89. *In epistolam ad Romanos* 4 (Frede and Stanjek, 111; PL 103:46c–47d).
90. *In epistolam ad Romanos* 7 (Frede and Stanjek, 159; PL 103:66b).

in different ways. There is, Sedulius says, culpable freedom and there is laudable servitude. To be free from justice is a crime, whereas to be a servant of justice is praiseworthy. This in turn pertains to matters of grace and free will. Those who are free from justice are so by their own choice, whereas those set free from sin are such purely by the grace of Christ.[91]

Last, when treating the matter of predestination in his Romans commentary (Rom. 9:11–20), Sedulius adopts a rather moderate stand, rooting predestination in divine foreknowledge. He contends that God chose to save by faith alone those whom he foreknew would believe. Hence God called those he foreknew would believe. In that sense, he foresaw their merits and predestined their reward.[92] In the case of Jacob and Esau, therefore, God knew what each one was going to do. Indeed, Sedulius says, God would condemn no one prior to sin, just as he would crown no one before they have been victorious. God even knows that those people who will persevere in the good may at some earlier time be evil, just as those who will eventually abide in evil may once have been good. In this way God remains an impartial judge who hands down a verdict in light of a person's final and freely chosen condition. Sedulius insists that God does indeed foreknow future works, and that knowledge forms the basis of his decision. Of course, the saved must rely on divine grace even as the damned get their just deserts. So it was that God loved Jacob through his gratuitous mercy, while he hated Esau through his due judgment.[93] Divine grace and human free will must ultimately work in tandem, according to Sedulius. It does not suffice for humankind to will alone; the mercy of God is needed. Yet the mercy of God by itself is not sufficient apart from human will; those who misuse their free will perish.[94]

Haimo of Auxerre

Now we arrive at perhaps the greatest of the Carolingian exegetes: the French monk Haimo of Auxerre, who in the middle decades of the ninth century built up a school of lasting renown.[95] Leaving the Abbey of St. Germain in 865 to become abbot of the monastery at Cessy-les-Bois, Haimo was succeeded

91. *In epistolam ad Romanos* 7 (Frede and Stanjek, 158–60; PL 103:63d–67d).
92. *In epistolam ad Romanos* 9 (Frede and Stanjek, 190–92; PL 103:79a–80a).
93. *In epistolam ad Romanos* 9 (Frede and Stanjek, 208–9; PL 103:87a–d).
94. *In epistolam ad Romanos* 9 (Frede and Stanjek, 213–14; PL 103:89a).
95. Some of this material on Haimo has been adapted from my previously cited essay, "Commentaries on the Pauline Epistles in the Carolingian Era," in *Companion to St. Paul in the Middle Ages.*

by his former student Heiric of Auxerre, whose work we will look at below.[96] At St. Germain, Haimo proved to be a prolific and original commentator on books of the Old and New Testaments, although it is his commentary on the Pauline epistles that stands above the rest. Modern scholars have found some of the principal characteristics of Carolingian spirituality exemplified in Haimo's meditation on Scripture and appeal to the fathers. It was in these commentaries that Haimo endeavored to increase understanding (*aedificatio intellectus*) and thus resolve questions (*solutio quaestionum*), all for the sake of exhortation and consolation.[97] It is a great irony, therefore, that Haimo's biblical commentaries had circulated for many years under the name of Haimo of Halberstadt and were so classified in Migne's Patrologia Latina (vols. 116–18), before being properly attributed to him in the early twentieth century.[98] Actually, the later *Collectanea* of Heiric also went a long way to cementing Haimo's authorship, as he seems to have drawn directly from his master's commentaries. In addition to the commentaries on the Pauline epistles, we may also now safely reckon to Haimo commentaries on Isaiah, the Revelation to John, the Song of Songs, Genesis, Ezekiel, and the minor prophets.[99]

Although Haimo's commentaries were not divided into interlinear and marginal glosses at the time of their composition, scholars have observed that his notations between the words are markedly similar to the interlinear comments found in the *Glossa Ordinaria* of the twelfth-century Laon school. Since many of the citations of the fathers found in the marginal Gloss have been drawn from Haimo, it seems clear that Haimo's explanation (*sententia*) had later been incorporated into the marginal Gloss. His commentaries are especially valuable to scholars of the history of biblical exegesis since they offer us a glimpse into the way the texts were actually being read in the

---

96. Édouard Jeauneau, "Les écoles de Laon et d'Auxerre au IXᵉ siècle," *Settimane di Studio del Centro Italiano di Studi sull'Altro Medioevo* 19 (1972): 510–11; and John Contreni, "Haimo of Auxerre, Abbot of Sasceium (Cessy-les-Bois), and a New Sermon on I John V,4–10," *Revue Bénédictine* 85 (1975): 303–20.

97. Henri Barré, "Haymon D'Auxerre," *Dictionnaire de Spiritualité*, ed. Marcel Viller et al., 17 vols. (Paris: Beauchesne, 1932–95), 7.1:91–97.

98. Edward Riggenbach, *Die älteste lateinischen Kommentare zum Hebräerbrief* (Leipzig: A. Deichert, 1907).

99. Riccardo Quadri, "Aimone di Auxerre luce dei 'Collectanea' di Heiric di Auxerre," *Italia medioevale e umanistica* 6 (1963): 1–48; Ermenegildo Bertola, "Il commentario paolino di Haimo di Halberstadt o di Auxerre e gli inizi del metodo scolastico," *Pier Lombardo* 5 (1961): 29–45. For analyses of Haimo's Old Testament commentaries, see Sumi Shimahara, "La représentation du pouvoir séculier chez Haymon D'Auxerre," in *The Multiple Meaning of Scripture: The Role of Exegesis in Early-Christian and Medieval Culture*, ed. Ineke van't Spijker (Leiden: Brill, 2009), 77–99; Elisabeth Mégier, "Spiritual Exegesis and the Church in Haimo of Auxerre's Commentary on Isaiah," in *Multiple Meaning of Scripture*, 155–75.

schools. When examining a passage, Haimo is willing to allow two or more interpretations to rest side by side and acknowledges that "this passage can be taken in two ways" (*hoc dupliciter intelligi potest*). In such cases, therefore, Haimo follows Augustine's principle that diverse interpretations are permissible so long as they are not contrary to the faith. After a particularly difficult passage, Haimo makes a note such as "the word order is this" (*ordo verborum est*) or "the construction of this verse is as follows" (*istius versiculi ista est constructio*). He reconstructs the wording of the Pauline text to make it more comprehensible and clarifies the meaning, the *sensus*. He often uses the expressions "That is the sense" (*sensus autem iste est*) or "The sense of the saying in this passage is . . ." (*sensus dictionis in isto loco*). Thus, even when the grammatical construction itself is clear, Haimo may still explain what Paul meant by a certain phrase. Furthermore, he offers theological speculation of his own to explain the apostle's meaning and thereby provide the *sententia*. We find already present in Haimo's work the division of *littera*, *sensus*, and *sententia* that (as we shall see) Hugh of St. Victor elaborated on in the twelfth century.[100] There can be little doubt as to Haimo's contribution to the greater history of medieval biblical exegesis. Ann Matter has stated that the work begun at Auxerre with Haimo, flourishing in later generations with Heiric and Remigius, is indicative of "an increasingly vital urban school tradition." She goes so far as to say that the tradition of glossing that eventually came to fruition in the *Glossa Ordinaria* may ultimately be traced back to the ninth-century school at Auxerre.[101]

For our purposes we will begin by examining Haimo's Pauline commentaries before taking a brief look at his commentary on the Song of Songs. Haimo did not write a general prologue to the epistles as such, but his prologue to Romans serves in that capacity. He also offers a brief thesis statement (*argumentum*) wherein he provides a reason for Paul's composition (*causa scribendi*), outlining the tension at Rome between the Jewish and gentile Christians. The apostle's central purpose in writing this letter is to lead the whole community into concord by showing that none of them will be saved by their own merits, but through the grace of Jesus Christ.[102]

In the prologue itself, Haimo begins by breaking down the word *epistola* into its constituent parts, noting that this Greek word could be rendered in Latin as *supermissa*, just as an epigram is a superscription or an epitaph is

---

100. Bertola, "Il Commentario Paolino di Haimo," 40, 45–47, 50–52; and Quadri, "Aimone di Auxerre luce dei 'Collectanea,'" 8–9.

101. E. Ann Matter, "Exegesis and Christian Education: The Carolingian Model," in *Schools of Thought in the Christian Tradition*, ed. Patrick Henry (Philadelphia: Fortress, 1984), 90–105.

102. *In epistolam ad Romanos, Argumentum* (PL 117:361c–62d).

located over a tomb. *Epi* thus means *super*, and *stola* is *missa*. His point is that the epistles are added over and above the Old Testament and the grace of the gospel in which perfect salvation consists. These letters have been sent to believers so as to curtail present and potential future vices, offering medicine to those who have transgressed against the gospel, so as to lead them down the road of repentance. Haimo goes on to note that just as Moses, lawgiver to the Israelites, handed down the Ten Commandments to those who had been liberated from Pharaoh, so Paul wrote ten letters to believers in Christ who had been freed from the spiritual Pharaoh. The four remaining letters were thus sent to his own disciples (Timothy, Titus, and Philemon).[103]

For Haimo the work of the Holy Spirit was absolutely integral to the exposition of Holy Scripture, thus maintaining in his Galatians commentary that Scripture was written through the dictation and revelation of the Holy Spirit, who is himself of one substance with the Father and the Son.[104] The faithful know that it was by the speaking of the Holy Spirit that the law and the gospel were written, for the Spirit is the Lord of the law and gospel (*spiritus dominus est legis et evangelii*). Commenting on 2 Corinthians (3:17), Haimo contends that it is through the Spirit that the faithful receive the faculty to understand the divine Scriptures. Because the Spirit is the Lord of Scripture, according to Haimo, and nothing contained therein is hidden from him; rather, the Spirit reveals its contents. Thus the presence of the Spirit liberates the soul and provides the faculty of understanding the Old and New Testaments. Whoever is filled with the Holy Spirit through the faith of Christ, therefore, possesses freedom of the soul and the ability both to discern the obscurities of the law and to penetrate the grace of the gospel.[105] Those who are filled with the grace of the Spirit are thus enabled to interpret the divine Scriptures and speak of the divine mysteries (1 Thess. 5:19).[106]

Haimo's interest in the persons of the Trinity also manifests itself in his treatment of justification. In his Romans commentary, he explained that the righteousness of God (Rom. 1:17) is in fact the righteousness by which God makes believers righteous; this is what has been manifested in the gospel. This is the righteousness by which all believers are justified through the gift of the Holy Trinity. Hence it is called the righteousness of God because, by imparting it to the faithful, God renders them righteous.[107] Indeed, Haimo is quite clear that the righteousness of God is that righteousness by which

103. *In epistolam ad Romanos*, prologue (PL 117:362d–63a).
104. *In epistolam ad Galatas* 5 (PL 117:691c).
105. *In epistolam II ad Corinthios* 3 (PL 117:621c–d).
106. *In epistolam I ad Thessalonicenses* 5 (PL 117:776a).
107. *In epistolam ad Romanos* 1 (PL 117:372d).

we are justified by God (Rom. 3:21–22).[108] This takes a christological turn, precisely because the righteousness of God the Father is none other than the Son himself, through whom we are justified.[109] Indeed, Haimo says, this righteousness is not that by which God is himself essentially (*essentialiter*) righteous, but rather Jesus Christ, by whose faith we are justified—together with good works (Rom. 10:3–4).[110] Although it can be said that it is Christ himself who justifies, Paul may also have in mind God the Father, who justifies those who believe in his Son.[111] Either way, Christ himself is clearly at the center of the righteousness that the believer receives as a divine gift. For God the Father promises his Son, in whom we find our justification (Rom. 3:26–27), that through faith in his passion we are justified and washed clean in the water of baptism.[112]

No doubt, for Haimo, we are indeed justified freely (*gratis*), which is to say without preceding merits. Pursuing this topic in his Romans commentary, he asserts that the person who comes to baptism having never done anything good to that point will be immediately justified. He is freely justified through grace, which is a gift of God. Yet Haimo is always keen to stress the vital soteriological role of the church's sacraments. We are redeemed and justified through the passion of Christ, which, joined to baptism, justifies one through faith and then later through penitence. As we lead our lives, we should adorn faith with good works, inasmuch as faith without works is dead (James 2:26).[113] For Haimo, as for so much of the medieval tradition, the Epistle of James—far from being in tension with Paul's gospel—was read as complementary. In the spirit of intertextuality, this passage from James lends clarity to Pauline texts that might otherwise be misunderstood.

Haimo definitely exhibited a concern for good morals within the new life of the believer. In that vein, he maintains that the law of Moses is twofold: it contains at once mysteries and precepts. Its mysteries and sacraments came to an end with the advent of Christ, because Christ is the end of the law. Yet the precepts remain and must be kept even now. "Works of the law" (Rom. 3:28), according to Haimo, refer to ritual demands such as carnal circumcision and Sabbath observance.[114] The law in its more expansive sense—understood as an expression of divine truth—is ultimately fulfilled in love for God; this

---

108. *In epistolam ad Romanos* 3 (PL 117:391a).
109. *In epistolam ad Romanos* 3 (PL 117:390d).
110. *In epistolam ad Romanos* 10 (PL 117:448d).
111. *In epistolam ad Romanos* 3 (PL 117:392b).
112. *In epistolam ad Romanos* 3 (PL 117:392c).
113. *In epistolam ad Romanos* 3 (PL 117:391c–d).
114. *In epistolam ad Romanos* 3 (PL 117:389c–d).

is the way to righteousness.[115] That the righteous now live by faith (Rom. 1:17) pertains to what is conceived in the heart, proclaimed by mouth, and adorned with good works. Thus the righteous person lives unto eternal life. Once more will Haimo invoke the Epistle of James: "Faith without works is dead" (James 2:17).[116] If one truly believes (Rom. 10:9), one's faith will be adorned with good works, lest it be rendered inoperative and thus reduced to a dead faith. Echoing Galatians 5:6, Haimo insists there that faith in Christ works through love.[117] Even as we stand in grace—referring to the faith of justification and the forgiveness of sins—we still labor strenuously in good works. Hence, while in the present age we are children of God in hope, in the life to come we will be such in reality—provided that we are found to be in good works at the hour of our death.[118]

The intersection of divine grace and human freedom within the soteriological process comes to the fore in discussions of predestination. When Haimo takes up the matter of predestination directly, he contends that those whom God foreknew (Rom. 8:29) refers to those whom God knew would believe and thus abide in the faith.[119] Yet their calling, justification, and glorification are all free acts of God's grace set in place apart from any preceding merits. The call comes from grace and justification by means of Christ's passion, which itself proceeds through baptism and a faith adorned with good works.[120] God exhibited his grace and mercy through Jacob, and his righteous justice was fulfilled through Esau (Rom. 9:11–20). We must be clear, though, that the election of Jacob and that of the gentiles was based not on their merits but rather on the grace of God. As to why Jacob was elected without any good works while Esau was hated apart from any evil works, only God knows; for he knows all things before they come to pass, and his judgment is always just. Both Jacob and Esau were tainted by original sin, Haimo says, but God loved Jacob out of his gratuitous mercy and rejected Esau out of his just judgment. Throughout it all, faith remains a gift: by calling a person to faith, God shows his mercy by granting faith so that the person will believe. This is only the beginning, however. God has mercy on a person so that the person might then live justly and persevere in the good works that will later be rewarded. Haimo nevertheless affirms that God gives the elect all of the necessary requirements: the good of willing, doing, and persevering. The good will of humankind

115. *In epistolam ad Romanos* 3 (PL 117:389d–90a).
116. *In epistolam ad Romanos* 1 (PL 117:373a).
117. *In epistolam ad Romanos* 10 (PL 117:451b).
118. *In epistolam ad Romanos* 5 (PL 117:402c).
119. *In epistolam ad Romanos* 8 (PL 117:436b).
120. *In epistolam ad Romanos* 8 (PL 117:437a–b).

alone does not suffice, Haimo says, unless the mercy of God comes first so as to give humans the good to will and the good to perform.[121]

Throughout his Pauline commentaries, Haimo insists on the essential role of the Christian sacraments in the life of the believer. With regard to the church and Eucharist—which is to say the body of Christ—Haimo speaks of the church simply as the body of Christ. Jesus Christ is the head directing the members, whom Haimo identifies as all the elect who have been brought to life (Eph. 1:22–23).[122] Yet the term "*corpus Christi*" is not exhausted by this one definition. When commenting on Paul's remark that believers have "died to the law through the body of Christ" (Rom. 7:4), Haimo declares that the body of Christ is at once the one assumed in Mary's womb, the whole church of the faithful, and the body that is daily consecrated in the church.[123] Then as Haimo reads 1 Corinthians 11:23–24, he points out that the body referred to in this eucharistic passage is the flesh of Christ assumed in Mary's womb—the *verum corpus* sacrificed for our salvation. Priests daily consecrate this body in church with the power of divinity that fills the true bread, which is the body of Christ. There are not two bodies, Haimo insists, namely, the flesh that Christ assumed and the bread; rather, they form the one true body of Christ. Even though the host is fractured and eaten, Christ remains whole and alive throughout. Just as the body that hung on the cross for our salvation was immolated, so daily for our salvation the bread is offered to God, which, although appearing to be bread, is indeed the body of Christ. The Lord left us this sacrament out of concern for our weakness; for even as we sin daily, we have a true sacrifice by which our sins can be expiated.[124]

Before taking our leave of Haimo, we turn to one of his other outstanding achievements, namely, his commentary on the Song of Songs, which has been called a "masterful compendium" drawing on such authors as Plato, Aristotle, Origen, Gregory the Great, Bede, and Alcuin. That Haimo gave only the most basic explanation of his exegetical method here as he dived into allegorical exposition shows how commonly accepted the multiple levels and spiritual expositions had become by this time.[125] In the prologue Haimo declares that Solomon was inspired by the Holy Spirit (*inspiratus divino spiritu*) as he composed this book about the marriage between Christ and the church. Written

121. *In epistolam ad Romanos* 9 (PL 117:443a–d).
122. *In epistolam ad Ephesios* 1 (PL 117:707a).
123. *In epistolam ad Romanos* 7 (PL 117:420c). See the classic study of this whole period by Henri de Lubac, *Corpus Mysticum: The Eucharist and the Church in the Middle Ages*, trans. Gemma Simmonds et al. (Notre Dame, IN: University of Notre Dame Press, 2006).
124. *In epistolam I ad Corinthios* 11 (PL 117:572c–d).
125. E. Ann Matter, *The Voice of My Beloved: The Song of Songs in Western Medieval Christianity* (Philadelphia: University of Pennsylvania Press, 1992), 103–4.

as though in a comedic style (*quasi comico stylo*), according to Haimo, it is a most obscure book, since no actual person is commemorated in it.[126]

The Song of Songs begins with the voice of the synagogue waiting for Christ and yearning for the sweetness of the gospel, which is like milk nourishing the infancy of believers. Thus as wine signifies the austerity of law, so the gospel's sweetness is the antidote to the law's bitterness, which provides no opportunity for repentance as its precepts proclaim the death of the sinner. The gifts of the Holy Spirit are fragrant, and the oil poured out is the grace given abundantly to all who have found the faith of Christ (Song 1:1–3 Vulg. [1:2–4 Eng.]).[127] The voice of the church (*vox ecclesiae*) then speaks to the bridegroom Christ, whom her soul loves, when she says, "Show to me the one whom I love." The church is calling out to Christ in the midst of her persecution and temptation; she seeks his help lest she wander among alien flocks, here identified by Haimo as conventicles of heretics (Song 1:6 Vulg. [1:7 Eng.]). And so she prays that she may recognize the elect and thus be able to distinguish true members of her flock from these false Christians.[128]

We find that the bride can also speak on behalf of the pagans: "Upon my bed through the night I have sought him whom my soul loves; I sought him but found him not" (Song 3:1). This bed, Haimo says, is the state of unfaithfulness and the ignorance of darkness. Many philosophers were ignorant of God, and yet with the greatest zeal they looked for him, wishing to understand the creator by way of the creation. Haimo admits that Plato has much to say of the soul in his *Timaeus*, and so too Aristotle and Socrates, all of whom sought the truth. And yet, Haimo concludes, they could not know God by way of worldly wisdom.[129]

Even as Haimo blithely pursues an allegorical reading of the Song of Songs, on occasion he does pause to acknowledge his exegetical methodology. Some passages seem to require a fuller explanation of the interpretive process. Hence when he addresses the chains of gold inlaid with silver (Song 1:10–11), he explores the etymology of the Latin *merenulae*, which, according to the letter (*iuxta literam*), are ornaments worn around the neck of a virgin or girl. They are so called, Haimo says, because they resemble a fish of the sea called a *murena*, which is a sort of eel. Mystically (*mystice*), however, these *murenulae*, or golden chains, are the perplexing dogmas of the Scriptures and are joined to the different sayings of the holy fathers. In this case the gold signifies charity according to the spiritual sense, as the bridegroom makes golden necklaces for

126. *Commentarium in Canticum Canticorum*, prologue (PL 117:295a).
127. *Commentarium in Canticum Canticorum* 1 (PL 117:295b–c).
128. *Commentarium in Canticum Canticorum* 1 (PL 117:297d–98a).
129. *Commentarium in Canticum Canticorum* 3 (PL 117:309a–b).

his bride when Christ instructs his church with the teachings of the fathers. Thus when the bride says "We will make chains of gold," she is speaking of Christ conjoining himself to the holy doctors through whom these necklaces are strung together for the adornment of his church.[130] Elsewhere the saints and the doctors are "the watchmen" (Song 3:3) who defend the city, which is the holy church, against the wiles of the infidel enemies.[131]

Haimo, as we mentioned above, clearly allows for multiple readings of the text where context permits. For instance, the "flower of the field" (2:1) may refer to the whole world decorated with the faith and knowledge of Christ, just as flowers adorn the fields and make them green. Although, again, the flower may be the son of the Virgin Mary, the shoot from the stump of Jesse, while the lily of the valley is Christ among his humble parents. For the Son of God came into the world choosing to be a poor man for our sake and so chose poor parents. He participated in our own poverty so that he might make us participants in his riches and glory.[132]

Haimo sometimes needs to explain the principle of an allegory, if not on the basis of etymology then on knowledge of the natural world. When the bride says, "My beloved is like a roe or young deer" (Song 2:9), Haimo explains that, although in their own nature these animals have many attributes that might suit the allegorical senses, here they have a single sense. These animals prefer the higher and more arduous places, where they are accustomed to dance. Rightly, therefore, they are likened to Christ, since no intellect can grasp his divinity and majesty. Yet Haimo extends the interpretive possibilities, observing that Christ is likened not only to the deer but also to the roe, one of the lesser animals, thus in keeping with the profound humility of his incarnation; he not only became man but a humble man at that.[133]

Christ's sacrifice for his bride the church is a consistent theme throughout Haimo's commentary. Thus when the bride speaks of her "dove in the clefts of the rock" (Song 2:14), Haimo has recourse to the words of the apostle Paul. Here is another instance in which a New Testament text opens up the meaning of the Old. For Paul had said that the rock was Christ (1 Cor. 10:4), and so the crevices of the rock must be the wounds that he sustained on the cross for our salvation. In these clefts there abides the dove, namely, the church, which dwells therein, since her hope for salvation rests in the passion of her redeemer.[134] The crown Christ has worn (Song 3:11) is the

---

130. *Commentarium in Canticum Canticorum* 1 (PL 117:299c–d).
131. *Commentarium in Canticum Canticorum* 3 (PL 117:309c).
132. *Commentarium in Canticum Canticorum* 2 (PL 117:301d–2a).
133. *Commentarium in Canticum Canticorum* 2 (PL 117:304d–5a).
134. *Commentarium in Canticum Canticorum* 2 (PL 117:307a).

flesh he assumed for our sake, the flesh by which he destroyed the kingdom of death and then rose from the dead. Thus we see Christ crowned with honor and glory through his passion. His mother too is said to be crowned, Haimo says, because she brought him forth from her own material flesh. "On the day of the wedding" therefore speaks to the time of the incarnation when Christ joined the church to himself that had neither spot not wrinkle. Or again, Haimo notes, it may also refer to when God was united to man in the incarnation.[135]

When the voice of Christ the bridegroom addresses his church, "You are beautiful, my friend" (Song 1:14–15 Vulg. [1:15–16 Eng.]), he indicates that she is indeed beautiful insofar as she is perfected in good works, by living justly and in holiness. Not seeking worldly glory, she has a simple intention of heart, praising God through her good works. Fittingly, then, the dove is the simplest of birds and thereby symbolizes the simplicity and innocence of the church.[136] And later when the bride says of herself, "I am a wall and my breasts are as towers" (Song 8:10), she is speaking as the church, which is built on the firm foundation of the rock and solidified by the glue of divine charity, although this verse may also refer to the church as built on the living and elect stones of the saints. Her breasts meanwhile will nourish her faithful with spiritual teaching as her towers defend them. The bride, however, is so strong not on account of her own merit or free will but rather by the gift and grace of the bridegroom. And so too the "peace" that she attains comes through Christ having shed his blood for his bride as he made propitiation to God the Father for her sake. In this way he dissolved the enmity between man and God and so put her at peace with heaven (cf. Col. 1:20).[137]

Finally, as the bride calls on her beloved bridegroom to "flee away" (Song 8:14), she beseeches him to make his way swiftly through the ascension so that he might return to the Father. She is saying to him, according to Haimo, "Flee now that you have fulfilled the mystery of your incarnation and passion, return to heaven, so that now—not as man but as God—I might begin to think of you above all things." And after he has ascended into heaven, the church begins spiritually to love, to contemplate, and to preach his divinity, for as the apostle Paul says, "No longer according to the flesh do we know him" (2 Cor. 5:16). He who is comprehensible through his humanity has thus become incomprehensible through his divinity.[138]

135. *Commentarium in Canticum Canticorum* 3 (PL 117:341b–c).
136. *Commentarium in Canticum Canticorum* 1 (PL 117:300d).
137. *Commentarium in Canticum Canticorum* 8 (PL 117:355d–56a).
138. *Commentarium in Canticum Canticorum* 8 (PL 117:357d–58c).

Heiric of Auxerre

As we mentioned above, Haimo's most illustrious student, the man who carried on his school, was Heiric of Auxerre. Heiric put together a scriptural compendium of sorts, the *Collectanea*, which offers us a close look at classroom instruction in the latter part of the ninth century. The succinctly arranged questions Heiric addresses are the sort of theological queries that arise from a careful reading of the biblical texts. And, again as stated, it seems clear that Heiric drew much of this material from the commentaries of his former master Haimo. The material covered in the *Collectanea* runs the gamut, from geographical notes on the Syro-Phoenician woman in the Gospel of Mark (7:26) to the clarification of biblical words. For instance, one reads in the book of Job (31:40) that "the words of Job have ended" (*Finita sunt verba Job*), and yet Job will actually speak later in the book. What, then, is one to make of the word *finita*? According to Heiric, in this case it should be taken to mean "perfect and complete" (*perfecta et consummata*), either because Job's friends did not later respond or because whatever he had said was perfect, as in "Christ is the perfection of the law" (*finis legis Christus*) as Paul asserts in Romans (10:4).[139]

There are also some more substantial theological treatments of Christ's eucharistic body in relation to his divine nature as well as resolutions of apparent contradictions that seem to arise in the reading of Scripture. Consider this question: How can the text "You have hated none of the things that you have made" (Wis. 11:24) be balanced against "Jacob I have loved and Esau I have hated" (Mal. 1:2–3)? Who, Heiric asks, can untie this knot (*qui nodus ita solvitur?*)? The answer is given as follows: God is the maker (*artifex*) of all creatures. Hence every creature is good and every man, insofar as he is a man, is a creature of God—yet not insofar as he is a sinner. Therefore as God is the creator of the human body and soul, neither of these is evil, nor does God hate them. For God hates nothing that he has made, nor does he hate anything in man except sin. As such, God does not hate Esau the man, but God does hate Esau the sinner.[140] That Heiric, or his own students, saw fit to collect these questions along with their magisterial answers testifies to the emergence of the "scholastic method" already in the ninth century. The age of the *quaestio* that blossomed in the twelfth century and flourished in the thirteenth has already budded here in northern France at the end of the Carolingian era.

---

139. Riccardo Quadri, *I Collectanea di Eirico di Auxerre* (Fribourg: University of Fribourg, 1966), esp. 113–34.

140. Ibid.

3

The Schools
of the Eleventh Century

From Bec to Reims

The forerunners to the universities of the thirteenth century were the cathedral schools that emerged by the tenth century and asserted themselves as increasingly important centers of learning by the later eleventh and early twelfth centuries. These schools were for the most part clustered in northern France in towns such as Reims, Chartres, and Laon. Attached to cathedrals as they were, they were staffed not by monks but by secular clerics. As instructors in the liberal arts as well as in Holy Scripture, these men were chiefly designated by the moniker "schoolman" or "scholastic" (*scholasticus*).[1] Their lives, according to Fulbert of Chartres (d. 1028), turned on the integration of classroom lectures, prayer, and learned study (*lectio, oratio, eruditio*). By no means insulated from the great debates of their day, these schoolmen were consulted by ecclesiastical officials on key questions of doctrine and church life. For example, when they weighed in on such heated issues as clerical chastity or the parameters of papal and imperial power, the masters collected and interpreted biblical texts to make the case for their respective sides.[2] Indeed,

---

1. Pierre Riché, "Les conditions de la production littéraire: Maîtres et écoles," *Mittellateinische Jahrbuch* 25/26 (1989/90): 413–22.

2. Guy Lobrichon, "The Early Schools, c. 900–1100," in *The New Cambridge History of the Bible* (Cambridge: Cambridge University Press, 2013), 2:536–54.

Holy Scripture proved integral to some of the most pressing debates of the day: all sides combed the sacred text in support of their arguments.[3]

The cathedral scholars were not, however, without their critics; the fiercest criticism emanated from the monasteries, where it was often alleged that the schoolmen were so enamored of their own dialectical and grammatical prowess that they had forsaken the sublime reasoning of the Scriptures. The Benedictine monk Otloh of St. Emmeram berated his opponents in the cathedral schools, contending that the true theological experts are those learned in Holy Scripture (*sacra scriptura*) rather than mere dialectics (*dialectica*). Scripture has its own way of speaking, Otloh insisted, that need not conform to the logic of Boethius. Central to this difference between the two logics—sacred and profane—was that in Boethian logic words bore only a single meaning, but in Scripture words could function metaphorically (*abusive*) in one case and properly (*proprie*) in another.[4] Such criticism coming out of the cloister, often delivered with great rhetorical flourish, was commonplace in the eleventh and twelfth centuries. Peter Damian appealed to the power of divine mysteries such as the virginal conception for evidence that the logical rules of the worldly philosophers might be transcended. He complained of cathedral schools luring good men away from the monasteries. These debates over secular learning could also spill into politics. The Augustinian canon Manegold of Lautenbach identified opponents of the papal reform program as "the philosophers" (*philosophi*)—that is, those whose reason was governed by pagan, rather then scriptural, principles. For all of their invective, however, many of these same men—whether Otloh, Peter, or Manegold—were actually quite well versed in the very methods they seemingly deplored.[5]

Criticism notwithstanding, the prominence of the cathedral schools only grew, attracting students from all over Europe who wished to acquire the skills necessary for lifetime employment in ecclesiastical or royal precincts. Students arrived in the cathedral towns, drawn by the possibility of studying

3. I. S. Robinson, "The Bible in the Investiture Contest: The South German Gregorian Circle," in *The Bible in the Medieval World: Essays in Memory of Beryl Smalley*, ed. Katherine Walsh and Diana Wood (Oxford: Blackwell, 1985), 61–84; Wilfried Hartmann, "Psalmenkommentare aus der Zeit der Reform und der Früscholastik," *Studi Gregoriani* 9 (1972): 315–66.

4. *Dialogus de tribus quaestionibus* (PL 146:60a–61b).

5. Irven M. Resnick, "Attitudes towards Philosophy and Dialectic during the Gregorian Reform," *Journal of Religious History* 16 (1990): 115–25; and Resnick, "'Scientia Liberalis': Dialectics, and Otloh of St. Emmeram," *Revue Bénédictine* 97 (1987): 241–52; Thierry Lesieur, *Devenir fou pour être sage: Construction d'une raison chrétienne à l'aube de la réforme grégorienne* (Turnhout: Brepols, 2003), 53–59; and Stephen Ferruolo, *The Origins of the University: The Schools of Paris and Their Critics, 1100–1215* (Stanford, CA: Stanford University Press, 1985), 47–92.

under specific scholars, who, in addition to their reputation for sheer erudition, tended to be rather charismatic men. There was a very personal quality to it all, therefore, as students would later recount with pride the scholar with whom they had studied rather than mentioning the place itself.[6] By the early eleventh century, Reims had secured a reputation as a school where a young man could learn not only classical texts (*litterae*) but also good manners (*mores*) and appropriate behavior (*honestas*). Meinhard of Bamberg reminisced in a letter (ca. 1057–67) about his days studying under Herimann (who also mentored Bruno of Cologne). At Reims, Meinhard had learned much in the presence of this master about the proper manner of living (*convictus*) and the cultivation of refined tastes (*elegantia*).[7] In addition to such moral pedagogy, however, cathedral masters were expected to come to the defense of the catholic faith, refute heretics, and otherwise support pure doctrine—this according to the tenth-century customs of Fleury.[8]

Lanfranc of Bec

Before returning to the cathedral school of Reims and the biblical exegesis that it produced, we need to take a look at one particular monastery. There were, in fact, schools attached to some monastic houses, most notably at the Norman abbey of Bec, where Lanfranc and his pupil Anselm combined the best of secular learning with monastic devotion.[9] Deeply learned, Lanfranc had received his training in dialectic in Pavia before moving north.[10] He had first proved himself to be a pioneer in the field of rhetoric, but from about 1055 forward Lanfranc turned his attention to Holy Scripture, specifically the Psalms and the Pauline epistles. In this vein a former student, Sigebert of Gembloux, remembered Lanfranc as a "dialectician" (*dialecticus*) and

---

6. R. W. Southern, "The Schools of Paris and the Schools of Chartres," in *Renaissance and Renewal in the Twelfth Century*, ed. Robert. L. Benson and Giles Constable (Cambridge, MA: Harvard University Press, 1982), 112–37.

7. See C. Stephen Jaeger, *The Envy of Angels: Cathedral Schools and Social Ideals in Medieval Europe, 950–1200* (Philadelphia: University of Pennsylvania Press, 1994), 56–62, for a specific discussion of Reims.

8. Riché, "Les conditions de la production littéraire," 416.

9. Sally N. Vaughn and Jay Rubenstein, "Introduction: Teaching and Learning from the Tenth to the Twelfth Centuries," in *Teaching and Learning in Northern Europe, 1000–1200*, ed. Sally N. Vaughn and Jay Rubenstein (Turnhout: Brepols, 2006), 1–16.

10. Charles Radding, "The Geography of Learning in the Early Eleventh-Century Europe: Lanfranc of Bec and Berengar of Tours Revisited," *Bulletino dell'Istituto storico italiano per Medio Evo e Archivo* 98 (1992): 145–72; and Charles Radding and Francis Newton, *Theology, Rhetoric, and Politics in the Eucharistic Controversy, 1078–1079: Alberic of Monte Cassino against Berengar of Tours* (New York: Columbia University Press, 2003), 8–9, 118–19.

specifically mentioned his application of the trivium to the Pauline epistles.[11] Even as Lanfranc made use of syllogistic reasoning in order to clarify Paul's arguments, he remained fundamentally cautious in the application of *artes* to Holy Scripture. As Cowdrey has observed, Lanfranc principally sought to explicate the biblical texts so as to further the moral instruction of his students; that was the chief responsibility of the monastic teacher, although it should be said that Lanfranc wrote his commentaries not solely for the sake of edifying monks but also for all Christian people, clergy and laity alike.[12]

There is little doubt that Lanfranc played an important role at a pivotal moment in the history of biblical exegesis. Gibson speaks of his "rhetorical exposition of Paul, strengthened by patristic theology," which paved the way for the Laon commentaries of the twelfth century. Constructing his own commentaries, Lanfranc seems to have drawn his Augustine material from the Carolingian collection compiled by Florus of Lyons, although he worked with Augustine's Galatians commentary directly. The writings of Jerome also had a major role to play in addition to Ambrosiaster, Theodore of Mopsuestia, and John Chrysostom.[13]

Recent scholarship has given increased attention to Lanfranc's sophisticated application of the liberal arts to biblical study. Scholars have observed the convergence of the rules of law and dialectic in Lanfranc's Pauline commentaries, principally under the influence of Cicero's *Topics*. For instance, Lanfranc can point to occasions when the apostle will "render a reason" (*reddere rationem*) in three different ways: to justify and prove, to determine the reason for things and show their cause, and to determine the reason or logical principle in the arrangement of words and things. To that end Lanfranc employed terminology that speaks in terms of the proofs and principles necessary for effective argumentation: *probat, probatio, comprobatio, causa cur,* and *ratio cur*.[14]

The dialectic located by Lanfranc in Paul's letters was thus judged to run contrary to that of Aristotle and Boethius. Theirs does not allow for apparent contradiction, whereas Paul's dialectic does, for the very fact that his reasoning transcends mere human ingenuity. Hence arises the preponderance of phrases such as "*per simile ostendit,*" "*alia similitudine probat,*" and "*conclusio a simili,*" which all express likeness. The frequently employed "as if one were

11. *Liber de scriptoribus ecclesiasticis* 155 (PL 160:582c).

12. H. E. J. Cowdrey, *Lanfranc: Scholar, Monk, and Archbishop* (Oxford: Oxford University Press, 2003), 46–59.

13. Margaret T. Gibson, *Lanfranc of Bec* (Oxford: Clarendon, 1978), 39–62; and Gibson, "Lanfranc's 'Commentary on the Pauline Epistles,'" *Journal of Theological Studies*, n.s., 22 (1971): 86–112; and Jean Châtillon, "La Bible dans les écoles du XIIᵉ siècle," in *Le Moyen Age et la Bible*, ed. Pierre Riché and Guy Lobrichon (Paris: Beauchesne, 1984), 169–70.

14. Lesieur, *Devenir fou pour être sage*, 103–4.

to say" (*quasi diceret*) also denotes similarity as one phrase explains another. For Lanfranc, just as the syllogism can be used for a proof, so too similitude. This has led Thierry Lesieur to conclude that "similitude is therefore the foundation of the dialectic which Lanfranc recognizes in the sacred text."[15] Lanfranc was proposing a new model of logic, a "dialectic of similitude," in opposition to the schools of Aristotle and Boethius.[16]

Consider Lanfranc's comments on the apostle Paul's words "If the Law were given that could make alive . . ." (Gal. 3:21). Lanfranc writes,

> Again [Paul] proves his point. The Law does not grant the inheritance because it does not grant life. For if the Law did grant life, then similarly [*a pari*] it would grant righteousness. But it does not grant righteousness, since Scripture says that all the Jews are confined under sin. Therefore the Law by a similar rationale [*a relatione*] does not grant righteousness. And so, in this same vein [*a pari*], neither does it grant life. Nor then does it grant inheritance. Thus it is only through faith that the inheritance, promise, and blessing is given.[17]

Lanfranc also appealed to the more rarified principle of "equipollence," a rhetorical construction whereby one produces equivalent forms of a given proposition so as to bolster its force. Southern has noted, moreover, that Lanfranc felt free to adapt this device to his own needs such that there does not have to be absolute parity, but only a basic congruity.[18] As it is, we find Lanfranc frequently employing the term in its adverbial form: "The Apostle states this equipollently when he says . . ." (*hoc est dicere aequipollenter/quod aequipollenter dicit*).[19]

Does such a sophisticated adaptation of classical methodology place Lanfranc the Benedictine at odds with his confreres? After all, we saw the unease that some monks had exhibited toward the use of the liberal arts in biblical exegesis—their fear that the subtleties of Scripture would be subjected to, and ultimately become subservient to, an alien logic. Lanfranc was alive to this danger and nonetheless trod lightly but steadily. It is true that at times his commentary on Paul presents some rather scathing remarks about dialectical methods, or more precisely perhaps, dialectics as practiced in the eleventh-century schools. Reading Colossians 2:8, "See to it that no one takes you

15. Ibid., 104–15, quote on 114.
16. Ibid., 140.
17. *Commentarius in epistolam ad Galatas* 3 (PL 150:273c).
18. R. W. Southern, *Saint Anselm: A Portrait in a Landscape* (Cambridge: Cambridge University Press, 1990), 51–52. See also Marcia L. Colish, *The Mirror of Language: A Study in the Medieval Theory of Knowledge* (Lincoln: University of Nebraska Press, 1983), 73.
19. *Commentarius in epistolam I ad Corinthios* 7–8 (PL 150:178b, 182b).

captive through philosophy and empty deceit, according to human tradition,"
Lanfranc directly equates deception through philosophy with the discipline of
dialectic, and human traditions specifically with the teachings of Aristotle.[20]
When commenting on 1 Corinthians, Lanfranc explains that Paul's claim not
to have preached the gospel "in eloquent wisdom" (1 Cor. 1:17) means that he
did not employ dialectic, for mere dialectic, Lanfranc says, cannot grasp the
subtle reasoning of the cross. And here, by way of example, Lanfranc spins
out the false reasoning of the dialectician: "God is immortal; Christ is God;
therefore, Christ is immortal. Yet if he is immortal, he cannot have died."
For all that, however, Lanfranc's position is more subtle than it may first appear. He goes on to maintain that, for those who carefully consider the virgin
birth and other divine mysteries, dialectic can actually prove to be a support
if properly grasped.[21] Hence it seems that, for Lanfranc, dialectic—as a part
of the trivium—may indeed be employed if done so responsibly, whereas
syllogizing carries the taint of destructive sophistry.

Commenting on 1 Corinthians, Lanfranc finds that by "lofty words" (1 Cor.
2:1) Paul is referring to logic (*vocat logicam*), which forms the backbone of
skillful oration. As for wisdom (*sapientia*), that refers to the quadrivium.
In fact, Lanfranc reckons that Paul chiefly has in mind the books of Plato,
although here designating the narrower species by the name of the broader
genus.[22] Yet in the context of the Epistle to the Colossians, "lofty words"
(Col. 2:4) carries a more negative connotation since it is associated with
syllogistic reasoning. Here it means speaking dialectically, or rhetorically,
by way of lofty arguments and syllogisms (*loquens dialectice, vel rhetorice
in sublimitate locorum et syllogismorum*).[23] Loftiness is associated with the
syllogism and other forms of disputation. At first blush this seems to bear the
stigma of the cathedral schools, because Lanfranc hastens to add that Paul
does not reject the art of disputation (*artem disputandi*) wholesale even as he
notes the danger of putting it to nefarious use.[24] Even as Paul may deny that
he is speaking with the erudite words of human knowledge (1 Cor. 2:13), his
writings are nonetheless imbued with subtle methods of disputation (*locorum
disputationum subtilitas*). However, we must be clear that the apostle was
employing such methods in a very different vein than might be pursued in
the schools. Lanfranc insists that Paul was not adhering to the rules of the
secular arts (*artium saecularium*), but rather was imbued with the teaching

20. *Commentarius in epistolam ad Colossenses* 2 (PL 150:323–24).
21. *Commentarius in epistolam I ad Corinthios* 1 (PL 150:157b).
22. *Commentarius in epistolam I ad Corinthios* 2 (PL 150:161b).
23. *Commentarius in epistolam ad Colossenses* 2 (PL 150:323–24).
24. *Commentarius in epistolam ad Colossenses* 2 (PL 150:323b).

of the Holy Spirit (*per doctrinam sancti Spiritus*), through whom comes all useful expertise.[25] And yet despite the fact that the apostle himself elsewhere claimed not to speak with wisdom or employ subtle discourse (cf. 1 Cor. 1:17), the careful reader (*perspicax lector*) will be able to pick up on it.[26]

Bruno the Carthusian

We conclude this chapter with a look at a master whose influence stretches into the future life of both the cathedral schools and monasticism. Bruno of Cologne is best known today as the progenitor, if not precisely the founder, of the monastic order of the Carthusians. Yet Bruno first built his reputation as a master at the cathedral school of Reims. Born in Cologne around 1030 to a family of noble standing, Bruno arrived at Reims as a student in the 1040s to study under the aforementioned scholar Herimann and eventually succeeded him as master in 1056. Before his departure in about 1077 for the eremitic life, Bruno had become one of the most illustrious schoolmen in northern France.[27]

The mortuary roll that circulated in the years following Bruno's death, in which colleagues penned remembrances, confirms that Bruno had indeed exhibited some of the most cherished characteristics of the cathedral master. Not only was he righteous (*iustus*), humble (*humilis*), and exceedingly wise (*sapiens nimis*), but he was also a man of charm and attractiveness (*venustus*).[28] He was an authentic teacher (*doctor verus*) and a genuine man (*sincerus*), known for his strict adherence to proper manners (*morum gravitate severus*).[29] Manners were prized in the cathedral schools, and Bruno, this lover of sacred virtue (*sanctae virtutis amator*), exhibited them impeccably (*morum corrector iustus . . . moribus ornatus*).[30] As Bruno was possessed of charm (*venustas*),

25. *Commentarius in epistolam I ad Corinthios* 3 (PL 150:163b).

26. *Commentarius in epistolam ad Hebraeos* 7 (PL 150:394b–c).

27. For sketches of the life of Bruno, see André Ravier, *Saint Bruno le Chartreux*, 3rd ed. (Paris: Lethielleux, 2003), 23–53, 144–45; Gordon Mursell, *Theology of the Carthusian Life in the Writings of St. Bruno and Guigo I*, Analecta Cartusiana 127 (Salzburg: Institut für Anglistik und Amerikanistik Universität Salzburg, 1988), 19–38; Bernard Bligny, *Saint Bruno: Le Premier Chartreux* (Rennes: Ouest-France, 1984), 13–32; *Lettres des Premiers Chartreux*, ed. A Carthusian, 2 vols., SC 88 (Paris: Cerf, 1962), 1:9–27. On the school of Reims, see John R. Williams, "The Cathedral School of Rheims in the Eleventh Century," *Speculum* 29 (1954): 661–77; and Williams, "Godfrey of Rheims: A Humanist of the Eleventh Century," *Speculum* 22 (1947): 29–45. For more on the state of the Reims school into the twelfth century, see Williams, "The Cathedral School of Reims in the Time of Master Alberic: 1118–1136," *Traditio* 20 (1964): 93–114.

28. *Tituli funebris* 2.32 (PL 152:564c).

29. *Tituli funebris* 2.31 (PL 152:564b).

30. *Tituli funebris* 6.150 (PL 152:595c).

so he was also hailed as a man who conducted himself well (*honestas*), a beacon to those around him: "Bruno, an eminently upright man and a jewel of wisdom [*gemma sophiae*]!"[31] Bruno's most fundamental characteristic as a man was again and again extolled—the *vir excellens* who pursued virtue and shunned vice (*probus et vitiosa repellens*).[32] Thus Bruno was reckoned a *vir bonus*[33] and could be addressed by his admirers as *vir sancte*.[34]

No doubt Bruno was a man of great charisma, therefore, who earned the respect of his students and fellow clerics by dint of such esteemed personal traits, but he was also hailed as a scholar of the first rank. He was a teacher of future schoolmen and a model of virtue (*doctor doctorum fuit, exemplarque bonorum*).[35] One student recounts that "the wisdom of Bruno shone so brilliantly that he was alone among the French stars, so that he might be here the flower among them all and the font of the philosophers [*fons philosophorum*]."[36] Another former student eulogizes "my teacher [*magister*] Bruno from whose mouth flowed sound instruction."[37] And yet another finds that he is "rightly counted among the ranks of the famous teachers."[38] He was "a leader of the way and a wellspring of philosophy [*fons philosophiae*] who taught not otherwise than he strived to live."[39] Bruno was hailed as a brilliant master both in the secular arts and in the study of Holy Scripture. He was known as a teacher of the trivium (*grammaticus, rhetor, dialecticus*) and even some aspects of the quadrivium (*astrologusque*), although he was notably remembered as the teacher of many grammarians (*multorum praeceptor grammaticorum*).[40] We are told that Bruno possessed true knowledge and wisdom of the liberal arts (*veram scientiam et prudentiam liberalium artium*).[41] Yet this man who was a "most illustrious philosopher" was also a "learned psalmist [*doctus psalmista*]."[42] Bruno, it is said, was "most brilliant in the Psalter and the rest of the sciences."[43] Repeatedly one finds that Bruno was well acquainted with the Psalter (*novit Psalterium*).[44] And he seems

---

31. *Tituli funebris* 3.74 (PL 152:576a).
32. *Tituli funebris* 3.83 (PL 152:578b).
33. *Tituli funebris* 4.124 (PL 152:588a).
34. *Tituli funebris* 3.78 (PL 152:576c).
35. *Tituli funebris* 3.77 (PL 152:576b).
36. *Tituli funebris* 4.131 (PL 152:589c).
37. *Tituli funebris* 3.79 (PL 152:577a).
38. *Tituli funebris* 3.78 (PL 152:576b).
39. *Tituli funebris* 4.124 (PL 152:588a).
40. *Tituli funebris* 6.156 (PL 152:597b).
41. *Tituli funebris* 6.173 (PL 152:602b).
42. *Tituli funebris* 4.107 (PL 152:583c).
43. *Tituli funebris* 6.173 (PL 152:602c).
44. *Tituli funebris* 6.175 (PL 152:603b).

to have been recognized for his adherence to true doctrine, proving himself a "standard of orthodoxy [*norma veri dogmatis*]."[45] Even this sampling of remembrances seems to bear out Steckel's conclusion that Bruno stood at a crucial turning point in the conception of the ideal cathedral schoolmaster, at once fitting the traditional model of the Christian gentleman known for holiness of life, but also the highly skilled man of letters adept in the latest methods of critical analysis.[46]

The major works attributable to Bruno of Cologne are the Psalter and epistles commentaries dating from his time as master at the Reims school. There has been some debate surrounding the authorship of these commentaries, which we cannot delve into here. Although there are solid arguments to be made on both sides, it seems more than likely that Bruno can be counted as the author of both.[47] Artur Michael Landgraf, for instance, believes that Bruno authored the Psalter commentary but not the work on the epistles. In a recent study, however, Gordon Mursell concurs with the earlier findings of Anselme Stoelen,[48] arguing for dating both commentaries to Bruno's years as a cathedral master.[49] Yet even as Landgraf rejects Bruno's authorship of the epistles commentary, he nevertheless concedes that the latter was a product of the Reims school, attributing it to one of Bruno's students, either Ralph of Laon or John of Tours. No matter the precise assignation of authorship, Landgraf is certain that Reims had a significant influence on the Laon school, which flourished in the first few decades of the twelfth century and produced the *Glossa Ordinaria*.[50] Along these lines, Beryl Smalley concludes that the

45. *Tituli funebris* 6.168 (PL 152:601a).

46. Sita Steckel, "Changing Concepts of 'Teaching' in the Mortuary Roll of Bruno the Carthusian (d. 1101)," in *Bruno the Carthusian and His Mortuary Roll*, ed. H. Beyer, G. Signori, and S. Steckel (Turnhout: Brepols, 2014), 83–116.

47. See my article, "Bruno the Carthusian: Theology and Reform in His Commentary on the Pauline Epistles," *Analecta Cartusiana* 300 (2013): 1–61, esp. 13–15; Martin Morard, "Le Commentaire des Psaumes et les écrits attribués à saint Bruno le Chartreux: Codicologie et problèmes d'authenticité," in *Saint Bruno et sa postérité spirituelle*, Analecta Cartusiana 189 (Salzburg: Institut für Anglistik und Amerikanistik Universität Salzburg, 2003), 21–39; Pascal Pradie, "L'appel à la vie contemplative d'après le commentaire des Psaumes attribués à Bruno le Chartreux," in *Saint Bruno et sa postérité spirituelle*, 41–50; Andrew Kraebel, "*Grammatica* and the Authenticity of the Psalms-Commentary Attributed to Bruno the Carthusian," *Mediaeval Studies* 71 (2009): 63–97; Damien van den Eynde, "Literary Note on the Earliest Scholastic 'Commentarii in Psalmos,'" *Franciscan Studies* 14 (1954): 124–28; and Van den Eynde, "Complementary Note on the Early Scholastic 'Commentarii in Psalmos,'" *Franciscan Studies* 17 (1957): 149–72.

48. Anselme Stoelen, "Les commentaires scripturaires attribués à Bruno le Chartreux," *Recherches de théologie ancienne et médiévale* 25 (1958): 177–247.

49. Mursell, *Theology of the Carthusian Life*, 19–38.

50. Artur Michael Landgraf, "Probleme des Schriftums Brunos des Kartäusers," *Collectanea Franciscana* 8 (1938): 542–90; and Landgraf, *Introduction à l'histoire de la littérature théologique de la scholastique naissante*, ed. and trans. Albert M. Landry and Louis B. Geiger (Montreal:

twelfth-century exegete Gilbert the Universal was deeply indebted to Bruno's Psalter commentary. Indeed, she says, "[Gilbert] must have written with a copy of St. Bruno before him, and he relies on it much as later scholars would rely on the *Gloss*. Not only the conceptions of Bruno are taken over, but often his very word and phrase."[51]

Constant J. Mews has recently stated that Bruno's Psalms commentary was unique for its period in its application of technical terms of grammar and rhetoric to this devotional text, thus building on what his students might have previously learned from the arts master Godfrey of Reims.[52] Bruno's prologue to the Psalter is quite sophisticated, seeming to fit the so-called C-type according to R. W. Hunt's standard classification, with its treatment of the work's intention, usefulness, method of proceeding, the name of the author, the title of the work, and to which part of philosophy it belongs (*intentio, utilitas, ordo/modus agendi, nomen auctoris, titulus, ad quam partem philosophiae*).[53] Bruno was keen to address the question of authorial intention, observing that although the whole Psalter resonates with the praise of God, the purpose (*intentio*) of this work is multifold. It pertains to the incarnation, nativity, passion, resurrection, and other acts of Christ, as well as to the salvation of the good and damnation of the wicked—all of which the psalmist intended to prophesy (*prophetare intendit*). Rightly, therefore, the Jews called this a book of hymns (*liber hymnorum*). More precisely stated, though, Bruno finds that the Psalms were composed in lyric meter (*lyrico metro*), a claim that he supports by appealing to the early Christian poet Arator: "*Psalterium lyrici composuere pedes*."[54] Thus Bruno may have been following in the footsteps of Remigius of Auxerre by treating the Psalms in poetic categories (*carmina, hymni,* and *cantica*) that call for grammatical exposition.[55] Whereas most twelfth-century Psalter commentaries were replete with patristic quotations,

---

Université de Montréal, 1973), 65–67. For more on the influence of eleventh-century commentators generally on the Laon school, see Beryl Smalley, "La Glossa Ordinaria," *Recherches de théologie ancienne et médiévale* 9 (1937): 365–400.

51. Beryl Smalley, "Gilbertus Universalis: Bishop of London (1128–34) and the Problem of the 'Glossa Ordinaria,'" *Recherches de théologie ancienne et médiévale* 8 (1936): 24–60, quote on 52.

52. Constant J. Mews, "Bruno of Reims and the Evolution of Scholastic Culture in Northern France, 1050–1100," in *Bruno the Carthusian and His Mortuary Roll*, 49–81.

53. Gilbert Dahan, "Les prologues des commentaires bibliques (XIIᵉ–XIVᵉ siècle)," in *Les prologues médiévaux*, ed. Jacqueline Hamesse (Turnhout: Brepols: 2000), 427–70, esp. 434–35. See R. W. Hunt, "The Introductions to the 'Artes' in the Twelfth Century," in *Studia mediaevalia in honorem R. J. Martin* (Bruges: Flandrorum, 1948), 84–112.

54. *Expositio in Psalmos*, prologue (PL 152:637b–38b).

55. Andrew Kraebel, "Prophecy and Poetry in the Psalms-Commentaries of St. Bruno and the Pre-scholastics," *Sacris Erudiri* 50 (2011): 413–59; and Kraebel, "The Place of Allegory in the Psalter-Commentary of Bruno the Carthusian," *Mediaeval Studies* 73 (2011): 207–16.

Bruno was especially attentive to grammar and rhetoric even as he employed this ancient material quite subtly.[56]

Here in his Psalter prologue Bruno observes that divine books, like their secular counterparts, are concerned partly with natural philosophy, partly ethics, and partly logic (a tripartite division of philosophy employed by Isidore of Seville).[57] Yet, Bruno says, the divine books that deal with matters of natural philosophy (*physica*) may also include figures, as with the Genesis account of creation and also Ecclesiastes, which treats the many natures of things in a mystical way (*mystice tractatur*). Some books, such as Job and certain psalms, tend toward ethics (*ad ethicam*), while others are concerned more with contemplation (*ad theoricam*). Such is the case with the Song of Songs, which deals with the divine mysteries; here God's relationship to the church, as husband to bride, is spoken of by way of a wonderful mystery (*mirabili mysterio*).[58] Discerning the different sorts of prophecy (*genera prophetiae*) present in Holy Scripture will also assist us in comprehending the Psalter. Some prophecies are effected through deeds (*per facta*), as with the exodus, thereby in keeping with Paul's dictum that "all these things happened to them *in figura*" (1 Cor. 10:11). Others work through words (*per dicta*), as God spoke directly to Moses and many other prophets through angels. And still others operate through revelation (*per revelationem*), as with the dreams of Daniel and Ezekiel. And then there are those that come about through the secret inspiration of the Holy Spirit (*per occultam Sancti Spiritus inspirationem*), which is the case with David's prophecies of Christ's life and death found in the Psalter. Here, then, we see the surpassing agility of the Holy Spirit, who presents prophecies of the future as though speaking of the present and the past. For all future happenings, Bruno says, are indeed present now to the Holy Spirit just as if he had known them as past events.[59] Prophecy, for its part, concerns continuous knowledge of future things, although not through figures, but solely by way of the inspiration of the Holy Spirit. Revelation, however, is a sudden knowledge of future things, as when one is taken up by the Holy Spirit in order to predict the future, because the Spirit will soon recede. Revelation, moreover, can also refer to the knowledge of the future through dreams, as with Daniel and Joseph, or through events (*per res gestas*), as happened with Noah.[60]

---

56. Constant J. Mews, "Bruno of Rheims and Roscelin of Compiègne on the Psalms," in *Latin Culture in the Eleventh Century: Proceedings of the Third International Conference on Medieval Latin Studies, Cambridge, September 9–12, 1998*, ed. Michael W. Herren, C. J. Mc-Donough, and Ross G. Arthur, 2 vols. (Turnhout: Brepols, 2002), 2:129–52.

57. *Etymologiarum* 2.24 (PL 82:141).

58. *Expositio in Psalmos*, prologue (PL 152:638b–39a).

59. *Expositio in Psalmos*, prologue (PL 152:639b).

60. *Expositio in epistolam 1 ad Corinthios* 14 (PL 153:198a).

If the Psalter was primarily regarded as a work of poetry, then grammar would prove most useful. The Pauline epistles, however, were rarely treated as poetry or as texts requiring allegorical interpretation. They were read as straightforward theological argumentation designed to establish Christian faith and morals. Therefore, it is rhetoric that predominates in Bruno's epistles commentary as he locates the different sorts of arguments that the apostle employed. Some of these arguments were admittedly hard to follow, which meant that the master had to break them down for his students by means of rhetorical techniques that isolate main themes and transition points so as to expose the inherent logic of Paul's teaching. Much of the methodology that Bruno applied to the epistles he would have learned from Cicero, most notably from the *De inventione* and *Topica*, as well as the pseudo-Ciceronian work *Ad Herennium*. Master Bruno was still moving in the world of Ciceronian rhetoric, therefore, rather than the Aristotelian-Boethian realm of the *logica vetus*. His epistles commentary does not betray the influence of the *Categoriae* and *De interpretatione*, nor is there a strict demarcation drawn between rhetoric and dialectic. Indeed, for Bruno all three arts (grammar, rhetoric, and dialectic) function together seamlessly for the larger purpose of explicating Paul's method of communication, and thus disclosing the intention of the sacred author (*ad mentem auctoris*).

One of the most striking features of Bruno's commentary is that it is replete with hypothetical interlocutors. This responsorial technique not only enables Bruno to bring the text to life for his students but also exposes the central issues at stake in any given section of the epistle. Many times the interlocutor is simply a generic "someone." Thus "someone might say" (*diceret aliquis*)[61] or "someone might object" (*opponeret aliquis*).[62] Or it could be the very people to whom the apostle is writing: "The Corinthians may ask why, . . . to which Paul responds" (*quaerere possent Corinthii, . . . ad hoc respondet Paulus*).[63] Paul is often placed in dispute with a Jewish opponent, especially in matters concerning the law. Here "a Jew might object that . . . and against this Paul states" (*opponeret Judaeus . . . contra hoc Paulus*);[64] "perhaps a Jew might say . . . against which Paul says" (*diceret fortassis Judaeus . . . contra quod Paulus*);[65] "but were a Jew to say . . . , Paul proves otherwise" (*sed diceret Judaeus, . . . contra Paulus probat*).[66] No doubt the students would recog-

---

61. *Expositio in epistolam ad Romanos* 1 (PL 153:18d).
62. *Expositio in epistolam ad Romanos* 5 (PL 153:51d).
63. *Expositio in epistolam I ad Corinthios* 7 (PL 153:159d).
64. *Expositio in epistolam ad Romanos* 2 (PL 153:31d).
65. *Expositio in epistolam ad Romanos* 3 (PL 153:40a).
66. *Expositio in epistolam ad Romanos* 7 (PL 153:65a).

nize their own scholastic milieu in the back-and-forth as Paul, the *maître extraordinaire*, deftly fields all manner of challenging queries.

The apostle is not simply presenting his views, however, but is proving his case as a skilled rhetorician in the public forum. "He has proven his case through an example" (*probavit per exemplum*);[67] "he begins to prove his case on the basis of an authoritative source" (*probare incipit per auctoritatem*).[68] He might accomplish this by way of his own authority (*probat iterum exemplo et auctoritate sua*)[69] or the authority of Scripture (*probat . . . ab auctoritate Scripturae*) or the testimonies of the Scriptures (*probavit per testimonia Scripturarum*)[70] or by the authority of Moses (*probat auctoritate Moysi*).[71] At one point Paul proves his case based on the authority of David, who is himself functioning "in the person of the martyrs" (*probat auctoritate David in persona martyrum agentis dicens*).[72] Paul might also make his case from the created order and the law of nature (*probavi per ordinem creationis, et per legem naturae*).[73]

Apart from the appeal to authority, Paul employs other methods of argumentation in order to deduce some conclusion from the given premises (*hanc autem consequentiam sic probat*).[74] A conclusion may "follow by necessity" (*sequitur ex necessitate*).[75] Or Paul may "prove his point through the many incongruities that would otherwise follow" (*et hoc probat per multa inconvenientia*);[76] "Paul wishes to prove the case through necessary principles and through incongruities" (*Paulus per necessarias rationes, per inconvenientia . . . vult illam approbare . . .*).[77] "He proves what he said moving from the lesser to the greater and then from the greater to the lesser" (*probat quod dixit a minori . . . a majori constat*).[78] "Paul proves his case through some comparison based upon resemblance" (*probat per similitudinem*)[79] and in this way "dismantles an opponent's argument" (*et hoc per inductam similitudinem Paulus destruit*).[80] In this vein, Bruno also appealed to the technique of equipollence

67. *Expositio in epistolam ad Romanos* 4 (PL 153:44c).
68. *Expositio in epistolam ad Romanos* 4 (PL 153:44d).
69. *Expositio in epistolam I ad Corinthios* 14 (PL 153:199c).
70. *Expositio in epistolam I ad Corinthios* 15 (PL 153:205b).
71. *Expositio in epistolam ad Romanos* 10 (PL 153:90c).
72. *Expositio in epistolam II ad Corinthios* 4 (PL 153:237d).
73. *Expositio in epistolam I ad Corinthios* 11 (PL 153:183a).
74. *Expositio in epistolam I ad Corinthios* 15 (PL 153:206a).
75. *Expositio in epistolam I ad Corinthios* 15 (PL 153:206a).
76. *Expositio in epistolam I ad Corinthios* 15 (PL 153:206c).
77. *Expositio in epistolam I ad Corinthios* 15 (PL 153:210b).
78. *Expositio in epistolam I ad Corinthios* 2 (PL 153:134d).
79. *Expositio in epistolam I ad Corinthios* 13 (PL 153:197c).
80. *Expositio in epistolam I ad Corinthios* 14 (PL 153:194c).

(as had his contemporary Lanfranc), most often in its adverbial form (*quod aequipollenter ait . . .*), showing how Paul confirms his point by restating it in another form to achieve the same meaning.[81] On occasion the apostle also employs more subtly persuasive rhetorical techniques, as when he uses irony (*ironia*) among other tools in dealing with the recalcitrant Corinthians. Paul had spoken to these people ironically (*ironice*) when calling them wise, and he will admonish them now softly (*blande*) and now harshly (*aspere*) as befits his children in Christ.[82]

We should remember that Bruno's epistles commentary is most likely the product of classroom instruction and thus a public exposition of an authoritative text (*praelectio*). There are even a few times when we seem to catch a glimpse of the Reims school in action as Bruno leads his students through the day's reading: "Now let us explicate the text" (*nunc litteram exponamus*),[83] or "let us return to the text" (*revertamur ad litteram*).[84] Bruno's first obligation to these students was to make sure that they could follow what they were reading, for it is easy to lose one's way amid the twists and turns of Paul's arguments. Bruno therefore pays very close attention to the sequence of these arguments as they unfold: "The text is put together like this" (*littera sic jungitur*).[85] "We might construe the text in the following way, but the meaning remains unchanged" (*vel ita construamus, non mutata sententia*).[86] Sometimes the apostle does not state something outright, but nevertheless implies it (*ipse quidem non ait . . . satis hoc innuit*).[87] And on some occasions Bruno needs to clarify intrascriptural citations, noting that 1 Corinthians 2:9 does not precisely correspond to the text of Isaiah 64:4 (*illud quod de littera Pauli est, et non Isaiae sic dicentis*).[88] This is also the case with Galatians 4:22, although it is close enough to capture the meaning of the Genesis passage (*haec autem verba non eadem inveniuntur in Genesi; sed aeque valentia*).[89]

Interestingly, Bruno does not reflect at great length on the various senses of Scripture, but there are some scattered remarks. When addressing the apostle's express employment of allegory in Galatians 4:24, Bruno defines the term in standard fashion as "some other understanding than what the literal sense here conveys" (*per allegoriam, id est per alium intellectum quam sit litteralis hic*

---

81. *Expositio in epistolam ad Romanos* 1–9 (PL 153:23c, 45c, 54a, 64a, 84c).
82. *Expositio in epistolam I ad Corinthios* 4 (PL 153:144a–b).
83. *Expositio in epistolam I ad Corinthios* 1 (PL 153:130b).
84. *Expositio in epistolam I ad Corinthios* 2 (PL 153:137c).
85. *Expositio in epistolam I ad Corinthios* 4–6 (PL 153:144d, 150a, 151d).
86. *Expositio in epistolam ad Ephesios* 4 (PL 153:338d).
87. *Expositio in epistolam II ad Corinthios* 4 (PL 153:238b).
88. *Expositio in epistolam I ad Corinthios* 2 (PL 153:134b).
89. *Expositio in epistolam ad Galatas* 4 (PL 153:306a).

habendum).⁹⁰ Elsewhere Bruno acknowledges three senses of Scripture, referring in one instance to the historical, moral, and allegorical understanding,⁹¹
and in another to the literal, moral, and allegorical.⁹² Like the twelfth-century
exegete Hugh of St. Victor,⁹³ therefore, Bruno's threefold schema makes no
explicit reference to an anagogical sense. At all events, epistles commentaries
tended by their very genre to stick to the literal sense of the text, since Paul
was seen to be offering a clear exposition of theological matters that might
otherwise have been conveyed by way of mystery or figure as in the Old Testament and even in the gospels.

Bruno did not compose a formal prologue to the Pauline epistles in the
manner of his work on the Psalter. It is still possible, however, to discover
a consistent presentation of Paul the apostle. Lecturing to men who would
go on to occupy some of the most important posts in Western Christendom
(a former student, Eudes of Châtillon, became Pope Urban II), it is not surprising if Paul emerges as the paradigm for ecclesiastical prelates: humble,
orthodox, and steadfast. At the opening of his Romans commentary, Bruno
observes that the apostle labors among the gentiles in humility as he seeks
to subject them to the grace of God. He is a humble servant of Christ and
thus presents himself as a model of perfect Christian servitude to the Lord.
Called by grace alone rather than for reasons of race or merit, he has been
constituted by God as an apostle whose authority should be obeyed.⁹⁴ Rather
than exulting in his apostolic status, however, Paul exhibits a subtle modesty
that we do well to observe.⁹⁵ When he speaks through grace, he is exercising
his apostolic authority and thereby offers an example to churchmen, for it is
better to draw people to the good by way of love than by resorting to coercion
and strict demands of obedience.⁹⁶

It is the grace belonging to his apostolic office (*apostolatus*) that enables
Paul to speak boldly and exercise his teaching authority (*magisterium*). Paul
may be said to glory in his apostolate, but this glory is always directed to
the Lord, who consecrated him, for it is none other than Christ who is at
work in Paul and speaks through him. In an allusion to valid clerical ordina-
tion, a pressing issue of the day, we see that Christ operates through Paul in
the power of the Holy Spirit, which is then dispensed through Paul's hands

90. *Expositio in epistolam ad Galatas* 4 (PL 153:306d).
91. *Expositio in epistolam ad Colossenses* 3 (PL 153:393c).
92. *Expositio in epistolam I ad Corinthios* 1 (PL 153:126c).
93. *De sacramentis*, prologue 4 (PL 176:184d–85a).
94. *Expositio in epistolam ad Romanos* 1 (PL 153:17b–d).
95. *Expositio in epistolam II ad Corinthios* 10 (PL 153:263a).
96. *Expositio in epistolam ad Romanos* 12 (PL 153:101c–d).

(*per impositionem manus*), something that false teachers (*pseudodoctores*) cannot accomplish.[97] Even in the midst of this struggle against heresy, Paul remains an exemplar of humility. He is a legate of Christ (*legatus Christi*) sent by God's good pleasure and who, unlike the false teachers, comes without presumption.[98] In the introduction to his commentary on 1 Corinthians, Bruno contrasts the wholesome frankness of Paul's teaching to the worldly reason of false teachers. Mere human reason (*ratio*) is set against the candor of faith (*simplicitas fidei*).[99] His own conscience is founded on the Holy Spirit (*conscientia fundatur in Spiritu Sancto*), and so he must speak the truth.[100]

From here we can look at how Bruno tackled some major themes in Paul's writings. An overarching topic for all medieval biblical exegesis was the relationship between the old law and the new law, hence the navigation of salvation history as it plays out across the Old and New Testaments. This was, of course, a major concern that Paul addressed in one form or another throughout virtually all of his letters. It will be instructive, therefore, to see how Bruno handles this question in the last quarter of the eleventh century. According to Bruno, in his Romans commentary, human salvation is a mystery that had remained hidden until disclosed through Christ in the time of grace. Thus it is through Christ that the prophetic writings of the Old Testament are at last understood.[101] The new law, moreover, possesses a divine immediacy that the old lacked. The old law was given through Moses and thus cannot properly be said to be of God, whereas God gave the new law in his very own person.[102] Bruno even goes so far as to assert in his Colossians commentary that the old law was a word of falsehood (*verbum falsitatis*), whereas the gospel is a word of truth (*verbum veritatis*).[103] Although Bruno makes no direct remarks about contemporary Jews or Judaism, he does contend that keeping the Mosaic law now constitutes a form of idolatry. Hence those who imagine that the law is necessary for justification are likened to idolaters assigning to their talisman what really belongs to God.[104] The shadow must retreat now that the truth has arrived; the carnal law thereby yields to the spiritual.[105]

Every medieval discussion of the old and new law is integrally connected to the exegetical staple of the letter and the Spirit. In classic tones, Bruno

97. *Expositio in epistolam ad Romanos* 15 (PL 153:117b–d).
98. *Expositio in epistolam I ad Corinthios* 1 (PL 153:125a).
99. *Expositio in epistolam I ad Corinthios* 1 (PL 153:123a).
100. *Expositio in epistolam ad Romanos* 9 (PL 153:79a).
101. *Expositio in epistolam ad Romanos* 16 (PL 153:122b).
102. *Expositio in epistolam ad Romanos* 1 (PL 153:18b).
103. *Expositio in epistolam ad Colossenses* 1 (PL 153:376d).
104. *Expositio in epistolam ad Galatas* 4 (PL 153:303c).
105. *Expositio in epistolam ad Romanos* 7 (PL 153:62b).

remarks on the fatal mistake of opting for the literal sense of the biblical text over the intended spiritual meaning. Circumcision of heart, therefore, speaks to fulfilling the law spiritually (*spiritualiter*) rather than literally (*litteraliter*).[106] The letter kills, but the Spirit—namely, the gospel given together with the Spirit's assistance—produces a life of righteousness. Through the hands of Moses, the precepts were given apart from grace; through Paul's imposition of hands, one receives the assisting grace (*gratia adiuvans*) of the Holy Spirit, which enables one to carry out the divine commands.[107] The gospel should really open up those things hidden within the figures (*in figuris*) of the old law, but human unfaithfulness shuts the heart and throws a veil over these symbols, a veil that can be removed only through faith in Christ.[108]

With regard to the purpose of the old law, Bruno adopted the standard medieval line: it was designed to prove to an otherwise prideful human race that it was actually impotent and thereby prompting it to seek the grace of God.[109] Yet Bruno will never go so far as to say that the law actually compelled humankind to sin. Hence he reads the apostle Paul's discussion of the topic in Romans 7 as an attempt to forestall any suggestion that Paul was claiming that the law itself is an efficient cause of sin. Rather, it is our own corrupt nature, not the law, that compels us to sin. Here Bruno proceeds to reconstruct the logic of Paul's argument: If we say that the law is sin, then we are asserting that the law is unjust, which would mean that we are accusing God of injustice, since he gave us a law that compels us to sin. It is not sin itself that comes through the law, however, but rather the knowledge of sin. In that sense the law is good, precisely because it reveals humanity's sinfulness to itself. Yet that very sin works concupiscence in us by way of the will, action, and custom of sinning.[110]

Hence Bruno extols the very law he seems to have denigrated elsewhere. For as Bruno continues his analysis of Romans 7, he contends that the law is indeed holy, since it commands fasts, almsgiving, and serving one's neighbor. Again, therefore, it is one's corrupt nature, along with the instigations of the devil, that leads to sin. To say that "the law is spiritual" (Rom. 7:14) means that it was given by the Holy Spirit or that it nourishes the human spirit; either way, though, it is not the cause of death. In fact, the law and the rational self consent to the good, but all this is undone when one is overcome by the corrupt aspect of one's own nature. Law and reason simultaneously agree to

---

106. *Expositio in epistolam ad Romanos* 2 (PL 153:35a).
107. *Expositio in epistolam II ad Corinthios* 3 (PL 153:232a–c).
108. *Expositio in epistolam II ad Corinthios* 3 (PL 153:233b–c).
109. *Expositio in epistolam ad Romanos* 3 (PL 153:40c–d).
110. *Expositio in epistolam ad Romanos* 7 (PL 153:63c–64a).

follow what is good, therefore, but carnality prevails. Bruno has a strong sense of such a dichotomous tension, one that leads him to posit the existence of both a carnal and a rational self. The rational self (*ego rationalis*) wills the good, while the carnal self (*ego carnalis*) pursues what the rational hates. The law teaches what is good, and the rational self wills to do it. Thus the inner rational human being (*interior homo rationalis*) wills the good although it cannot accomplish it. Here three things must be considered: law, rationality, and carnality. The first two are overcome by the third, yet carnality itself will then be overcome by grace. And this in turn means that the good can be accomplished only through grace. The law could not liberate the Jew any more than natural reason could liberate the gentile; both were deficient in themselves. Here Bruno speaks of a double will (*duplex velle*) that is operative in the human person. One facet wills the good according to natural reason, which has been oppressed by the corruption of sin; its will to do the good is not sufficient to accomplish it. The other facet wills according to the inspiration of the Holy Spirit, through which the so-called tinder of sin (*fomes peccati*) is suppressed in order that we may then do the good. Through the gift of grace, therefore, human free will is strengthened against this tinder, this impulse to sin, so that it may now both do the good that it wills and constrain the impulse to sin. Bruno's emphasis on human free will in the salvific process comes to the fore at this point, for he says that even as a person is redeemed by grace, God does not completely separate the person from the impulse toward sin, since that would remove human merit from the equation. If someone no longer sinned because constrained by necessity, there would be no merit (*meritum*) on account of which one ought to be saved. Thus the tinder does remain, albeit in a weakened form, such that one can actively subject it to reason. A key point to bear in mind here is that, although someone may now be redeemed from sin, one is still not restored to the full dignity that Adam enjoyed before the fall. In fact, abiding in this imperfect state prevents humankind from becoming proud in its happiness only to fall again irreparably. So it is that this memory of sin, this penalty of sin (*poena peccati*), remains with humankind to keep everyone humble. All the while, though, one receives the power of the Holy Spirit, by whose help the rational self can subject the carnal. Thus the impulse to sin, over which human reason formerly had no power, is now subject to reason—if one so wills (*si velit homo*).[111]

As we have just seen, certain biblical texts can elicit sustained analysis as major themes are traced with the hope of resolving apparent incongruities. Thus we find that Bruno's fullest discussion of predestination was driven by

---

111. *Expositio in epistolam ad Romanos* 7 (PL 153:66d–68a).

a series of questions and responses (*quaeritur cur . . . ad hoc respondetur*)
arising in his commentary on Romans 9. Here Bruno begins by stressing
the sheer gratuity of God's call, even to the exclusion of human merit. The
story of Jacob and Esau, as evoked by Paul, makes clear to Bruno that it is
only by divine election that anyone becomes good; election has nothing to
do with preceding merit. Election is first and foremost an act of divine grace
apart from merit (*sine merito*). This is why Paul specifically excluded the
possibility that the two boys could have merited anything while in the womb.
Hence Jacob's election can be ascribed solely to the grace and good pleasure
of God, who called him (*ex gratia et beneplacito vocantis Dei*).[112] The key
here is that preceding, but not necessarily future, merits are excluded from
consideration; in himself Jacob was undeserving of God's grace. Yet if Jacob
was elected solely on the basis of divine mercy, Esau was nonetheless denied
grace as a matter of divine justice. This is because God foreknew (*praescivit*)
that he would not have cooperated with grace had it been offered. Thus if
it is asked why Jacob was chosen and Esau rejected, it is because Jacob was
elected through mercy and Esau reprobated through justice. By sinning, one
makes oneself unworthy of God's grace, and therefore God owes that person
nothing; one has no right to complain if bereft of grace. And if we ask why
both brothers were not condemned by justice on account of original sin, it
is because God foreknew that Jacob would cooperate with grace (*cooper-
aturum gratiae praescivit*), while Esau's unwillingness to cooperate was also
foreknown.[113] As with his patristic forebears, Ambrosiaster and Pelagius, to
whom Bruno seems indebted, divine foreknowledge proves to Bruno to be a
central component in the process of election and reprobation.[114]

A briefer discussion of election and reprobation is found in the comments
on 1 Timothy 2:4, "It is God's will that all be saved." Bruno admits that some
may well ask why Paul commands us to pray for all people when some will
surely be damned. It might even offend God if we pray for those he chooses
to condemn. Bruno replies that God, out of his kindness and mercy, does
indeed will that all be saved, since this is an expression of his nature. It is
only the injustice of the wicked, therefore, that averts God's kindness. Within
God there is actually a "double will" (*duplex voluntas*): one the kindness and
mercy by which he wills all to be saved, and the other the will of his justice
by which he reprobates the wicked and elects the good. It is according to the

---

112. *Expositio in epistolam ad Romanos* 9 (PL 153:81b–c).
113. *Expositio in epistolam ad Romanos* 9 (PL 153:81d–82b).
114. Cf. Ambrosiaster, *Commentarius in epistolam ad Romanos* 8 (PL 17:134c); and Pelagius,
In Romanos 9, in *Pelagius's Expositions of Thirteen Epistles of St. Paul*, ed. Alexander Souter,
2 vols. (Cambridge: Cambridge University Press, 1926), 2:75.

will of God's kindness, therefore, that the apostle commands us to pray for all.[115] Here again, for Bruno, human free will plays a central role. As God is the creator of all, there is no reason why he denies his kindness to one creature and gives it to another creature except that the impious creatures deny it to themselves. God does want to extend his saving kindness to all—a truth that is clearly expressed in the actions of Christ the mediator, who wills the good of all equally. The incarnation is therefore a striking testimony to God's will to save: Christ, although so glorious in his divinity, became man so vile and subject to violence, precisely that he might save the human race. The very name Jesus indicates that he is the savior of all, and thus he paid a sufficient price for the salvation of all men—if all men will to be good (*si omnes boni esse vellent*).[116]

We can now examine more precisely how Bruno's reading of Paul formed his thinking on Christ's salvific work. According to Bruno, to say that "Christ knew no sin" (2 Cor. 5:21) means that he had no personal experience of having sinned himself (*per experientiam*), although he would have understood the concept of sin (*per scientiam*). Furthermore, that "Christ was made sin" means not that he actually became a sinner but rather that he bore the penalty for sin. Bruno likens this to an innocent man being called a thief, not because he actually committed a crime, but because he suffered the punishment meted out to thieves.[117] In a similar vein, Christ may be called sin on account of the sacrifice he offered up for the sins of the human race. More than this, however, Christ "condemned sin" (Rom. 8:3) when he overcame Satan. And this takes us into a central feature of Bruno's soteriology: Christ's defeat of the devil, which is often depicted in terms of justice and rights. Bruno maintains that the devil had a right (*ius*) over every human being on account of original sin. Yet he possessed no such right over Christ, who bore no guilt and thus was free from concupiscence of the flesh. When seizing upon Christ, the devil therefore had usurped a right unduly (*indebitum ius usurpavit*) and thereby forfeited the rights that had once been conceded to him over all men.[118]

Some decades later, in 1098, Anselm of Canterbury would pointedly reject the notion that the devil had any rights over humankind (*Cur Deus homo* 1.7). Yet Anselm's argument for the logical necessity of human redemption (*Cur Deus homo* 2.1) bears some similarity to what we find already in Bruno's Hebrews commentary. According to Bruno, the whole of creation would have

115. *Expositio in epistolam I ad Timotheum* 2 (PL 153:435d–36a).
116. *Expositio in epistolam I ad Timotheum* 2 (PL 153:437a–c).
117. *Expositio in epistolam II ad Corinthios* 5 (PL 153:244a).
118. *Expositio in epistolam ad Romanos* 8 (PL 153:70b).

been rendered futile (*frustra*) had humankind perished unredeemed. Every earthly creature serves humankind so that we might be able to praise God. If humankind were not saved, however, this divine arrangement would have failed, since condemned humanity would be unable to glorify the God who had created all things to his own glory. Yet it is precisely because the God through whom all things are made must be glorified that it was necessary that his plan be fulfilled (*consilium impleri oportuit*). Indeed, it would be irrational (*absurdum*) for his creation not to be saved.[119]

Continuing in his Hebrews commentary, Bruno says Paul has proved that it was eminently suitable for Christ to bring all things to their consummation through his own sufferings. Bruno regards this as a direct refutation of those who reckoned it unfitting that the author of salvation and judge of all would subject himself to the ignominy of the passion (an objection Anselm also recites in *Cur Deus homo* 1.3). Christ the man was subject to the power of God, just as those who are saved through him. And Christ the sanctifier placed his trust in God, just as those who are sanctified by him, for the sanctifier and the sanctified are dependent on one source: God the Father. Thus it was necessary (*oportuit*) for Christ to suffer as the author of human salvation, for through his act of sanctifying participation with the human race, he thereby united with humans in their mortality and passibility. This need for Christ to enter into such intimate union with humans cannot be understood apart from the central hypothesis that the devil possessed rights over humankind. Although created pure and free, humankind had willingly entered into the servitude of the devil; corrupted by sin, they had no power to release themselves. Since humankind became slaves through their own actions, if they had been liberated by someone other than a human being, it would have been an act of violence, with the result that the devil could have reclaimed them justly (*iuste*) for the injury done to himself. That humankind might finally be redeemed, therefore, it was essential to find a human being in whom there was no sin, so that the devil would attempt to usurp what he had no claim on. The devil would infer that Christ was a sinner precisely on account of his death, which is itself the penalty for sin. Yet this presumptuous act on the devil's part would then lead to the forfeiture of all the human beings that he had hitherto justly (*iuste*) possessed. Christ was uniquely suited for this role, since no other sinless human being could be found, given that all others are born in concupiscence. Nor, however, could this plan have proceeded by way of an angelic nature becoming human, since both angels and humans are subject to sin, which means that salvation could not have been assured. The

---

119. *Expositio in epistolam ad Hebraeos* 2 (PL 153:499d–500a).

only way in which a human nature could be preserved from sin was by union with a divine nature. God willed to become human, therefore, so that through this act he might render humankind all the more indebted to his love.[120] In fact, the incarnation must have been the only means of salvation, Bruno says, for if humankind could have received eternal beatitude by any other means, this entire process would have been superfluous, and Christ would not have gone through with it.[121]

Here it is worth reflecting on the genuinely transformative effect that Christ's act of self-giving has on the human heart. Recognizing that it was on the basis of love alone that Christ died for us, Bruno says, we will then strive to be configured to his death.[122] In fact, Bruno speaks of this event in what we might call "Abelardian" terms many decades before Peter Abelard devoted a *quaestio* to Christ's sacrifice in his own Romans commentary (ca. 1137). For reasons of love alone (*pro sola dilectione*), Christ suffered for our sake, thereby setting our hearts on fire (*accensi dilectione*) so that we might hasten to him.[123] If we understand that which we love and thereby grasp its goodness, we are all the more set ablaze (*diligenda accendimur*) by what must be loved.[124] We are now glowing hot with Christ's love (*ferventes amore*),[125] that supernal love that is manifested in the very dimensions of his cross, for when Paul speaks of the "breadth, length, height, and depth" (Eph. 3:18), this all refers to the crucifixion. Breadth from right to left signifies the fullness of Christ's love, by which he prayed for his enemies; length from head to foot signifies the perseverance of his love as he loved us to the end; height is the part above his head where Pilate inscribed the title "King of the Jews," thereby signifying that Christ had done the will of his Father in heaven; and the depth was the part of the cross fixed in the ground, designating the hidden grace of God by which Christ had multiplied good things for those who could not have imagined such largesse.[126]

We mentioned above that Bruno had exhibited a strong commitment to clerical reform and doctrinal orthodoxy in keeping with his position as a cathedral schoolmaster. His comments on the Eucharist in both his Psalter and epistles commentaries do seem to be directed at perceived threats to eucharistic orthodoxy as it came to be defined in the last few decades of the

120. *Expositio in epistolam ad Hebraeos* 2 (PL 153:500c–501b).
121. *Expositio in epistolam ad Hebraeos* 11 (PL 153:555b).
122. *Expositio in epistolam ad Philippenses* 3 (PL 153:367b).
123. *Expositio in epistolam ad Colossenses* 2 (PL 153:383c). Cf. Peter Abelard, *Comm. in Ep. Pauli ad Romanos*, CCCM 11:117–18.
124. *Expositio in epistolam ad Ephesios* 3 (PL 153:333b).
125. *Expositio in epistolam ad Romanos* 8 (PL 153:77b).
126. *Expositio in epistolam ad Ephesios* 3 (PL 153:332d–33a).

eleventh century.[127] Yet we also find here a constructive and sophisticated eucharistic theology, built up through commentary on biblical texts. Commenting on Psalm 21 Vulg. (22 Eng.)—"My God, my God, look upon me; why have you forsaken me?"—the words that Christ cried out from the cross (Matt. 27:46), Bruno offers an extended christological reading that focuses on the Lord's passion and, in that context, the Last Supper. He begins with a comment on the title of the psalm, "Unto the end [*in finem*], for the morning protection, a psalm for David." As Bruno reads it, the psalm speaks to Christ's own perseverance unto the end, namely, his victory, which is the end of his course of obedience. Aware that the Latin translation made from the Septuagint differs from that of the Hebrew, Bruno observes that "where we have '*finem*,' the Hebrews have '*victori*.'" Nevertheless, he says, whether one reads "end" for victory or for perseverance, the point is made: the title of this psalm proclaims Christ's resurrection in the morning and thus his transition from humility and mortality to glory and everlasting life.[128]

As Bruno traces the passion and ultimate victory of Christ over death, he reaches the verse "With you is my praise in a great church [*ecclesia*]; I will pay my vows in the sight of those who fear him" (Ps. 21:26 Vulg. [22:25 Eng.]). Bruno takes this as Christ's pledge to give his body and blood for the salvation of the faithful. These are the ones who fear the Lord, those of pure faith who believe that the sacraments are truly transferred (*veraciter translata*) into the body and blood of Christ. Here one is not dealing with mere similitudes (*imaginaria tantum*) as certain heretics falsely claim when they perversely explicate Christ's words, "Do this in memory of me." The heretics think this is only a memorial (*solam memoriam*) of the Lord's body and blood, thereby lacking in reality (*absque realitate*), even as they are reproved by Christ himself when he says "This is my body which is handed over for you. . . . This is my blood which is poured out for you" (Luke 22:19). Here, then, the New Testament lends further clarity to this prophetic psalm as Christ most clearly (*apertissime*) testified to the presence of his body and blood. It is at this point, after having established their presence, that Christ then added the words, "Do this in remembrance of me." There can be no doubt as to this fact, therefore, if one construes the apostle's meaning in a catholic way (*catholice*) when he reports Jesus as saying: "As often as you

127. See Levy, "Bruno the Carthusian," 54–60; and also Josef Geiselmann, "Zur Frühmittelalterlichen Lehre vom Sakrament der Eucharistie," *Theologische Quartalschrift* 116 (1935): 323–403; and Gary Macy, "Some Examples of the Influence of Exegesis on the Theology of the Eucharist in the Eleventh and Twelfth Centuries," *Recherches de théologie ancienne et médiévale* 52 (1985): 64–77.

128. *Expositio in Psalmos* 21 (PL 152:718c).

eat this bread and drink this cup, you proclaim the Lord's death" (1 Cor. 11:26).[129]

Bruno explains that, according to Christian truth (*christiana veritate*), the elements can be called bread and wine, not insofar as their nature is concerned (*quantum ad naturam*) but with regard to their appearance (*ad speciem*). This is the one who assumed flesh in the Virgin's womb, which he was able to unite to the Word personally and ineffably, the one who is capable of rendering our mortal bodies immortal. And so Christ is also able to transfer (*transferre*) the matter of bread and wine into the nature of his body and blood. These mystical sacraments are rightly called signs, therefore, not because they are signs of themselves, but rather because they function as signs for us.[130] Great and mystical signs are indeed contained in these things. That matter (*materia*), namely, the bread from which the Lord's body is confected by a spiritual blessing, is ground from many grains and joined together by a sprinkling of water. And the wine that is transferred into blood is made from many grapes crushed in the press. As the grains and grapes are brought forth (*procreantur*) by the cooperative labor of the farmers, so we are re-created (*recreati*) in faith by the cultivation of preachers. And later, having been ground down by fasts and vigils, we are formed into the one body of Christ, joined together by the sprinkling of baptism. This is in keeping with Paul's words, "We who are many are made one in Christ" (Rom. 12:5). These sacraments are down payments (*arrha*) on the eternal beatitude that we will receive if we worthily partake of them. The water that is added to wine also functions as a figure for us: as we flow along toward death like rushing water, by enacting the mystery of the Lord's passion, we are joined to Christ by the adoption of grace. Surely this body received by the faithful is a sign of our mortal bodies renewed through Christ's passion, and through the reception of the blood is signified the renewal of our souls. Bruno is alert in emphasizing here that, although the sacrament is divided into parts, it always remains whole and intact (*totum ubique tamen est integrum*).[131]

Bruno also addresses the Eucharist when commenting on Psalm 77:20 Vulg. (78:20 Eng.): "Because he struck the rock, and the waters gushed out, and the streams overflowed. Can he also give bread, or provide a table for his people?" As the New Testament so often unlocks the fuller meaning of the Old, so Bruno appeals to Paul's own spiritual reading of the exodus account that is also recounted in the psalm, thus applying this passage to Christ. And

129. *Expositio in Psalmos* 21 (PL 152:725a–b).
130. *Expositio in Psalmos* 21 (PL 152:725b–c).
131. *Expositio in Psalmos* 21 (PL 152:725c–26a).

as Christ was the rock in the wilderness that God provided to the Israelites (1 Cor. 10:4), so Bruno links the distrust of the Israelites in the desert to heretics who continue to sin after baptism. They tempt God in their hearts and cast doubt on his omnipotence when they question whether he could offer his body to be consumed under the species of the bread (*sub panis specie corpus suum*). They may speak of Christ's body and blood, but they are bereft of true belief (*sola voce non corde*) as they recite the Lord's Prayer: "Give us this day our daily bread" (Luke 11:3), which refers to the Lord's own body and blood. This body and blood is the one indivisible and incorruptible food, even as it appears to be broken under the species of the bread and crushed in the teeth of the faithful. The wording here, "*sub specie panis videatur frangi et a dentibus fidelium conteri*," is virtually identical to the 1059 eucharistic confession written by Cardinal Humbert of Silva Candida and forced on Berengar of Tours: "*tractari et frangi et fidelium dentibus atteri*." Having made the theologically subtle yet crucial distinction that Christ's body only appears (*videatur*) to be crushed, Bruno readily admits that why Christ's body appears to be broken and crushed while in actuality remaining indivisible remains an insoluble mystery, yet one that must be firmly believed. Heretics will say that Christ departed from this life corporeally when he ascended into heaven and that heaven is where he remains (i.e., not on the altar). Yet catholics know that God can indeed "prepare the table" with his body, having performed an even greater miracle when the water of spiritual grace flowed from the rock in the wilderness. And so in his passion Christ the rock (1 Cor. 10:4) poured out a flood of spiritual grace.[132]

Moving on to the epistles commentary, we find that Bruno addresses the Eucharist in a few separate places within 1 Corinthians. He explains that when speaking of Christ our Pasch (1 Cor. 5:7), the apostle "sends us to the historical record" (*mittit nos ad historiam*) where the children of Israel were commanded to place the lamb's blood on the doorposts (Exod. 12:7). That unblemished lamb signified Christ the true lamb, whose blood has anointed our minds so as to liberate us from the plague of the persecuting angel. Thus the church daily convenes to celebrate this meal of the lamb. Through this Passover (*transitus*) to the very truth of the thing itself (*ad veritatem rei*)—now employed under the species of bread and wine—we believe that the elements have genuinely passed into the true substance of Christ's body and blood (*revera transire in veram substantiam*) so that we too will pass over into eternity.[133]

132. *Expositio in Psalmos* 77 (PL 152:1038c–39d). For the 1059 *Ego Berengarius* confession, see *Enchiridion Symbolorum*, ed. H. Denzinger and A. Schönmetzer (Rome: Herder, 1976), 690.
133. *Expositio in epistolam I ad Corinthios* 5 (PL 153:147d–48a).

Commenting on Paul's words, "The cup of blessing that we bless, is it not a sharing in the blood of Christ? The bread that we break, is it not a sharing in the body of Christ?" (1 Cor. 10:16), Bruno observes that the blood of Christ, worthily consumed, liberates us from previous sins and strengthens against future temptation. Confirming once more the central role of the clergy, Bruno states that God himself blesses and consecrates the chalice through the ministry of the priesthood (*per sacerdotum ministrum*). Partaking of Christ's blood, we are united to Christ and thus conformed to him. Here is the true body of Christ (*verum corpus Christi*), which is received under the outward appearance alone of the bread (*sub specie sola panis*). And here, as in the Psalter commentary, Bruno makes the important point that the breaking (*frangimus*) occurs only on the level of appearance (*licet ita videatur*) while the body of Christ remains one in truth (*unum est in veritate*), since it cannot be torn apart. This fundamental unity thereby signifies that we who are diverse people are made one in Christ, for we are incorporated into Christ's body. God instituted this sacrifice in the two substances of body and blood, and by means of these sacraments God transfers us into a state of incorruption. It is through the flesh on the altar that Christ redeems our flesh and through his blood he redeems our soul, since blood is the seat of the soul. Here Bruno also confirms the doctrine of concomitance (even if he does not employ that precise term), for even as the Eucharist is distributed in two substances (*in duas substantias*), the person who receives the blood or body alone still receives the whole, and the person who receives communion under both kinds receives no more than the person who receives only one. Yet again Bruno emphasizes that the body of Christ, which is offered under the species of bread (*sub specie panis*), is torn and divided into parts only on the level of outward appearance (*per solam speciem atteritur*), while remaining incorruptible and indivisible in truth (*in veritate incorruptibile*). This discussion of real presence remains anchored, however, in the ecclesial unity of the church as the body of Christ, for it is through the reception of Christ's body and blood that we are united to him—united in faith, hope, and charity, serving one another in the unity of love.[134]

It should already be clear that Bruno affirms a strong doctrine of real presence. Commenting directly on the Last Supper as recounted by the apostle Paul (1 Cor. 11:23–26), Bruno observes that Christ had taken the true substance of bread (*veram substantiam panis*) in his hands. Through those words by which Christ gives thanks to the Father, the substance of the bread and wine on the altar pass into (*transire*) his true flesh and blood (*veram carnem et*

---

134. *Expositio in epistolam I ad Corinthios* 10 (PL 153:176a–c).

verum sanguinem). Thus when Christ says "This is my body," the pronoun "this" (*hoc*) refers to what was bread a little while ago but now is the immortal and impassible body that Christ offers to the apostles.[135] Bruno sees no problem in Christ handing over his immortal self into mortal hands. This event is likened to the transfiguration, in which Christ's body—at the time still mortal—was shown to Peter, James, and John in the glory of its immortality and impassibility.[136] For Bruno, moreover, real presence and effective sacrifice go together. Christ commands that we continue to do this in memory of him, not in enjoyment and drunkenness, but in commemoration of his passion, so that we in turn might be willing to suffer for his sake. Here, then, the cup that had a short while ago been the true substance of wine now becomes the blood of the new promise. As opposed to the carnal happiness offered by the old covenant, therefore, the sacrament of the body and blood presents a new reality (*rem novam*). It is a New Testament that can never be altered. The point is again made that this is the true body (*verum corpus*) of Christ even as the appearance and taste (*speciem et saporem*) of bread remain so as not to horrify those who consume it.[137]

The amount of space devoted to the Eucharist and the genuine depth of the discussion in Bruno's Psalter and epistles commentaries reveal just how important this cathedral schoolmaster thought it was for his students to understand the prevailing orthodox position. It would not be too long before these men were teaching students of their own, advising bishops, and eventually presiding over synods. Moreover, with regard to the history of biblical exegesis, we observe the willingness of the scholastic exegete to delve into central theological questions at length within the confines of the commentary. As we shall see in chapter 6, these questions arising from the biblical text were eventually treated in a separate forum, as their breadth and complexity demanded.

---

135. *Expositio in epistolam I ad Corinthios* 11 (PL 153:184b–d).
136. *Expositio in epistolam I ad Corinthios* 11 (PL 153:184c–85a).
137. *Expositio in epistolam I ad Corinthios* 11 (PL 153:185a–b).

4

The Monks
of the Twelfth Century

Some of the exegetes we looked at in previous chapters were monks, while others were secular masters, but this chapter is devoted entirely to the monastic biblical commentators. The twelfth century was a remarkable period and, like the Carolingian era, is very often spoken of as a time of "renaissance." In light of the varied and prodigious exegetical work produced in this century, we will devote three separate chapters to its different facets. Although the first will be given to the monks, to be followed by the canons, and finally the cathedral schools, this order is not dictated by any strict walls of separation. Despite some tensions, these different groups of scholars were not at odds with one another; in fact, they had a great deal in common and can even be said to have complemented one another's work. Nevertheless, we begin with the men and women of the cloisters, those whose lives were devoted above all else to prayer.

The Benedictine Monks

If we are to begin to understand the mind-set of the medieval monk, which informed his biblical exegesis, there is no better place to begin than with the Benedictine Rule. That rule formed the locus around which monastic life was centered. Consider first the prologue to the rule as it addresses the monk directly:

Listen, my son to the precepts of your master [*praecepta magistri*] and incline the ear of your heart [*aurem cordis*] to the advice of a loving Father. . . . Let us encompass ourselves with faith, and the practice of good works, and guided by the Gospel, tread the path he has cleared for us. . . . We are about to open a school [*schola*] for God's service, in which we hope nothing harsh or oppressive will be directed. . . . As our lives and faith progress, the heart expands, and with the sweetness of love we move down the paths of God's commandments. Never departing from his guidance, remaining in the monastery until death, we patiently share in the sufferings of Christ so that we might be found worthy to be coheirs with him in his kingdom.[1]

As we see, the monks have entered into a sacred school where they will be inculcated into the life of holiness that conforms them ever more deeply to the Lord Jesus Christ. This life of work, prayer, reading, and contemplation was driven by the aspiration to attain eternal peace in the heavenly homeland.

The way to heaven begins with humbleness of heart. In chapter 7 of the rule, wherein the monks are exhorted to guard themselves against pride and thus comport themselves in all humility, it is a mystical reading of Scripture that exemplifies this foundational principle. This is hardly surprising given that the rule is absolutely saturated with scriptural quotations and allusions. Here the monks are told to erect a ladder like that which appeared to Jacob in his dream as he watched the angels ascending and descending the rungs (Gen. 28:12). Applying the moral sense of the passage, therefore, the monks are to understand it as the descent that comes by pride and the ascent by way of humility. The ladder itself is likened to life in the present world, through which the humble heart ascends by the Lord's assistance into heaven. The monk's body and soul constitute the two sides of this ladder, into which the divine calling has inserted various degrees of humility or discipline for the monk to climb. Having ascended all of these degrees of humility (*humilitatis gradibus ascencis*), the monk will then arrive at the perfect love of God that casts out fear (1 John 4:18). And now, transformed by the love of Christ (*amore Christi*), he will take pleasure in virtue and begin to keep the commandments effortlessly by force of habit.[2]

Daily life in the monastery is focused around prayer: through his prayer life the monk is immersed in Scripture, most especially the Psalms. In fact, the medieval monks chanted all 150 psalms each week. The schedule of prayer

1. *The Rule of St. Benedict: The Abingdon Copy*, ed. John Chamberlain (Toronto: Pontifical Institute Press, 1982), 18–20; *The Rule of St. Benedict*, trans. Anthony Meisel and M. L. Mastro (New York: Image Books, 1975), 43–45. I have altered the translation in places as needed.

2. *Rule*, chap. 7, pp. 28–33 (Meisel and Mastro, 56–61).

that forms the center of the monastic life is itself drawn from the words of the psalmist: "Seven times a day I have given praise to Thee" (Ps. 118:164 Vulg. [119:164 Eng.]). "We will fulfill this sevenfold sacred number if we perform the offices of our service at Lauds, Prime, Tierce, Sext, None, Vespers, and Compline." The Psalter, which would soon be committed to memory by sheer repetition, thus formed the soul of the monk. Here the whole of the Christian spiritual life was displayed: sorrow, repentance, hope, joy, and yearning for God.[3]

Books, whether read or heard, also formed a mainstay of monastic formation. Although it is true that the monks were forbidden personal ownership (no monk was to possess even a book, writing tablet, or pen), they were nonetheless actively reading and writing daily.[4] This might be while alone or while listening to sacred books read aloud during their meals.[5] In Lenten season the monks were to be employed in reading from morning until the third hour. They would thus receive books from the library, which they were to read through in order.[6] The rule makes clear the inestimable value of sacred reading in the quest for perfection.

> For what page or what utterance of the divine authority of the Old and the New Testament is not a most upright standard of human life [*rectissima norma vitae humanae*]? Or, what book of the holy catholic fathers does not proclaim that by a straight path we may find our Creator? So, too, the Collations of the Fathers, and their Institutes and Lives, and the rule of our holy Father, Basil; what are they except the monuments of the virtues of exemplary and obedient monks?[7]

The great modern scholar of monastic culture, Jean Leclercq, has highlighted the way in which the monks embraced the life of study even as they allowed it never to become an end unto itself but rather a means to spiritual perfection. Hence, like their founder, Benedict, the monks in their studies were, paradoxically, "knowingly ignorant and wisely unlearned" (*scienter nescius et sapienter indoctus*). The principal occupation of the monk was rumination on biblical and patristic texts, the practice often summed up in the term *lectio divina*. It speaks not only to the sacred content of what is being read but also to the prayerful act of reading itself. To read (*legere*) meant also to listen intently or understand (*audire*), and then furthermore to meditate

3. *Rule*, chap. 16, pp. 36–37 (Meisel and Mastro, 66).
4. *Rule*, chap. 33, p. 45 (Meisel and Mastro, 76).
5. *Rule*, chap. 38, pp. 48–49 (Meisel and Mastro, 79–80).
6. *Rule*, chap. 48, pp. 54–55 (Meisel and Mastro, 86–87).
7. *Rule*, chap. 73, pp. 72–73 (Meisel and Mastro, 106).

(*meditari*) on what one read. To meditate, in turn, implied a preparation to fulfill what one was contemplating, a desire to conform oneself to the lessons of the holy reading.[8] These insights apply not only to the individual monk as he seeks God in prayerful reflection but can also be seen in corporate actions. It has been said that medieval monks "acted out and in some ways even incarnated the Bible." Eight hours each day were devoted to the liturgy, chants, and prayers that read like a catena of biblical texts. The monks, moreover, re-created scenes from the New Testament in their processions marking holy days such as Ash Wednesday and Palm Sunday.[9]

Robert of Tombelaine and Bruno of Segni

Holy Scripture also found immediate application to momentous issues of the day, as we find in the late eleventh century when ecclesiastical and imperial interests clashed in the investiture contest. Staunch proponents of the Gregorian reform effort, two Benedictine monks, Robert of Tombelaine and Bruno of Segni, located within the Song of Songs a prophetic message of spiritual purity, as true Christians would need to fend off assaults leveled by secular forces against the virgin bride of Christ.[10] We see here how these monks were able to weave together the call to personal sanctity and the papal cause: the holy ones cling to their Savior while the corrupt forsake his body for worldly gain. Commenting on the opening verse of the Song of Songs, Robert finds in the mouth of the bridegroom the "inspiration of Christ"; the kiss of the mouth is thus the sweet love of that inspiration.[11] The two breasts refer to love of God and neighbor; it is from these breasts that Christ feeds his bride with the milk of piety. Whoever refreshes himself with the charity of God, according to Robert, senses the fragrance and sweetness of the spiritual gifts.[12] It is the holy soul that is the bride of Christ: she who exults in the delights of the bridegroom, putting away carnal things so that she might hide herself in the spiritual. The soul remembers the charity with which Christ loved the bride, redeeming her with his blood as he was dying on the cross, and now daily nourishing her from the bosom of

8. Jean Leclercq, *The Love of Learning and the Desire for God: A Study of Monastic Culture*, trans. C. Misrahi (New York: Fordham University Press, 1988), 12–17.

9. Isabelle Cochelin, "When the Monks Were the Book," in *The Practice of the Bible in the Middle Ages*, ed. Susan Boynton and Diane Reilly (New York: Columbia University Press, 2011), 61–83, quote on 61.

10. E. Ann Matter, *The Voice of My Beloved: The Song of Songs in Western Medieval Christianity* (Philadelphia: University of Pennsylvania Press, 1992), 106–11.

11. *Commentariorum in Canticum Canticorum* 1.1 (PL 150:1364c–d).

12. *Commentariorum in Canticum Canticorum* 1.2 (PL 150:1365a).

mother church.[13] Robert therefore stresses the call to holiness: one must follow along the path of truth and seek the works of virtue. Now there are those who rightly love Christ, but others are distorted by their vices; they offend his rectitude and cannot altogether love Christ, the very author of righteousness.[14] Some (i.e., imperial apologists) do not dwell within Christ's pasture but roam outside, lacking the spirit of Christ. Then there are the so-called companions of Christ, the false Christians who bear the name and even receive the sacraments, but are really like irrational animals. They persecute the elect (i.e., supporters of papacy), who must suffer them and thereby be proved true by their endurance.[15]

In his own Song of Songs commentary, Bruno of Segni imagines the words of the bride, who is said to exclaim, "I have Moses, Elijah, Jeremiah, and David, and all the others who announced his coming to me. I believe in their words and yet languish in my heart. I am ready now; the laws have come to an end. Moses was wine to me, and yet the wine that the prophets gave me was bitter, austere, and sour to drink." Thus she yearns for the preaching of Christ that will finally convert this acrid wine to sweet milk, the milk therefore of the New Testament.[16] Amid such rejoicing in the sweet milk of Christ, Bruno sounds a warning as he comes upon the verse, "Like a lily among the thorns" (Song 2:2). What is especially noteworthy about his treatment of this verse is his application of the senses of Scripture. For Bruno, the literal reading of the text (ad litteram) actually refers to the church of his own day, which is presently afflicted by heretics and schismatics who have been born from the font of baptism. Thus it seems that the prophetic message applicable to the eleventh-century church is not the spiritual meaning as one might expect. In fact, Bruno specifically states that this verse read spiritually refers to Christ among the Jews, although it also serves as a more general moral reference to the just among sinners.[17]

Honorius Augustodunensis

Now we can turn to a less controversial, although no less interesting, work on the Song of Songs composed by the German Benedictine Honorius Augustodunensis. His commentary has been described as "a relentless application of the four levels of biblical interpretation described by Cassian," although not

---

13. *Commentariorum in Canticum Canticorum* 1.7 (PL 150:1366c–d).
14. *Commentariorum in Canticum Canticorum* 1.8 (PL 150:366d).
15. *Commentariorum in Canticum Canticorum* 1.14 (PL 150:1368b).
16. *Expositio in Canticum Canticorum* 1 (PL 164:1235a).
17. *Expositio in Canticum Canticorum* 2 (PL 164:1243d–44a).

without variation and creativity.[18] It is not surprising to find that Honorius's prologue, written in the twelfth century, presents an *accessus ad auctorem*, wherein he outlines the author, subject matter, and intention of the work. Thus the author is the Holy Spirit, speaking through the vessel of wisdom, Solomon, the writer (*scriptor*) of this book, who was the most wise king and preeminent prophet. Honorius observes that Solomon published three books in heroic meter, which cover the three parts of philosophy: ethics, physics, and logic. The Song of Songs falls under logic, since here Solomon wished for the rational soul to be joined to God through love.[19] The subject matter is the bridegroom and bride, namely, Christ and the church. Christ is called the bridegroom by way of likeness (*per simile*). Just as the bridegroom is carnally joined to the bride that they may become one, so Christ through the flesh he assumed is conjoined to the church, and she through the consumption of his (eucharistic) body is incorporated into him. So it is that through faith and love the head and body are united.[20] Indeed, the intention of this work is the conjoining of the church, or any human soul, to Christ through love. This unitive love is itself twofold, thereby covering both the love of God and love of one's neighbor.[21]

Honorius finds, furthermore, that the Song deals with marriage according to all four scriptural senses: historically, allegorically, tropologically, and anagogically. By way of history, there is the mingling of the flesh or just betrothal: the former referring to Solomon and the daughter of Pharaoh, the latter to Joseph and Mary. Allegorically, there are two ways to read the text: it can refer (1) to the incarnation as the Word of God conjoined himself to flesh or (2) to Christ, the God-man, united in fellowship to the universal church. Tropologically, the soul is joined to Christ through love. And by way of anagogy, the new man ascends to heaven after the resurrection as he joins the whole church in the vision of divine glory.[22]

Honorius will pursue the four senses throughout his commentary, applying them to almost every line, which results in a massive work. For our purposes, one example will have to suffice. By way of history, he explains that "Solomon" means "peaceful" and that Solomon built the temple in Jerusalem in seven years. Allegorically, Solomon's name thus refers to Christ, while Jerusalem, the vision of peace, is the church, which Christ made a temple for himself through the seven gifts of the Holy Spirit. Then, by way of tropology, Honorius

---

18. Matter, *Voice of My Beloved*, 58–76.
19. *Expositio in Canticum Canticorum*, prologue (PL 172:347d–48d).
20. *Expositio in Canticum Canticorum*, prologue (PL 172:349a).
21. *Expositio in Canticum Canticorum*, prologue (PL 172:350a).
22. *Expositio in Canticum Canticorum*, prologue (PL 172:349b–c).

finds that the temple constructed from wood and stones may be likened to the faithful person who renders his soul a temple for God, built from the good works and examples of the saints. And anagogically, the precious stones that also went into the temple's construction speak to Christ building his temple in the heavenly Jerusalem from all the elect.[23]

Rupert of Deutz

One of the more prolific writers of the early twelfth century was the Benedictine monk Rupert of Deutz, some of whose works, including his highly original Song of Songs commentary, we will look at below. Because as a matter of principle he maintained that biblical exegesis should always be useful (*utilis*) as opposed to speculative, Rupert was willing to extend his sights beyond the fathers if that meant finding an interpretation of even greater usefulness to religious life in his own day.[24] The first of his writings that we can examine is *On the Holy Trinity and His Works*, where Rupert looked to God's acts of creation and redemption as recorded in Scripture to learn about the trinitarian God. As Rupert composed this work, he would have had access to almost all the patristic texts that the Laon school had utilized for the production of the *Glossa Ordinaria*, although there is no evidence that Rupert had himself read the Gloss. Most of *On the Holy Trinity* is devoted to the work of the Second Person of the Trinity, with more attention to Christ as revealed in the mysteries of the Old Testament than as recorded in the gospels. When Rupert did look at the role of the Holy Spirit from the time of the incarnation up until the final judgment day, he found that the monks have now taken the place of the apostles and martyrs of the early church; they are the new vanguard.[25]

As a commentator, Rupert leads the reader through the book of Genesis and reveals all of its embedded christological mysteries. Abel was the first witness to God's only begotten Son, and by faith in his passion Abel offered the firstborn of his flock so as to prefigure that great and final sacrifice (Gen. 4:4). Abel is himself a figure of Christ, the good shepherd (cf. John 10:11) who is held in contempt and then slain by those who belong to the body of Cain. Thus while "Cain offered gifts to the Lord from the fruits of earth, which were inanimate and without faith, a dead sacrifice of insentient things, Abel made an offering from the firstborn of his flock and from their fat."[26] Here

23. *Expositio in Canticum Canticorum* 1 (PL 172:359c–d).

24. John Van Engen, *Rupert of Deutz* (Berkeley: University of California Press, 1983), 67–72.

25. Ibid., 81–94.

26. *De Sancta Trinitate et operibus eius* 2–5 (CCCM 21:282–87); *The Bible in Medieval Tradition: The Book of Genesis*, trans. and ed. Joy Schroeder (Grand Rapids: Eerdmans, 2015), 87–92.

then is the sacrifice instituted by Christ the high priest, which, although bread and wine in appearance, is truly the Lamb of God. The presence of the fat, moreover, is a sign that not only flesh and blood are present but also the true Word of God in his divinity. That the whole likeness might be perfected (*tota similitudo perficiatur*), just as Abel the dutiful priest was slain by Cain following his sacrifice, so Christ, who is both priest and sacrifice, was betrayed and seized following the most holy supper.[27]

In the midst of writing on the Trinity, Rupert began to work on a commentary on John, which he finished by the middle of 1116. In this age of antagonism between schoolmen and monks, Rupert counted knowledge (*scientia*) as a blessing of the Holy Spirit, although he cautioned that it should not be confused with the higher wisdom (*sapientia*) that one could learn only from Christ. Rupert was supremely confident that he was able to match the sophisticated learning of the schoolmen, and he felt compelled to counter what he regarded as their near-heretical excesses. His commentary on John was written to that end, as he sought to shore up the unity of the person of Christ, the God-man, whom he thought some schoolmen were dividing through their overly strict distinction of natures. Christology therefore was the focus of this commentary: Rupert took up the tough questions that had arisen around the doctrine of the hypostatic union. He was concerned that the human nature of Christ, Christ the man, was being radically subordinated to the divine Christ so that there were almost two Christs. This issue was especially important for the devotional life of the monk; Rupert wished to adore the crucified Savior, the crucified God. He insisted, therefore, that the Son of Man and Son of God were "one and the same" (*unus idemque*).[28]

When Rupert addresses the opening verse of John's Gospel, "In the beginning was the Word" (1:1), he maintains that the Word should not be taken here in the childish mode (*pueriliter*) of its basic etymological sense, the sort that schoolboys learn from reading Donatus, wherein a word is said to be formed from reverberations in the air and the movement of the tongue. For this Word abode from all eternity, before there even was any air at all and thus before all things were made. This Word is perpetual reason, eternal wisdom, incomprehensible understanding, and incommutable truth. Drawing on Augustine's discussions in his own Johannine commentary, Rupert likens the eternal Word to our own equivocal use of the term "word," which applies to both the articulated word (*vox*) and the unspoken counsel of the mind.[29]

27. Ibid.
28. Van Engen, *Rupert of Deutz*, 95–134.
29. *Commentaria in Evangelium Sancti Iohannis* 1.1 (CCCM 9:9–10).

From the outset, Rupert was keen to show how the Johannine text refutes the heresies of the Patripassianists, Sabellians, and Arians. When John says "And God was the Word" (John 1:1 Vulg.), he supports the homoousians, those "confessors of consubstantiality" who neither confuse the persons nor divide the substance of the Trinity. And when John writes "Through him all things were made" (John 1:3), we see that the entire Trinity is already revealed. "For if you were to ask [*si quaeras*], who made all things? the answer is God. And through what? Through himself, namely, the Word. And if you ask Why? Because it is good, for the goodness of the Father and Son is itself the Holy Spirit." Thus you have, Rupert says, the whole Trinity (*tota Trinitas*).[30]

"And it was the light of men" (John 1:4) prompts a discussion of human rational faculties. The Word, Rupert says, is the eternal principle of reason (*ratio*), and thus the light of the best part of all human beings. This is the light that illuminates human nature; its image is expressed in the soul of all people. Thus the universal light of human reason shines in both the good and the bad equally, for although one may fall into the darkness of sin, one cannot be deprived of the light of reason. Yet there is another light that can be lost: this is the glory of the likeness of God. For God made man not only according to his image (*ad imaginem*) but also his likeness (*ad similitudinem*); the former pertains to rationality, the latter to goodness. Thus "the light that shines in the darkness" (John 1:5) is the discernment of reason that shines in the conscience, which has grown dark through the practice of evil. That is why, according to Rupert as he appeals to Paul, both Jews and gentiles were without excuse (Rom. 1:19–20) when they failed to properly glorify God. While the gentiles possessed the light of reason (*lux rationis*), the Jews had both reason and the Scriptures to guide them.[31] Along these lines, then, when it is said, "He was the true light which illuminates every man coming into this world" (John 1:9), this speaks to the brilliant illumination of divine grace. And yet, Rupert says, not all children of Adam follow after this grace of divine light. Indeed, many are justly left behind; they have erred along the path of truth, and the sun of righteousness has not risen upon them. Thus it as if the gospel writer were to say, Christ was the true light apart from which no one is illuminated among all who come into this world.[32]

Rupert's discussion of the eucharistic passages of John's Gospel gave him a chance to present a sophisticated analysis of some key principles of exegetical method, specifically the subtle distinctions inherent to figurative discourse.

30. *Commentaria in Evangelium Sancti Iohannis* 1.1 (CCCM 9:10–11).
31. *Commentaria in Evangelium Sancti Iohannis* 1.4 (CCCM 9:16–17).
32. *Commentaria in Evangelium Sancti Iohannis* 1.9 (CCCM 9:22).

Addressing John 6:32, "My Father gives to you true bread from heaven," Rupert argues against a so-called adversary (perhaps the recently deceased Berengar of Tours, d. 1088) who states that the bread on the altar is actually a figure of the living bread who descended from heaven; it is not the living bread himself. This is an argument that Rupert regards as devoid of "canonical authority," for it was the living bread himself who said of the bread that he was holding in his hands, "This is my body." Apparently Rupert's adversary claims that the admonition "Unless you eat the flesh of the Son of man and drink his blood, you will not have life in you" (6:54) must be read figuratively. Yet, Rupert says, even were one to grant that this is a figurative locution, it still does not destroy the truth of the thing itself (*veriatem rei*) any more than the words of a parable undermine the fundamental truth of what the parable communicates. This is in keeping with the definition of figurative discourse, according to Rupert: when one thing resonates in the word (*in voce sonat*) while some other thing should be understood (*aliud intelligendum est*). Thus even as the aforementioned verse is a figure of speech (*locutio figurata*), the Jews heard one thing while Christ meant another. In fact, not only did the figure not destroy the reality, but one might even say that the figure itself is undone by the abiding reality, as Christ says of the bread and wine, "This is my body." It is the so-called Jewish sense (*sensus iudaicus*) that is destroyed here, according to Rupert, since the Jews were thinking that he was speaking of flesh present to the five senses as one might be said to eat the flesh of a lamb. Here is an instance, therefore, in which the figure is undone and the fitting sense of the word (*sensus verbi consonus*) remains, namely, that the bread will be converted into the true substance of his body by divine power.[33]

When Rupert arrives at Christ's promise, "The bread which I give you is my flesh for the life of the world" (John 6:52), he argues that this proposition is convertible and thus makes sense in two ways. On the one hand, one could predicate the flesh of the bread such that it reads "The bread which I give to you is my flesh or my body." On the other hand, if one were to predicate the bread of the flesh, Christ would be saying "My flesh, which was swallowed up into the dead stomach of the earth, is bread because it is going to grant life and resurrection to the dead who are fed by it." Thus, however one turns the phrase, the meaning (*sententia*) is true, although Rupert favors a reading whereby the bread is the subject and the flesh the predicate. At this point Rupert makes what became a very controversial remark: "The Word, that is the bread of angels, was made flesh, not having been changed into flesh, but by assuming flesh; so that same Word previously made flesh becomes

---

33. *Commentaria in Evangelium Sancti Iohannis* 6.32 (CCCM 9:331–32).

the visible bread, not having been changed into bread, but by assuming and transferring the bread into the unity of his person."[34] On the strength of this statement Rupert was accused of heresy. His apparently overly literal reading led to an interpretation that his adversaries, principally Alger of Liège, labeled impanation, for here it seems that Rupert had identified the person of Christ with the bread itself.

On less controversial ground we turn to Rupert's reading of the Song of Songs, which he read as a paean to the Virgin Mary, the one who made possible Christ's incarnation. In his commentary, Mary is either speaking for herself or is being personally addressed. Allegorically, Mary is presented as the embodiment of the church, and on the tropological level she is the example of humility, virginity, and obedience.[35] Thus in his prefatory letter to Thietmar of Verden, Rupert says that he has dictated this little work on the Song of Songs "in contemplation of the face of our Lady Mary, holy and perpetual Virgin."[36] One finds, however, that Rupert remained true to the historical sense of the text by tracing the story of Mary, as presented in the gospels, from the time of the annunciation to her visit with Elizabeth and beyond, often weaving gospel passages into the text so as to explicate the meaning of the Song. Hence "we will exult and rejoice" (Song 1:3 Vulg. [1:4 Eng.]) finds its fullest expression in Luke's narrative: "I and the child in my womb exult in joy from the voice of your salvation" (cf. Luke 1:44). And so, Rupert says, we too may sing these same words; for while Eve made us weep, Mary makes us exult.[37]

In the prologue to the commentary, Rupert draws on the imagery of Jacob wrestling with the angel, whom he will not let go until he receives a blessing (Gen. 32:22–28). Similarly, Rupert says, the faithful soul must grapple with the word of God until able to draw out the blessing of the Holy Spirit, which is the true and useful understanding of the mysteries contained in Scripture. This is no easy task, so Rupert calls on his lady, the mother of the Word of God (*O domina Dei genetrix*), so that, armed with her merits and none of his own, he might struggle with the Song of Songs to her glory and the glory of the incarnate Lord. First, though, Rupert must address the very title of the work: Why is it called Song of Songs in the plural rather than the singular, as is standard practice in the rest of Scripture? Rupert proceeds to list six individual songs, beginning with the Song of Moses extolling the liberation of the children of Israel as they crossed the Red Sea (Exod. 15:1–19). Finally, we reach the seventh, the song of love, that sings of the greatest of all God's

---

34. *Commentaria in Evangelium Sancti Iohannis* 6.52 (CCCM 9:357).
35. Matter, *Voice of My Beloved*, 159–63.
36. *Epistula ad Thietmarum* (CCCM 26:4).
37. *Commentaria in Canticum Canticorum* 1.3 (CCCM 26:16–17).

beneficent acts as he descended into the Virgin Mary that she might bear a son, Jesus Christ, man and God. As he concludes the prologue, Rupert informs the reader that he remains cognizant of the history, or actual events (*historiae sive res gestae*), which form the foundation on which the mystery is built. For the mystical exposition (*expositio mystica*) will stand all the more solidly, he observes, if grounded in a record of times and events that can be reasonably substantiated.[38]

In keeping with his Marian reading of the Song, the bride's initial plea, "Let him kiss me with the kiss of his mouth" (Song 1:1 Vulg. [1:2 Eng.]), are the words of the Virgin Mary. Here is the great and sudden exclamation, Rupert says, the torrent of joy and power of love. And now Rupert addresses Mary directly (*O Beata Maria*): "You have beheld what 'eye has not seen and ear has not heard, nor has it entered into the heart of man' (1 Cor. 2:9); you have said to the angel, 'Behold the handmaid of the Lord; let it be done with me according to your will' (Luke 1:38). What was that word; what had he said to you? It was the angel's report: 'You have found favor with God. Behold you will conceive and bear a son, and you will call his name Jesus'" (1:30–31). And he thereupon tells her that "The Holy Spirit will come upon you, and the power of the Most High will overshadow you" (1:35). Surely, Rupert says, the word of the angel was the word and promise already present in the kiss of the Lord's mouth. And here he compares "Let him kiss me" with Mary's words in the gospel, "Behold the handmaid of the Lord; let it be done with me"; in each case these are the words of a jubilant and exultant heart. "Is not the meaning [*sensus*] the same," Rupert asks, "even as the words or expressions [*verbis seu vocibus*] are different? For just as you heard and believed, and thus beseeched God that this 'might be done with me,' so God the Father has kissed you 'with the kiss of his mouth.'" Continuing to address Mary directly, Rupert exclaims: "What eye has seen this? What ear has heard this? Into whose heart has it entered? To you, Mary, he has revealed himself, the one kissing, the kiss, and the mouth of the one kissing. . . . How great you are, O blessed one, in the reception of this singular gift, when the Holy Spirit came upon you and the power of the Most High overshadowed you, and you received this revelation."[39]

Hildegard of Bingen

We conclude this section on the Benedictines with a look at one of the most remarkable women of the twelfth century, Hildegard of Bingen. She was born in 1098 near Mainz, joined the Benedictine convent at Disibodenberg

38. *Commentaria in Canticum Canticorum*, prologue (CCCM 26:5–9).
39. *Commentaria in Canticum Canticorum* 1.1 (CCCM 26:10–11).

in 1112, and was elevated to the position of teacher (*magistra*) there in 1136. Soon thereafter, in 1141, Hildegard had a mystical experience in which she was called to speak and write about her vision. She was not motivated by a desire to say new things, however, so much as she wished to recover the teachings of the holy doctors in response to the sort of novelties being produced in the schools. There can be no doubt that Hildegard was a deeply learned exegete, even though she may have attributed her insights to divine revelation: "And suddenly I knew the meaning of the exposition [*intellectum expositionis*] of the Psalter, the Gospels, and other catholic books from the volumes of the Old as well as the New Testaments." So esteemed was Hildegard as an interpreter of Scripture that in 1176 the monks of Villers sent her a set of questions on a variety of biblical texts. Conversant with the range of literal and spiritual meanings, Hildegard favored the moral, or tropological, exposition that undergirded the monastic life.[40] The questions themselves, let alone the ingenious answers, provide us with a wonderful glimpse into the intellectual world of twelfth-century monastic life. One imagines the monks at Villers hashing out these scriptural conundrums in their daily chapters or perhaps while about their daily chores.

Among other topics, the monks ask Hildegard what sort of speech God would have used when speaking to the first human being, to which she replies that God would have spoken an angelic language (*angelicis verbis*) that Adam could have understood. In fact, having received from God both wisdom and the spirit of prophecy, Adam would have already known all the languages that future human beings would speak.[41] In this vein, the monks then ask what sort of eyes the first parents would have had, having seen the tree prior to their trespass. Hildegard opines that Adam and Eve had spiritual eyes (*spiritales oculos*), but as a result of their fall lost their spiritual vision, at which point their fleshly eyes (*carnales oculi*) were opened.[42]

And when they ask why Jonathan's eyes were said to be illumined when he ate from the honey (1 Sam. 14:27), Hildegard first compares him to a rich and fruitful land that is easily overturned with a plow and brings forth useful crops. Jonathan is further described as a man of even temperament, just and true. A person with such a character has sound humors, which are nourished by the foods that restore the brain, veins, and marrow. He is not beset by melancholy and anger, for the gift of God is present within him, causing him to germinate and grow as when dew falls on the land. The melancholy

40. See Beverly Mayne Kienzle, *Hildegard of Bingen: Solutions to Thirty-Eight Questions* (Collegeville, MN: Liturgical Press, 2014), 1–38, quote on 4–5. For the Latin text, see PL 197:1037–54.

41. *Solutions*, q. 4 (PL 197:1041c–d; Kienzle, 44).

42. *Solutions*, q. 6 (PL 197:1042b–c; Kienzle, 47).

man, however, is like the hard earth that is not easily plowed. And unless such people can master their feelings, they will be overwhelmed by sadness and anger, which will rob them of joy in all of their pursuits. Like the first sort of person, Jonathan—a man of sound humors—was therefore strengthened by the honey that he ate.[43]

The monks also inquire as to what sort of bodies the angels who visited Abraham might have had (Gen. 18:8–9). Hildegard replies that they appeared in human form, for otherwise a mutable human being (*mutabilis homo*) could not have seen such immutable spirits. That we cannot see such spirits is itself a result of the fall, Hildegard says, as Adam was deprived of his spiritual eyes and thus led the rest of the human race into this state of blindness. The angels conversed with Abraham not in angelic speech but in human language that he could understand. Regarding the flour, calf, butter, and milk that Abraham placed before the angels and they ate, Hildegard explains that they ate as human beings eat but that the food evaporated like the dew that falls on the grain and instantly dissolves in the heat of the sun.[44]

Continuing in Genesis, these inquisitive monks ask why Abraham had ordered his servant to place his hand under his thigh to swear an oath (Gen. 24:9). Hildegard says that this event prefigured (*praesignavit*) the sacred humanity of Christ descended from Abraham's own offspring, who would then destroy the counsel of the ancient serpent by liberating the human race.[45] And then addressing the wish of the patriarchs to be buried in a double cave (Gen. 23:9), Hildegard determines that by this the old law and the new law are symbolized (*figuratur*): just as the soul is hidden in the body, so the new law is hidden within the old. Indeed, already in their day the patriarchs recognized the advent of the new law, seeing as they did Christ prefigured (*significabatur*) in their sacrifices.[46]

Looking at one more question, we should examine a particularly remarkable passage that exemplifies the way in which Hildegard may be said to have internalized the biblical text. A trinitarian question had arisen in light of two passages in the Gospel of John (8:42 and 15:26) that apply the term "procession" at once to the Son and then also to the Spirit. What is the difference between these two processions, and what is the distinction between the generation of the Son and procession of the Spirit if they both come about from the Father? In her response, Hildegard begins by speaking in the voice of Christ: "My Father is power, and I sounding forth his Word,

---

43. *Solutions*, q. 30 (PL 197:1050c–d; Kienzle, 79–80).
44. *Solutions*, q. 8 (PL 197:1043a–c; Kienzle, 50–51).
45. *Solutions*, q. 9 (PL 197:1043c–d; Kienzle, 52).
46. *Solutions*, q. 10 (PL 197:1044a; Kienzle, 53).

proceeded from him when he created all creatures through me. The Holy Spirit proceeded from him, namely, my Father, when I came down into the womb of the Virgin, whose flesh was not wounded by the serpent's deception. I donned humanity from her after I had been conceived by the same Holy Spirit."[47]

When she was not answering the questions of monks, Hildegard, in keeping with her responsibilities within the monastery, composed fifty-eight sermons for her fellow nuns, covering twenty-seven different gospel passages. The modern editors of these sermons have observed her innovative exegesis: "Uncovering and analyzing the *magistra*'s use of sources in the *Expositiones evangeliorum* reveals the newness of her writing: although she does borrow from the patristic tradition, she constantly innovates and creates a unique exegetical voice." It is, moreover, important to remember that Hildegard's monastic audience would have been familiar with many of these patristic texts, not only from their own private reading but also from having heard them read during the night office.[48]

Commenting on the angel's announcement to Joseph that he should take the holy family to Egypt (Matt. 2:13–15), Hildegard offers a decidedly moral reading. The "angel of the Lord" is the admonition of the Holy Spirit, who speaks to Joseph, representing as he does all human beings. His warning that Joseph must get up and take the boy and his mother to Egypt to remain until he receives further word is a call to awaken one's intellect to the knowledge that one must descend into affliction for the correction of one's sins and remain in this state until such time as God reveals his grace to the repentant sinner. All the while the devil, represented by Herod, works to destroy the knowledge (*scientia*) that leads to repentance. Thus the words of the prophet Hosea (Hosea 11:1) quoted by the evangelist, "Out of Egypt I will call my son" (Matt. 2:15), signal God's promise that, from the affliction and darkness of sins, he will lead faithful souls to safety, away from eternal death.[49]

Along the lines of moral interpretation, Hildegard's reading of the parable of the prodigal son (Luke 15:11–32) is an account of human free will and the capacity to choose good or evil. The "certain man having two sons" is God, according to whose image and likeness the human race was created. And his "two sons" speak to the knowledge of good and evil that he gave to human beings. The younger brother, with an unsteady moral foundation, is more prone to evil. When he seeks his share of the inheritance, the father, God,

47. *Solutions*, q. 23 (PL 197:1047d–48a; Kienzle, 69).

48. *Expositiones Evangeliorum* in *Hildegardis Bingensis Opera Minora*, ed. P. Dronke et al., CCCM 226 (Turnhout: Brepols, 2007), 137–44, quote on 140–41.

49. *Expositio* 11 (CCCM 226:217–18).

renders glory and honor to the one who would adhere to knowledge of the good, while permitting the one who coveted to go his own way. As the wayward brother grew hungry for lack of the food of life, having filled up his will with evil desires, his desperate need resulted from having squandered the hope of life in the abundance of his vices. When the son finally returns to his father in repentance, confessing that he is a transgressor unworthy "to be called your son" (i.e., to receive his original inheritance), he expects no wage but seeks only the grace of God. The father's summoning of his servants is then a call to the virtues by which man serves God, and the robe that the son receives is the innocence that Adam lost in paradise. To don this robe is to be clothed in "the justice of innocence." The ring he receives is "the comprehension of good works," while the shoes are those by which he will renounce the devil as he walks the straight path.[50]

When Hildegard turned to the Gospel of John and Christ's declaration "I am the good shepherd" (John 10:11), she read this in a vein of high Christology, as the Word of the Father declared himself the good creator of all creatures, "for they all proceed from me and I feed them all in plenitude." The life that the Word lays down is the very life that sustains all things, and he lays it down in corporeal form for the sake of his elect. The hired hand, in turn, is the devil who deceives the sheep, which are not his own, since he neither made them nor can redeem them. The wolf that he sees is rationality, which in evil human beings behaves as a wolf inasmuch as it contradicts God in the ways of knowledge of good and evil. The wolf, therefore, attacks knowledge of the good and scatters the sheep by dissipating them in perversity. As for the hired hand, he flees from the truth, while the good shepherd, the Word who made all things, knows all the elect who abide in him.[51]

Yet this christological reading of the Johannine passage does not exhaust its spiritual significance, for this same passage, according to Hildegard, can be taken another way (*alio modo*), so that it is a lesson in the moral order of the believer. The good shepherd is actually faith, here speaking for itself as the foundation of the virtues. The hired hand is thus unfaithfulness, who does not care for the sheep (the virtues); when he sees the coming wolf, who threatens the soul, he deserts the sheep by rejecting the virtues and fleeing, thereby withdrawing his help, since he has no ability to assist them in the good. The good shepherd, however, knows his own, and those virtues know him, because they are born of faith.[52]

50. *Expositio* 26 (CCCM 226:260–63).
51. *Expositio* 30 (CCCM 226:274–75).
52. *Expositio* 31 (CCCM 226:275–76).

The Cistercian Monks

Taking our leave of the Benedictines, we now look at two of the most illustrative commentators of the Cistercian monastic order: Bernard of Clairvaux and William of Saint Thierry.[53] The Cistercians, called "white monks" for the undyed wool of their habits, were devoted to the reform of the monastic life. Constituted in the early twelfth century, the monks of Citeaux purposefully eschewed the worldly glory of the Benedictines at the Abbey of Cluny (Cluniacs) for a rigorously ascetic regimen. The Cistercians, however, also developed a rich intellectual life and a unique brand of deeply personal spiritual reflection. Nowhere is that more evident than in Bernard of Clairvaux's Song of Songs commentary, which we will look at below, in addition to the profoundly affective writings of his confrere William of Saint Thierry.

Bernard of Clairvaux

Bernard of Clairvaux was born in 1090 to a noble family in Burgundy; along with his brothers, he entered the monastery at Citeaux in 1112. At the time it was simply known as the "new monastery" (*novum monasterium*) since the Cistercian order itself had been founded only some ten years earlier, in 1098. By 1115, however, Bernard was the abbot of a daughter house at Clairvaux.[54] The Cistercian tradition developed as it did in part due to its methods of recruitment. While the Benedictine monks traditionally received their members as oblates who were formed within the order from early childhood, the Cistercians accepted their new recruits as adults. These men were very often knights, many had been married, and most would have had some sexual experience before entry into the religious life. At the very least they would have been familiar with love literature of the sort recounted by the troubadours. As we stated, Bernard himself had joined the Cistercians from the ranks of secular knighthood, and it fell to him to compose sermons and tracts that could hold the attention of former knights by drawing on their experience and expectations of love. Bernard's genius, according to Leclercq, was in recognizing that "monastic love for God can and must be expressed in terms of human love; it can assume, retrieve, and integrate images, representations of human love, and even memories of its accomplishment." Bernard knew,

---

53. For two recent essay collections on Bernard and William respectively, see *A Companion to Bernard of Clairvaux*, ed. Brian Patrick McGuire (Leiden: Brill, 2011); and *Unity of Spirit: Studies of William of Saint-Thierry*, ed. F. Sargent, A. Rydstrøm-Poulsen, and M. Dutton (Collegeville, MN: Liturgical Press, 2015).

54. See Brian Patrick McGuire, "Bernard's Life and Works: A Review," in *Companion to Bernard of Clairvaux*, 18–61.

furthermore, that if these men within the cloister were to form a genuine community, the monastery itself would have to function as a sort of "school of charity" (*schola caritatis*), where they would learn the ways of true love for God and one another.[55]

This sort of affective appeal to the monks was borne out within Cistercian biblical commentaries. Ann Astell observes that twelfth-century Song of Songs commentators, such as Bernard and William, read the text not so much in terms of the soul attaining to some greater level of intellectual illumination but as the believer being moved to love God more dearly. "Their exegesis moves beyond an exposition of hidden learning [*allegoria*] to tropological exhortation—that is, they apply the interpreted text to the concrete life situation of their auditors and use the affective force of the Song's literal imagery to move them to virtuous action."[56] It is evident that Bernard's eighty-six sermons on the Song of Songs, written over a span of eighteen years beginning in Advent 1135, reflect a deeply personal reading of the Song that is directly concerned with achieving mystical union with God.[57] The result is a work of rhetorical, psychological, and religious genius. It is no wonder that his commentary has been called a "synthesis of the whole of his spiritual teaching."[58]

At the outset of his course of sermons, Bernard advises his fellow monks that they are mature enough now that they should be ready to feed on bread rather than milk (cf. 1 Cor. 3:1–2). Solomon has given us delicious bread; let us bring it forth now and break it.[59] The monks had been prepared for the Song by having read Solomon's other books of wisdom: Ecclesiastes and Proverbs. These two "loaves" have thus taught them how to recognize and to overcome misguided love of self and the world. And so, Bernard says, having warded off those two evils, they may start reading this contemplative work, which is delivered up to well-prepared ears and minds. In fact, this "reading" will come through the ears and then enter into the heart.[60]

The solid food that these more learned and spiritually mature monks are ready to consume will require of them something much more than mere

---

55. Jean Leclercq, *Monks and Love in Twelfth-Century France: Psycho-Historical Essays* (Oxford: Clarendon, 1979), 8–23, quote on 23.

56. Ann Astell, *The Song of Songs in the Middle Ages* (Ithaca, NY: Cornell University Press, 1990), 8.

57. Matter, *Voice of My Beloved*, 124–26.

58. See the introduction to Bernard's *Song of Songs*, introduction by M. Corneille Half-lants, trans. Kilian Walsh and Irene Edmonds, 4 vols. (Kalamazoo, MI: Cistercian Publications, 1971–80), 1:ix–xxx.

59. *Sancti Bernardi Opera*, ed. J. Leclercq, C. H. Talbot, and H. M. Rochais, 8 vols. (Rome: Cisterciensis, 1957–77), sermon 1, 1.1 (1:3; Walsh, 1:1).

60. *Sancti Bernardi Opera*, sermon 1, 1.2 (1:3–4; Walsh, 1:1–2).

intellectual prowess, for in taking up the Songs, they would be engaged in nothing less than an exploration of the self. The monks, Bernard says, must now turn their attention inward and read from "the book of our own experience" (*in libro experientiae*).[61] An introspective quest this may be, but by no means a dour one. Bernard is almost ecstatic at times as he rallies the monks: "Hear of the joy that which I have experienced. Yet it is your joy also. Hear of it then and rejoice. I experienced this joy in just one word of the Bride; and I was, as it were, lapped in its fragrance."[62] Struck by the magnitude of the task of leading the monks through such a sublime work, Bernard calls upon the assistance of the Word himself.[63] Apart from divine guidance there can be no progress. And so, Bernard says, "We implore his presence [the bridegroom] that we may worthily trace the words of his Bride, . . . for we cannot worthily consider and study such words as these unless he is present to guide our discourse. For her words are pleasant and lovely, . . . and they are deep in mystery."[64]

What is the subject matter (*materia*) of the Song? For Bernard, it is the sacred love that exceeds the limitations of language and thus must be expressed instead in deed and truth. Here in the Song, "love speaks everywhere [*amor ubique loquitur*]; if anyone desires to grasp these writings, let him love, . . . for a cold heart cannot catch fire [*capere ignitum*] from its eloquence."[65] Putting himself in the place of the bride, the monk seeks after the one she loves, all the while remembering that it was she who was first sought and first loved. Indeed, it is because of the bridegroom's initiative that she can now both seek and love.[66] The soul that yearns to recover the intimacy with the divine Word that she has felt so deeply then speaks in the person of the bride: "It was not by any of my senses that I perceived that he had penetrated to the depths of my being. Only by the movement of my heart, as I have told you, did I perceive his presence." Indeed, as Bernard continues, he asks, "When I have had such experience of the Word [*experimentum de Verbo*], is it any wonder that I take myself back to the words of the Bride, calling him back when he has withdrawn? . . . From the burning desire of my heart [*ardenti desiderio cordis*] I will not cease to call him. . . . I will implore him to give me back the joy of his salvation, and restore himself to me."[67]

61. *Sancti Bernardi Opera*, sermon 3, 1.1 (1:14; Walsh, 1:16).
62. *Sancti Bernardi Opera*, sermon 68, 1.1 (2:196–97; Walsh and Edmonds, 4:17).
63. *Sancti Bernardi Opera*, sermon 74, 1.1 (2:239–40; Walsh and Edmonds, 4:85).
64. *Sancti Bernardi Opera*, sermon 67, 1.1 (2:188; Walsh and Edmonds, 4:4).
65. *Sancti Bernardi Opera*, sermon 79, 1.1 (2:272; Walsh and Edmonds, 4:138).
66. *Sancti Bernardi Opera*, sermon 84, 1.4 (2:304–5; Walsh and Edmonds, 4:191).
67. *Sancti Bernardi Opera*, sermon 74, 1.6 (2:243; Walsh and Edmonds, 4:91).

Bernard the exegete was alive to every turn of phrase and captured all the rhetorical nuances of the text. He seems to delight in texts that first perplex him, recognizing that they must be all the richer in meaning for their difficulty. At the very first verse, "Let him kiss me with the kiss of his mouth," Bernard is immediately struck by its abruptness and wonders aloud how he can explain it. He identifies this as a delightful play of speech (*iucundum eloquium*), a way for Scripture to entice the reader to find pleasure in the laborious pursuit of its hidden message. This fascinating theme will serve only to sweeten the fatigue of research. Such turns of speech, though, only point up the Song's divine authorship: this is a work composed not by human reasoning (*humano ingenio*), Bernard says, but the rhetorical skill of the Spirit (*Spiritus arte ita compositum*).[68] One might say that the Holy Spirit is the consummate master of the *artes liberales*; his skills in the trivium are unmatched.

To interpret a work so sublime clearly demands more than a keen intellect; the reader will have to be conformed to the eternal author. The very title, "Solomon's Song of Songs," speaks to the necessary disposition of the exegete. Only the touch of the Spirit can inspire a song like this, Bernard insists, and only personal experience (*experientia*) can unfold its meaning. Let those who are versed in the mystery revel in it; let all others burn with desire (*inardescant desiderio*) to attain this experience (*experiendi*) rather than merely learn about it (*cognoscendi*).[69] And as the name Solomon means "peaceful," so only men of peaceful minds, who achieve mastery over the turmoil of the passions and the distracting burden of daily chores, are invited to study such a sublime book.[70] Solomon himself was directed by a divine impulse to celebrate the praises of Christ and his church, the gift of holy love, and the mystery of endless union with God. Here too, though, one will find expressed the mounting desires of the soul, its marriage song, and the exultation of the spirit poured forth in figurative language (*elogio figurato*) pregnant with delight.[71] One is struck too by the immediacy, and even intimacy, that Bernard has achieved with the text. Indeed, it has been keenly observed that Bernard expertly inserted the commentator, the preacher, into biblical scenes, "making himself part and parcel of what is going on inside the text." Speaking as the "I," Bernard became a protagonist in the drama that he recounts for his hearers.[72]

68. *Sancti Bernardi Opera*, sermon 1, 3.5 (1:5; Walsh, 1:3–4).
69. *Sancti Bernardi Opera*, sermon 1, 6.11 (1:7–8; Walsh, 1:6).
70. *Sancti Bernardi Opera*, sermon 1, 4.6 (1:5; Walsh, 1:4).
71. *Sancti Bernardi Opera*, sermon 1, 4.8 (1:6; Walsh, 1:5).
72. On Bernard's literary style, see M. B. Pranger, "Bernard the Writer," in *Companion to Bernard of Clairvaux*, 220–48, quote on 234.

When Bernard proceeds to parse the initial verse, he discovers therein some essential theological distinctions. The mouth that kisses is the Word who assumed human nature; the nature assumed thus receives this kiss. And the kiss that takes its being from both the giver and receiver is the one person formed by both: the mediator Jesus Christ. That is why the saints will not say "Let him kiss me with his mouth" but rather "the kiss of his mouth," for the mouth of the Word impressed itself on the human nature of Christ alone.[73] The believer, however, cannot immediately ask for even this kiss of the mouth. One must advance by degrees to a higher and holier state, thus from the feet to the hand, before arriving at the face of the bridegroom.[74] First there must be a genuine conversion of life. As one makes spiritual progress, the believer approaches the hand, while the final kiss of the mouth remains an experience only for the most perfect.[75]

Such spiritual advancement can be accomplished, however, only insofar as one relies on divine grace. And the more one grows in grace, the more confident one becomes. One begins to love with greater ardor and to knock on the door with greater assurance to gain what one still lacks. Yet this confidence born of grace is the fruit of a quest that itself must begin in humility. As we have seen when examining the rule, this is the essential disposition apart from which no such ascent is possible. The humble soul seeks not its own strength but places all its hope in God's mercy. God, Bernard says, will not refuse that most intimate kiss of all to the humble of heart; he will not fail to bestow this gift of his supreme generosity and ineffable sweetness (*mirae suavitatis*).[76] The language of not only emotional experience but also tactile sensation is vividly drawn by Bernard throughout the commentary, whether invoking the heat and burning feeling of love that frees one from the coldness (*frigiditas*) of emotional torpor or tasting (*gustare*) the sweetness (*dulcedo/suavitas*) of Christ.[77] To be sure, this is biblical language, especially that of the psalms, but Bernard internalized it and created a way of speaking that was uniquely his own.

The mystical union into which we have been called takes on markedly trinitarian dimensions as Bernard delves more deeply into the kiss that the bride so passionately seeks. He observes that even though we cannot be kissed by the mouth of the eternal Word directly, we can be kissed by the kiss, which is nothing less than the gift of the Holy Spirit, who is the mutual love between

---

73. *Sancti Bernardi Opera*, sermon 2, 2.3 (1:10; Walsh, 1:10).
74. *Sancti Bernardi Opera*, sermon 3, 2.4 (1:16; Walsh, 1:18–19).
75. *Sancti Bernardi Opera*, sermon 4, 1.1 (1:18–19; Walsh, 1:21).
76. *Sancti Bernardi Opera*, sermon 3, 3.5 (1:17; Walsh, 1:19).
77. *Sancti Bernardi Opera*, sermon 74, 1.7 (2:243–44; Walsh and Edmonds, 4:92).

Father and Son. As the Father kisses and the Son is kissed, so the kiss is the Holy Spirit; he is their undivided love and their indivisible unity.[78] This means that the kiss of the Spirit is itself the kiss of participation, which enables us not only to know God but also then to love the Father, who is never fully known (*plene cognoscitur*) until he is perfectly loved (*perfecte diligitur*). Reception of the Holy Spirit in the form of a kiss, therefore, allows believers to participate in the divine life of the Trinity.[79]

To experience the joy of the Trinity, to participate in this eternal communion of love, is what the monks desire above all else. And yet, for even the most devout, it often seems to be a desire unfulfilled. The bride says, "I cannot rest . . . unless he kisses me with the kiss of his mouth." Bernard speaks then on her behalf: "There is no question of ingratitude on my part, it is simply that I am in love." She has striven for years to lead a chaste and sober life, to concentrate on spiritual studies and pray often, to resist vices, and recount all the years of bitterness in her soul.[80] Bernard knows very well that this is something to which his fellow monks can relate. "Many of you too, as I recall, are accustomed to complain to me in our private conversations about a similar languor and dryness of soul." These men find that their best efforts can be frustrated; they yearn to be kissed and attain what they desire.[81] Even men of frequent prayer experience this dullness of spirit; we approach the altar to pray, Bernard writes, but our hearts are only lukewarm (*corde tepido*). He urges them not to lose hope, for "if we persevere, there comes then an unexpected infusion of grace [*infunditur gratia*], our breast expands as it were, and our interior is filled with an overflowing of love [*pietatis inundatio*]."[82]

The very best of men in the monastery might begin to grow restless. With all good intentions many fall prey to subtle temptations that can draw them away from their original vows. The Song speaks to such dangers as Bernard reads of the little foxes found among the vineyard (Song 2:15). Here he immediately puts aside the literal sense of the passage and searches out the spiritual meaning of the text: "*Littera quidem istud. Spiritus quid?*" Indeed, Bernard patently rejected the literal interpretation as absurd (*ineptum*), even deeming it unworthy of inclusion in holy and authentic Scripture. This passage is certainly not to be read, Bernard says, as a lesson on how to defend one's crops against wild animals. Putting aside the carnal meaning in favor of the spiritual, therefore, one readily recognizes that souls rather than crops are what must be

---

78. *Sancti Bernardi Opera*, sermon 8, 1.2 (1:37; Walsh, 1:46).
79. *Sancti Bernardi Opera*, sermon 8, 7.9 (1:41–42; Walsh, 1:52).
80. *Sancti Bernardi Opera*, sermon 9, 2.2 (1:43; Walsh, 1:54).
81. *Sancti Bernardi Opera*, sermon 9, 2.3 (1:43–44; Walsh, 1:55).
82. *Sancti Bernardi Opera*, sermon 9, 5.7 (1:46; Walsh, 1:58).

safeguarded.[83] Here we find the enemies of the monk, like cunning little foxes, waging stealthy attacks on their sanctity in order to sow confusion. Bernard recounts the many men who began their journey so promisingly down the path of virtue only to be tripped up by these little foxes.[84] Sometimes a little fox comes in the form of seemingly reasonable notions: "If I were at home, I could share with so many of my brothers, kinsfolk, and acquaintances the good that I here enjoy alone. . . . There is nothing to fear in a change of environment. As long as I am doing good, it does not matter where I am." This man then leaves for home, "like a dog returning to his vomit" (2 Pet. 2:22), thereby losing his own soul without even saving others.[85] And then there are those who leave the monastery for the solitary life of the hermit, thinking they will grow in the spiritual life, only later to become lukewarm, slack, and dissolute. Once again, Bernard warns, "a little fox has plainly been at work when such havoc has been caused in the vineyard."[86]

Under assault from demonic forces and faced with his own frailty, the monk will not be able to complete the spiritual pilgrimage by his own strength alone. He needs the daily support of his brothers to help him weather these periods of ennui and desperation. Thus, having spoken of the two ointments of contrition and devotion (Song 1:3), Bernard proceeds to speak of a superior ointment, that of loving-kindness; its elements are the needs of the poor, the anxieties of the oppressed, the worries of the sad, and the misfortunes of all who endure affliction.[87] Such loving-kindness is essential to foster a truly cohesive life within the monastery. The monks need to share with their companions the spiritual gifts they have received from above. "If you are at all times courteous, friendly, agreeable, gentle and humble, you will find men everywhere bearing witness to the perfumed influence you radiate." Bernard therefore calls on the monks to patiently bear with their weaker brethren, to inspire and encourage them, and so give forth a good odor "like a rare and delicate perfume."[88]

William of Saint Thierry

Bernard's confrere William of Saint Thierry was born into the nobility at Liège around 1085 and seems to have studied as a young man at the cathedral

---

83. *Sancti Bernardi Opera*, sermon 63, 1.1 (2:161–62; Walsh and Edmonds, 3:161–62).
84. *Sancti Bernardi Opera*, sermon 64, 1.1–2 (2:166–67; Walsh and Edmonds, 3:170).
85. *Sancti Bernardi Opera*, sermon 64, 1.2 (2:167; Walsh and Edmonds, 3:170).
86. *Sancti Bernardi Opera*, sermon 64, 1.4 (2:168; Walsh and Edmonds, 3:172).
87. *Sancti Bernardi Opera*, sermon 12, 1.1 (1:60–61; Walsh, 1:77).
88. *Sancti Bernardi Opera*, sermon 12, 3.5 (1:63–64; Walsh, 1:81).

school of Laon (although possibly at Reims). With a solid education in hand, William entered the Benedictine abbey of St. Nicaise in Reims, before being named abbot of the nearby monastery of Saint Thierry. Amid a good deal of tension between the Benedictines and the newly formed Cistercians at this time, William had befriended Bernard, even defending him against attacks leveled by fellow Benedictines. William, for his part, greatly admired the reform efforts of the Cistercians and wished to join their ranks. In fact, he would have done so sooner had not Bernard himself insisted that William stay put. Finally, though, in 1135 William left Saint Thierry for the Cistercian house at Signy, where he was heartily received by the prior and monks.[89]

Near the end of his life, in 1144–45, William sent a letter to the Carthusian House of Mont-Dieu, which had been founded only a decade earlier. This masterpiece of spiritual guidance, which has come to be known as the Golden Epistle, betrays such a deep familiarity with the life of these semi-hermetical monks that we may assume William had spent a fair amount of time with these men.[90] It is worth looking at this letter first since it offers us genuine insight into William's own sense of the spiritual life, which is then reflected in his biblical commentaries. Here William commends the life these Carthusians have taken on for themselves, their sublime profession (*altissima professio*), as they pass into heaven, the equal of angels and imitative of angelic purity.[91] They have been blessed not only to believe, know, love, and revere God, but also more intimately still to taste, understand, become acquainted, and enjoy him (*sapere, intelligere, cognoscere, frui*). And so, in their great love for God, they will pledge themselves to great things, and may then trust in his grace to accomplish what is otherwise beyond their own strength.[92]

Addressing monks who spend much of their day as virtual hermits, William assures them that in their spiritual quest heaven (*caelum*) may be brought near to the cell (*cella*) in their loving devotion. Indeed, the cell functions as a sacred

89. Jean Marie Déchanet, *William of St. Thierry: The Man and His Work*, trans. Richard Strachan (Spencer, MA: Cistercian Publications, 1972), 1–46.

90. *Epistola Domini Willelmi ad Fratres de Monte Dei*, following the Latin critical edition with accompanying French translation, *Lettre aux Frères du Mont-Dieu*, ed. Jean Déchanet, SC 223 (Paris: Cerf, 1975). For an English translation, see *Golden Epistle*, trans. Theodore Berkeley (Kalamazoo, MI: Cistercian Publications, 1980). See also CCCM 84 for a critical edition of the Latin text. On the circumstances of the letter, see Jean Déchanet's introduction to the edition as well as his *William of St. Thierry*, 94–105. I have changed Berkeley's English translation in places as seemed warranted.

91. *Epistola Domini Willelmi ad Fratres de Monte Dei*, introduction 15 (SC 223:154; Berkeley, 14).

92. *Epistola Domini Willelmi ad Fratres de Monte Dei*, introduction 16 (SC 223:156; Berkeley, 14–15).

symbol (*sacramentum*) of heaven itself, where the celestial life is played out.[93] The cell cherishes, nourishes, and enfolds the son of grace, leading him to fullness of perfection so that he may be worthy to converse with God.[94] The cell, according to William, is itself holy ground (*terra sancta*), on which the Lord and his servant often talk together as a man does with his friend (cf. Exod. 33:11). And then invoking the imagery of the Song of Songs, William continues: here the faithful soul is united to the Word of God (*fidelis anima Verbo Dei conjungitur*), as the bride in the company of the bridegroom, as the heavenly is united to the earthly, and the divine to the human.[95]

The monastic life is a project of re-formation. In this vein William reminds the Carthusians that human perfection is found in conformity to the likeness of God (*similitudo Dei*), which is itself made possible by the Holy Spirit.[96] When the object of one's thought is God and all that relates to God, and the will reaches the stage at which it becomes love (*amor fiat*)—it is then that the Holy Spirit, the very Spirit of life, infuses himself by way of love and gives life to everything (*per viam amoris infundit se Spiritus Sanctus, spiritus vitae, et omnia vivificat*). The Spirit will lend his assistance in prayer, in meditation, or in study. Immediately the monk's memory will become wisdom and will taste the good things of the Lord, while his thoughts are brought to the intellect so as to be formed into affections. It is then, William says, that understanding becomes the contemplation of one who loves and then shapes this contemplation into an experience of divine sweetness.[97]

In this letter William defines love (*amor*) as a strong inclination of the will toward God; dilection (*dilectio*) is a clinging to, or union, with God; and charity (*caritas*) the enjoyment of God.[98] Yet as man seeks unity of spirit with God, he will find himself being lifted up into the life of the Holy Trinity. This is because the Holy Spirit himself effects this union. The Spirit is the love (*amor*) of the Father and Son, their unity, their sweetness, their kiss, and all that they have in common. And for this reason he may become for man what he is for the Father and Son: that bond of love that will unite man to God. It is through the Holy Spirit, therefore, that the soul will find its happiness standing midway within the embrace and kiss of the Father and Son. Then, William says, in a manner that exceeds description, man will be found worthy

93. *Epistola Domini Willelmi ad Fratres de Monte Dei*, introduction 32 (SC 223:170; Berkeley, 21).

94. *Epistola Domini Willelmi ad Fratres de Monte Dei*, introduction 34 (SC 223:170–72; Berkeley, 21).

95. *Epistola Domini Willelmi ad Fratres de Monte Dei*, introduction 35 (SC 223:172; Berkeley, 22).

96. *Epistola Domini Willelmi ad Fratres de Monte Dei* 1.45; 2.259 (SC 223:78–80, 350; Berkeley, 27, 95).

97. *Epistola Domini Willelmi ad Fratres de Monte Dei* 2.249 (SC 223:342; Berkeley, 92).

98. *Epistola Domini Willelmi ad Fratres de Monte Dei* 2.257 (SC 223:348; Berkeley, 94).

to become through grace what God is by nature (*homo ex gratia quod Deus ex natura*).[99] What comes through so powerfully in this work is, as one scholar has observed, William's conception of love as a gift; in humbling himself, the person thus receives the love that God graciously bestows.[100]

William, like Bernard, also wrote an *Exposition of the Song of Songs*, even if one not so long. Still, it is a marvelous work, redolent of Cistercian affective piety.[101] William begins with a prayer of wondrous admiration: "O splendor of the highest good, you ravish with desire every rational soul; the more the soul burns for you the purer it is in itself; and the purer it is the freer from bodily things so that it might then turn to spiritual things."[102] William then calls on God to set our love free so that the bride that is the soul may love God chastely and further sing her love songs amid the wearisome sojourn in this strange land.[103]

Humankind could not possibly grasp the sublimity of the Song apart from divine assistance, and so William asks God for the gift of love that will unlock the Song: "We beseech you O Holy Spirit that we may be filled, O Love, with your love so that we might then understand this canticle of love." Here love is revealed as the hermeneutical key that unlocks the mysteries of the sacred text, as the monk prays that he might become a participant in the holy conversation of bridegroom and bride.[104] Indeed, William's preface to the Song is a veritable hymn to love: "Come to us that we may truly love you, that whatever we think and say may flow from the fountainhead of your love. May the canticle of your love be read by us in such wise as to kindle in us love itself. Yes, may love itself show us the meaning of its own canticle."[105]

For William, therefore, the Holy Spirit does not simply provide the requisite illumination to correctly interpret the Song. It is love itself, in the person of the Holy Spirit, that breaks open the text. Moreover, one seeks not merely to understand but also to actively participate in a divine conversation; to do this one must be able to love above all else. So William insists that he has no pretension to delve into those deeper mysteries in the Song that pertain to Christ and the church and thus seek an allegorical reading pertaining to

99. *Epistola Domini Willelmi ad Fratres de Monte Dei* 2.263 (SC 223:354; Berkeley, 95–96).
100. Aage Rydstrøm-Poulsen, "The Way of Descent: The Christology of William of Saint-Thierry," in *Unity of Spirit: Studies on William of Saint-Thierry*, 78–91.
101. *Expositio super Canticum Canticorum*, ed. Paul Verdeyen, CCCM 87 (Turnhout: Brepols, 1997); *Exposition of the Song of Songs*, trans. Mother Columba Hart (Shannon: Irish University Press, 1970).
102. *Expositio super Canticum Canticorum*, Invocatio Trinitatis 1 (CCCM 87:19; Hart, 3).
103. *Expositio super Canticum Canticorum*, Invocatio Trinitatis 2 (CCCM 87:20; Hart, 5).
104. *Expositio super Canticum Canticorum*, Invocatio Trinitatis 3 (CCCM 87:21; Hart, 6).
105. *Expositio super Canticum Canticorum*, Invocatio Trinitatis 3 (CCCM 87:21; Hart, 7).

doctrine. Rather, William will follow a far more personal route, seeking the moral, or tropological, sense that concerns Christ and the Christian soul. And for his labor he asks no other reward than the subject matter of the Song: love itself.[106]

William makes clear that this Song treats the love of God, whether it be the love whereby God is loved, or the love whereby God himself is called love. Yet William is not overly concerned by the multiplicity of terms (*amor, caritas, dilectio*) that can be rendered as "love," even though (as we have seen) he did observe the finer distinctions. Love, William says here, seems to indicate a certain tender affection on the part of the lover, indicating striving; charity is defined as a certain spiritual affection or the joy of the one who has attained fruition; and dilection is reckoned the natural desire for an object that gives delight. Nevertheless, he concludes, they all find their source in one and the same Spirit, who is the love of the bridegroom and the bride.[107]

The Holy Spirit, who is the true author of Songs, has determined that he would clothe this account of spiritual love in exterior images borrowed from carnal love. And because it is love alone that fully understands divine things, the Spirit began this ascent to the divine on the level of the flesh. Carnal love would thus be led onward and upward so that it may be transformed into the love of the spirit, since it is impossible that genuine love, pining for the truth, should be content for very long with mere images. It will soon pass by a path known to itself into what it had imagined.[108] Of course, such an ascent will be possible only when the faithful soul is led by Love itself, the Holy Spirit: "O Love from whom all love, even that which is fleshly and degenerate takes its name, O Love, holy and sanctifying, pure and purifying! . . . Show us the meaning of your holy canticle, reveal the mystery of your kiss and the inner pulsing of your murmured song wherewith to the hearts of your sons you chant the power and the delights of your sweetness."[109] Hence when the bride says "Show me O you whom my soul loves" (Song 1:6 Vulg. [1:7 Eng.]), she prays that the Holy Spirit would now help her weakness, for the Holy Spirit is that very love, that very desire (*ipsa dilectio*), by which she speaks these words.[110] "Filled with the spirit of his mouth, she loves you, Lord Jesus, and she loves you only through yourself, who are the very love wherewith she loves you."[111]

---

106. *Expositio super Canticum Canticorum*, Invocatio Trinitatis 4 (CCCM 87:21; Hart, 7).
107. *Expositio super Canticum Canticorum*, Praefatio 5 (CCCM 87:21–22; Hart, 8).
108. *Expositio super Canticum Canticorum*, Praefatio 21 (CCCM 87:29–30; Hart, 18).
109. *Expositio super Canticum Canticorum*, Praefatio 22 (CCCM 87:30; Hart, 19).
110. *Expositio super Canticum Canticorum*, 10.50 (CCCM 87:44–45; Hart, 43).
111. *Expositio super Canticum Canticorum*, 10.51 (CCCM 87:45; Hart, 44).

Taking our leave of the Song of Songs, we will touch on a portion of William's commentary on the Epistle to the Romans wherein he similarly extols the outpouring of divine grace and charity. In keeping with his greater theological vision that we have traced above, William observes here that the very faith by which man is justified is itself a gift from God. "Being justified by faith" (Rom. 5:1) prompts the rhetorical question "Made just by whom? By him who gave the faith which made us just."[112] And when William reaches the verse "Because the charity of God is poured forth in our hearts by the Holy Spirit" (Rom. 5:5), we encounter even more clearly William's theology of unitive love. It is the Spirit, William says, who reveals the persons of the Trinity and draws humans into that eternal divine communion. As he so often does throughout the commentary, William addresses God directly in a hymn of praise: "When he comes into us by your gift, he teaches us all truth, making known to us that in you, O Father, is the source of the highest divinity; in you, O Son, the eternal birth of eternal consubstantiality; in you, O Holy Spirit, the holy union of the Father and the Son; and in the Three the one simple equality of the holy OMOUSION [i.e., homoousion]." Having thus given glory to this sacred communion of persons, William then praises the mercy of God, who has called man to share in this life: "And what, O Lord, is the glory of your sons, what is the hope of their journey, what is the solace of their exile, no matter how prolonged, except that you wish us to have communion among ourselves and with you through that which is common to you, holy Father, and holy Son. You gather us into one through that gift which you both possess in common."[113]

Once more we see that, for William, the very love that unifies the persons of the Trinity, the Holy Spirit, is that love by which humans participate in the eternal communion. Knowledge of the truth is not sufficient; we must love: "Just as we learn through truth [veritate discimus], so we love through charity [caritate diligimus]." For only in love can we savor the sweetness of what we have learned. God wishes that we might love him through God's own love, the Holy Spirit, which God gives man as a gift so as to enable our participation in the divine life: "That precious substance by which we love you is not from ourselves, but from your Holy Spirit whom you give us."[114]

The world, moreover, has been redeemed through love. And so when Paul writes "Scarcely anyone will die for a just man" (Rom. 5:7–11), William turns

112. *Expositio super Epistolam ad Romanos* 3 (CCCM 86:62). See the English translation *Exposition on the Epistle to the Romans*, trans. John Baptist Hasbrouck (Kalamazoo, MI: Cistercian Publications, 1980), 93.
113. *Expositio super Epistolam ad Romanos* 3 (CCCM 86:63–64; Hasbrouck, 94–95).
114. *Expositio super Epistolam ad Romanos* 3 (CCCM 86:64; Hasbrouck, 95).

once more to address God the Father: "What, is there no other exit from sin for me except through the death of Christ your son? None. For great love [*magnus amor*] must be set against great hate, the love of the son against the hatred of the enemy." More than that, however, Christ has thereby rendered human love once again pure, thus enabling humans to hold fast to God in this renewed love. "By these mysteries and the affections of these mysteries, the love by which we go to God and cling to him was to be purified. Without this love [*amor*] completely cleansed and purified [*mundato et puro*] there is no return to God, no clinging to God."[115] The whole life of Christ, from his birth through his passion, was an expression of charity that could awaken man to love him in return, "for love is drawn most strongly by love [*fortius enim amor amore trahitur*]." Christ not only loved, therefore, "but he wished to be loved by those whom he undertook to save." In fact, William says, people could not be saved unless they too loved, unless they loved Christ who loved them, "those whose measure of salvation is in the measure of their love."[116]

Whence this love by which we love God? Coming full circle now, William returns to the gift of the Holy Spirit (Rom. 5:5): "Our love [*amor*] for him is the Holy Spirit, whom he gives us, through whom the charity [*caritas*] of God is poured forth in our hearts. He commended his charity toward us by loving us first. We were loved first in order that we might be made worthy to love and to be loved even more."[117] For William, it is clear that human salvation rests in love, the love for God that is itself a gift from God. Divine love in the person of the Holy Spirit is setting us ablaze (*accendendo*) as we are propelled forward to the source of love itself. Indeed, it seems that God, above all else, desires to be loved by humans, and so God gave them the means to love him and thereby partake of the eternal communion of love that is the divine Trinity. In this William might be said to capture the essence of monastic biblical exegesis in the twelfth century: a way of reading Scripture whose ultimate end is the affective union between human reader and divine author.

115. *Expositio super Epistolam ad Romanos* 3 (CCCM 86:65; Hasbrouck, 96).
116. *Expositio super Epistolam ad Romanos* 3 (CCCM 86:65; Hasbrouck, 97).
117. *Expositio super Epistolam ad Romanos* 3 (CCCM 86:66; Hasbrouck, 98).

5

The School of St. Victor

From the monks we now turn to the ranks of the canons regular, men who lived by a rule in community, although without withdrawing to the countryside. Their life was a hybrid of sorts that anticipated the mendicant orders of the thirteenth century: priests running their own school in the city apart from the cathedral. When Peter Abelard's onetime teacher William of Champeaux founded the Abbey of St. Victor in Paris at the outset of the twelfth century, he established a community that would live by the Rule of Augustine. The influence of Augustine on the canons of St. Victor was indeed pervasive. This saint was not simply read for study in the abbey but was also heard at meals and was thus part of the communal listening that was central to the life of these canons. Specifically mentioned in the *Liber ordinis* (48, *De lectione mensae*), they would have listened to Augustine's sermons and biblical commentaries along with other patristic authors such as Origen and Gregory.[1] The Augustinian mind-set was deeply entrenched, therefore, and this was no more felt than in the field of biblical exegesis. It was most notably Augustine's *De doctrina christiana* that helped to form the larger vision of the leading exegetes that the abbey produced in the first half of the twelfth century.[2]

---

1. Grover Zinn, "The Augustinian Tradition of Sacred and Secular Reading Revised," in *Reading and Wisdom: The "De doctrina christiana" of Augustine in the Middle Ages*, ed. Edward English (Notre Dame, IN: University of Notre Dame Press, 1995), 61–83. See also Beryl Smalley's pioneering treatment of the Victorine school in *Study of the Bible in the Middle Ages* (Notre Dame, IN: University of Notre Dame Press, 1964), 83–195.
2. Margaret T. Gibson, "The *De doctrina christiana* in the School of St. Victor," in *Reading and Wisdom: The "De doctrina christiana" of Augustine in the Middle Ages*, 41–47.

Hugh of St. Victor

No single master was as influential on the entire exegetical enterprise pursued at St. Victor as master Hugh. Within Hugh's *De institutione novitiorum*, as well as the *Liber ordinis Sancti Victoris*, the novices received not only a course in liberal arts (*studium legendi*) but also instruction in proper behavior (*studium vivendi*). Here one found a program of formation for the whole person: cultivation of the inward spiritual life complemented by the outward practice of good manners. The canons were thus schooled in what Jaeger terms an "ascetic Ciceronianism" that lay midway between the secular ethic of the royal courts and the piety of the new monasticism.[3] In this vein scholars have located a program of reform at the heart of Hugh's work. The study of Scripture was to be undertaken within a greater life of prayer and spiritual discipline, which was likened by the canon to the construction (*aedificatio*) of a dwelling place for God in the human heart, which in turn led to the re-formation (*reformatio*) of the entire human person.[4] The process of re-formation, however, was not primarily the recovery of a lost nature so much as the ascent to something even better (*reformatio in melius*).[5] When Hugh spoke of the great work of restoration outlined on the divine page, he was speaking in terms of a process of beautification (*pulchrum esse*), whereby the creature is brought into conformity with Jesus Christ, the eternal Wisdom of God.[6] As we shall see below, this transformative process of the whole person is ultimately grounded in the study of Holy Scripture, wherein the contemplative reader comes to rediscover his original calling and true self.

At the opening of his *Didascalicon*, an introduction to the very task of reading, Hugh exhorts his students to seek Wisdom above all, who illuminates humans so that they may know themselves (*sapientia illuminat hominem ut seipsum agnoscat*), for the mind, having been numbed by the physical world, is seduced by sensible forms and has forgotten (*oblitus*) its own true self. We must therefore be restored though learning (*reparamur autem per doctrinam*); only in this way can we recover our true nature and the very purpose for which we were made.[7] To that end Hugh outlined an order of reading (*ordo legendi*). It begins with the letter (*littera*), which is the suitable arrangement of words

---

3. C. S. Jaeger, "Humanism and Ethics at the School of St. Victor in the Early Twelfth Century," *Mediaeval Studies* 55 (1993): 51–79.

4. Boyd Taylor Coolman, *The Theology of Hugh of St. Victor: An Interpretation* (Cambridge: Cambridge University Press, 2010), 3–4.

5. Ibid., 16–17.

6. Ibid., 24–25.

7. *Didascalicon* 1.1, in *Hugonis de Sancto Victore Didascalicon de Studio Legendi: A Critical Text*, ed. C. H. Buttimer (Washington, DC: Catholic University of America Press, 1939), 4–6.

(*congrua ordinatio dictionum*) that we call grammatical construction. From there one reaches the sense (*sensus*), which is the simple and clear signification (*aperta signifcatio*) that the letter displays on the surface. Finally one reaches the meaning (*sententia*), namely, the deeper understanding (*profundior intelligentia*) that is discovered through exposition and interpretation. Only when one has moved through these three in due order is exposition complete (*perfecta est expositio*).[8] Yet, as Harkins observes, the "*ordo*" that Hugh proposes here pertains to something far greater than a correctly organized reading strategy. Its goals are ultimately soteriological; by following this path, readers will embark on a process of reordering and thus restoring their fallen nature.[9]

It soon becomes clear that reading means far more than scanning a page and amassing a set of facts; it is a meditative process. Hugh describes meditation as constant reflection with a purpose (*meditatio est cogitatio frequens cum consilio*) that seeks the cause and origin, the mode of being, and the usefulness of each thing. It begins with reading, to be sure, but it is bound by none of its precepts. Rather, meditation delights to run in open areas, where it fixes its keen and unrestrained vision on the contemplation of truth. The beginning of learning is reading, therefore, but its completion is meditation (*consummatio in meditatione*). It is meditation that renders life pleasing and provides comfort in times of tribulation. And meditation, in turn, can be broken into three sorts: careful consideration of morals, examination of the commandments, and the investigation of divine works. Ultimately, Hugh says, one habituates oneself (*consuevit*) to meditating on the wonders of God.[10]

Closely aligned with meditation is the cultivation of memory, which itself forms the heart of the exegete. The process of recollection, Hugh says, safeguards what we have so painstakingly read by gathering it all up, by recollecting it (*memoria colligendo custodit*). We must gather up the things we have analyzed in the process of learning and then entrust these things to memory (*commendanda memoriae*). More precisely, recollection is a process whereby we reduce the things that have been written or discussed at greater length to a certain concise and compendious summary. This may not be easy at first; cultivating memory is itself a skill that must be practiced. With everything that we learn, Hugh advises his students, we should gather some

---

See the new translation in *Interpretation of Scripture: Theory*, ed. Franklin Harkins and Frans van Liere, Victorine Texts in Translation (Turnhout: Brepols, 2013), 82–84.

8. *Didascalicon* 3.8 (Buttimer, 58; Harkins and van Liere, 124–25).

9. Franklin Harkins, "Hugh of St. Victor: Didascalicon on the Study of Reading," in *Handbuch der Bibel-Hermeneutiken: Von Origenes bis zur Gegenwart*, ed. Oda Wischmeyer (Berlin: de Gruyter, 2016), 135–48.

10. *Didascalicon* 3.10 (Buttimer, 59–60; Harkins and van Liere, 125–26).

brief and specific principles to be stored in the little box of memory (*arcula memoriae*). In tones reminiscent of Gregory's image of ruminating on the cud of Scripture, Hugh tells them that they must then go over and over these principles, frequently bringing them back up from the stomach of memory (*de ventre memoriae*) into the mouth so as to taste them. Hugh is training these young men not to be impetuous, but to be patient and deliberative learners. And so he cautions them not to rejoice too much because they have read many things (*multa legeris*), but rather that they have understood them (*multa intellexeris*), and not merely understood but retained (*retinere*) them in memory.[11]

The cultivation of memory played such a central role in the life of the medieval biblical scholar that we need to address a short work that Hugh wrote for his students on this very topic.[12] Master Hugh explains to the novices that wisdom is like a treasury and their heart a strongbox (*archa*). In the process of their studies, students will store up incorruptible treasures that must be rightly ordered in the heart like precious stones and jewels, each piece stored in its proper place (*locus*). Correct arrangement (*dispositio*) and the right placement (*disponere*) will lead to what Hugh terms "the enlightenment of thought" (*illustratio cognitionis*). However, he warns that "the confusion of ignorance is the mother of forgetfulness" (*confusio ignorantiae et oblivionis mater est*). Thus the novice must cultivate an attitude of discernment (*discretio*) that illuminates one's understanding and also confirms one's memory.[13]

The student, therefore, ought to prepare his heart and give thought to how he plans to arrange the precious contents that he will place within it. Order is essential precisely because a scholar must ultimately be able to draw on this treasury and retrieve what he has stored up. So it is then that the better ordered the treasures, the easier they will be to locate through memory (*facile per memoriam invenire*) as they are needed. This is a craft and thus encompasses certain practices that facilitate its exercise. In the process of learning new things, Hugh counsels that one should always pay attention to number, place, and time. For instance, one should learn to imagine a line of numbers as though extended before one's eyes; when one hears the number ten, therefore, one should imagine ten points. Or one might remember the psalms in order by tagging their opening lines to a number: "*Beatus vir*" is the first psalm,

---

11. *Didascalicon* 3.11 (Buttimer, 60–61; Harkins and van Liere, 126–27).

12. *De tribus maximis circumstantiis gestorum*, ed. William Green, "Hugo of St. Victor: *De tribus maximis circumstantiis gestorum*," *Speculum* 18 (1943): 484–93. See the classic study by Mary Carruthers, *The Book of Memory: A Study of Memory in Medieval Culture* (Cambridge: Cambridge University Press, 1990), esp. 156–88.

13. *De tribus maximis circumstantiis gestorum*, 488.

"*Quare fremuerunt*" the second psalm, and so forth.[14] It is important, however, to keep things manageable, for "memory always rejoices in both brevity of space and fewness in number." When one has to memorize a long series, it is best to break it into a few sections.[15] Contextual cues are also very useful: we remember one thing by virtue of its connection to another. Thus when we read books, Hugh advises, pay attention not only to the number and order of the verses, but also to the color, shape, and position of the letters on the page: let us strive to impress these things on our minds through the imagination of memory (*per imaginationem memoriae imprimere studeamus*).[16]

There really is no learning apart from a well-formed memory, for just as it is useless to hear if one does not understand, so it does no good to understand if one cannot, or will not, retain these things in memory. What one retains in memory, and thus can recall, is the basis of further learning. Here Hugh speaks of the foundation stones of knowledge (*fundamenta scientiae*), which, when firmly impressed on the memory (*memoriae firmiter impressa*), make all the rest more easily clear.[17] When rightly ordered and laid down through memory, Hugh says, all the rest that is built on this foundation will be solid.[18] Indeed, for Hugh, as Boyd Coolman has observed, "the well-formed memory is the foundation of the remaining soul-construction process, which will involve theological reflection and moral action."[19]

Returning now to the *Didascalicon*, we find that as the soul of the student is being re-formed through the process of deep reading and recollection, so every aspect of his life must reflect this transformation. To that end Hugh laid down precepts for living (*praecepta vivendi*) that are integrally bound to precepts for learning (*praecepta legendi*). One's way of life (*modus vitae*) cannot be separated out from one's course of study. In fact, Hugh says, knowledge that is polluted by a shameless life is certainly not worthy of praise.[20] The disposition to be cultivated before all others is humility, for it is the beginning of discipline. And this means, in turn, that his students must consider no written work useless or be ashamed to learn from anyone.[21]

Receptivity to what the text is offering, apart from the prejudice born of pride, is essential for the study of Scripture, a text in which no passage is devoid of sacred teaching. Therefore, Hugh compared the divine writings

14. *De tribus maximis circumstantiis gestorum*, 489.
15. *De tribus maximis circumstantiis gestorum*, 490.
16. *De tribus maximis circumstantiis gestorum*, 490.
17. *De tribus maximis circumstantiis gestorum*, 490.
18. *De tribus maximis circumstantiis gestorum*, 491.
19. Coolman, *Theology of Hugh of St. Victor*, 162.
20. *Didascalicon* 3.12 (Buttimer, 61; Harkins and van Liere, 127).
21. *Didascalicon* 4.1 (Buttimer, 61–62; Harkins and van Liere, 127).

to a honeycomb; they may appear to be dry on account of the simplicity of their discourse (*simplicitatem sermonis*), but they are sweet on the inside (*intus dulcedine plena sunt*).[22] Hugh then proceeds to outline three levels of signification: history, allegory, and tropology. Some things are written to be understood only in a spiritual sense, while others have to do with morals and some with the simple sense of history. Hugh cautions, however, that we ought not to seek all three meanings in every biblical passage but rather should look for them as reason requires. Some passages may indeed contain all three levels; hence the truth of the historical narrative (*historiae veritas*) can be the basis for the allegorical introduction of something pertaining to one of the sacred mysteries, while simultaneously revealing tropologically what the reader should be doing.[23]

Aware of the different levels of meanings, readers must trace the trajectory of the signs they encounter, thereby allowing themselves to be led into the deeper truths that the text reveals. In a manner reminiscent of Augustine in his *De trinitate* (15.11), Hugh observes that an idea in the mind can be called an internal word (*ratio mentis intrinsecum verbum est*), which is revealed by the sound of the voice, namely, the exterior word (*verbo extrinseco*). This human process seems to be patterned on an eternal trinitarian reality, wherein the divine wisdom, which the Father brought forth from his heart, while invisible in himself, is recognized in and through the created universe. For Hugh, this serves to highlight the profundity of meaning to be found in Scripture: the reader comes through the word or expression to a basic concept, through the concept to the thing, through the thing to an idea, and finally through the idea to truth: "*per vocem ad intellectum, per intellectum ad rem, per rem ad rationem, per rationem pervenitur ad veritatem.*" Failure to acknowledge this chain of meaning leaves the reader impoverished. Those who are less learned and consider only the outward appearance of the letter (*solam litterae superficiam*) will miss the force of the truth (*virtutem veritatis*) that is therein conveyed.[24]

As exegetes must begin with the proper disposition if they are to understand Scripture in its deeper levels, so they must let themselves be transformed by that reading. Hugh thus speaks of the fruit of sacred reading (*fructus divinae lectionis*) that at once instructs the mind with knowledge and also adorns it with morals. We are delighted by what we learn in the pages of Scripture, but then we are beckoned to imitate the examples we have found.[25] One might even say that Scripture serves as a kind of instruction manual in

22. *Didascalicon* 4.2 (Buttimer, 70–71; Harkins and van Liere, 133–34).
23. *Didascalicon* 5.2 (Buttimer, 95–96; Harkins and van Liere, 150–51).
24. *Didascalicon* 5.3 (Buttimer, 96–97; Harkins and van Liere, 151–52).
25. *Didascalicon* 5.6 (Buttimer, 104–5; Harkins and van Liere, 157).

holiness. So it is, Hugh says, that the one who seeks knowledge of the virtues and an upright way of life in the divine writings ought to read primarily those books that urge contempt for this world and thus set the soul aflame with love for its creator (*ad amorem conditoris sui accendunt*). Because we ultimately seek spiritual ascent, our reading of these books should not be concerned so much with the arrangement of words but rather the beauty of truth (*veritatis pulchritudo*).[26]

Just persons are undergoing a training course as they immerse themselves in Scripture, honing their skills in the four crafts by which they are raised to future perfection: learning, meditation, prayer, and action (*lectio sive doctrina, meditatio, oratio, et operatio*). Yet above these four, there follows a final, fifth stage: contemplation (*contemplatio*), in which the just person can enjoy even now a foretaste of the future rewards for good work. Reading is for beginners, Hugh says, but contemplation is for the perfect. It must be recognized, however, that this whole process of ascent requires the assistance of grace, apart from which we can do nothing good. Grace will illuminate the path before us and direct our feet on the way of peace. This nevertheless remains a cooperative effort, for while it is true that the one who acts alone accomplishes nothing, if it were entirely God's doing, we would merit nothing.[27]

We have seen that Hugh had warned novices not to despise the mundane, and here again he counsels that they will never really understand allegory unless they are first grounded in history. They must diligently commit to memory the deeds that have been done, noting when, where, and by whom; they should never despise what seems of little importance. After all, he reminds them, if they had scorned the study of the alphabet when they began their education, they would barely be a student of grammar by now. Eager as these novices may be to attain to the level of lofty and sublime truths, they must resist the urge to start philosophizing right away, for many things in Scripture seem at first glance to offer nothing of value, and yet when read in the context of surrounding passages are shown to be indispensable. One must be patient and proceed in an orderly fashion: just as the shadow leads us to the object casting that shadow, so we must begin by learning how to read the symbol (*figura*) if we hope to reach the truth (*veritas*) that it signifies. That is why the history must never be neglected; it forms the foundation and is the beginning of sacred learning, from which the truth of allegory (*veritas allegoriae*) is extracted like honey from a honeycomb.[28]

26. *Didascalicon* 5.7 (Buttimer, 105–8; Harkins and van Liere, 157–58).
27. *Didascalicon* 5.9 (Buttimer, 109–11; Harkins and van Liere, 161–62).
28. *Didascalicon* 6.3 (Buttimer, 113–17; Harkins and van Liere, 164–65).

Having reached the level of allegory, one is not then given free rein to construe the text as one likes. Attaining a genuine understanding of allegory is a rigorous exercise, requiring sober judgment that is attuned to the subtleties of the text. Hugh likens allegory to solid food: if not chewed thoroughly, it cannot be swallowed. Or again, the biblical exegete is like a mason, who lays down the right stones and hews them to fit with one another. This work is clearly a painstaking and deliberate process that Hugh envisions as a spiritual superstructure being trained upward into the sky, constructed with as many measures of stones as there are mysteries contained in Holy Scripture. Students must not be presumptuous, therefore, imagining that they know far more than they do. They are to be instructed and informed, he tells them, so that they can lay that solid foundation of unwavering truth on which the whole superstructure can be erected. Nor should they presume to teach themselves, lest they lead themselves astray with their own dodgy allegories. Let them instead seek out teachers who can instruct them in the ways of allegorical exegesis. Having duly admonished them, Hugh then presents his students with a list of books most suitable for allegorical reading: Genesis on the work of the six days, the last three books of Moses on the sacraments of the law, the prophet Isaiah, the beginning and end of Ezekiel, Job, the Psalter, Song of Songs, the Gospels of Matthew and John, the Pauline epistles, the canonical epistles, and the Apocalypse. Hugh recommends the epistles of Paul especially, which, because of their number (fourteen), indicate the perfection of the two Testaments: seven plus seven.[29]

How should the careful reader plan to tackle the study of these various and sundry books? Hugh lays down the basic principle that while history follows the order of time (*ordinem temporis*), the order of learning (*ordo cognitionis*) pertains more to allegory. Thus when it comes to learning, the teacher ought to start with what is already clear and better known rather than what seems obscure. Hugh's point is that many of the mysteries contained in the Old Testament cannot be grasped straightaway, but require recourse to the New Testament first, even though the historical events recorded in the Old Testament preceded those in the New. Thus when it comes to allegorical reading, Hugh says, we turn to the New Testament, where the truth is clearly proclaimed (*manifesta praedicatur veritas*), before reading in the Old Testament, where that same truth is foretold within the shadow of many figures. Hence one first reads in Luke's Gospel that the angel Gabriel was sent to the Virgin Mary and told her that she would bear a son; one then recalls the prophecy of Isaiah, "Behold a virgin shall conceive" (Isa. 7:14).[30] The New Testament, therefore,

29. *Didascalicon* 6.4 (Buttimer, 117–22; Harkins and van Liere, 167–72).
30. *Didascalicon* 6.6 (Buttimer, 123–25; Harkins and van Liere, 173–74).

has revealed the fuller implication of Isaiah's words; apart from faith in the gospel their spiritual import could not have been recognized by the reader.

As readers attempt to navigate the Scriptures, they find that some passages are clearer, or more plainly stated, than others. As touched on above, to bring a measure of order to the discussion of proper, metaphorical, and mystical discourse Hugh established three basic categories: letter, sense, and meaning (*littera, sensus, sententia*). One will find that the letter (*littera*) is sometimes complete (*perfecta*), such that there is no need for further interpretation in order to grasp what the writer intended to signify. Take, for instance, the statement "All wisdom is from the Lord" (Prov. 2:6). It is clear enough as it stands.[31] On other occasions, however, the meaning of the words may be clear (*aperta verborum significatio*), but there still seems to be no sense (*nullus tamen sensus esse videtur*). This may be because of an unfamiliar mode of expression or some detail of the text that hinders our full comprehension. For example, in the prophet Isaiah one reads, "In that day seven women will cling to one man" (Isa. 4:1). Maybe the reader does not understand what the prophet intended to say here and thus concludes that there is no literal meaning, in which case the reader jumps right to the spiritual sense. Yet the prophet was not speaking mystically here; he was actually signifying something by the letter. He had been speaking previously about the ruin of sinful people: there would be so few men left that the women would hardly find even one man, although they had been previously accustomed to having one husband each.[32] As for meaning (*sententia*), since it permits no contradiction, it is always suitable and true (*semper congrua est, semper vera*). Now sometimes there is one meaning (*una sententia*) for a single expression (*enuntiationis*) and sometimes multiple meanings (*plures sententiae*). There may also be one meaning for many expressions and even many meanings for multiple expressions. Quoting Augustine,[33] Hugh states that even if we cannot uncover the authorial intention, we should at least settle on one meaning that the scriptural context does not rule out and that accords with sound faith. All the while we ought to be careful, however, lest we impose our own meaning on the text—what we wish to be the case, rather than what Scripture itself really supports.[34]

Among Hugh's lasting contributions to the biblical scholarship of the twelfth century was his attention to the literal sense of the text. Although he was certainly willing to pursue the spiritual senses, he insisted that they be founded on a solid literal-historical foundation. To learn more about how

---

31. *Didascalicon* 6.9 (Buttimer, 126; Harkins and van Liere, 175).
32. *Didascalicon* 6.10 (Buttimer, 126–28; Harkins and van Liere, 175–76).
33. *De Genesi ad litteram* 1.21 (CSEL 28:31).
34. *Didascalicon* 6.11 (Buttimer, 128–29; Harkins and van Liere, 177–78).

Hugh conceived the relationship of the different senses of Scripture, we can turn to his *On Sacred Scripture and Its Writers*. In fact, it has been observed that this work reads like a prologue to the study of Scripture, a sort of *accessus ad auctores*.[35] Hugh begins by addressing the nature of Holy Scripture itself before turning to questions of method. Here at the outset he asserts that logic, mathematics, and music all teach truth to a certain degree, but they do not teach the truth that pertains to the salvation of the soul, apart from which all is in vain. Hugh acknowledges that the pagan philosophers have portrayed the virtues as if truncated from the body of goodness. Yet it remains the case that the members of the virtues cannot live without the body of God's charity (*sine corpore caritatis Dei*). This is because all the virtues make up one body, the head of which is charity, and they cannot be brought to sensation (*sensificentur*) apart from their connection to this head. Scripture alone is really alive; it is given breath (*aspirita*) through the Spirit of God. Furthermore, it is administered by those who have spoken through the Spirit of God, and it makes human persons holy (*divinum*) as it re-forms (*reformans*) them according to the likeness of God. This is because Scripture not only instructs us on how to know God but then also exhorts us to love the God whom we know. The key to distinguishing Scripture from other writings, according to Hugh, is found in the subject matter: what it is about and that of which it consists. It is actually the knowledge of things that enables one to arrive at an understanding of words. We more easily understand what is said when we can first grasp why it is said.[36]

We have seen that Hugh directly acknowledged three scriptural senses—the historical, allegorical, and moral—even as he found a place for the anagogical sense by subsuming it under the allegorical. Now, when Hugh speaks of the historical sense, it is important to recognize the expansiveness of this designation. History, for Hugh, is not confined only to what has happened, but more broadly includes the senses that words have in their primary meanings, that is, when they refer to things (*ex significatione verborum ad res*). From there one may move to the allegorical sense, which can be subdivided into simple allegory (*simplex allegoria*) and anagogy. The former is an instance of a visible fact signifying some invisible fact. The latter is defined as a leading upward as one invisible reality is indicated by another invisible reality. Hugh offers an example wherein all three senses are at work in one scriptural passage: in this case, Job sitting atop a dunghill (Job 2:8). The historical sense is clear and straightforward enough. Yet with respect to the allegorical sense, one will note

35. *Interpretation of Scripture: Theory*, ed. Harkins and van Liere, 205–11.
36. *De scripturibus* 1.1 (PL 175:10c–d; Harkins and van Liere, 213).

that the name "Job" means "mourning" and thus signifies Christ. Although equal with God the Father in glory, Christ nevertheless descended into our misery and sat humbled on the dunghill of this world. And with respect to the moral sense, Job may signify the penitent soul as it makes a dunghill out of all of its sins and meditates unceasingly on them.[37]

Now with regard to the literal sense and its foundational status for all subsequent exegesis, Hugh marvels that some people present themselves as teachers of allegory when they do not even understand the first meaning of the letter (*primam significationem litterae*). No doubt recounting the gist of actual debates, if not their precise words, Hugh records his opponents saying, "We read Scripture, but we do not read the letter. We do not care about the letter [*non curamus de littera*], for we teach allegory." This is not to say, of course, that they do not recognize that there is a letter at the base of Scripture, for they claim to read that letter even as they read it not according to the literal sense (*secundum literam*) but rather allegorically (*secundum allegoriam*). The issue, therefore, is not whether the text has a literal sense but what constitutes the literal sense and what its relationship is to the spiritual senses. Hugh is charging his opponents with making an illicit move that jumps from the word itself directly to the spiritual signifi-cate, bypassing the necessary intermediate step of establishing the word's primary meaning. For example, Hugh says, the word "lion" does not actu-ally signify Christ; rather, it is the animal, primarily signified by the word, that signifies Christ. It is not the name of the animal (*nomen animalis*) but the animal itself (*animal ipsum*) that bears the spiritual signification. Words cannot function as signs if one does not know what they mean at their first level of signification. Only by first grasping the primary meaning of words can one then meditate on them and gather from the similitudes what one needs to build up faith and good morals. In our quest for spiritual ascent we must never despise the humility of God's word, since it is the very means to reach enlightened divinity (*per humilitatem illuminaris ad divinitatem*). One must begin, therefore, with visible things before ascending to the invisible. Only by following the exterior forms conveyed in the narrative can we hope to draw out, as from a honeycomb, the sweetness of spiritual understanding by meditating on it.[38] One is struck by the consistent reference to meditation (*meditatio/meditari*); we begin with the literal-historical level so that we may eventually come to contemplate, mull over, and dwell on the deeper reality of what we are reading.

---

37. *De scripturibus* 1.3 (PL 175:12a–c; Harkins and van Liere, 214–15).
38. *De scripturibus* 1.5 (PL 175:13b–15a; Harkins and van Liere, 217–18).

Hugh may be best known today for his comprehensive theological work *The Sacraments of the Christian Faith*, which he regarded as a guide to understanding the sacred doctrine contained in Holy Scripture. Hugh begins by laying out a basic exegetical methodology, precisely because it was understood that the discussion to follow was determined by a correct reading of the biblical text. In his prologue, along lines that we have seen above, Hugh declares that the foundation of learning in "sacred eloquence" (*sacri eloquii*) is "historical reading" (*historica lectione*). It is the foundation for understanding the faith that all the rest is built on, "whether by reading or by listening" (*vel legendo vel audiendo*). Notice here too how oral and written communication are treated perhaps synonymously, thus evoking the lecture hall where the master "lectured" on an authoritative text and the students listened, in that way reading along with him. And here also Hugh returns to the theme of personal formation; learning itself, he says, is a construction project (*superaedificare*), a process of building up the whole person.[39]

In keeping with the tradition of the "*accessus ad auctores*," which we have encountered above, Hugh first inquires into the subject matter (*materia*) around which our treatment (*tractatio*) will turn.[40] In the case of the divine Scriptures, the subject matter is nothing less than the works of human restoration (*opera restaurationis*). The Scriptures also address the "work of creation," which concerns the bringing into being of what was not, and then the "work of restoration," the improvement of that which was perishing. We should be clear that the work of restoration, accomplished in Christ and his sacraments, has been under way since the fall. This means, according to Hugh, that there were followers of Christ's banner before the incarnation. Indeed, all the faithful across the ages of nature, law, and grace have been following the banner of their one king.[41]

If this is the subject matter, then with regard to its manner of treatment, Hugh locates the "triple understanding" (*triplicem intelligentiam*) that comprises history, allegory, and tropology.[42] It should be remembered that sacred eloquence is a question not only of the subject matter itself but also of the manner in which that subject matter is handled (*in modo tractandi*). This is where the subtlety and profundity of the Scriptures come to light: not only in words (*voces*) but also in the things (*res*) signified by those words. Hence the need to be well trained in the liberal arts: to understand the text one

---

39. *De sacramentis*, prologue; *Hugonis de Sancto Victore: De sacramentis Christiane fidei*, ed. Rainer Berndt (Monasterii Westfalorum, Münster: Aschendorff, 2008), 31; *On the Sacraments of the Christian Faith*, trans. Roy DeFerrari (Cambridge, MA: Medieval Academy, 1951), 3–7.

40. *De sacramentis*, prologue 1 (Berndt, 31; DeFerrari, 7–8).

41. *De sacramentis*, prologue 2 (Berndt, 31–32; DeFerrari, 8).

42. *De sacramentis*, prologue 4 (Berndt, 33; DeFerrari, 9–10).

must pay attention to pronunciation, which belongs to the art of grammar; whereas signification belongs to dialectic; and when both are considered at once, rhetoric. From the trivium we move to the quadrivium, which is essential for the understanding of things (*cognitio rerum*), their form and nature, namely, their exterior disposition and interior quality.[43] All the natural arts, therefore, ultimately serve sacred knowledge (*divina scientia*), as the inferior wisdom is properly ordered to the superior. History deals with the signification of words in regard to things and thus calls upon the services of grammar, dialectic, and rhetoric; allegory and tropology pertain to the signification of things, and so invoke arithmetic, music, geometry, and physics. Among the spiritual senses, then, allegory leads to right faith, while tropology leads to good work. Thus we have both knowledge of truth and the love of virtue (*cognitio veritatis et amor virtutis*), which in turn lead to the true renewal of the human person (*vera reparatio hominis*).[44]

Hugh's *Ark of Noah* is a masterful exploration of this process of restoration and re-formation, employing a detailed analysis of the Genesis account of the ark's construction to outline humankind's spiritual renewal. Thus the ark is proclaimed an "exemplar of the spiritual building" that the soul inwardly constructs.[45] Hugh observes that humankind was created to contemplate the presence of the face of the Creator. By always seeing our Creator, we would always love him; by always loving him, we would always adhere to him and, finally, by adhering would possess life everlasting. This is the one and true good of humankind, according to Hugh: full and perfect knowledge of our Creator. On account of sin, however, we have been cast from the face of the Lord and thus find ourselves immersed in blind ignorance. Our hearts are now unstable and ill at ease; the cause of our sickness is love of the world (*amor mundi*), and the remedy is love of God (*amor Dei*).[46] Thus while love of the world begins sweetly even as it ends in bitterness, the love of God may begin bitterly but is finally fulfilled in sweetness.[47]

Hugh pursues a spatial theme as he examines the way in which God can be said to be present at once to the whole universe and to the individual human person. First we can say that God inhabits the world as an emperor in his kingdom, then inhabits the church as a paterfamilias in his household, and finally inhabits the soul as a bridegroom in his wedding chamber.[48] God,

43. *De sacramentis*, prologue 5 (Berndt, 33; DeFerrari, 10).
44. *De sacramentis*, prologue 6 (Berndt, 34; DeFerrari, 10–13).
45. *De arca Noe* 1.2 (PL 176:622b).
46. *De arca Noe* 1.1 (PL 176:619–20).
47. *De arca Noe* 1.1 (PL 176:619a).
48. *De arca Noe* 1.1 (PL 176:621a).

according to Hugh, inhabits the human heart through knowledge and love. The heart constitutes a single dwelling since no one can love what he does not know, and yet these two facets remain distinct insofar as knowledge (*scientia*) attained through cognition of the faith builds the structure, while love (*dilectio*) attained through virtue is like the color painted on the house. Enter now, Hugh says, into the inner chamber of one's heart (*secretum cordis*) and make a dwelling place for God. Make a temple, a house, a tabernacle; make an ark of the covenant and an ark for the flood. Whatever name one may give, it is still the one house of God.[49]

Hugh then embarks on a painstaking exegetical foray into the historical ark's construction and all that it symbolizes. First, though, he examines Scripture itself and the ways in which it ought to be interpreted. Turning to the text of Isaiah 6:2, wherein the six-winged seraphim are depicted, Hugh finds that the seraph signifies Holy Scripture. The three pairs of wings are the three senses of Scripture: history, allegory, and tropology. The two wings covering the body of the seraph constitute the historical sense, which, through the veil of the letter, covers over the mystical senses. The two wings extending to the head and feet are allegory, Hugh says, because when we learn the mystical things of divine Scripture up until the knowledge of the divinity itself, we penetrate through the illumination of the mind. The two wings by which the seraph flies signify tropology, because through the reading of divine Scripture we are instructed in good works as though lifted up on wings to high places.[50]

In keeping with his commitment to the principle that history must support all mystical readings of the text, Hugh first examines the account of the ark *secundum litteram*. Having laid this solid foundation, he now turns his attention to the "ark of the church." Nothing in the ark's construction is without significance, beginning with its dimensions. Hugh finds that the length of three hundred cubits designates this present age, which comprises three times: one period each of the natural law, the written law, and grace. Through these ages the church, from the beginning of the world until the end, moves from present life to future glory. The fifty cubits in width signify all the faithful under the one head, who is Christ. This is fitting because the number fifty consists of seven sevens, or forty-nine—the number designating the universal gathering of the faithful—and one superadded, Christ the head of the church. As for the height of thirty cubits, this signifies the volumes of the divine page: the twenty-two books of the Old Testament and the eight

---

49. *De arca Noe* 1.2 (PL 176:621d–22a).
50. *De arca Noe* 1.2 (PL 176:624c–25b).

of the New, within which is contained all that God has done and is going to do for the sake of the church.[51]

And when Hugh turns to the column in the midst of the ark, he finds that it symbolizes both the tree of life and the book of life. The whole of divine Scripture, Hugh says, constitutes the one book that is the very book of life. All of this is ultimately drawn back to Christ, the one divine person in two natures, who may be designated either the book of life or tree of life according to either his divine or human nature. This is especially the case according to his assumed humanity with respect to the book of life, however, as he presents us in his manhood with the perfect example of how we ought to live. According to the form of divinity, Christ was made the tree of life, since it was by virtue of his divinity that he presented us with a remedy for our current condition.[52]

As Hugh proceeds to the three mansions in the ark, he finds that they designate shadow (*umbra*), body (*corpus*), and spirit (*spiritus*). These in turn correspond to figure (*figura*), reality (*res*), and truth (*veritas*). According to Hugh, shadows are the things that, before the advent of Christ, had taken place corporeally and visibly in the times of the natural and written law. They were intended to prefigure the things that now, after the coming of Christ and in the time of grace, occur visibly. Hence they are called shadows, because they were at once corporeal in themselves and yet also figures of other corporeal things. By this schema, therefore, the Christian sacraments may be called the body, since they are visibly performed in the church. The Spirit, however, is what is accomplished invisibly by the grace of God. For example, the crossing of the Red Sea prefigured Christian baptism, such that the Red Sea functions as shadow and figure, the baptism of visible water as body and reality, and the cleansing of sins as spirit and truth.[53] In this way, Hugh has integrated his central theme of restoration through Christ and his sacraments by tracing their presence, even if in foreshadowings, throughout the entirety of sacred Scripture.

In his *Ark of Noah*, Hugh extols Scripture as a perfect revelation of the divine will, which by its very nature transcends all earthly texts. When Hugh compares the sorts of books written by God and human beings, he observes that the latter are written on animal hides, that is, corruptible material that will eventually disintegrate. No one will find life through those books, and so they are more fittingly called books of death. Yet the book of God is of eternal origin and of an incorruptible essence. Its writing is indelible and its

51. *De arca Noe* 1.4 (PL 176:629d–30b).
52. *De arca Noe* 1.9 (PL 176:643a).
53. *De arca Noe* 4.9 (PL 176:679a–b).

knowledge is sweet. And while its words are innumerable, they all really make up just one Word: the book of life.[54]

Given this wonderful paean to the sublimity of Holy Scripture, we might then ask which sacred writings Hugh counted among its ranks: which books actually belonged to the biblical canon? This is a fundamental question that was consistently addressed in the High and late Middle Ages. In the *Didascalicon*, Hugh says that the Scriptures comprise those books that have been produced by persons who practiced the catholic faith and those that have been approved by the authority of the universal church. In addition to these, there are many small works written by devout men, and while not sanctioned by the authority of the church, they are still included among the divine writings because they are not inconsistent with the divine faith and teach some useful things.[55] Here Hugh also affirms that all of Holy Scripture is contained within the two books of the Old and New Testament. He thus follows Jerome in dividing up the Old Testament into the law, prophets, and sacred writings. And again, in keeping with Jerome, Hugh lists the apocryphal books, which can be read but do not belong to the canon. Hugh's treatment of the canon in the *Didascalicon* did indeed rely largely on Jerome and Isidore of Seville, often quoting large sections of their work verbatim. Hugh was certainly aware of the ambiguities of authorship surrounding books such as Wisdom, Sirach, Judith, and others as well as the doubts about the Pauline authorship of Hebrews. Yet he does note that among all the "gospels" floating around that lacked the Holy Spirit, the fathers—who were themselves "taught by the Holy Spirit"—received only four as authoritative. Quoting Isidore directly, Hugh declares that the authors of the sacred books spoke through the Holy Spirit, whereas the apocryphal books bear no such authority. Apocryphal books may contain some truth, he concedes, but they are also mixed with falsehood and are therefore lacking in all canonical authority (*canonica auctoritas*). Even though some of these books bear the names of legitimate prophets and apostles, diligent examination has ultimately shown them to be untrustworthy.[56]

What Hugh has to say about the New Testament is more interesting, however, given its expansiveness. He divides it into three parts as well: gospel, apostles, and fathers. After the four gospels and fourteen letters of Paul, the canonical epistles, the Apocalypse, and Acts, there are then the papal decrees, followed by the writings of the holy fathers and doctors of the church, including Jerome, Augustine, Gregory, Ambrose, Isidore, Origen, Bede, and

---

54. *De arca Noe* 1.11 (PL 176:643c–d).
55. *Didascalicon* 4.2 (Buttimer, 70–71; Harkins and van Liere, 134–36).
56. *Didascalicon* 4.4–7 (Buttimer, 73–78; Harkins and van Liere, 137–39).

many others. The order of the New Testament parallels the Old with its three categories, the last of which includes the doctors. Hugh points out that, in fact, "the full and perfect truth" can be found in each individual book of the two Testaments, although nothing there is ever superfluous.[57] This is what Hugh says about the canon in the *Didascalicon*, but in his *De sacramentis* he makes an important distinction: although he still counts the fathers within the New Testament along with the gospels and apostles, he now qualifies their presence. Here Hugh says that the writings of the fathers do not actually belong to the body of the text (*in corpore textus*). This is because they add nothing to the deposit of revelation; rather, they merely clarify the same material contained in the other books.[58] This position, moreover, would be repeated in the *Sententiae de divinitate*, a twelfth-century work that was likely written by Hugh or is at least of the Victorine school.[59]

Andrew of St. Victor

Nowhere was the Victorine interest in the literal-historical sense of the text more insistently pursued than in the exegetical works of Andrew of St. Victor. More remarkable, however, was that Andrew's pursuit of the literal sense, specifically with regard to Old Testament books, led this Augustinian canon into the world of rabbinic exegesis. Not since Jerome had a Christian exegete been so interested in Jewish interpretations of their own sacred texts. The modern scholar Michael Signer had located a concurrence in the exegetical methods being developed in the early twelfth century by the Victorines and the Jewish scholars of northern France. Both schools were seeking the so-called plain sense, which relied principally on reading passages in their broader biblical contexts and paying close attention to the sequence of the narrative. In fact, the interaction between the two communities seems to have spurred each one to make further advances in these methods. This closer attention to context and sequence also allowed each community to pursue readings of the text that were not necessarily governed by their respective interpretative traditions.[60]

57. *Didascalicon* 4.2 (Buttimer, 71–72; Harkins and van Liere, 134–36).

58. *De sacramentis*, prologue 7 (Berndt, 34–35). See also *De scripturis et scriptoribus sacris* 6 (PL 175:16a).

59. *Sententiae de divinitate*, edited in Ambrogio M. Piazzoni, "Ugo di San Vittore: 'Auctor' delle 'Sententiae de divinitate,'" *Studi Medievali* 23 (1982): 861–955, on 917–18.

60. Michael Signer, "*Peshat, Sensus Litteralis*, and Sequential Narrative: Jewish Exegesis and the School of St. Victor in the Twelfth Century," in *The Frank Talmage Memorial Volume*, ed. Barry Walfish (Haifa: Haifa University Press, 1993), 1:203–16.

The renowned Rabbi Solomon ben Isaac of Troyes, known as Rashi (1040–1105), had pioneered the aforementioned plain sense, or *peshat*, and thereby displaced the more fanciful method of midrash. Rashi's successors, including his grandson Rabbi Samuel ben Meir, known as Rashbam, then took up the *peshat* mantle, while Rabbi Eliezer of Beaugency explored further literary analysis of the text, such as foreshadowing (prolepsis) and flashback (analepsis). As with the Victorines, there was among these twelfth-century Jewish exegetes a marked appreciation for the human contribution to the text, a recognition of the personal agency of the human author possessing his own authorial style.[61]

Agreeing with Jerome that one had to grasp the original language first, Andrew peppered his commentaries with references to the Hebrew language and Jewish exegetes. Andrew believed, therefore, that the Jewish community ought to be consulted for the correct reading of the Old Testament text, even if these Jews were regarded as lacking the true faith. Their lexical erudition made them indispensable resources for Christian exegetes.[62] To that end, there are hints of oral communication between Andrew and the French rabbis in his use of Old French glosses that can also be found in Jewish biblical commentaries of the period. Andrew, for his part, would signal such vernacular glosses in his own commentaries with such phrases as *"francorum lingua"* or *"gallorum lingua."*[63]

Andrew's own degree of facility with the Hebrew language has been a source of much scholarly discussion, with the consensus being that he possessed only a limited grasp of Hebrew at best. The Jewish commentary tradition to which he appealed had not been translated into Latin, which makes it likely that he relied on direct conversations with French rabbis who could have distilled the material for him. What Andrew knew of Rashi, for instance, would have come by way of oral communication. As it is, therefore, Andrew's chief written sources were the commentaries of Jerome and the recently produced Gloss from Laon. Nevertheless, it must be said that Andrew did manage to incorporate a lot of contemporary Jewish exegesis into his own commentaries, which in turn allowed him to temper those

61. Robert Harris, "Jewish Biblical Exegesis from Its Beginnings to the Twelfth Century," in *The New Cambridge History of the Bible* (Cambridge: Cambridge University Press, 2013), 2:596–615.

62. Michael Signer, "From Theory to Practice: The *De doctrina christiana* and the Exegesis of Andrew of St. Victor," in *Reading and Wisdom: The "De doctrina christiana" of Augustine in the Middle Ages*, 84–98. See also Smalley's extensive treatment of Andrew in *Study of the Bible in the Middle Ages*, 112–95.

63. See Signer's discussion of Andrew's knowledge of Hebrew and use of Jewish sources in *Expositio in Ezechielem*, ed. Michael Signer, CCCM 53e (Turnhout: Brepols, 1991), xxi–xxvii.

Christian texts as he endeavored to remain true to the historical sense of the Old Testament Scriptures.[64] We can catch some of the flavor of Andrew's exegetical method with a brief look at his Exodus commentary. Scattered throughout the commentary we find phrases that signal his reliance on Jewish biblical exegesis in one form or another: "*sicut in hebraeo est*";[65] "*secundum Hebraeos*";[66] "*secundum eosdem Hebraeos*";[67] "*dicunt Hebraei*";[68] "*ut aiunt Hebraei*";[69] "*in hebraeo nusquam legitur*";[70] and "*Hebraeus sic exponit.*"[71] Sometimes the Jewish exegetes help uncover the deeper significance of a passage. Thus "the Hebrews say" that the Lord appeared to Moses in a burning bramble bush lest the Jews be tempted to make an idol from it, for God always removes occasions for idolatry.[72] Andrew sometimes cites an alternative translation: "the Hebrews say that the Hebrew word in the place where we have 'ceremonies' (Exod. 12:25) actually means 'precepts.'"[73] Analysis of the underlying Hebrew may clarify the otherwise ambiguous Latin. Hence, when commenting on Exodus 15:16, "Terror and dread fell upon them," Andrew observes that the Latin words "*formido et pavor*" do not seem to signify different things. But the Hebrew words (*hebraica verba*) do allow for a distinction: the one signifying the dread of some imminent danger and the other danger still far off.[74] Looking at Exodus 20:3, "You will have no other gods before me," Andrew points out that in Hebrew there are many passages employing "against" (*contra*) where we have "before" (*coram*). The meaning (*sensus*), Andrew says, would be as follows: you are not to have idols and images of gods who are foreign to me, nor will you worship the gods of the gentiles, for that would be to act against me (*contra me*). It is, as Andrew goes on to explain, "an idiom of the Hebrew language to employ the future indicative in place of the present imperative."[75]

A brief look at some of the prologues that Andrew wrote for different Old Testament books will reveal something of how he understood the composition and the study of divine Scripture. Now it should be said that, for all his

64. See the discussion by Liere and Zier in *Expositio super Duodecim Prophetas*, ed. Frans van Liere and Mark Zier, CCCM 53g (Turnhout: Brepols, 2007), xxvii–xxviii.
65. *In Exodum* 13.3 (CCCM 53:115).
66. *In Exodum* 1.11 (CCCM 53:97).
67. *In Exodum* 13.3 (CCCM 53:115).
68. *In Exodum* 3.14 (CCCM 53:99).
69. *In Exodum* 3.8 (CCCM 53:99).
70. *In Exodum* 3.1 (CCCM 53:98).
71. *In Exodum* 4.10 (CCCM 53:100).
72. *In Exodum* 3.2 (CCCM 53:98).
73. *In Exodum* 12.25 (CCCM 53:113).
74. *In Exodum* 15.16 (CCCM 53:121).
75. *In Exodum* 20.3 (CCCM 53:131).

attention to the primary sense of the texts, Andrew was still very much the twelfth-century Christian exegete for whom the whole Bible was replete with the mysteries of the Triune God. In his prologue to the Heptateuch, Andrew comments that Moses wished to rouse the people to devotion by recounting the great benefits of God's creation recorded in Genesis so that they would be more ready to receive the law. Moses did not speak explicitly about the Trinity, however, lest the people be tempted to polytheism by mysteries that surpassed their comprehension. Thus Moses only insinuated the works of the Trinity in the creation account. On the one hand, that Moses could have known all about the creation is possible if one grants that he saw these events under the inspiration of the Holy Spirit (*spiritus sancti gratia*). On the other hand, Andrew opines, he may have received the traditions of the fathers that had been handed down from Adam, whether by oral or even written means (*narrratione vel etiam scripto*).[76]

In his general prologue to the prophets, Andrew chooses Psalm 17:12 Vulg. (18:11 Eng.) as his theme: "And he made darkness his covert, his pavilion round about him; dark waters in the clouds of the air." This text gave Andrew the opportunity to address the required disposition of the faithful exegete as he confronted his labors. The sharpness of our mind, Andrew says, is in some way covered over by a certain darkness. Yet the one who told light to come forth from darkness can pour such light on our otherwise dark hearts and enlighten our eyes. Let us therefore dedicate ourselves entirely to the laborious, but ultimately joyful and salvific, pursuit of divine wisdom. Andrew then addresses his readers directly, surmising their proclivities: "You are fearful and weak; you flee from danger. You are lazy and would rather read the works of others than produce your own. But then, to avoid the labors is to be deprived of the rewards. Although it must be admitted that when you do produce such work, there are bound to be those who envy you and thus criticize your work." Notwithstanding, Andrew says, "I do not labor for the fastidious ears of others who cling to the ancient and disdain all that is new; I work for myself." Giving us a glimpse into his own working conditions, Andrew states that he must take care of his poverty, which does not always provide ready access to commentaries and glossed books (*libros glosatos*). In other words, he cannot always rely on the ancient insights of the fathers to guide him when producing his own commentaries on the prophets. He must sometimes be content to gather what is scattered throughout these books pertaining to the historical sense (*ad historicum sensum*).[77]

76. *Expositio super Heptateuchum*, prologue, ed. Charles Lohr and Rainer Berndt, CCCM 53 (Turnhout: Brepols, 1986), 4–5. Translation in Harkins and van Liere, *Interpretation of Scripture: Theory*, 277–78.

77. The Latin text has been transcribed by Smalley in *Study of the Bible in the Middle Ages*, 375–77; translation in Harkins and van Liere, *Interpretation of Scripture: Theory*, 278–80.

Richard of St. Victor

We conclude this chapter with a few words about Richard of St. Victor, who, along with Andrew, was among the contingent of English scholars at the abbey. In his capacities as a master there, Richard composed a *Book of Notes* to serve as an introductory guide for students as they waded into biblical exegesis. It was not unlike Hugh's *Didascalicon*, although Richard extended the discussion beyond the literal into the allegorical and tropological senses.[78] Richard begins the *Notes* with a brief discussion of human nature and destiny, thereby providing the greater context within which all biblical study must find its true purpose. He points out to the novices that since God is supremely good, he wished to share his beatitude with a rational creature. Moreover, he made humankind with reason and with love, thus in keeping with his likeness. And by virtue of the fact that human beings were made in the divine image, they would come to know and love God, with the result that they could eventually possess God and achieve eternal beatitude.[79] This being the case, it is not surprising that, like Hugh before him, Richard identifies the subject matter of sacred Scripture as the work of creation and restoration: the former taking place over six days and the latter across six ages.[80] Richard likewise observes the three senses of history, allegory, and tropology. He explains that, just as knowledge of words is necessary for determining the meaning that lies between words (*voces*) and things (*res*), so knowledge of things is needed for the meaning that occurs between things and the mystical realities that they signify.[81]

The hallmark of Richard's exegetical method, however, is his emphasis on experience. Whoever is zealous for wisdom and divine knowledge, Richard declares, can acquire the fruit of reading more by his own experience (*experimento*) than by another's instruction. "In reading," Richard says, "the mind of the reader possesses the good of worthy occupation and the skill of meditation; he finds perseverance in prayer, fervor in devotion, and clarity in heavenly contemplation." Once the deceit of falsehood has been rejected, and the malice of iniquity driven away, one is then led to genuine knowledge of the truth and the love of goodness. "Yet whoever refuses to eat the food of Sacred Scripture," he cautions, "already begins to lose the life of his soul." Thus one could say of such people that their soul abhors all food and that they have advanced all the way to the gates of death (Ps. 106:18 Vulg. [107:18 Eng.]).[82]

78. Harkins and van Liere, *Interpretation of Scripture: Theory*, 289–96.
79. *Liber Exceptionum* 1.1, ed. Jean Chatillon (Paris: J. Vrin, 1958), 104; translation in Harkins and van Liere, *Interpretation of Scripture: Theory*, 299.
80. *Liber Exceptionum* 1.2.1 (Chatillon, 114; Harkins and van Liere, 310).
81. *Liber Exceptionum* 1.2.3 (Chatillon, 115–16; Harkins and van Liere, 311–12).
82. *Liber Exceptionum* 2, prologue (Chatillon, 213; Harkins and van Liere, 318–19).

A writer of great mystical works, such as the *Benjamin Major and Minor*, Richard was impatient with what he regarded as Andrew's overreliance on Jewish exegesis. Thus in the prologue to his *De Emmanuele*, Richard outlines his plan to refute the assertions regarding Isaiah 7:14 put forward by master Andrew. Richard complains that in many places Andrew sets forth the meaning assigned by the Jews (*sententia Judaeorum*) as though it were not so much a Jewish reading of the text as the proper reading, and therefore true. Thus rather than attribute the text to the Virgin Mary, Andrew maintains that it refers to the wife of the prophet Isaiah.[83] Richard proceeds to recount Andrew's arguments, one of which is straightforwardly linguistic: the Jews point out that the Hebrew text reads *almah*, which translates not as "virgin" but as "young woman" (*juvencula*).[84] For his part, Richard vows to wage his fight not only against the blindness of the Jews but also against the deafness of "our own Judaizers" (*judaizantes nostri*), meaning those Christians who were interpreting Old Testament texts in the manner of Jewish exegetes.[85]

To that end Richard appealed to a Christian candor (*Christiana simplicitas*) that finds the clear path as opposed to what he deemed Jewish faithlessness. The Christian, according to Richard, has been illuminated and would rather die than disavow the truth.[86] Who can fail to understand the voice of the prophet or hear the sense of the one explaining its meaning? Hear the prophet: "Behold a virgin shall conceive" (Isa. 7:14). And then pay attention, Richard says, to the explanation supplied by the evangelist Matthew: "This was to fulfill what was written through the prophet" (Matt. 1:22–23). As Matthew clearly speaks of the prophecy being fulfilled in Mary, who would dare to contradict this? If you do not understand what you read, Richard pleads, then at least believe with your heart. We find, moreover, that the gospel account supplies additional information that serves to clarify the original prophecy. It was the angel Gabriel whose address to Mary revealed her to be the true mother of Immanuel (Luke 1:28).[87] The great sign was seen, therefore, to have been fulfilled precisely in the incarnation, the advent of the God-man, and thus the miraculous sign of God with us, the Immanuel. The gospel narratives thereby testify to the substantive fulfillment of Isaiah's prophecy.[88]

We should be clear that here Richard was not appealing to a mystical reading of the Isaiah text as though eschewing the literal sense. Rather, he

83. *De Emmanuele*, prologue (PL 196:600–602).
84. *De Emmanuele*, prologue (PL 196:601a).
85. *De Emmanuele* 1.2 (PL 196:607c).
86. *De Emmanuele* 1.1 (PL 196:605d).
87. *De Emmanuele* 1.1 (PL 196:607a–b).
88. *De Emmanuele* 1.13 (PL 196:622a–d).

believed that his reading was the correct literal-historical interpretation over and against Andrew's misinterpretation of the literal sense. That Andrew and Richard could clash in this regard may be traced to some of their fundamental exegetical premises, namely, what counts as historical. As Dale Coulter observes, whereas Andrew limited the application of history (*historia*) to the immediate circumstances of the narrative, Richard allowed the term to cover the full range of salvation history. Hence, for Richard, the literal sense (*sensus litteralis*) of Isaiah 7:14 could be brought into conformity with Matthew's Gospel, for the very fact that by their words the prophet and the evangelist were referring to the same reality (*res*).[89]

This is not to say that Richard believed that the genuine literal-historical sense would be immediately obvious to any reader. He is keen to acknowledge the loftiness of the divine secrets (*arcani divini*) hidden within the enigma of the words (*verborum ambage abscondi*).[90] As we have touched on above, there must be recourse to the context of the passage itself (*circumstantia litterae*). Even then, however, the mysteries of Christ will remain partly obscured under the veil of figures and the ambiguity or obscurity of the text (*littera*) itself. That is why, Richard says, one will ultimately have to rely on the Holy Spirit to interpret the text and understand how it speaks of Christ.[91] The truth may well be submerged within the depth of ambiguity (*ambiguitatis profundo veritas tegitur*); it remains to be raised up by those who seek it with faith and simplicity of heart. "Surely," Richard says, "the sublime heights of divine wisdom should be hidden from the faithless and thus reserved for the faithful."[92] Thus we are brought back once more, in true Victorine fashion, to the requisite disposition of the exegete. For the hard of heart everything remains opaque, but to those who meditate on the sacred page, who surrender to its mysteries in deep contemplation, the honeycomb reveals its sweetness.

89. Dale Coulter, *Per Visibilia ad Invisibilia: Theological Method in Richard of St. Victor (d. 1173)* (Turnhout: Brepols, 2006), 97–102.
90. *De Emmanuele* 1.6 (PL 196:613b).
91. *De Emmanuele* 1.8 (PL 196:614c–d).
92. *De Emmanuele* 2.19 (PL 196:654c).

6

The Schools of the Twelfth Century

From Laon to Paris

Our last chapter to treat the twelfth century brings us back to the world of the cathedral schools that we had left with Bruno at Reims. Here we will begin in Laon before following the action to Paris. First, what was it like to study at the cathedral schools at this time? A recent analysis of Peter Abelard's lively description of his student days at Laon, as recounted in his *Historia calamitatum*, reveals the inner workings of the cathedral school classroom in the first decades of the twelfth century. Although this was a period of transition as the predominantly oral world of learning began to cede ground to the authority of written text, the vital interplay between spoken and written communication is still very much in evidence. Abelard peppers his account with many of the key terms that we have come to associate with the schools of this period: *lectio, sententiarum collationes, glosae, magister, expositiones, expositor.* Abelard has opened a window for us into the world of learning that he and his contemporaries knew so well. Here we find that *lectio* formed the basis of teaching in the classroom as the *magister* read aloud from a set text and added his own interpretation of that text as he proceeded. At this time magisterial instruction in Scripture came in the form of a lecture, therefore, as the master incorporated patristic authorities into his explanation of the biblical text. The master most likely composed the entire day's lecture in his head, without the assistance of written notes. Such was his power of memory and his immersion in the art of rhetoric and his own training in the trivium. Students, likewise, would have simply listened to the master and committed to memory what he had said that day. The master may have had a student taking notes on a wax tablet that, in later consultation with the master, would have been written up and then circulated among the students. Still, it seems that in Abelard's student days the circulating written version was intended not as a substitute for attending the *viva voce* lecture but as more of a preview of what sort of teaching one could expect from a given master. The master made no money from the copying of his glosses but only from actual paying students in the classroom. This was where the real learning took place, in the presence of a renowned scholar. In fact, Abelard's onetime student Robert of Melun contended that the written form of a lecture was a poor substitute for hearing the master speak for himself. Written texts, Robert warned, can be easily misconstrued; better to hear for oneself what the master has to say so that one can catch what he really means. This concern also speaks to the fear that the master will inevitably lose control of the written text, which will then acquire a life of its own apart from what the master had originally intended. Masters were rightfully wary about what they allowed to be copied, therefore, lest their text be used against them at some later date. To that end, some twelfth-century masters pointedly stated that they had removed certain remarks from the written text (*in legendo*) that they had felt free to pursue orally in the midst of classroom discussion (*in disserendo*). Finally, a master may well have taught a given biblical book in the schools without leaving behind a written commentary. Hence the absence of an extant text does not rule out the possibility of oral instruction; not all teaching was committed to writing.[1]

Now as the "words of the master" (*verba magistri*) could acquire a life of their own, detached from their original speakers, there arose different methods of regulating magisterial discourse. This might result in the call for direct oral debate, as a master would request a face-to-face meeting with those reckoned to be circulating theological errors. The master might respond to his nemesis in writing, penning a countertract to correct perceived errors. A formal synod might even be convened where some schoolman would have to

---

1. Here I have followed Michael Clanchy and Lesley Smith, "Abelard's Description of the School of Laon: What Might It Tell Us about Early Scholastic Teaching?," *Nottingham Medieval Studies* 54 (2010): 1–34. See also Martin Morard, "Étienne Langton et les commentaires-fantômes: Le cas du commentaire des Psaumes," in *Étienne Langton: Prédicateur, bibliste, théologien*, ed. Louis-Jacques Bataillon, Nicole Bériou, Gilbert Dahan, and Riccardo Quinto (Turnhout: Brepols, 2010), 241–84; and Jean Châtillon, "Abélard et les écoles," in *Abélard en son temps: Actes du colloque international organisé à l'occasion du 9e centenaire de la naissance de Pierre Abélard, 14–19 mai 1979*, ed. Jean Jolivet (Paris: Les Belles Lettres, 1981), 133–60.

defend his writings before ecclesiastical judges. An example of the first method was taken up by Rupert of Deutz, who planned to travel from his monastery in Liège to the school at Laon in an effort to correct what he believed was a distortion of the original teachings of Anselm and William of Champeaux. Rupert, for his part, had never actually heard either of these men teach in person but knew of their teachings by way of oral tradition. As an example of the second method, Walter of Mortagne took issue with theological positions proposed by Peter Abelard in his *Theologia scholarium* and so wrote a letter to him seeking a written response. Walter was apparently wary of oral debate, which he thought only obscured matters; better, therefore, to clear up these issues in writing. Finally, there might be an appeal to a council for the sake of restoring true doctrine, which afforded the indicted master the chance to speak for himself rather than let his words be distorted by others. Peter Abelard was thus summoned to the Council of Soissons in 1121 and Gilbert de la Porrée to Reims in 1148.[2]

The Laon School and the *Glossa Ordinaria*

As we have seen above, teaching in the schools involved commenting on authoritative texts, and thus sometimes proposing controversial readings of Scripture and the fathers in an effort to gain greater insight into such knotty theological topics as the Trinity or incarnation. The schools were constantly adopting new methods and terminology to keep pace with the lively discussions of the schoolmen. By the twelfth century, the preferred term for a commentary was *glosa* rather than *commentum*. The classic review of this distinction was presented by William of Conches: "Nowadays we call '*commentum*' only an explanatory text. Hence it is different from the '*glosa*,' for a '*commentum*' deals only with the '*sententia*.' It says nothing about the '*continuatio*' or the '*expositio*' of the '*littera*.' But a '*glosa*' takes care of all these factors. That is why it is called '*glosa*.'" It seems that, for William, a *commentum* sums up the content of the author's teaching, whereas the *glosa* examines individual words and their context. The term *glosa*, therefore, does not speak to the physical layout of the text but to the method of interpretation. To gloss a text, whether secular or sacred, is to present a verse-by-verse explanation of some authoritative work. By the latter half of the twelfth century, Parisian scholars such as Peter Comestor

2. Cédric Giraud, "*Per Verba Magistri*: La langue des maîtres théologiens au premier XIIe siècle," in *Zwischen Babel und Pfingsten: Sprachdifferenzen und Gesprächverstandigung in der Vormoderne (8–16 Jahrhundert)*, ed. Peter von Moos (Zürich: LIT, 2008), 357–73.

and Peter the Chanter drew a further distinction between the patristic *expositor* and the later *glosator* who had arranged the earlier material into an organized gloss.[3]

The contemporary masters continued to add their own insights, however; their glosses were not merely patristic replications, and this meant that the glossed text was always a living text. Thus, when discussing glosses and the activity of glossing, we must remember that the assignment of authorship becomes a difficult proposition. This is the case for a number of reasons, not the least of which is because the glosses themselves were often anonymous, and the glossed text itself remained fluid. Each succeeding generation of masters added to and altered the glosses to suit the immediate needs of classroom instruction.[4] If an authoritative text—whether it be Boethius or the Bible—formed the core of the magisterial lecture, it stands to reason that the masters will constantly be updating the explanatory notes so as to provide their students with the latest and best thinking on the topic. Not unlike modern college professors, the schoolmen were not "glossing" for posterity; they were preparing notes for the day's class.

We can now turn our attention specifically to some of the major breakthroughs in the glossing of Holy Scripture. For this we look to the Laon school, which may fairly be considered the source of what has come to be known as the *Glossa Ordinaria*, or "Standard Commentary." This was a highly organized commentary on the entirety of Holy Scripture, comprising comments, or glosses, drawn from the works of the fathers, as well as more recent authorities such as the Venerable Bede. The *Glossa Ordinaria*'s appearance, its *mis-en-page*, was pioneered already in the eleventh century, presenting a system of interlinear glosses written between the lines of the biblical text with more extensive comments written in the margins. The brief interlinear glosses clarified the meaning of individual words or phrases, while the more substantial marginal glosses provided theological reflection on important passages. Culling material largely from earlier Carolingian commentaries, which themselves incorporated massive amounts of patristic material, the compilers of the Laon Gloss provided lecturers on Scripture with the best the tradition had to offer, all for the sake of breaking open the biblical text. The staying power of the Gloss was extraordinary. Even in the first decades

---

3. Nikolaus Häring, "Commentary and Hermeneutics," in *The Renaissance of the Twelfth Century*, ed. Giles Constable (Cambridge, MA: Harvard University Press, 1982), 173–200, quote on 179.

4. Anne Grondeux, "*Auctoritas et Glose*: Quelle place pour un auteur dans une glose?," in *Auctor et Auctoritas: Invention et conformisme dans L'écriture médiévale*, ed. Michel Zimmermann (Paris: École des Chartes, 2001), 245–54.

of the sixteenth century, the Augustinian friar and professor of sacred Scripture Martin Luther was still consulting it when he delivered his lectures on the Psalms and Pauline epistles.[5]

There can be no precise determination as to which scholars were responsible for which individual books, but modern scholarship has traditionally credited Anselm of Laon (d. 1117) with directing the project. One leading scholar, Alexander Andrée, does not find solid evidence of Anselm's direct involvement with the construction of the Gloss, which was likely left to his colleagues Ralph of Laon (d. ca. 1133) and Gilbert the Universal (d. 1134), along with some other scholars whose identity remains unknown. This is not to say that Anselm was therefore unconnected to the Gloss; his method of exposition and the commentaries that he did leave on a number of books do indeed stand behind the Gloss. In fact, it seems that Anselm's own lectures on the Gospel of John were copied and later incorporated into the Gloss on John. So it is that Anselm's *Glosae super Iohannem* provides a glimpse into what biblical exposition looked like at the Laon school in the early twelfth century. One finds that Anselm himself had drawn principally on the previous exegesis of Alcuin of York and Heiric of Auxerre. Now Alcuin had in turn drawn on Augustine's Johannine sermons as well as Gregory the Great and the Venerable Bede. And Heiric, for his part, had used some of the same material as Alcuin in addition to Alcuin's own John commentary. The final product, as it comes to us in Anselm's gloss, is a carefully crafted whole that bears the unique stamp of the master. In the words of his editor, Andrée, "Anselm's art was such that he was able to construct an apparently seamless narrative out of authoritative texts and glosses, and his method, which was both traditional and innovative, managed to provide a digest, succinct and useful, of the highlights of the previous commentary tradition."[6]

5. For a published edition of the Gloss, which retains the traditional layout, see the facsimile edition: *Biblia Latina cum Glossa Ordinaria*, ed. Karlfried Froehlich and Margaret T. Gibson, 4 vols. (Strassburg, 1480/81; repr., Turnhout: Brepols, 1992). For the history of the Gloss, see Lesley Smith, "The Glossed Bible," in *The New Cambridge History of the Bible*, 4 vols. (Cambridge: Cambridge University Press, 2013), 2:363–79; E. Ann Matter, "The Church Fathers and the *Glossa Ordinaria*," in *The Reception of the Church Fathers in the West*, ed. Irena Backus (Leiden: Brill, 1997), 1:83–111; Robert Wielockx, "Autor de la 'Glossa Ordinaria,'" *Recherches de théologie ancienne et médiévale* 49 (1982): 222–28; and Beryl Smalley, *Study of the Bible in the Middle Ages* (Notre Dame, IN: University of Notre Dame Press, 1964), 46–66.

6. *Anselmi Laudunensis Glosae super Iohannem*, ed. Alexander Andrée, CCCM 267 (Turnhout: Brepols, 2014), ix–xliv, quote on xli. See also Alexander Andrée, "Laon Revisited: Master Anselm and the Creation of a Theological School in the Twelfth Century," *Journal of Medieval Latin* 22 (2012): 257–81. For a thorough assessment of Anselm's career and legacy, see Cédric Giraud, *Per Verba Magistri: Anselme de Laon et son école au XIIe siècle* (Tunhout: Brepols, 2010), esp. 35–101.

As we look at Anselm's text, we find, not surprisingly, that it still bears the marks of the lecture hall even after it had been more formally prepared for later written circulation. There is the use of the second-person singular, as though addressing the hearer directly; the first-person singular, as the lecturer puts himself in the place of the one speaking within the biblical narrative; the rephrasing of the biblical text, "as if he were to say" (*quasi diceret*); and the question: "someone might ask" (*quaeritur*). When Anselm comments on the opening verse of the gospel, "In the beginning was the Word," he addresses the listener/reader directly in the second-person singular as he compares the eternal Word to that inner word that "you have [*habes*] in your heart [*corde tuo*], as though a counsel born in your mind [*mente tua*]." And he continues: "Do you wish [*vis*] to see how it is that the counsel of God is the Lord Jesus Christ, that is, the Word of God? Look at the construction of the world; see [*vide*] those things that would have been made through the Word and then you will know [*scies*] what the Word is like."[7] This rhetorical strategy creates an aura of intimacy between lecturer and hearer/reader that the third person could never convey.

Here one also catches a glimpse of some of the more sophisticated theological discussions that arose from the study of the sacred page. Having established that the Word is coeternal with the Father and of the same essence, Anselm writes: "And lest anyone think that the Son subsists in the Father in such way that there would be no difference between them, he [John] adds: 'And the Word was with God.' It is as if to say: The Son subsists in the Father in unity of essence although also by personal division."[8]

Moving on to the wedding feast at Cana (John 2:1–11), Anselm has an opportunity to present spiritual readings of the text that go beyond the letter. So it is that spiritually (*spiritualiter*) this wedding signifies the marriage of Christ and the church as God became man and wished to sanctify the church through the mystery of his body and blood. That the wine is recorded as having been depleted mystically (*mistice*) signals that with the appearance of Christ in the flesh, the carnal interpretation of the law began to lose its sweetness little by little. But the Lord then converted water into wine: when the literal understanding (which was tasteless) had been put aside, he revealed how the law might be spiritually understood. Now the teaching of the gospel was transforming the outward appearance of the legal letter.[9] And again, the water in the stone jars of purification mystically (*mistice*) signifies the

7. *Glosae super Iohannem*, prothemata 1 (CCCM 267:3).
8. *Glosae super Iohannem* 1.1–2 (CCCM 267:6–7).
9. *Glosae super Iohannem* 2.3 (CCCM 267:38).

knowledge of Holy Scripture, which washes away the filth of sins and sati- ates its hearers from the font of divine understanding.[10] The servants who are told to "fill the jars with water" are the disciples and doctors of the New Testament, who do not construct the Scriptures but are given the task of spiritually interpreting them.[11]

The crucial text of John 6:56—"Whoever eats my flesh and drinks my blood . . ."—prompts an important comment on eucharistic reception. Here, Anselm says, Christ explains (*exponit*) what it means to eat his body and drink his blood. To eat this food and to drink this blood is for a believer to abide in Christ while Christ is understood to abide within the believer. Thus sinners who do not abide in Christ, and in whom Christ does not abide, although they may carnally eat and visibly press down on the sacrament of the body with their teeth, nevertheless do not spiritually consume the Lord's flesh. In fact, such persons who come to the Eucharist unclean, eat and drink to their own judgment.[12] Here we see the ecclesiological reading of this text, with its emphasis on moral cohesion with the body of Christ, rather than a detailed discussion of eucharistic presence.

Finally, as Anselm comments on Christ's exchange with Peter at the end of the gospel (John 21:15–17), the emphasis is placed squarely on love and pastoral self-sacrifice. Notably absent is any discussion of papal authority. When Christ asks, "Do you love me more than these?" Anselm claims that he is commending to Peter the virtue of perfect love, which is thus defined as that by which we are commanded to love God with our whole heart and our neighbor as ourselves. And neither of these loves, Anselm asserts, can be perfect apart from the other. It is not possible for God to be loved without one's neighbor, nor the neighbor without God. Thus the command to "feed my sheep" exhibits the proof of one's love for God, which is exhibited in love for one's neighbor. Peter's response, "You know that I love you," prompts an explanation as Anselm, observing Peter's measured response (*simplici voce*), speaks in Peter's stead: It is as if he were to say (*quasi dicat*), "I know that I love you with a whole heart as you well know. Although I do not know how much others may love you." As Christ proceeds to tell Peter once more to "feed my sheep," Anselm switches into Christ's role: "My sheep not yours. . . . Seek my glory in them not your own. You are not to love yourself, but me, so that you might not be a mercenary. You are not to seek after riches, nor cave into fear, nor elevate yourself to a place of honor, for you must not

10. *Glosae super Iohannem* 2.6 (CCCM 267:39).
11. *Glosae super Iohannem* 2.7 (CCCM 267:41).
12. *Glosae super Iohannem* 6.56–57 (CCCM 267:121).

be afraid even to suffer death for the sheep." For Anselm, Christ's admonition, far from being a unique sign of papal prerogative, is spoken to Peter as a symbol (*figura*) of all teachers.[13]

Peter the Lombard

Anselm died by 1117, but the Laon school continued and had glossed almost the entire Bible by the middle of the twelfth century. It was not long before the glosses on the Psalter and Pauline epistles were being revised and expanded: scholars speak of three stages (*parva, media,* and *magna*), although this process is quite complex. Hugh of St. Victor's former student, Peter the Lombard, produced the so-called *Magna Glossatura*, which very quickly became a mainstay in the curriculum of the Paris cathedral school, which by this time had eclipsed Laon. We turn first to Peter's Psalter gloss. Drawing on a range of holy doctors—from Cassiodorus to Jerome, Augustine, and Remigius of Auxerre—Peter extols David as the greatest of prophets who spoke under the inspiration of the Holy Spirit; indeed he was a *"tuba Spiritus Sancti."*[14] Addressing first the very word *Psalterium*, Peter finds that it takes its name from a musical instrument. This literally (*ad litteram*) was a ten-stringed instrument played to accompany David's singing of his songs before the ark in the tabernacle of the Lord. Yet according to the spiritual sense (*juxta spiritualem intelligentiam*), the ten strings symbolize that this book teaches observance of the Ten Commandments. And just as this instrument produces a superior sound, so this book teaches us how to do good, not on earthly terms but rather with regard to the celestial things that are from above. That there are 150 psalms is also not without significance; for instance, three times fifty speaks to the three states of the Christian religion: repentance, righteousness, and eternal life.[15]

The Psalter, the most frequently used book within the divine offices, offers "the consummation of the whole theological page," according to the Lombard, for here are described the rewards given to the good, the punishment of the wicked, rudiments for beginners, progress of the mature, perfection of those who have arrived, the active life, and the speculations of the contemplatives.[16] Moreover, in the Psalter we see the mercy of God for the penitent: David, the murderer and adulterer, became by way of his repentance both a teacher and

---

13. *Glosae super Iohannem* 21.15–17 (CCCM 267:349–50).
14. *Commentarium in Psalmos*, preface (PL 191:55a).
15. *Commentarium in Psalmos*, preface (PL 191:55d–57a).
16. *Commentarium in Psalmos*, preface (PL 191:57b).

a prophet. In that way he can be likened to Saul the Pharisee, who after his conversion was promoted by God's mercy to the place of an apostle. And while it is true that all the prophets speak of Christ's death and resurrection at least obscurely and enigmatically, David alone revealed these things most clearly (*evidentissime*), such that one might say of him that he "evangelized" more than he prophesied.[17]

Both the *Magna Glossatura* on the Psalter and that on the epistles begin with the C-Type prologue that we have encountered already in the later eleventh century. Peter the Lombard thus turned to methodically address the title of the work, its subject matter, intention, and manner of treating its subject. The first thing he mentions is that this is called a "book" (*liber*) in the singular, rather than the plural "books" (*libri*), for we read "*Incipit Liber Hymnorum.*" He makes this point against those who have said that there are really many books here owing to the five distinctions of psalms. Actually, Peter says, the Psalter is like the epistle collection of Paul, which also constitutes just one book. David himself makes this clear as he speaks in the person of Christ (*Christi persona*): "*In capite libri scriptum est de me*" (Ps. 39:8 Vulg. [40:7 Eng.]). And again, we read in the Acts of the Apostles, "*Sicut scriptum est in libro psalmorum*" (Acts 1:20).[18] That this is a book of "hymns" designates that it is suited for lauding God in song; hence this book of hymns teaches us how to praise God.[19]

Peter was keen to establish not only the inherent unity of the work itself but also the singleness of its authorship. "Of the Prophet," without any attached proper name, can be taken for David alone, therefore, just as Paul is known simply as "the apostle." Here Peter specifically seeks to refute those who claim that there were multiple writers or authors (*scriptores vel auctores*) of the Psalms despite the names of Asaph, Heman, Ethan, and Idithum appearing in some titles. These were not, Peter insists, "*auctores psalmorum.*" Their names were instead meant to signify the mysteries that, from the interpretation of names, can be perceived.[20] The subject matter of the Psalter is the whole Christ (*totus Christus*): head and body, bridegroom and bride. And its intention (*intentio*) is that the human race deformed in Adam would then be conformed to Christ the new man. Yet the manner of discussion (*modus tractandi*) is such that the Psalter may treat Christ the head sometimes, his body the church at other times, and sometimes both at once.[21] One might say

17. *Commentarium in Psalmos*, preface (PL 191:57c–d).
18. *Commentarium in Psalmos*, preface (PL 191:57d–58a).
19. *Commentarium in Psalmos*, preface (PL 191:58a).
20. *Commentarium in Psalmos*, preface (PL 191:59b).
21. *Commentarium in Psalmos*, preface (PL 191:59c–d).

that for Peter, in the good Victorine tradition, the Psalter principally guides us along the path of re-formation; it is a work of restoration.

In the *Magna Glossatura* on the epistles, known also as the *Collectanea*, Peter begins with the observation that in order to attain a fuller knowledge of things, we must first grasp their foundational principles (*principia rerum*). The exegete must demonstrate the underlying methods and rationale (*modum et rationem*) of these letters if he is to disclose their truth. As in his prologue to the Psalter, here the Lombard points out the similarities between David and Paul as human beings who were called to be instruments of the divine will. As David was both an adulterer and murderer and yet recovered the spirit of prophecy through repentance, so Paul the onetime persecutor of the church was now an apostle and preacher who excelled all other letter writers in the profundity of his work, proclamation of faith, and commendation of grace. And as with the Psalter, here too Peter addresses the subject matter (*materia*), intention (*intentio*), and manner of discussion (*modus tractandi*). The general subject matter of all the epistles is the teaching of the gospel, while their intention is to admonish recipients to obey evangelical teaching. Beyond these two basic criteria, each letter has its own specific subject and purpose. In the case of the Epistle to the Romans, for instance, the subject matter is the sin of the Roman congregation along with the benefits of God's grace to which Paul calls them. His intention, or purpose, here is to rebuke them for their vices in order that they would humble themselves under the hand of grace and so achieve true peace and fraternal harmony. And his manner of discussion is to begin, in the custom of all skilled letter writers, with a greeting so as to introduce himself and to gain their good will (*capat benevolentiam*). From there Paul proceeds to demonstrate that salvation comes not from the law but through faith in Christ, and he concludes with some moral instruction along with an expression of thanksgiving.[22]

Peter Comestor

The Paris master Peter Comestor, an illustrious student of Peter the Lombard, made a major contribution to the field when he produced a historical commentary on Scripture known as the *Historia scholastica*. In this work Peter provides readers with the sort of geographical, biographical, and linguistic information that they would need to establish a solid grounding in the

22. *Collectanea in Omnes D. Pauli Apostoli Epistolas* (PL 191:1297–1302). On the Psalms and epistles, see Marcia L. Colish, *Peter Lombard*, 2 vols. (Leiden: Brill, 1994), 1:70–89 and 1:192–225 respectively.

literal-historical sense of the biblical text. The *Historia scholastica* proved to be an invaluable resource for generations of scholars. Moreover, the continuity and expansion of scholarship at Paris is evinced by the fact that Comestor had drawn substantially on Peter the Lombard's *Sentences* as he composed the *History*, and his own student Stephen Langton would then lecture on Comestor's work for years to come in the Paris schools. Actually, the *Historia scholastica* appears to have been an ongoing project that Comestor himself continued to revise throughout his career, even as it was further revised by Langton, who had produced one commentary on the text by 1176 and then another in 1193. In keeping with our earlier discussion of the living gloss tradition, the *History* was continually absorbing new glosses into the body of text. This phenomenon makes it especially difficult to reconstruct the "original" text, if there ever really was one, amid the ongoing revisions, all of which testifies to the central place of the *History* in the day-to-day teaching at Paris. Its popularity carried over into the next century as the newly formed Dominican school at Paris headed up by Hugh of St. Cher drew on Langton's work when producing its own commentary on the *History* in the 1230s. It seems clear, therefore, that in the latter part of the twelfth century and first decades of the thirteenth, Comestor's *History* was a staple of the Paris curriculum, along with the glossed Bible and Peter Lombard's theological textbook, the *Sentences*. Yet, as the Franciscan master Roger Bacon would later lament, Comestor's orderly narrative of biblical history finally gave way to the *Sentences*, which came to dominate theological discourse well into the fourteenth century.[23]

In his prologue to the *History*, Comestor speaks of God as an emperor whose palace contains three dwellings: the auditorium, which is the whole world that he governs according to his will; the bridal chamber, wherein he inhabits the souls of the righteous; and the dining room of Holy Scripture, where he inebriates his faithful ones so that he might then render them sober. Comestor proceeds to describe the construction of this dining room in keeping with the different senses of Scripture. History is its foundation, of which there are three sorts: daily, monthly, and yearly accounts. Allegory forms the supporting walls whereby one fact signifies another fact, and tropology constitutes the roof as what has been done implies what we ought to be doing. Thus the first sense is plainer, the second sharper, and the third sweeter.

---

23. The leading authority on Comestor's *History* is Mark J. Clark, *The Making of the "Historia Scholastica," 1150–1200*, Mediaeval Law and Theology 7, Studies and Texts (Toronto: Pontifical Institute of Mediaeval Studies, 2015). Roger Bacon's observations appear in his *Opus minus*, in *Opera quaedam hactenus inedita*, ed. J. S. Brewer, Rerum Britannicarum medii aevi scriptores 15 (London: Longman, Green, Longman and Roberts, 1859), 1:322–59.

Comestor then presents a set of examples of scriptural allegory: it may be when some person, such as Isaac or David, signifies Christ. It could also apply to cases in which something that is not a person (with person defined here, in keeping with Boethius, as an individual substance of a rational nature), such as a slaughtered sheep, signifies Christ's suffering humanity. Allegory may furthermore be applied to inanimate objects, numbers, places, seasons, and deeds. In the last case, for instance, David's slaying of Goliath (1 Sam. 17) can signify Christ's victory over the devil. Tropology is further defined as transformative discourse (*sermo conversivus*) pertaining to the moral life of the soul. It is more stirring than allegory, which has to do with the church militant. And finally anagogy makes an appearance here, pointing to the church triumphant and the Holy Trinity.[24]

Weaving together the four gospels, Peter proceeds methodically through the life of Christ depicted therein, beginning with the birth of John the Baptist as recorded in the Gospel of Luke. Although Peter is principally devoted to a literal-historical account, he occasionally offers an allegorical reading of the text alongside when it serves to highlight some aspect of the church's liturgy. Thus in Mary's song, the Magnificat, the words "He has regarded the humility of his handmaid" (Luke 1:48) are seen to refer to the church as well as to Mary herself. The historical referent is not displaced, therefore, but there is a further spiritual component. This occurred in the sixth age, Comestor claims, and therefore is sung at vespers, which is the sixth office, whereas the song of Simeon is sung at the seventh office, compline, as Simeon prays that he may be dismissed in peace (Luke 2:29). Because these are both gospel canticles, we sing them standing.[25] As even these brief comments reveal, the study of the sacred page was for these masters fully integrated into their own lives of prayer and devotion.

Within the *History* we also encounter material drawn from medieval legend and hagiography as well as references to current liturgical customs. For they can serve not only to better illustrate the biblical texts but also to demonstrate their relevance to the contemporary church. When discussing Christ's nativity, for instance, Comestor claims that the hay in which Jesus was laid had been taken to Rome by Saint Helen and is now located in the church of St. Mary the Greater. Comestor also opines that Joseph may have originally constructed Jesus's manger for an ox and ass that he had brought along, thereby fulfilling the words of the prophet (Isa. 1:3). He reports that one will see this very scene painted in the churches today, as pictures function like books for

24. *Historia scholastica, In Evangelia*, prologue (PL 198:1053–56).
25. *Historia scholastica, In Evangelia* 3 (PL 198:1538c).

the laity (*quasi libri laicorum*).[26] Further discussion of the nativity presents the possibility that the shepherds "keeping watch at night" might refer to a custom among the ancients during both solstices to observe a night vigil in veneration of the sun. Perhaps, then, this custom was also adopted by Jews influenced by the practices of their neighbors.[27] And when addressing the visiting magi (Matt. 2:1–2), coming from Persia and the Chaldees, Comestor recounts John Chrysostom's comment that the star would have appeared to them quite a while before Christ was born, thereby allowing time for them to make their long journey. It is possible, Comestor says, that it would have taken them about thirteen days of sitting on dromedaries to make the journey to Bethlehem.[28]

In his efforts to afford students a solid historical foundation so that they might comprehend the literal sense of the biblical text, Comestor not only turns to hagiographical and patristic writings but also makes ample use of the work of the first-century Jewish historian Josephus, whose *Antiquities* provides a meticulous account of such political facts as the distribution of territory among Herod the Great's sons and the subsequent exile of Archelaus, whose region was placed under the control of a Roman prefect. The succession of emperors, prefects, and high priests is also duly recounted.[29] As it was, Comestor worked his way through the life of Jesus as recorded in the gospels and tackled tough questions as they arose. The wedding feast at Cana (John 2:1–12), for instance, prompts a discussion of Joseph's whereabouts, since he had not been invited to the wedding even though Mary was present. Comestor reports that some say Joseph was dead by this time and so Mary had passed into the care of her son. But even if he was not dead at the time of the wedding, he was certainly dead by the time of Christ's passion, when she was commended to the Beloved Disciple (John 19:27). Some opine, further, that this was the wedding of John the evangelist, and so Mary was called because she was his aunt and Jesus his cousin.[30]

A discussion of the Last Supper, as narrated in the synoptic gospels, prompts a reference to the canon of the Mass: By virtue of the words "This is my body," there occurs a transubstantiation (*fit transsubstantiatio*) of the elements. Hence it is credible, Comestor says, that when Christ spoke these words originally, he changed the bread and wine into his body and blood and thereupon conferred this same power on these words for later generations. Thus the text (*littera*),

26. *Historia scholastica, In Evangelia* 5 (PL 198:1540a).
27. *Historia scholastica, In Evangelia* 6 (PL 198:1540d).
28. *Historia scholastica, In Evangelia* 7 (PL 198:1541c).
29. *Historia scholastica, In Evangelia* 22–29 (PL 198:1549a–51d).
30. *Historia scholastica, In Evangelia* 38 (PL 198:1559a).

Comestor says, might be construed such that the record of Christ blessing the bread (*benedixit*) is to be taken as implied within his statement "This is my body" (*hoc est corpus meum*). Or perhaps Christ first said "This is my body" and then proceeded to bless the bread by means of a blessing that has not been passed down to us. Yet later, at the institution of the apostles, the power of the blessing (*vis benedicendi*) was handed down from the Lord with these words: "This is my body."[31]

Christ's final words on the cross, recorded by Matthew in the original Aramaic (Matt. 27:46), are first explained by Comestor before he makes the further point that the words of the psalm quoted here by Jesus (Ps. 22:1) are indeed intended to refer to him rather than to David (*ex persona David*). And because the Romans did not understand Hebrew/Aramaic, according to Comestor, they imagined that Christ was calling on Elijah. There is, however, a larger christological point to be made: When Jesus cried out that he had been forsaken by his Father, this should not be taken to mean that his divinity could have been separated from his humanity. Rather, it refers to the fact that he had been handed over by the Father to such misfortunes and thus might appear to have been forsaken, since his passion seemed at the time ineffective for human redemption.[32]

Comestor also sets himself to explain apparent anomalies, as when biblical authors seem to offer varying accounts of the same episode. For example, Matthew is alone among the evangelists in recording Christ's entrance into Jerusalem on both a colt and an ass (Matt. 21:7), which prompts Comestor to surmise that Christ may have begun on the former and switched to the latter since the colt might not have been tame enough to ride.[33] And if the evangelists seem to have made mistakes (as the pagan Porphyry alleged), Comestor follows Jerome's lead and blames the copyists for introducing errors into the text (*sed scriptor corrupit*).[34] Reliance on the fathers was central to a correct reading, and there are times when even the patristic expositors appear to disagree (*videtur contrarietas esse in verbis expositorum*), although such discrepancies can be resolved with a little ingenuity.[35] That his readers were already working with a glossed Bible is clear, as Comestor advises them to check the Gloss for a certain comment on Luke's account of the transfiguration (*super Lucam invenies glossam quae dicit*)[36] or a gloss on Mark regarding the hanging of

31. *Historia scholastica, In Evangelia* 152 (PL 198:1618b–c).
32. *Historia scholastica, In Evangelia* 176 (PL 198:1632b–c).
33. *Historia scholastica, In Evangelia* 117 (PL 198:1599c).
34. *Historia scholastica, In Evangelia* 162 (PL 198:1625c).
35. *Historia scholastica, In Evangelia* 86 (PL 1981582c–d).
36. *Historia scholastica, In Evangelia* 86 (PL 198:1582c).

Judas (*glossa quae est in Marco*).[37] In this vein, there are also references to the *Glossa Ordinaria* precisely as an authoritative text in its own right: *glossa super Exodum*;[38] *glossa super Mattheum*;[39] and *hic plane in glossa*.[40] Such was the status of the Gloss at the Paris school by the second half of the twelfth century.

Not everyone at this time was so happy with the prominence of the Gloss. The twelfth-century scholar Robert of Melun complained of an overreliance on, even a veneration of, the Gloss to the point that scholars were now reading the biblical text merely for the sake of the Gloss (*textus propter glosam legitur*) rather than for what it revealed about Holy Scripture. The Gloss, Robert claims, is simply being recited in the classroom while genuine exposition of Scripture is passed over, the result being that nothing is really taught and nothing learned. And so it is, according to Robert, that knowledge of the Gloss is now supplanting genuine facility with the biblical text itself. These people are so enamored of the latest technology that they have lost the very exegetical skills required to uncover the meaning (*sententia*) of the sacred text that they are supposed to be studying.[41] Robert's misgivings notwithstanding, the Gloss had become a mainstay in the medieval schools. He nevertheless put his finger on a larger issue that did not go away: the ordering and treatment of authoritative sources.

Peter Abelard and His Students

In the prologue to his *Sic et Non*, Robert's teacher, Peter Abelard, tackles the thorny topic of sources, observing that the sayings of the saints (*sanctorum dicta*) appear not only diverse at times but even contradictory. Given the indispensable role reserved for the church fathers in the interpretation of Holy Scripture, there would have to be some means of reconciling apparent conflicts and errors. Abelard cautions that one must begin by adopting an attitude of humility: the saints were writing under the inspiration of the Holy Spirit, which is lacking to contemporary schoolmen. Having admitted that, one then needs to be attentive to the fact that the saints employed a varied discourse such that their words could signify different things in different places.[42] The

---

37. *Historia scholastica, In Evangelia* 162 (PL 198:1625d).

38. *Historia scholastica, In Evangelia* 19 (PL 198:1601d).

39. *Historia scholastica, In Actus Apostolorum* 40 (PL 198:1669b).

40. *Historia scholastica, In Actus Apostolorum* 10 (PL 198:1651b).

41. *Sententiae*, vol. 3/1 of *Oeuvres de Robert de Melun*, ed. R.-M. Martin and R. M. Gallet, 4 vols. (Louvain: Spicilegium Sacrum Louvaniense, 1932–52), 12.

42. *Sic et Non*, prologue; *Sic et Non: A Critical Edition*, ed. Blanche B. Boyer and Richard McKeon, 2 vols. (Chicago: University of Chicago Press, 1976–77), 89.

very real possibility of textual corruption was also a factor; what appears to be an error on the part of a saint may actually be the fault of a scribe. For if, Abelard says, even the gospels themselves have been corrupted by negligent scribes (*per ignorantiam scriptorum*), it stands to reason that the writings of the fathers—which possess far less authority (*longe minoris sunt auctoritatis*) than Holy Scripture—may also be corrupt.[43] Abelard's observation is noteworthy not only for what it says about the general awareness of textual problems but also for its unequivocal affirmation of Scripture's preeminent position in the medieval schools.

Some of Abelard's general observations on the structure of Holy Scripture are also worth mentioning, for they make an appearance among his disciples. In the prologue to his Romans commentary, Abelard observes that all Scripture, in the custom of the rhetoric of oration, intends either to teach or to move. It teaches by insinuating what it is fitting to do or to avoid; it moves our will by its holy admonitions either dissuading us from doing the evil or persuading us to do the good. Thus we might wish to fulfill what we were taught that we should fulfill and also avoid the contrary.[44]

Abelard states, furthermore, that perhaps everything the gospels handed down concerning faith, hope, love, and the sacraments was itself sufficient for salvation, apart from the apostolic institutions and teachings of the fathers. Yet, he says, the Lord nevertheless willed that certain precepts and dispensations from the apostles and fathers might be added for the further edification of the church. Christ saw fit, therefore, to reserve certain disciplines for later implementation at the authority of future teachers.[45] It is the intention of the gospels to teach us all things that are necessary for salvation, therefore, while the intention of the epistles is to move us to obey the teaching of the gospels and to fortify us more securely in the salvation that they hand down.[46]

We can return now to Robert of Melun, an Englishman who, like many of his fellow countrymen in the twelfth century, made the pilgrimage to Paris to study at its illustrious schools.[47] Among Robert's works are a collection of *Sentences*, a set of *Questions on the Divine Page* mainly to do with the Gospel of Matthew, and his *Questions on the Epistles of Paul*. In the first book of his

43. *Sic et Non*, prologue (Boyer and McKeon, 91–92).
44. *Commentaria in Epistolam Pauli ad Romanos*, prologue, ed. E. M. Buytaert, CCCM 11 (Turnhout: Brepols, 1969), 41.
45. *Commentaria in Epistolam Pauli ad Romanos*, prologue (CCCM 11:42–43).
46. *Commentaria in Epistolam Pauli ad Romanos*, prologue (CCCM 11:43).
47. See David Luscombe, *The School of Peter Abelard* (Oxford: Oxford University Press, 1971); and Astrik Gabriel, "English Masters and Students in Paris during the Twelfth Century," in *Garlandia: Studies in the History of the Medieval University*, ed. A. Gabriel (Notre Dame, IN: University of Notre Dame Press, 1969), 1–37.

Sentences, Robert takes up the pivotal exegetical question of signification. Here he observes that as the figure (*figura*) properly precedes the truth (*veritas*) in the act of existence, so in the act of explication it should also be considered first. Thus to return from the truth to the figure is to go backward, since it is the figure that signifies, while the truth is that which is signified. This means, in turn, that as long as the figure remains unknown to us, we will not be able to reach the truth that it signifies.[48] This basic principle could then be applied to the relationship between the Old and New Testaments. We hold the Old Testament in high esteem owing to its figures whose truth is revealed in the New Testament. Indeed, Robert says, to reject the figure (*figura*) is tantamount to despising the thing that it represents (*rem figuratum*). There is a transition, however, as one passes from the level of sign to reality, as one epoch yields to another. Looking to the verse, "There is one who sows and another who reaps" (John 4:37), Robert surmises that the sowers are the doctors of the Old Testament, namely, Moses and the prophets, while the reapers are the evangelists of the New Testament, as well as the doctors of the church, who confirm by their preaching what is established in the New Testament with the authorities of the Old.[49]

Veneration of the Old Testament leads, naturally enough, to the question of whether the law should still be kept. Should we not observe the precepts of the law, since such precepts are the very confirmation of the New Testament? After all, the argument runs, who would accept something as confirmation while at the same time claiming that this very thing must be refuted? To this Robert responds that the law should actually be regarded as the name of a writing (*scripturae nomen*), not the name of real things (*rerum*). Hence the law should not be kept according to the letter but rather observed spiritually. The spiritual understanding of the law deals not with precepts, which are only words, but with the things signified by those words. Thus we do not keep the precepts anymore, since they merely testified to the greater spiritual reality that was to be fulfilled, which is narrated in the gospel. As Robert points out, if the gospel apart from the law were not sufficient for salvation, then the teaching of Christ is not perfect, and Christ himself does not constitute the fullness of our reconciliation.[50]

Robert proceeds to aver that signification in sacred Scripture occurs on two levels: the level of words (*vocum*) and the level of things (*rerum*). The

48. *Sententiae* 1.1, *Oeuvres de Robert de Melun*, 3/1, ed. Martin, 159–60. Translation in *Interpretation of Scripture: Theory*, ed. Franklin Harkins and Frans van Liere, Victorine Texts in Translation (Turnhout: Brepols, 2013), 445.

49. *Sententiae* 1.2 (Martin, 3/1:160–62; Harkins and van Liere, 445–46).

50. *Sententiae* 1.3 (Martin, 3/1:162–67; Harkins and van Liere, 447–50).

signification of words amounts to what Robert calls their historical meaning (*historica vel historialis*). Yet "history" can actually be quite an expansive term when applied to Scripture, for it may refer, on the one hand, to something being narrated that existed in fact but also to something that is signified parabolically or hyperbolically, or again to something being shown through some other figure of speech. On the other hand, the signification can be mystical, or hidden (*mistica id est occulta*), when it is subject to comprehension of the intellect alone apart from the senses. And this in turn may be classified as allegory or tropology, Robert says, noting here that some people add anagogy to the list, although we include that under the sense of allegory.[51]

Robert also takes up the question of Scripture's subject matter and its course of study. Like Hugh of St. Victor, he finds that the subject matter (*materia*) is the incarnate Word and the sacraments, which both precede and follow Christ. With respect to the study (*studium*) of Scripture, Robert states that Scripture is understood through a course of reading (*per lectionis exercitationem*), under which he likely includes attending lectures on Scripture. Yet this course of study is then fulfilled through a course of action (*operis executione*). Thus for Robert the *studium scripturae* is of a composite nature: it is understood through reading but only completed when what has been understood is then put into practice.[52] Again, therefore, we see that the study of Scripture in the schools was always undertaken for the purpose of re-forming the reader through the inculcation of virtues and the acts of piety that resulted.

When addressing the contents of the New Testament, Robert observes that some people divide it into three parts, the last of which includes the writings of the fathers: Jerome, Augustine, and all the other "expositors" of the Old and New Testaments. Other people, however, do not wish to include the fathers, so their tripartite New Testament places the gospels in part 1, the canonical and Pauline epistles in part 2, and Acts of the Apostles and the Apocalypse in part 3. These people reason that the New Testament should include only books in which nothing could be corrected or changed, for as Augustine pointed out,[53] if something is found in these Scriptures that appears to be contrary to the faith, the fault must lie either in a faulty manuscript or our own lack of comprehension. Such is not the case with the writings of the fathers, however, as they themselves confess. Indeed, as Robert reports, Augustine freely admitted in his *Retractationes* that on many occasions he had erred or at least misspoken. Thus whereas the authors of Scripture possess an inherent

---

51. *Sententiae* 1.6 (Martin, 3/1:170–79; Harkins and van Liere, 452–55).
52. *Sententiae* 1.8 (Martin, 3/1:181).
53. *Epistula* 82.1 (PL 33:276–77).

authority that renders their works immediately authentic (*autentica*), the expositors (*expositores*) derive their authority from having been confirmed by the church.[54]

As we have mentioned, the explication of Scripture in the classroom yielded theological questions that often merited special consideration in their own right. Robert's introduction to his questions on Romans actually serves as a general prologue to the study of Scripture. Here he asserts that erudition depends on the study of texts (*scripturae*), whether they be Holy Scripture or the writings of the pagans. Drawing on the works of both Hugh of St. Victor and Peter Abelard, Robert observes that it is within the pagan writings that one is taught about the composition of discourse (*sermonum compositio*) and the arrangement of things (*rerum proprietas*), the first of which is dealt with in the trivium and the second in the mathematical disciplines that treat both the extrinsic and intrinsic qualities of things. The quadrivium, Robert says, is concerned with the exterior figures, whereas physics tackles the intrinsic natures of things. We must be acquainted with all of this before we attempt to understand the divine Scriptures.[55]

The Scriptures, although divided into the Old and New Testaments, have a single subject matter, namely, the incarnate Christ and his sacred mysteries (*sacramenta*). Their intention, befitting the custom of rhetorical discourse (*more rhetorice orationis*), is to teach and to persuade. Robert proceeds to subdivide the Old Testament into the law, prophets, and holy writings; while the New comprises the gospels, epistles, Acts of the Apostles, the Apocalypse, and—at least according to some people (*secundum quosdam*)—the writings of the fathers. In general, though, one might say that the gospels provide instruction, while the epistles follow up on that instruction by way of admonitions informed through examples. Each epistle, in turn, has its own subject matter and intention.[56]

Turning to his Questions, the lasting influence of Robert's teacher, Peter Abelard, is most noticeable in the emphasis placed on conscience as the determining factor in establishing moral culpability. Thus in his Questions on Romans, when discussing what the gentiles might have known about God from the created order, and their subsequent duties to God (Rom. 1:20–22), Robert acknowledges that the question has arisen (*queritur item*) as to why the pagan philosophers were not excusable when they knew as much as they were able to know about God through natural reason. How had they not glorified

---

54. *Sententiae* 1.12 (Martin, 3/1:191–92).
55. *Questiones de Epistola ad Romanos*, vol. 2 of *Oeuvres de Robert de Melun*, ed. R.-M. Martin and R. M. Gallet, 4 vols. (Louvain: Spicilegium Sacrum Louvaniense, 1932–52), 1–2.
56. *Questiones de Epistola ad Romanos* (Martin, 2:2–4).

God? Was it because they had not understood the mystery of the incarnation? But by natural reason they could not possibly have understood this mystery. Why they should bear guilt (*culpa*) for not glorifying God is not clear, for if they did as much as they were able to do, it seems that they do indeed have a valid excuse. In fact, though, they did not do as much as they were able to do, for if they had done what they were supposed to do, God would surely have given them the grace they needed to understand what they could not grasp through nature. That God may have revealed this saving knowledge to some of them is certainly possible, Robert says, although we should not go so far as to assert that this was the case. What we do know, however, is that most of the pagan philosophers did not do all that they were capable of doing. Rather, they took the wisdom that God had given them and turned it to their own glory, thus preferring themselves to God. They were not ignorant of the fact that their wisdom was from God, since natural reason is sufficient to grasp that all things come from God. But because they used that wisdom pridefully, they became fools (cf. Rom. 1:22). Since they ascribed their wisdom to themselves, therefore, they lapsed into error.[57]

The question then arises as to why God handed the pagans over to the desires of their hearts (Rom. 1:24). Some say, according to Robert, that "hand over" (*tradere*) should be taken to mean "permit to be handed over" (*permittere tradi*). And this in turn prompts the question as to just what sort of permission this constitutes. Some say that to permit means not to impede, while others refine the definition even further: it means not to impede even though God could have impeded them. And this could be said of any sin; for when we sin God hands us over to the desire of our heart. That is to say, God does not impede us, although he could, such that we would not sin. In that sense, according to some people, Paul is really not saying anything special. Here Robert asserts that the apostle is treating the penalty for sin (*pena peccati*), which hinges on preceeding actions. Thus "to hand over" must have some other force (*vis*) here than does "to permit" in the case of other sins. In this case, it is argued that "to hand over" (*tradere*) means "to make happen" (*operari*), along the lines of what Augustine means when he says that God is at work in the hearts of some people to incline their wills to the good by his mercy, and at work in others to incline their wills to the evil by his justice. Even as God's judgment may be hidden at times, it is always just.[58] Here, then, God handed them over in the sense of inclining their wills to evil by proposing to them the occasion by which they might be moved

---

57. *Questiones de Epistola ad Romanos* (Martin, 2:28–29).
58. *De gratia et libero arbitrio* 21 (PL 44:909).

interiorly to the evil. The people themselves are still responsible, however, for their own demise. For instance, when Jesus arrived in Jerusalem to much fanfare, this provoked envy that was already in the hearts of some of the Jews. Jesus himself did not sin by doing what he did; indeed, he did what he should have done, for he should not have desisted from his good action even though it would be the occasion of others' evil action. Thus in answer to the question, God only presented the opportunity to the pagans to follow their own wicked path, one that had already been set by their previous sins. And so when God exercises his wrath on them, it is just.[59]

Can we nevertheless grant that God is somehow implicated in the sin that people commit if he is indeed at work in the hearts of men inclining their will to evil? On the one hand, God does indeed withdraw his grace from some people so as to leave them to themselves and thus to reap what they deserve. And moreover, by inclining their wills he works wrath against them as he should. Nevertheless, through all of this, it is the man himself who has persevered in his own wickedness, as he delights in the evil that he does and does not repent. The work itself is man's evil, therefore, not God's, for what comes from God is good because it is just, while evil proceeds from man. For instance, one might enter a church for sake of stealing or praying. The action (*opus*) of entering the church in itself is neither good nor evil; it is the intention that makes it one or the other.[60]

Yet one is left to ask whether God does not act cruelly by withdrawing the very grace that one needs in order not to sin. If by this very fact one cannot avoid being damned, how then is one guilty? Indeed, it seems that the person has been damned unjustly. The answer is that it was their own guilt (*culpa*) that put them in this situation to begin with. They willingly (*volens*) sinned and so were justly damned by God for that sin. Does this mean that God consents to the bad acts of sinners, since he knows the evil and could prevent it? It seems that if we were to see another person sin and yet not stop that person although we could do so, we would be consenting and thus would be culpable (*reus*). This is not true, Robert says. We see many things take place that we could stop and yet should not stop, for such things do not concern us. In the same way, when God could stop some evil act from occurring, he still should not. The consent that implies liability, therefore, only applies in those situations when we should prevent some evil act and yet do not.[61]

---

59. *Questiones de Epistola ad Romanos* (Martin, 2:30–31).
60. *Questiones de Epistola ad Romanos* (Martin, 2:34–35).
61. *Questiones de Epistola ad Romanos* (Martin, 2:35–36).

These discussions of divine justice would not be complete without addressing Paul's invocation of the brothers Jacob and Esau (Rom. 9:11–15) in his discussion of divine election. Now it seems, according to Robert, that God would be unjust if he neither rewards the one nor damns the other on account of their merits. Here Robert offers a distinction, observing that the question has its origin in two distinct things: the election that occurs from all eternity and those things that happen in time, namely, the conferral or withdrawal of grace. It is agreed that nobody can be just apart from divine predestination and that nobody could merit such predestination inasmuch as the temporal cannot be the cause of the eternal. Hence the question remains as to why God would choose Jacob rather than Esau, since there was nothing in either brother that could cause God to choose or reject one or the other. And yet apart from predestination, salvation is impossible. Nor, Robert says, could future sin be the cause of reprobation since it is only on account of predestination that one could avoid sin. Moreover, no temporal thing—in this case a sinful act—can be the cause of the eternal will. So again we are left to ask: If neither brother were able to merit grace, without which it is impossible to be saved, why did God give grace to one and withhold it from the other? It seems unjust that he damns the one from whom he has withheld the very grace needed to avoid sin. Here Robert provided an example from everyday life: I should not be blamed if I fail to carry out an assigned task if I could not accomplish this task without a horse, the very horse that I could get only from you. In the same way, it is not the person from whom grace has been withdrawn who should be blamed for sinning but rather the one who could have conferred the assistance and yet did not, the very assistance apart from which there was no way to avoid sinning.[62]

Yet regarding divine predestination, Robert says, we really do not know how to assign a cause for why God preordains one person to salvation and another not. This simply exceeds human cognition. What we do know, however, is that God does act justly by both electing and reprobating, for God knows what benefits will come from the election of one person and the damnation of another. Thus God offers salvation by his grace and damnation by justice. This justice, nevertheless, remains hidden to us. Robert reports that some people, such as his own teacher Peter Abelard, have attempted to solve this by proposing that God cannot do other than he does. Robert, however, rejects this opinion. Yet to the person who takes offense and seeks a reason why God elects this one and not that one, Robert responds that it is not right to seek a cause for the divine will; it is as foolish a question as asking why God exists.[63]

---

62. *Questiones de Epistola ad Romanos* (Martin, 2:121–22).
63. *Questiones de Epistola ad Romanos* (Martin, 2:122–23).

On the question of grace itself, Robert canvasses various opinions that try to balance the relative grace and merit involved in the salvific process. As opposed to those who say that grace is offered to all people generally, Robert states that divine grace is indeed offered to each person, but not equally to each person. Rather, it is given to each person as will be sufficient for each to merit salvation. Just because God offers grace to someone does not mean that he/she will take hold of it; the light of grace may be poured out to someone even as they close their eyes to it. From such a person, then, grace is rightly withdrawn. As is the case in the natural order, no eye can see apart from the light of the sun. Yet while it is true that the sun cannot illuminate an eye that does not possess the nature and power of seeing, it is also possible that a stone wall might prevent one from seeing, despite the shining sun. In the same way, then, the soul materially possesses the power of meriting and yet cannot exercise that power apart from being touched and even moved by the splendor of grace. Merit is not excluded, therefore, even as no good can be accomplished apart from grace. Robert offers another example: a young boy is not yet able to walk by himself; yet if someone takes hold of him and leads him, he walks. Of course, the boy could not have done this unless he already had the natural power of walking. Yet when he does walk, everything is said to be from the one who leads him. The boy has the natural power of walking, it is true, and yet cannot walk apart from the parent leading him. And again, Robert says, I have the power to ride, but I do not have the power to ride without a horse. In this vein, then, the rational soul has the natural power of meriting and doing the good, but not apart from grace.[64]

As this brief look at Romans suggests, the schoolmen were increasingly interested in matters of grace and free will, matters that this epistle in particular bring to the fore. These questions that arose in the course of reading Scripture were not, however, mere abstractions. At their heart they touched, in one form or another, on moral liability. At a time when canon law, no less than theology, was parsing the limits of what a rational person could and could not be held responsible for, both in the internal forum of the confessional and the external forum of the episcopal court, this sort of painstaking reflection on the sacred page was more necessary than ever. In that vein we turn to Robert's first question from Galatians. It concerns Paul's persecution of the church (Gal. 1:13), which by his own admission he had carried out with a fervent zeal. It is asked, Robert says, whether Paul sinned in persecuting the church, since he had a zeal for the law and believed that he was serving God. Many catholics, Robert tells us, believe that when one's conscience dictates

64. *Questiones de Epistola ad Romanos* (Martin, 2:124–26).

that one must do something for God's sake, it would be a sin not to do it, for one would then be acting against conscience. Yet to persecute the church is itself a sin. Hence there are those who say that Paul would have sinned either way. Robert concludes that, while Paul's intention (*voluntas*) was good, since he wanted to exhibit his obedience to God, his actual deed (*opus*) was evil and born of error, having been executed based on the dictates of an erroneous conscience. Because the zeal and fervor of Paul's love was good in itself, his erroneous deed can be excused.[65] We see, therefore, that the intention of the actor is the deciding factor in such cases. This is what must be given the greatest weight in the confessional.

The issue of conscience arises again with Paul's confrontation of Peter at Antioch (Gal. 2:11). The question is whether Peter really was reprehensible for having abstained from eating with the gentiles in the presence of the Jewish Christians. Because Peter believed that he had to do this to avoid a scandal, he would have acted against his own conscience had he not abstained. Therefore it seems that not only did he not sin but he actually acted meritoriously. Robert responds that, while Peter was morally good insofar as he acted out of a righteous zeal, he still erred in this instance, and thus Paul correctly rebuked him. Although it is true that Peter had erred (*erraverit*), it is still true that he had not actually sinned (*peccaverit*), and so his deed was not reprehensible, since righteous zeal excuses error. Here Robert also reports that some people are distressed over the disagreement between Jerome and Augustine on this matter and want to smooth it over. He sees no cause for alarm, however, since these fathers themselves admit that they disagree. Robert assures the reader that the Christian faith is in no danger from this disagreement, though, for both fathers are speaking in the same Spirit.[66]

A fellow member of the Abelardian school seems to have been the anonymous author (known as the "Commentator") of the so-called *Commentarius Cantabrigiensis*, or Cambridge Commentary (ca. 1141) on the epistles of Paul, which takes it name from its sole manuscript in Trinity College, Cambridge.[67] The commentary begins with a prologue for Romans, which attempts to fit the epistles as a whole into the larger plan of the biblical canon before offering more specific remarks about Romans itself. The prologue is quite similar in

---

65. *Questiones de Epistola ad Galatas* (Martin, 2:245).

66. *Questiones de Epistola ad Galatas* (Martin, 2:245–46). Cf. Jerome, *Comm. in Epist. ad Galatas* (PL 26:339–39); and Augustine, *Expositio ad Galatas* (CSEL 84:70).

67. *Commentarius Cantabrigiensis in Epistolas Pauli e Schola Petri Abaelardi*, ed. Artur Michael Landgraf, 3 vols. (Notre Dame, IN: University of Notre Dame Press, 1939). This section on the Cambridge Commentator has been adapted from a section that I wrote for *The Bible in Medieval Tradition: The Letter to the Romans*, ed. I. Levy, P. Krey, and T. Ryan (Grand Rapids: Eerdmans, 2013).

places to Robert of Melun's prologue to his own *Questions* on the epistles, beginning with a broad view of biblical studies. Just as the entire universe was created to serve the human race, and human beings to serve God, so all the liberal arts are meant to assist in the grander study of Holy Scripture. Grammar, dialectic, and rhetoric (the trivium) chiefly, but also the arts that comprise the quadrivium, are attendants of the discipline of theology. It is along these lines that the Commentator extols the benefits to be gleaned from ancient philosophical and poetical works, for no matter the original intention of their authors, the Holy Spirit had all along determined to direct them to the greater purpose of serving Scripture.[68]

Having addressed the necessity of learning the liberal arts, the Commentator observed that both the Old and the New Testaments intend to teach and to influence behavior with the aid of rhetorical methods. It soon becomes clear that this treatment of the two Testaments has substantial bearing on the meaning of the Epistle to the Romans. The Old Testament can be divided into the law, prophets, and histories. The principal function of the law is to teach what must be done and to prohibit what must not be done. The prophets and histories, however, seek to influence human attitudes toward such obligations. They are additions to the law, designed to entice believers into a willing observance of what the law commands. One could say that the prophets and histories were added to the law in order to remedy what the Commentator takes to be a central deficiency in the law itself. It could not lead people to perfection, for it contains nothing about loving one's enemy. This is not to say that the law was wrong; it was merely incomplete in its instruction. Hence one had to wait for Christ, who came not to destroy the law but to fulfill it when he declared, "Love your enemies" (Matt. 5:44).[69]

The New Testament comprises the gospels, epistles, Acts of the Apostles, and the Apocalypse. The gospel, whose function is to teach, takes the place of the law. Although it does move people by example on occasion, that is not its primary purpose. The epistles and the Apocalypse deal with promises concerning the final days, while Acts offers numerous examples of good conduct. The central goal of these latter three sets of books is to entice people into observing the evangelical precepts. Given the sufficiency of the gospel, providing as it does all necessary instruction, one may wonder what need there is for the epistles. Drawing on the analogy of a city, the Commentator explains that the precepts laid down by Christ in the gospel can be compared to fortifications that keep a city secure. They are essential; there is no salvation apart from

68. *Commentarius Cantabrigiensis*, vol. 1, *In Epistolam ad Romanos* (Landgraf, 1).
69. *In Epistolam ad Romanos*, prologue (Landgraf, 1:1–2).

obedience to these precepts. The epistles, however, provide ornamentation in the form of counsels, which inspire believers to fulfill the evangelical precepts. Helpful as they are, obedience to these counsels is not strictly necessary for salvation. An example of such counsels, therefore, would include Paul's teaching on marriage and virginity (1 Cor. 7:12–31).[70] While all the epistles are intended to influence behavior (*intentio movere*), each epistle has its own specific intention or subject matter. In the case of Romans, it is the bitter dispute between Jewish and gentile believers in that city's church. In order to resolve this tense situation, therefore, the apostle Paul sets out to undercut claims of human merit while extolling divine grace.[71]

The apostle Paul's opening salutation to the Christian community at Rome provides a lesson in the ancient art of letter writing (*ars dictaminis*). As we have seen, such attention to style is indicative of the practice already in place by the latter part of the eleventh century as Paul is treated specifically as an author (*auctor*) and his letters as carefully crafted literary productions. Hence the Commentator observes that it is the custom of letter writers to begin with a greeting through which they show their affection for the recipients and thereby pave the way for an exhortation to good conduct. One begins an oration in this way to render the audience at once attentive and well-disposed to what will follow.[72] What is more, by demonstrating his affection for the Romans, Paul can draw them closer to himself on a personal level. Thus when he begins to rebuke them severely, they will see that he does so out of love. In this vein, Paul is likened to the wise physician who first applies a soothing balm to the wound before gradually adding the more bitter medication. All of this is consistent with Paul's overall apostolic commission, according to the Commentator, which consists in stirring the Romans to the obedience of faith (Rom. 1:5) through his preaching so that they willingly submit themselves to what must be believed about God.[73]

Larger issues of Christology soon come to the fore when the apostle states that Jesus Christ "was made . . . according to the flesh" (Rom. 1:3). The Commentator observes that, although one can say that the Son of God was "made" with regard to his human nature, and is therefore less than his Father in that regard, he is still fully equal to the Father with respect to his divine nature. To say he was made with regard to his human nature, therefore, is a way of saying that the Word united that human nature to his singular divine person.[74] And so, in this vein, when Paul speaks of Christ being "predestined

---

70. *In Epistolam ad Romanos*, prologue (Landgraf, 1:2–3).
71. *In Epistolam ad Romanos*, prologue (Landgraf, 1:3–4).
72. *In Epistolam ad Romanos* 1 (Landgraf, 1:6).
73. *In Epistolam ad Romanos* 1 (Landgraf, 1:13–14).
74. *In Epistolam ad Romanos* 1 (Landgraf, 1:10).

. . . according to the flesh" (Rom. 1:4), we attribute such predestination to the human nature rather than the divine Word.[75]

In the twelfth century there was much discussion regarding the precise language that could be employed concerning the filial relationship of Christ's human nature to his divine nature. The complexity of this matter precludes an extended discussion. Here, though, we can note that the Commentator blithely employs the term "assumed human being" (*homo assumptus*), which was pivotal to the debates: "One might ask whether that assumed human being is the Son of God through adoption, through nature, or through grace." The Commentator rules out the first option, since that would presuppose the existence of some human being prior to his adoption by God. Nor, however, can he be the Son of God through nature, since, with respect to his humanity, he is not of the same substance as the Father. Thus he must be Son of God through grace, since all that he had was acquired by grace.[76]

Such christological questions, important as they surely are, remained at a more speculative level than some of the more mundane concerns that the Commentator also addresses. Medieval society was held together to a great extent by the swearing of oaths in different contexts: feudal allegiances, judicial proceedings, and religious vows. Addressing the church at Rome, Paul had invoked God as his witness (Rom. 1:9) when proclaiming his own fidelity. Thus it seems that Paul was swearing an oath in this instance. But had not Christ himself forbidden the swearing of oaths (Matt. 5:33–37)? Here one must ask whether the apostle thereby contradicted the teaching of Christ. The answer to this question is no mere scriptural conundrum; it was a matter of concern for people throughout twelfth-century Europe. Indeed, the circumstances, conditions, and validity of vows consumed the efforts of canon lawyers. The Commentator concludes that Christ never intended to forbid all oath swearing but only warned that one must not actively desire to swear an oath. The reason for this is that oath swearing is an inherently risky enterprise. There is the danger of perjuring oneself or somehow failing to accomplish what one has vowed. Hence the oath should be sworn only in matters of necessity, when some greater good makes it worth such a risk.[77]

We have seen already in the eleventh century a certain ambivalence regarding the legitimacy of applying logical analysis to biblical texts. Such unease lingered into the twelfth century and could place schoolmen on the defensive against their monastic critics. The Commentator's own teacher,

75. *In Epistolam ad Romanos* 1 (Landgraf, 10:11).
76. *In Epistolam ad Romanos* 1 (Landgraf, 1:12).
77. *In Epistolam ad Romanos* 1 (Landgraf, 1:15).

Peter Abelard, had been attacked by Bernard of Clairvaux and William of Saint Thierry for supposedly subjecting the mysteries of faith to the tests of human reason. Thus when the apostle Paul says that he is "not ashamed of the gospel" (Rom. 1:16), the Commentator mentions that some people are ashamed even today when they find themselves incapable of presenting good arguments on behalf of the catholic faith. These people claim that the faith must not be examined, and in their own defense they invoke Gregory the Great's remark that faith has no merit in matters that human reason can grasp through experience.[78] In other words, some things have to be taken on faith without any rational argumentation to support them. Yet the Commentator finds that such an attitude runs contrary to the apostle Paul's own example. After all, he observes, nobody would have accepted Paul's proclamation of Christ's resurrection from the dead had he not been able to offer a coherent and reasonable defense.[79]

Such confidence in human reason, at the service of faith and not at the expense of it, is also borne out in a discussion of what can be known about God apart from divine revelation. The Commentator contends that the ancient philosophers living prior to Christ could have recognized God, not only in unity but even as a trinity of persons. Yet it must be admitted that they could not have reasoned their way to the incarnation of the Word. Much can be known of God through an examination of the great work of creation itself. As the greatest of all artisans, the invisible God was known by philosophers through the masterpiece that is the world. The philosophers, according to the Commentator, had discerned God's supreme craftsmanship in the world's great beauty and harmonious order. Consequently, seeing how God arranged all things so fittingly to human advantage, they came to recognize God as supremely kind. What is more, though, Paul implies that the philosophers not only understood the distinction of trinitarian persons, but even their procession, such that three different things could be shown to subsist in one reality.[80]

For all that might have been known about God, however, Paul still makes the case that Jews and gentiles are altogether inexcusable. Neither people can reckon anything to their own merits, but instead must ascribe everything to divine grace. Both groups stand condemned, therefore, but on different charges. When Paul contends that "the wrath of God is revealed from heaven against all ungodliness and unrighteousness" (Rom. 1:18), the commentator observes that Jews are ungodly, whereas gentiles are unrighteous. To be

78. *Hom. in Evang.* 2.26 (PL 76:1197).
79. *In Epistolam ad Romanos* 1 (Landgraf, 1:18).
80. *In Epistolam ad Romanos* 1 (Landgraf, 1:21–23).

ungodly is more serious than being unrighteous. This distinction pertains to one's intentions. Properly speaking, the ungodly person is someone who knowingly acts against God. Thus defined, the Commentator concludes that Jews, with their superior knowledge of the divine will, were reckoned guilty under both the written law of Moses and the natural law. The gentiles, while not ungodly, were still unrighteous as they sinned only against the natural law, which is common to all humankind.[81]

If both Jew and gentile stand condemned, it remains to be seen how anyone is saved. According to the Commentator, the gospel is the "power of God" (Rom. 1:16) through which God justifies the human person. Here he plays on the Latin word *virtus*, which can mean both "power" and "virtue." The gospel can be called "power" (*virtus*), because just as virtues (*virtutes*) make one righteous, so the gospel instructs believers in all things necessary for salvation. Hence, in keeping with what he said in his prologue, the gospel constitutes a separate teaching apart from the law as it revealed to humankind the way to perfection. "The power of salvation," therefore, means justification for all who accept this gospel teaching and find comfort in it.[82]

Proceeding to the next verse, the Commentator finds that "the righteousness of God" (Rom. 1:17) refers to God's just recompense, whether for punishment or for glory. Yet the principles of God's remuneration are not based on someone's works, but rather on the basis of someone's will. This, he believes, marks the crucial difference between law and gospel. The criterion of righteousness before God is not based on exterior works, but interior disposition.[83] The Commentator returns to this theme in later chapters, noting that the chief deficiency of the old law was its inability to lead anyone to moral perfection because it was wholly concerned with exterior actions. The law simply commanded "Do not kill," but the person living by the gospel knows that one must not even wish to kill. This, in turn, is what it means to live by faith, and therefore be justified by faith; it means conforming one's will, not just one's actions, to Christ. In genuine Abelardian fashion, the Commentator concludes that God will judge all people on the basis of their interior selves, what they intended in their hearts, no matter whether they actually refrained from murder or theft in fact.[84] No doubt God is pleased by good works, but only those works that arise from a good will (*voluntas*).[85] Under this system one cannot draw a crude distinction between works and faith.

81. *In Epistolam ad Romanos* 1 (Landgraf, 1:21).
82. *In Epistolam ad Romanos* 1 (Landgraf, 1:19).
83. *In Epistolam ad Romanos* 1 (Landgraf, 1:19–20).
84. *In Epistolam ad Romanos* 2 (Landgraf, 1:36–37).
85. *In Epistolam ad Romanos* 4 (Landgraf, 1:55–56).

All Christians are called to do good deeds and live holy lives. It should be remembered that the moral law remains in force even as the ceremonial law has reached its conclusion. The real contrast, therefore, is between exterior works demanded by the law, on the one hand, and on the other hand a deeper interior disposition constituted by faith in Christ. God's judgment will turn on whether one has replaced reliance on exterior dictates of the old legal code with a renewed heart conformed to Christ in love. To believe in Christ is to love Christ, and by loving Christ to direct one's life in his service and so be incorporated into his body as a living member. Thus, for the Commentator, to be "justified freely by grace" (Rom. 3:24) is to be justified through the love of God infused into one's heart (cf. Rom. 5:5).[86]

The Biblical Moral School

The later decades of the twelfth century witnessed the emergence in Paris of what has come to be known as the "biblical moral school." It was spearheaded by Peter Comestor's former student, Peter the Chanter, along with such notable scholars as Stephen Langton and Robert Courson. These men were dedicated to applying the fruit of their scriptural studies to the concrete concerns of medieval society; speculative queries were to pay pragmatic dividends.[87] Thus in his *Verbum Abbreviatum*, Peter the Chanter laid out the formation and duties of the schoolman. His training in Holy Scripture would first consist of careful explication of the biblical text (*lectio*), which formed the solid foundation for the tasks that followed. Next, one attached the walls of scholastic disputation (*disputatio*), since nothing can be fully understood or faithfully preached unless it has first been mashed up in the teeth of disputation. These two activities serve the final, indeed the greatest, task of preaching (*praedicatio*), which constitutes the roof that protects the faithful against the winds of vice.[88]

Yet Peter the Chanter found that all three components were in dire need of reform within the schools of his day. The exposition of Scripture was being overwhelmed, he complained, by a torrent of prolixity. Saints of old such as Jerome had explicated Scripture by means of the biblical text itself, but present masters were lost in a sea of useless commentary (*superfluitatis glossarum*). We should be clear, however, that Peter was not opposed to biblical commenting

---

86. *In Epistolam ad Romanos* 3 (Landgraf, 1:38–46).
87. See John W. Baldwin, *Masters, Princes, and Merchants: The Social Views of Peter the Chanter and His Circle*, 2 vols. (Princeton: Princeton University Press, 1970); and Beryl Smalley, *The Gospels in the Schools: c. 1100–c. 1280* (London: Hambledon, 1985), 99–118; and Smalley, *Study of the Bible in the Middle Ages*, 196–263.
88. *Verbum Abbreviatum* 1 (CCCM 196:9).

as such, for he not only produced commentaries of his own but also made ready use of the *Glossa Ordinaria* in his lectures. Rather, he was disturbed by the profusion of those superfluous explanations and useless remarks that only proved onerous and wearisome to the reader.[89]

As for the task of disputation, Peter the Chanter reminds his fellow scholars that the true knowledge to be gleaned from Scripture consists in the teaching of faith and morals (*doctrina fidei et morum*). Masters and students, therefore, must not waste their time disputing frivolous matters that are only tangentially connected to genuine theology. These men have a duty to bear fruit for the sake of the church and should take care that they do not grow sterile, languishing in pointless and empty questions.[90] The deeper problem, as Peter sees it, is that scholars are forcing heavenly wisdom to suit human predilections, and this has dangerous consequences. Some are narrowing the applicability of general divine precepts, thereby easing the rigorous demands of Holy Scripture through their indulgent interpretations (*carnali expositione*).[91]

Exegesis, for Peter the Chanter, proved to be inseparable from personal sanctity, since pious exposition must bear fruit in the holy life (*sanctitas vitae*) of the preacher himself. In fact, he goes so far as to say that preaching will be futile if the preacher is not a living example of holiness: "He who does not burn with sanctity will never set others ablaze." Thus according to Peter, those who take up the word of God—whether in reading, disputing, or preaching—without first securing a foundation in sanctity are like the men of Sodom hopelessly banging on Lot's door (Gen. 19:9–11).[92]

Also at Paris was the English master of theology Stephen Langton, who went on to become archbishop of Canterbury. His commentaries as we have them appear to have been the notes from his lectures given at the Paris school. In addition to Langton's forays into textual criticism, engagement with patristic sources, and the answering of scholastic *quaestiones*, there seems to be a clear connection between his biblical commentaries and his preaching activities. Smalley observes that as Langton explored the spiritual meaning of the text, one finds within the manuscripts marginal notes designating appropriate sermon material for specific occasions, such as the feast of the ascension and the like. As an exegete, Langton formally recognized four senses of Scripture, but for all intents and purposes he followed Hugh of St. Victor's three-sense model, thereby folding the anagogical into the allegorical and moral senses. Langton's standard modus operandi was to first explain the literal sense, before

89. *Verbum Abbreviatum* 2 (CCCM 196:9–11).
90. *Verbum Abbreviatum* 3 (CCCM 196:15–16).
91. *Verbum Abbreviatum* 4 (CCCM 196:27).
92. *Verbum Abbreviatum* 6 (CCCM 196:34–39).

moving on to the allegorical, and concluding with the moral sense. Interestingly, though, Langton would also speak of a "moral-literal sense" (*moralitas iuxta litteram*), namely, some useful moral advice that can be gleaned from the literal sense of the biblical text. Langton was also willing to include christological prophecies within the literal sense of the Old Testament, hence not relegating them to the level of allegory. When, for instance, Numbers 24:17 reads, "A star shall arise from Jacob," Langton declares this to be a "clear prophecy regarding Christ" (*aperta prophetia de Christo*) and therefore dismisses the need to search for some other literal sense (*alium sensum litteralem*) of this prophecy. Christ is himself the star. Langton does concede, however, that the prophecy was literally fulfilled under David (*ad litteram*) while mystically (*mistice*) through Christ, but all of this still belongs to Langton's treatment of the letter of the text. The next section is devoted to spiritual exposition and presents allegorical readings along the lines that the star signifies Christ's divine nature or even the Virgin Mary.[93]

Perhaps the sort of fluidity, or even ambiguity, that one finds in Langton's engagement with the various senses of Scripture should not surprise us, for as Gilbert Dahan has stated, Langton never composed a work specifically devoted to exegetical method, although he does present methodological considerations within his many prologues written for various biblical books. Langton stood at a pivotal moment between the age of the cathedral schools and the universities, as the prologues of the former structured around categories of *accessus ad auctores* began to yield to the thematic prologues of the latter. Langton, moreover, seemed to be aware of his own place within a larger and ongoing exegetical tradition. He employed procedures that had been pioneered by his predecessors, even as he applied them in a very systematic way and with great attention to detail. In his prologues we find Langton utilizing such central terms as *utilitas*, *materia*, and *intentio*. The categories of *materia* and *intentio* could then be divided into the intrinsic and extrinsic. Hence the *materia extrinseca* of the book of Numbers can refer to the number of the sons of Israel coming into the promised land, while its *materia intrinseca* is christological, in the case of Joshua, referring to Christ and his deeds. There may also be an anagogical reading of the intrinsic subject matter such that this passage signifies our entrance into the heavenly fatherland. Along similar lines, then, *intentio extrinseca* recalls God's generosity and the ingratitude of the Israelites, whereas the *intentio intrinseca* is to exhort us to progress along the stages of virtue so that we might finally see God. Or again, as Langton

93. Beryl Smalley, "Stephen Langton and the Four Senses of Scripture," *Speculum* 6 (1931): 60–76. See here Smalley's transcriptions of MS Trinity, Oxford, fol. 241v.

states, "The exterior intention is to describe the deeds of Joshua, whereas the interior intention concerns Christ and his deeds [*Intentio exterior: describere facta Iosue. Interior: Christus et eius facta*]." Thus, while certainly acknowledging the importance of the literal sense, Langton's exegesis was marked by the letter-spirit dichotomy running through both Testaments of Scripture. Ultimately, for Langton, all biblical exegesis was intended to serve the larger goal of effective preaching; it belonged to what Dahan aptly calls Langton's "pastoral program."[94]

In the next chapter (chap. 7) we will have the opportunity, when discussing magisterial inaugural sermons (*principia*), to examine Langton's reading of the ten plagues visited on the Egyptians in the book of Exodus. Here, though, we can take a look at the prologue to his moral commentary on the Pentateuch, where Langton addresses the discussion of the tabernacle and its ten curtains in Exodus 25–26. As the tabernacle symbolizes the church militant, so one set of its five curtains is made up of the five books of Moses literally understood (*litteraliter intellecti*), which protect the church from the enticements of the vices and decorate her with virtues, as well as providing defense against the intemperance of malign spirits. The different colors assigned to the curtains by the Lord signify the four ways of reading (*modus legendi*) Scripture: historically, allegorically, tropologically, and anagogically. Langton's descriptions of the four senses are standard fare, and he even invokes the traditional Jerusalem example first offered by John Cassian. Langton then declares that the other set of five curtains refers to the five books of Moses understood spiritually (*spiritualiter*). And so, as he explains, these curtains were joined to one another by loops, because through the promises of the Old Testament and the promises of the New the spiritual understanding is conjoined with the literal.[95]

Langton looks to the table in the tabernacle on which the twelve loaves of the bread of presentation were placed (Exod. 25:23–30) in order to discuss the four senses of Scripture. As we mentioned, the tabernacle is a symbol of the church militant, the gathering of the faithful living under the articles of faith and fighting mightily against the devil. Just as Moses had built the tabernacle, so the church militant is constructed in this present life through faith, erected by hope, and joined together by charity and the gifts of the Holy Spirit. The table within the tabernacle is Holy Scripture within the church, having twelve loaves that indicate the catholic teaching of the twelve apostles

---

94. Gilbert Dahan, "Les commentaires bibliques D'Étienne Langton: Exégèse et herméneutique," in *Étienne Langton: Prédicateur, bibliste, théologien*, ed. Bataillon et al., 201–39.

95. MS Paris, BnF lat. 355, fol. 1r-v as transcribed by Dahan in "Les commentaires bibliques D'Étienne Langton," 237–39.

and the faith of the Holy Trinity preached throughout the four regions of the earth. They are called, moreover, loaves of presentation because the word of salvation should always be set forth. As for the construction of the table itself, with its four feet, these are the four divine rules of Scripture: history, allegory, tropology, and anagogy. History, Langton says, is when things that have been said or done (*res dicta et gesta*) are then plainly narrated. It is a literal account (*ad litteram*): in this case, the liberation of the Israelites from Egypt and the building of the tabernacle in the desert. Allegory is when some other thing, by word or deed, is signified with regard to Christ and the church. Thus the liberation of the people from Egypt through the blood of the lamb signifies the liberation of the church from the power of darkness through Christ's passion. Tropology is moral discourse (*moralis locutio*), when morals that should be formed within ourselves are either openly (*aperte*) or figuratively (*figurate*) shown. Thus in 1 John 3:18 it is displayed openly, "Little children, let us love, not in word or speech, but in truth or action," while in Ecclesiastes 9:8, it is figurative: "Let your garments always be white," that is, let your body be chaste. And anagogy pertains to discourse that leads to things above, namely, heavenly heights. Notice, then, that the eternal reward and the life to come in heaven can be spoken of openly in the gospel, "Blessed are the pure in heart for they shall see God" (Matt. 5:8), or figuratively in the Apocalypse, "To the one who conquers I will give the hidden manna" (Rev. 2:17), which speaks to eternal life. As Langton concludes his exposition of the four rules, he pays a fitting tribute to his mentor, Peter Comestor. He declares that it was the first rule, history, that "the master of venerated memory" had worked through, as though laying a foundation or providing milk for infants when they were being introduced to the study of theology (*in facultatem theologicam*).[96] The twelfth-century Paris cathedral schoolmasters, no less than their successors in the universities of the thirteenth century, never lost sight of the foundational nature of the literal-historical sense for all subsequent biblical exegesis. They recognized, as we have seen, that only by addressing with the utmost seriousness the acts of God in history among the people of Israel could the prophecies, types, and figures find their lasting meaning. Only then could one ever fully appreciate the significance of God's own entrance into history in the person of Jesus Christ.

96. See the *Prologus generalitatum magistri Stephani de Longatonia*, transcribed by Riccardo Quinto, "Stefano Langton e i quattro sensi della scrittura," *Medioevo* 15 (1989): 67–109; for the text, see 103–9.

7

Exegesis in the Universities of the Later Middle Ages

As we enter into the thirteenth and fourteenth centuries, we leave behind the monasteries and cathedral schools for the universities, chiefly Paris but also Oxford. It was to these newly formed institutions that the theological and exegetical weight had shifted. Universities were a corporation, that is, a union of masters with a set of rights and privileges that one would expect of any medieval guild. This body of masters determined the curriculum and the requirements for advancement within the faculties of arts, theology, and law. Our specific concern is with the theology faculty, and more specifically the means by which a student might attain to the rank of master of the sacred page (*magister sacrae paginae*). There were many levels through which a prospective candidate for this illustrious position would have to pass, all the while engaging in formal disputations and the presentation of lectures commending the subject matter of his studies. Finally, upon completion of the curriculum, a master of theology would have to prove his proficiency in biblical exegesis to the satisfaction of the reigning masters at the university.

First, on the way to promotion to master of the sacred page, both the mendicant friars and the secular clergy had to lecture on Scripture as bachelors of theology. This was a rapid reading that did not treat doctrinal questions but stuck to basic grammatical and textual issues. Their job was to explain the literal sense of the text and to clear up the ambiguities and anomalies, making use of the Gloss along the way. The bachelor was not to venture into the mystical senses of the text, which were reserved for the masters of theology.

Mendicant lecturers at this stage were known as *biblici*, while seculars were referred to as *cursores*. The former could lecture on whatever biblical book they chose, whereas the latter lectured on one Old Testament book for a year and then one book from the New Testament the next year.[1]

These biblical lectures formed the final stage of preparation at Oxford, but at Paris the bachelors would then lecture on Peter Lombard's *Sentences*. When all the stages were complete, these men were now ready to incept formally as masters of theology. The inception ceremony itself took place in three stages: vesperies, the *aula*, and finally the resumption.[2] In the bishop's hall (*aula*) the incepting master received his license to read and dispute theology and to teach in the sacred theology faculty anywhere in the world. The first stage, the vesperies, was a disputation that occurred the night before the inception ceremony. The actual inception ceremony the next day took place in the *aula*, and at this time the master delivered his *principium*. This was a formal commendation of Holy Scripture, examples of which we will soon consider. There then followed some more disputations. Finally, at the resumption, the master completed the *principium* that he had begun in the *aula* and also completed the full round of disputations. He was now a master of the sacred page and was ready to begin his two-year regency as a master at the university.[3] By 1233 the papacy was granting universities the right to issue an official license to teach throughout Christendom (*licentia ubique docendi*), which was to be formally conferred by the chancellor.[4] As it was, then, the term *magister* appplied to those who had been received into the company of fellow masters, those who had received the *licentia docendi*. They bore this title even if they were not actively teaching, hence the distinction between a reigning and nonreigning master (*magister regens / non regens*).[5]

It was standard practice for the *principium in aula* to begin with a short scriptural passage that formed the theme to which the master would hark back throughout the lecture. He was free to choose the passage from anywhere in

---

1. Nancy Spatz, "Principia: A Study and Edition of Inception Speeches Delivered before the Faculty of Theology at the University of Paris ca. 1180–1286" (PhD diss., Cornell University, 1992), 25–29; and Palémon Glorieux, "L'enseignement au moyen âge: Techniques et méthodes en usage à la faculté de thélogie de Paris, au XIIIᵉ siècle," *Archives d'histoire doctrinale et littéraire du moyen âge* 35 (1968): 108–19.

2. Spatz, *Principia*, 29–34; See also Thomas Prügl, "Medieval Biblical *Principia* as Reflections on the Nature of Theology," in *What Is "Theology" in the Middle Ages? Religious Cultures of Europe (11th–15th Centuries) as Reflected in Their Self-Understanding*, ed. Mikołaj Olszewski (Münster: Aschendorff, 2007), 253–75.

3. Spatz, *Principia*, 39–48.

4. Mariken Teeuwen, *The Vocabulary of Intellectual Life in the Middle Ages* (Turnhout: Brepols, 2003), 88–91.

5. Ibid., 95–97.

Scripture, although Wisdom texts and Psalms were the most popular since they allowed for a simple transition into the study of Scripture as the pursuit of wisdom. Some masters chose texts such as Revelation 10:10–11, "I took the book from the hand of the angel," which naturally ties in with the ceremony itself in praise of Scripture. While Scripture certainly formed the bulk of the references and was the chief authoritative text, the masters also invoked pagan authors, most frequently Aristotle. Moreover, the newly incepting masters emphasized the personal qualities necessary for the study of theology and considered the nature of theology itself in comparison to other disciplines. Having thus commended Scripture in the *aula*, the masters proceeded to divide and classify the books of Scripture in their concluding resumption on the following day.[6]

Stephen Langton

Although the *principium* was a staple of the late medieval university, it actually had its roots in the cathedral schools of the later twelfth century, and so we will begin with a look back at a man we considered in the previous chapter. In 1180 Stephen Langton delivered his *principium* upon ascension to the magisterial chair (*cathedra magistralis*) at Paris. It was an occasion for Langton to outline the proper disposition of the master, this man who would assume responsibility for the theological formation of the students under his care. As we find below, Langton's goal was to foster humility, devotion, and a sense of sacred mission among men who might too easily be led astray by the temptations of power and entitlement that their prestigious positions afforded them. Langton took as his principal text the Exodus account of the ten plagues and subsequent flight from Egypt (Exod. 7–13). For each plague, Langton found the moral sense of the text beneath the letter; we can survey them briefly. The first plague, the flowing water changed into blood, teaches that in this present world the corruption of a fleshly life abounds in place of the consolation of good deeds. As for the frogs, they are the vain boastings of this age; the river poured them forth as worldly excess produces and fosters words of vanity. The sting of the gnat is the sharp prick of hurtful speech; the flies are a preoccupation with worldly anxiety or a tormenting conscience. The death of cattle signifies people Jude regarded as irrational animals corrupted by what they do not understand (Jude 10). The swollen boils mark the inflation of pride, not having been bandaged by the commandments or cured

6. Spatz, *Principia*, 130–55.

by the medicine of repentance or washed with the oil of divine mercy. The onrush of hail is the secular power that oppresses the poor, while the feeding locust is the sort of soothing flattery that must have marked court life. And here is a call to action, for the darkness that follows the locusts speaks to those who touch only gently upon another's sin and so blind that very sinner with their flattery. Finally, the death of the firstborn refers to the powerful in Egypt, while the children of Israel flee. They flee from a world that openly mounts up hardship and for this reason must not be loved.[7]

Having issued this moral admonition, Langton turns his attention directly to Scripture. The manna that the Israelites find in the desert is Holy Scripture; its sweetness is the kindness of divine mercy. God looked on the human race through the eyes of kindness, Langton says, when he illuminated the darkness of our mortality with the brightness of heavenly Scripture: "Your word is a lamp to my feet. Your commandment is full of light" (Ps. 118:105 Vulg. [119:105 Eng.]). If the manna is Scripture, then it is the master's duty to break it open. Or, more precisely, as the manna is ground down by a pestle, so Scripture is broken into small pieces by the pestle of exposition until its meaning is revealed. Its small flakes represent Scripture's subtlety, which thus requires magisterial acumen to unfold. Simple readers, according to Langton, think that Scripture can be easily understood, even as experts discover within Scripture an inexhaustible supply of subtle discourse. From here we come to ordering of the curriculum, the schedule of classes. As manna is gathered in the morning, so Scripture is also studied at that time, when the powers of intellectual discernment are still fresh. This was the case, in fact, as the best hours of the day (7:00–9:00 in the morning) were reserved for the magisterial exposition of the sacred page.[8]

All such expertise must pay dividends in the sort of holy life that Langton has sketched above. "Those who gathered" (Exod. 16:18) speaks to the fact that the more Scripture you can gather up, the more likely you are to understand it, and the more that you have, the more you will display in your deeds. We gather manna correctly, Langton advises his fellows, when we intend to acquire the food of Scripture in order to refresh our inner self (*homo interior*) with its nourishment. Thus manna melted by the sun signifies the sun of righteousness, and the fire that hardened it is the grace of the Holy Spirit. Grace, Langton observes, sometimes melts because, by the heavenly distribution of grace, our understanding of Holy Scripture can become clear

---

7. *Epistola Magistri Stephani de .x. plagis* 1–11, in *Selected Sermons of Stephen Langton*, ed. Phyllis B. Roberts (Toronto: Pontifical Institute of Mediaeval Studies, 1980), 17–23.

8. *Epistola Magistri Stephani de .x. plagis* 12–16 (Roberts, 23–25).

and open. Yet it can also harden when, unmindful of our weakness, we become proud of our own intellectual acumen. Succinctly outlining a threefold method for the biblical exegete, Langton finds that Scripture is ground down with the millstone of reading, crushed with the pestle of disputation, and then finally boiled in the pot of the mind through persistent meditation (*assidua meditatione*).[9]

Just as Langton offered a moral reading of the Exodus plagues, he now presents his audience with a clear agenda as he sets forth the basic principles necessary for both the learning and the teaching of Holy Scripture. The student will need a pure life, simple heart, attentive mind, humble disposition, and gentle spirit: a pure life, because wisdom will not enter a malevolent soul or dwell in a body overcome by sin; a simple heart, because wisdom, which is God himself, cannot be received unless one ceases to concern oneself with fleshly thoughts; an attentive mind, since Scripture must be consumed with a spiritual hunger (cf. Rev. 10:9); a humble disposition, as Christ said, "I praise you, Father, for you have hidden these things from the wise" (Matt. 11:25); and finally, the gentle spirit of those endowed with the grace of humility in the abundant pastures of Holy Scripture (cf. Isa. 30:23).[10]

As for the teacher, he will have to exhibit knowledge, a good life, humility, and gentleness. In fact, Langton says, virtually every syllable of Holy Scripture testifies that its teachers must lead meritorious lives. Like the prophet Ezekiel, who saw the glory of the Lord (Ezek. 2:1–2 Vulg. [1:28b–2:2 Eng.]), so is the man who has contemplated the secret mysteries of Scripture. Ezekiel saw this glory and then fell on his face, subjecting himself to the yoke of humility after gazing on the wondrous things of God. Humility is an essential quality for those who would set forth the word of the Lord; it befits a good life (James 3:13). We may well ask, "Who among you, inasmuch as he is wise through life's training, would dare to assume the teaching office for himself? Let him first learn good deeds before venturing to teach others; let him do this with a gentle spirit lest he end up despising others on account of his own wisdom and virtuous acts (cf. 1 Pet. 3:15–16)." Langton concludes his address on a personal note: "And yet what can I say, since I possess neither excellent life, nor outstanding knowledge, even as I ascend the magisterial chair? Yet I set my sights on the inexhaustible mercy of divine goodness rather than mere human presumption, and now turn my tongue to the service of my Redeemer and commit my purpose and myself to his grace."[11]

9. *Epistola Magistri Stephani de .x. plagis* 17–19 (Roberts, 25–28).
10. *Epistola Magistri Stephani de .x. plagis* 20–25 (Roberts, 28–31).
11. *Epistola Magistri Stephani de .x. plagis* 26–30 (Roberts, 31–34).

Thomas de Chobham

Some decades after Langton, around 1220 at Paris, Thomas de Chobham chose for the theme of his magisterial inception a passage from Genesis: "And when Jacob awoke from his sleep, he said: Indeed the Lord is in this place, and I knew it not. And trembling he said: How terrible is this place; this is no other but the house of God and the gate of heaven" (Gen. 28:16–17). Thomas likened himself to Jacob, having been roused from his slumbers and exhorted to wakefulness. Now he must be instructed even as he is awed by reverence for the magisterial role that he has assumed; he must be led to the gates and taken into the house of God. As Jeremiah saw a "rod watching" (Jer. 1:11–12), Thomas is like a body awakened from sleep by the rod of his teacher, and this rod is Holy Scripture. In fact, Thomas says, this may be a rod made from the almond tree, the husk of which is bitter while its fruit is sweet, thereby appealing to the gloss on this passage (*Unde ibi glosa . . .*), which speaks of the bitter roots of the text that will nevertheless yield sweet fruit. Let the teacher (*doctor*) therefore be aroused by the rod of castigation, lest he feel the blows of the rod of punishment (cf. Prov. 23:13–14). Indeed, Thomas says, one who reads the sacred page must be willing to submit himself to the magisterial rod. Then, appealing to the Gospel of Mark, Thomas compares the master (*magister*) to a doorkeeper (*ianitor*): "Even as a man who, going into a far country, left his house, and gave authority to his servants over every work, and commanded the doorkeeper to watch" (Mark 13:34). It is the teacher of Holy Scripture (*sacrae scripturae doctor*) who is called upon to teach how it is that the catholic is to be admitted and the heretic excluded from the corridor, the hall, and the bedchamber. Many will knock on the door, such that he must remain vigilant as he examines the multitude who seek entry.[12] Thus here at the outset of the thirteenth century, we find Thomas emphasizing the vital role that university theologians will come to play in the determination of catholic doctrine and the concomitant judgment of heresy. The submission of suspect propositions to the evaluation of the masters was commonplace throughout the Middle Ages and into the Reformation era.

As Thomas then addresses the text, "Now there was no smith to be found in all the land of Israel, for the Philistines had taken this precaution, lest the Hebrews should make them swords or spears" (1 Sam. 13:19), he once more appeals to the *Glossa Ordinaria* (*Et dicit ibi glosa . . .*), which was itself firmly entrenched in the university curriculum by this time. Here the Gloss reports

---

12. Sermon VIII in *Thomas de Chobham Sermones*, ed. Franco Morenzoni, CCCM 82a (Turnhout: Brepols, 1993), 88–90. Cf. *Biblia Sacra cum Glossa Ordinaria*, 6 vols. (Venice, 1603), 4:586.

that pagans prohibited Christians from studying the liberal arts, and heretics convinced princes that defenders of the church should be exiled so that the people would be left destitute and thereby easily deceived. Thomas takes this opportunity to compare the respective tasks of the different faculties. Teachers of the liberal arts (*doctores liberalium artium*) fashion for us weapons constructed from our own eloquence, Thomas says, whereas teachers of the sacred page (*doctores sacrae paginae*) are like goldsmiths constructing golden vessels and ornaments of wisdom. In fact, Thomas opines, if such wisdom had reigned in the land of the Albigensians (a heretical sect in southern France), it would not now be controlled by a multitude of infidels, thus fulfilling the words, "When prophecy shall fail, the people shall be scattered abroad" (Prov. 29:18). Here again Thomas emphasizes the responsibility of the theologian in combating heresy and thus his obligation to keep his affections rightly ordered. The theologian will have to keep at bay any desire for vain glory and perverse teachings. Citing a legend drawn from the *Passion of Saints Peter and Paul*, Thomas recounts how Simon Magus had attempted to fly by means of artificial wings, only to crash to the ground. Such wings might be compared to the sophistical questions that some rush to construct before they have acquired the natural wings of books and a foundation in the arts. They wish to fly to the cathedral but end up falling to earth. Evoking here the account of the Philistine god Dagon, who collapsed before the ark of the Lord (1 Sam. 5:1–4), Thomas compares Dagon to the ignorant teacher, or ecclesiastical official, who collapses like a mute statue when placed before the ark, that is, Holy Scripture. Following Jerome's etymology, he explains that Dagon means "fish of sadness." Those who go fishing at the behest of the devil draw up only the evil fish that are not caught in the nets of Peter, the nets that are the precepts of Holy Scripture. So it is, then, that the theologian must be willing to speak truth to power, even correct his ecclesiastical superiors, if he is to properly carry out his job. After all, Thomas writes, John the Baptist was not afraid to confront Herod, telling him that it was unlawful to have the wife of his brother (Mark 6:18). Nor then can the theologian afford to be timid. He must be willing to call to account the wicked doctor or prelate; he must tell him that it is not lawful to adulterate the word and bride of the Father.[13] What Thomas enunciates here also became a staple of magisterial identity: the right of the master, precisely as *"magister sacrae paginae,"* and thus a licensed expert in Holy Scripture, to weigh in on matters of faith and morals when the powers that be have gone astray. Having just incepted as a master himself, Thomas is assuring his colleagues that he is indeed up to the task.

13. Sermon VIII (CCCM 82a:92–93). Cf. *Biblia Sacra cum Glossa Ordinaria*, 2:394.

Robert Grosseteste

The Englishman Robert Grosseteste might also be counted as part of the so-called biblical moral school that emerged from the cathedral school of Paris. Grosseteste returned to his native England, however, where he was to serve as a beloved teacher to the newly arrived Franciscans before being installed as bishop of Lincoln in 1235. It was at Oxford around 1230 that he delivered his inception sermon. It appears that, in the wake of the backlash against Aristotelian natural philosophy at Paris, Grosseteste had wanted to commend the study of the *libri naturales* as useful for the study of Scripture. All the while, though, he made it clear that such texts find their value only insofar as they assist in the building up of faith and charity.[14] Grosseteste took as his text a passage from the prophet Ezekiel (2:9–10): "And I looked, and behold, a hand was sent to me, wherein was a book rolled up: and he spread it before me, and it was written within [*intus*] and without [*foris*]." Identifying this book with Holy Scripture, Grosseteste proceeds to extol the superiority of Scripture over all other texts. While other texts are only written outwardly, Scripture contains inner meanings beyond the outer level of the signifying words that express the historical sense. Here are the realities (*res*) signified by the history: allegory, tropology, and anagogy. And yet, despite such mystical depths, we are right to study the miraculous feats of God that Scripture conveys by way of created things, for it is through the discernment of the outward things that we ascend inwardly to knowledge of the truth.[15]

Grosseteste explicitly invokes and builds on Augustine's famous maxim that Scripture teaches all that is useful and condemns all that is harmful.[16] Like Augustine, he makes the case for drawing on the natural science contained in the quadrivium to better understand Scripture's mysteries. And so, again in an Augustinian vein, Grosseteste appeals to the fundamental goodness, and thus usefulness, of God's created order. Knowledge of creation in its inception and its workings can serve to promote the light of faith and fervor of love. There is no question of the natural sciences excelling Scripture, which is a thoroughly sufficient book that contains all the truth to be found in the other sciences. We just need to explicate Scripture faithfully, so as to instruct in matters of faith and to build up charity. For in fact, Grosseteste says, every word of Scripture intends to convey these virtues.[17]

14. The text has been edited by James Ginther, "Natural Philosophy and Theology at Oxford in the Early Thirteenth Century: An Editon and Study of Robert Grosseteste's Inception Sermon (*Dictum*) 19," *Medieval Sermon Studies* 44 (2000): 108–34.

15. Ibid., 125–26.

16. *De doctrina christiana* 2.42.63 (CCSL 32:76–77).

17. Ginther, "Natural Philosophy and Theology at Oxford in the Early Thirteenth Century," 127–29.

Throughout his work Grosseteste makes a great deal of the two aspects of the human soul that he calls the *aspectus* and the *affectus*. Basically, by these terms Grosseteste is identifying the intellect and the will. He compares these two faculties to the exterior and interior of the book of Holy Scripture, which he had sketched above. The *aspectus* can be considered exterior because nothing that passes into the interior *affectus* has not first been located in the *aspectus*. After all, nothing is loved (by the will) unless it is first known (by the intellect). What through cognition is described in the *aspectus* is like something depicted outwardly in the book, but the love of the knower is then configured in the *affectus* and thus inwardly written. The knowledge of Holy Scripture, according to Grosseteste, must be inscribed on the human mind, since it is through the medium of the outer *aspectus* that the inner *affectus* is shaped. As we see, meditation on Scripture, when approached in this vein, is a salvific act, for when inscribed on the human heart, Scripture conforms man to God (*conformat hominem Deo*), restoring the honor that had been lost in the fall back to its deiform state (*deiformem*) and thereby initiating the re-formation (*reformatio*) of the image of the creator within the creature. And this internal imprinting will, in turn, burst forth through the light of works into the open, as one's exterior works function as a sign, as though an outward text, signifying the inner man. As a result, the light of good works will then fully reilluminate the *aspectus* more expressly and inscribe more formatively what had first been inscribed. So begins a circular process, an inner turning, that can be fittingly compared to a wheel.[18] By vivifying the spirit, life is made that much more alive. Only Holy Scripture, among all writings, is able to accomplish this profound ordering of human affections; no other text so perfectly configures the *affectus* to the highest beauty. In fact, merely human texts do not illuminate the *aspectus* but actually darken it. They do not form the *affectus* but rather deform it. Scripture alone, inscribed in the human mind, elevates one all the way to God and so makes one alive to God in unity of spirit.[19]

Holy Scripture is obviously no ordinary book; this book that is written inwardly and outwardly is nothing less than the Word Himself and the Wisdom of the Father. What was sent forth from his hand, Grosseteste asks, except the Word through whom all things were made? Within the eternal Word, through whom all things were made, subsist the eternal principles (*rationes eternae*) of all things that have been made. This book remains rolled up (*involvitur*) so long as the eternal principles remain hidden in the secret Word of the Father.

18. Cf. Ezek. 1:15–21; Gregory, *Homiliae in Hiezechihelem Prophetam* 1.6.15 (CCSL 142:75).
19. Ginther, "Natural Philosophy and Theology at Oxford in the Early Thirteenth Century," 130–31.

This same book is then unfolded (*expanditur*) when the eternal reasons are recognized in the created order, which is patterned after them. Yet the rolled-up book can also be said to be unfurled when the Word, who was with God from the beginning, was manifested to the world in the incarnation. In the hand was sent the book of Holy Scripture, according to Grosseteste, for in the incarnate Word is found the consummation of the totality of Scripture. The book that was rolled up under the shadow of figures in the Old Testament is now unfurled in the refulgent light of the New, folded up in all its allegorical discourse (*in omnibus verbis allegoricis*) to be later unfurled in plain speech (*in verbis nudis*). Here in this unique book we see the harmonization of contraries (*concorditer contraria*) as it is simultaneously rolled up and unfurled, signifying and manifest, inner and outer. Scripture in all its multifarious glory will speak to man at every level of spiritual development: it is the milk of babes, bread for the mature, the restoration of vision to the blind, and a superfusion of light to those who already see.[20]

The Mendicant and Secular Masters

Although we will be looking at the work of some very important secular masters in this chapter, it will be the exegetes of the mendicant orders who must claim the bulk of our attention. The newly created orders of mendicant friars began to arrive at Paris and Oxford within a decade of their formation, first the Franciscans and Dominicans, then in time the Carmelites and Augustinians. The mendicants had a system of education all their own, however, with convents and provincial schools for the training of their biblical students. Even though they had a studium at Paris, they were not, strictly speaking, part of the university itself. Only the few, the elite within the order, actually attained their doctorate in theology at Paris. Given the limited number of magisterial chairs available to the mendicants at the universities in the thirteenth century, they tended to limit the regency of their masters to one or two years, thereby opening up the position to the next incepting master. From the middle of the thirteenth century the mendicants produced biblical commentaries at a prolific rate, even as their secular counterparts lagged behind. This is not to say that secular theologians abandoned the Bible; they still lectured on Scripture, and it informed all of their preaching and speculative theology. Nevertheless, it was among the friars that some of the greatest strides in biblical scholarship were made.[21]

20. Ibid., 132–34.
21. William J. Courtenay, "The Bible in Medieval Universities," in *The New Cambridge History of the Bible*, 4 vols. (Cambridge: Cambridge University Press, 2013), 2:555–78; and

The Dominican exegete Hugh of St. Cher and his team of friars at the St. Jacques Priory in Paris managed to produce a complete commentary on the Bible by 1236, known as the *Postillae in universa Biblia secundum quadruplicem sensum*. Actually, the use of the term *postilla* to refer to a biblical commentary seems to have come into fashion following the publication of this work.[22] It is clear that Hugh used the *Glossa Ordinaria* as the base text on which he elaborated; sometimes he simply quotes one of the fathers by way of the Gloss, while at other times the Gloss itself is subject to exposition. Hugh also employs the *Historia scholastica* of Peter Comestor and draws on Peter the Chanter, Stephen Langton, and Andrew of St. Victor, among others, thereby taking advantage of the most recent biblical work produced in the Paris schools. While it is true that Hugh remained indebted to the biblical moral school, his postil was constructed with its own grand purpose in mind, namely, to assist the preaching mission of the newly founded Dominican order.[23] Hugh's postil was a boon to the members of his order, not only in terms of classroom instruction in the Scriptures but even more for their preaching duties. Dominican preachers could turn to a given passage and find authoritative exegesis to provide ballast for their sermons. Perhaps the most useful feature was the inclusion of biblical distinctions, as Hugh's team laid out schemata tracing the various figurative meanings attached to frequently occurring words—such as "cup," "son," and "crown"—as they appeared across the Old and New Testaments.[24] "Cup," for instance, might symbolize learning, blessing, suffering, labor, judiciary power, or earthly pleasure, in addition to its plain material use. For each referent, a suitable scriptural example was provided. Thus suffering is exemplified by Matthew 26:42, "Father, if it could be so, let this cup pass from me"; judiciary power by Psalm 74:9 Vulg. (75:8 Eng.), "Because the cup is in the hand of the Lord"; and so on. Hugh also traces the many ways in which a given word, when employed figuratively, might apply to one referent. Psalm 17:15 Vulg. (18:14 Eng.) states, "[The Lord] sent forth his arrows." Here, Hugh says, "arrows" might be taken to mean "preachers," since the preacher ought to embody many features of the arrow: he should be light through contempt for temporal things, slender through

---

Bert Roest, "Mendicant School Exegesis," in *The Practice of the Bible in the Middle Ages*, ed. Susan Boynton and Diane Reilly (New York: Columbia University Press, 2011), 179–204.

22. Teeuwen, *Vocabulary of Intellectual Life in the Middle Ages*, 307–8.

23. See the collection of essays in *Hugues de Saint-Cher: Bibliste et théologien*, ed. Louis-Jacques Bataillon, Gilbert Dahan, and Pierre-Marie Gy (Turnhout: Brepols, 2004). See also Beryl Smalley, *The Gospels in the Schools c. 1100–c. 1280* (London: Hambledon, 1985), 125–43.

24. Already, in the preceding generation, the scholars Peter of Capua and Alan of Lille had produced works that alphabetically organized such biblical distinctions.

chastisement of the flesh, capable of putting wolves and thus demons to flight, and feathered with virtues and also curved at the head and thus humble.[25] It should be recognized, moreover, that Hugh's influence was not confined to the Order of Preachers. Franciscan theologians such as Alexander of Hales, John of La Rochelle, and St. Bonaventure all utilized Hugh's postil to one degree or another when composing their own sermons and commentaries.

Thomas Aquinas

When the Dominican friar Thomas Aquinas delivered the *aula* portion of his magisterial inception lecture at Paris in 1256, he took up the words of the psalmist, "You water the hills from your upper rooms; the earth shall be filled with your works" (Ps. 103:13 Vulg. [104:13 Eng.]).[26] Thomas begins by echoing Pseudo-Dionysius's *Ecclesiastical Hierarchy* as he declares, "The King and Lord of Heaven has established his law from all eternity, such that the gifts of his providence flow down through stages to the lowest reaches of creation." This law, Thomas says, concerns not only spiritual things but the corporeal as well. Thus by this psalm the Lord proposed that the afore-mentioned law in the communication of spiritual wisdom might be observed under the metaphor (*sub metaphora*) of corporeal things, hence the "watering of the hills." Fittingly for an inaugural magisterial sermon, Thomas likens the fructification of the land through the rains to the pouring out of divine wisdom on the minds of teachers, who, Thomas informs us, are signified by these hills. By their ministry the light of divine wisdom will then reach the minds of those who attend their lectures and hear their sermons. Thomas proceeds to treat four components of this effusion of divine wisdom: the loftiness of spiritual teaching, the dignity of its teachers, the condition of its hearers, and the order of its communication.[27]

We will just sketch his discussion, which is itself rather brief. Spiritual teaching (*spiritualis doctrina*) is lofty, due first to its celestial origin but also to the subtlety of its subject matter and the sublimity of its final cause, namely, eternal life. That the hills of the psalm signify its teachers speaks to their own dignity. Indeed, the very loftiness of this sacred teaching requires that

25. M. Michele Mulchahey, *"First the Bow Is Bent in Study . . .": Dominican Education before 1350* (Toronto: Pontifical Institute of Mediaeval Studies, 1998), 480–526.

26. *De commendatione et partitione sacrae scripturae*, in *Opuscula Theologica*, ed. R. Verardo, 2 vols. (Turin and Rome: Marietti, 1954), 1:441–43. For more on the dating and circumstances of Thomas's inception, see Jean-Pierre Torrell, *Saint Thomas Aquinas*, trans. Robert Royal, 2 vols. (Washington, DC: Catholic University of America Press, 1996), 1:50–53.

27. *De commendatione et partitione sacrae scripturae* (Verardo, 1:441).

the teachers themselves be elevated as well, rising above the earth into the heavens. And just as the hills receive the splendor of the sun's rays, so too are the minds of the teachers illuminated by the rays of divine wisdom. And then just as mountains are strong enough to provide a defense against enemies, so the church's teachers will defend the faith against error. Teachers of sacred Scripture, Thomas says, have an obligation to attain to such heights through esteemed conduct so that they may prove effective preachers. What of their audience? Those listening to the teachers are like the earth that is watered by the rains from above; they are lowly and thus humble, for humility is required of anyone who would be taught and then bear the fruit of their sacred lessons. Finally, with respect to the order, Thomas points out that the minds of the teachers cannot possibly contain the whole of divine wisdom. Thus they should be aware of their own limitations and not overwhelm the simpler members of their audience. Teachers should remember, moreover, that this is not their own wisdom but God's; they are merely his ministers, and cognizant of their awesome task, they must not rely on their own wits alone but place their hope in God.[28]

Later in his *resumptio* lecture, Thomas takes as his lead text Baruch 4:1, "This is the book of the commandments of God, and the law that is forever; all those who keep it shall come to life." Appealing then to St. Augustine's *De doctrina christiana* (4.12), the friar points out that Augustine—following Cicero—had said that the key components of erudite eloquence were to teach, to delight, and to persuade. Holy Scripture, Thomas says, fulfills these categories most completely. It teaches firmly through its eternal truth, delights sweetly through its utility, and persuades people efficaciously by means of its authority, which it derives from its divine origin. The truth of Scripture's teaching is secured by the fact that it is immutable and eternal, for as Christ assured the church, "My words will not pass away" (Matt. 24:35). Scripture is, moreover, supremely useful as it disposes one to the life of grace, justice, and glory.[29]

Having commended Scripture as surpassing all other texts, Thomas proceeds to offer a *divisio textus*, or breakdown of its contents into discrete parts. First, he observes that the whole of Scripture is principally divided into two parts: the Old and New Testaments. The Old Testament, in turn, consists of law, which functions as a precept issued by a king; prophets, who are like heralds speaking to the people on behalf of God and thus inducing them to observe the law; and sacred writings, which are inspired by the Holy Spirit and speak, not on behalf of God, but as though in their own right. Thomas states

28. *De commendatione et partitione sacrae scripturae* (Verardo, 1:441–43).
29. *De commendatione et partitione sacrae scripturae* (Verardo, 1:435–36).

that Jerome had posited a fourth category, namely, the apocrypha. Such is the designation when the Catholic Church receives some books whose meaning is not in doubt, even as their authorship cannot be verified. It is not that the authors of these books are themselves unknown, Thomas observes, but that those men were not of notable authority. Hence the strength of these books is based not on the authority of the authors but rather on the reception of the church herself.[30]

Turning then to the New Testament, Thomas finds that it is ordered toward eternal life, not only through precepts but also through the gift of grace. And it too is divided into three parts. First, there is the origin of grace, namely, Christ himself found in the gospels; second, the power of grace in the epistles of Paul (cf. Rom. 1:16–17); and finally, the leading of a virtuous life, which is treated throughout the rest of the New Testament books. It is this last category that speaks to the progress of the church that began in the Acts of the Apostles and continues on to the end, as depicted in the Apocalypse when the bride is wedded to Jesus Christ and participates in the glorious life to which Christ himself leads all members of the church.[31]

Thomas, like his fellow masters, was self-consciously a teacher of Scripture and a defender of catholic truth. Holy Scripture formed the basis of the science of theology for Thomas; it was the supreme authority in the determination of sacred doctrine. In fact, as one reads the opening articles of his *Summa theologiae*, one is struck by his willingness to employ the terms *sacra doctrina* and *sacra scriptura* almost interchangeably. In article 8 of the first question in the *Summa*, Thomas points out that the proper authorities employed by sacred teaching (*sacra doctrina*) are the canonical Scriptures. One argues from the canonical Scriptures of necessity (*ex necessitate*), whereas arguments based on the doctors of the church, valuable as they are, only carry probable force (*probabiliter*). In fact, the Christian faith depends on the revelation made to the apostles and the prophets, which they then wrote down in the canonical books. Here Thomas had recourse to Augustine's statement to Jerome that he honors only the books of the Scriptures that are called canonical, since none of their authors erred when writing them. No other authors, no matter how holy or learned they may be, can attain to that status.[32]

In article 9 of that same question, it is asked whether it is fitting for Scripture to employ metaphor. Thomas therefore has to justify the use of figurative language in a text that formed the foundation of a science, which by

---

30. *De commendatione et partitione sacrae scripturae* (Verardo, 1:436–38).

31. *De commendatione et partitione sacrae scripturae* (Verardo, 1:439).

32. *Summa Theologiae* 1, q. 1, a. 8, ed. P. Caramello, 4 vols. (Rome: Marietti, 1950), 1:7–8. See Augustine, *Epistula* 82.1 (PL 33:277).

definition was supposed to yield certain knowledge. If anything, metaphors and similitudes seem to obscure the truth, not elucidate it. But Holy Scripture itself validates the practice when God said, "I have multiplied visions, and I have used similitudes by the ministry of the prophets" (Hosea 12:10). Indebted to Pseudo-Dionysius's *Celestial Hierarchy*, Thomas proceeds to argue for the fittingness of Scripture's communication of spiritual matters by way of corporeal likenesses. God provides for all as befits their nature, and it is natural for human beings to arrive at intelligible realties by way of sensible things. We need not fear, Thomas says, that the radiance of divine revelation will be destroyed by the sensible figures in which it is enveloped. In fact, the minds of those who receive the revelation will not remain on the level of the figures, but will be elevated beyond them so as to grasp the higher intelligible things they signify.[33] In short order, Thomas makes the case for the continued legitimacy of the spiritual exposition of Scripture and the possibility of multiple senses. Moreover, as Prügl has observed, Thomas's willingness to devote an entire article to metaphorical speech points to his keen awareness of the "linguistic-philosophical" (*sprachphilosophische*) component that is inherent in scriptural interpretation.[34]

It is in article 10, though, that Thomas offers his most famous and influential remarks on scriptural exposition: "The primary signification, by which words signify things, pertains to the first sense, which is the historical or literal sense. Yet that signification by which things are signified by words and again signify other things is called the spiritual sense, which is founded on the literal and presupposes it."[35] This would seem relatively straightforward were it not for the fact that, beyond the inspired human author, there stands the divine author, the Holy Spirit. If the divine author has many meanings in mind—all of which must be true—does that mean there could be more than one literal sense in any given passage of Scripture? After all, Thomas goes on to say, "The literal sense is that which the author intends. Now the author of Holy Scripture is God, who comprehends all things within the divine intellect simultaneously. Thus it is not unfitting, as Augustine says in Book Twelve of his *Confessions*, if in keeping with the literal sense there would be many senses in one letter of Scripture."[36] Given these parameters, Thomas also states in

33. *Summa Theologiae* 1, q. 1, a. 9 (Caramello, 1:8).
34. Thomas Prügl, "Thomas von Aquin: *Summa theologiae* I,1,9–10," in *Handbuch der Bibel-Hermeneutiken: Von Origenes bis zur Gegenwart*, ed. Oda Wischmeyer (Berlin: de Gruyter, 2016), 191–206.
35. *Summa Theologiae* 1, q. 1, a. 10 (Caramello, 1:8–9).
36. *Summa Theologiae* 1, q. 1, a. 10 (Caramello, 1:8–9). See Augustine, *Confessiones* 12.42 (CCSL 27:240–41).

another work: "Even if the expositors adapt some truths to Holy Scripture that the [human] author does not understand, there is no doubt but that the Holy Spirit, who is the principal author of Divine Scripture, did understand. Thus every truth that, without violating the circumstance of the letter, can be adapted to the Divine Scripture is the sense of Scripture."[37] These statements have created some confusion—and indeed some controversy—over whether Thomas believed that Holy Scripture contains multiple literal senses.[38] It may be that Thomas did believe in the plurality of the literal sense, such that the Holy Spirit, as well as the human author, might have intended to convey multiple meanings through the same words. The human author of a given biblical text need not understand all the meanings contained in the letter, but under the inspiration of the Holy Spirit it is possible. Either way, however, the Holy Spirit will have intended all the true readings of the text.[39]

Aristotle's works had been translated into Latin by the early thirteenth century and soon made their way—not without controversy—into the university curriculum. The schoolmen soon recognized that the Philosopher's fundamental structuring of reality according to a set of four causes could also be applied to Scripture. Every substance in the world is composed of matter and form and is directed toward its final end by a system of efficient causes. Each thing has a purpose for which it was created and possesses the means to achieve it; the goal of each thing, therefore, is to maximize its own potentialities, to become most fully itself. So it is that Holy Scripture must also comprise these four causes: material, formal, efficient, and final. Scripture was thus understood to have been written for a reason and provided with its basic structure by the divine author working in tandem with his inspired scribes. We can get a good sense of Thomas's exegetical methodology in the prologue to his commentary to the Psalter, in which he applied this increasingly popular *accessus ad auctores* known as the "Aristotelian Prologue," which identifies the four causes inherent to the different books of Scripture. Moreover, we will see it applied in one way or another by numerous exegetes across the thirteenth and fourteenth centuries.

When commenting on the Psalms, Thomas explains that while all the individual canonical books have their own special subject matter, this book

---

37. *De potentia* 4.1, in *Opera Omnia*, 34 vols. (Paris: Vives, 1871–80), 13:119.

38. For a history of the controversy, see Henri de Lubac, *Exégèse médiévale: Les quatre sens de l'écriture*, 2 vols. (Paris: 1959–64), 2/2:277–85.

39. Mark F. Johnson, "Another Look at the Plurality of the Literal Sense," *Medieval Philosophy and Theology* 2 (1992): 117–41. See also Thomas Prügl, "Thomas Aquinas as Interpreter of Scripture," in *The Theology of Thomas Aquinas*, ed. Rik Van Nieuwenhove and Joseph Wawrykow (Notre Dame, IN: University of Notre Dame Press, 2005), 386–415.

has for its subject the whole of theology. It pertains to all of God's works: creation, rest, governance, reparation, and glorification. In fact, Thomas says, that is why the Psalter is so frequently used in church, because it contains the totality of Scripture. Its universality is further confirmed inasmuch as its subject matter is Christ and his members—thus the principle of the "whole Christ" (*totus Christus*). With regard to the Psalter's mode or form, Thomas begins by noting that there are actually many sorts of form to be found in the Scriptures. There is the narrative one encounters in the historical books; the admonitory, exhorting, and preceptive in the law and prophets; the disputative in Job and also the apostle Paul. Here in the Psalter, however, we have the deprecative or laudative. And yet the adoption of this single mode does not compromise its universality, for whatever in the other books is spoken in the aforementioned modes is here posited by way of praise and prayer. Indeed, the end (*finis*), or final cause, of this book is the prayer that lifts us up to the sacred heights. More precisely, the soul is lifted up to God in wonder, faith, love, and righteousness. And with respect to its authorship, Thomas draws an essential distinction between Holy Scripture and the other sciences. The latter are produced by human reason, while Scripture is the product of divine inspiration, the revelation of the Holy Spirit.[40]

Thomas then sets himself to consider three general questions before proceeding to an examination of the text. First, there is the question of translation, of which he notes there are three. Thomas dutifully recounts the different stages and versions of the Psalms in Latin. There was one version, he says, dating to the apostolic period, but this had become corrupted through scribal error by Jerome's day. So it was that Pope Damasus called on Jerome to correct the Itala version of the Psalter. But because this translation contained discrepancies with the Greek, Jerome—at the request of Paulinus—translated the Greek version into Latin, which Damasus ordered to be sung in France (hence the so-called Gallican Psalter). This text, according to Thomas, agreed with the Greek word for word (*de verbo ad verbum*). Later, however, Sophrinus was disputing with Jews who claimed that the translation from the Greek had introduced material not found in the Hebrew original. Hence Sophrinus asked Jerome to translate from the Hebrew text directly into Latin. And this translation, Thomas says, agreed entirely with the Hebrew. Although this version was not being sung in the churches, many nevertheless possessed copies of it.[41]

Coming to the exposition of the text, Thomas lights upon one of the most crucial aspects of Old Testament hermeneutics: its typological, specifically

40. *Expositio in Psalmis Davidis*, prologue (*Opera Omnia*, 18:228–30).
41. *Expositio in Psalmis Davidis*, prologue (*Opera Omnia*, 18:230).

christological, import. In that vein, he says that with the Psalter, as with the other prophets, one must address an error that had been condemned at the Fifth Ecumenical Synod. To be refuted was the claim made by the Antiochene exegete Theodore of Mopsuestia that in the prophetic books of Scripture there is nothing expressly (*expresse dicitur*) said of Christ, but instead such things have subsequently been adapted to Christ (*adaptaverunt Christo*). For instance, when it is said "They divided my garments" (Ps. 21:18 Vulg. [22:18 Eng.]), this was not about Christ but instead literally (*ad litteram*) about David. Thomas preferred to follow Jerome's advice given in his Ezekiel commentary: when handling prophetic material as we find in the Psalms, we observe the apostle Paul's remark that "all these things happened to them in a figure" (1 Cor. 10:11). Hence there are deeds recounted in the prophetic books that are to be interpreted as figures pointing to Christ and the church. The prophets do indeed speak of events happening in their own day. Yet we need to recognize that they were nevertheless not speaking principally about such events but rather insofar as they were figures of future events. And this takes us back to the question of authorship, namely, the principal authorship of the Holy Spirit. For the Spirit ordained that when the prophets spoke of these events—true as they may have been—certain other things would be inserted that exceeded the condition of the narrated events (*res gestae*) in order that the soul might be elevated beyond them to what the events symbolized. For instance, in the book of Daniel many things are said about Antiochus Epiphanes that also speak figuratively of the antichrist (*in figuram Antichristo*). Much of what Daniel recounts did not completely transpire in that time; it would be realized therefore only in the time of the antichrist. And so too then when we read of David and Solomon; things that were not fulfilled during their earthly reigns will be fulfilled during the reign of Christ. Their own reigns can serve as a figure, therefore, of the final reign of Christ.[42]

None of this is to suggest that the Psalter has no literal-historical sense, only that this sense does not exhaust its meaning. Thomas observes that while some psalms do touch on historical events, they are not arranged according to the order of history. Thus a psalm dealing with Saul may be placed after one having to do with Absalom, and thus be out of strict historical order; this is because these psalms signify certain truths that transcend the bare historical record. According to Thomas, the first fifty psalms pertain to the state of penitence, which means that the tribulation and liberation of David can be treated figuratively as well as historically. This division on the literal level (*ad litteram*) can thus pertain to David's prayers when he faced battles

42. *Expositio in Psalmis Davidis*, prologue (*Opera Omnia*, 18:230).

and persecution within his own kingdom. These same psalms, however, can further signify the persecution faced by Christ and his church.[43]

Bonaventure

A direct contemporary of Thomas Aquinas, the Franciscan theologian Bonaventure of Bagnoregio had been schooled at Paris, where he studied under the illustrious master Alexander of Hales. We will dip into just a few works of this prolific scholar and mystic, who also served as his order's minister general from 1257 until his death in 1274. Bonaventure's work commonly known as the *De reductione artium ad theologiam* appears to have served as his magisterial *principium*, which he would have delivered in 1254 upon promotion to master of theology.[44] Here the Franciscan took as his lead text the words of James: "Every good gift and every perfect gift is from above, coming down from the Father of lights" (James 1:17). It is in this vein that Bonaventure speaks of four lights—exterior, interior, inferior, and superior—thereby corresponding to artifacts, natural forms, intellectual truth, and saving truth. Thus one can move in ascending order through the mechanical arts, sensitive and philosophical cognition, and culminate in the "light of Holy Scripture." It is Scripture that manifests the things that transcend human reason and therefore must be revealed through the inspiration that descends from the "Father of lights." The presence of God permeates creation, and his wisdom rests within all understanding of that creation. Yet whereas divine wisdom is present to varying degrees in man's comprehension of nature, this same wisdom has been clearly handed down in Holy Scripture. The light of Scripture, therefore, allows us to understand the natural world in ways that otherwise remain beyond our grasp. It is designated as superior because it leads us to higher things that transcend reason and cannot be found except by the inspiration that descends from the Father of lights. Although it is one with respect to its literal sense, it is threefold in its mystical, or spiritual, sense, for in the books of Holy Scripture there are—beyond the literal sense, which words exteriorly express (*exterius verba sonant*)—the allegorical, moral, and anagogical senses. In fact, according to Bonaventure, the whole of Sacred Scripture teaches three foundational truths: the eternal generation and incarnation of Christ, the order of living, and the soul's union with God. Hence the first has to do with faith, the second with morals, with the last as the goal of both

43. *Expositio in Psalmis Davidis*, prologue (*Opera Omnia*, 18:231).
44. See Joshua Benson, "Identifying the Literary Genre of the *De Reductione Artium ad Theologiam*: Bonaventure's Inaugural Lecture at Paris," *Franciscan Studies* 67 (2009): 149–78.

faith and morals. These three categories correspond to the work of doctors, preachers, and contemplatives. Bonaventure even has a set of examples from both ancient and more recent history. In the first category there is Augustine, who was followed by Anselm of Canterbury; then Gregory the Great, followed by Bernard of Clairvaux; and finally Dionysius the Areopagite, followed by Richard of St. Victor. Yet, Bonaventure says, it was Hugh of St. Victor who encompassed all three categories. As Bonaventure concludes his sermon, he once again emphasizes the greater purpose, or intention (*intentio*), of Sacred Scripture: it is love (*caritas*). All the sciences coalesce in Scripture, where faith is built up, morals are formed, and consolation found in the union of Bridegroom and bride. It is this union that is effected by love (*per caritatem*), apart from which all knowledge (*cognitio*) is in vain, for no one comes to the Son except through the Holy Spirit, who is himself the very love of God and teaches all truth.[45]

In the prologue to his *Breviloquium*, a compendium of theology produced 1256–57, Bonaventure makes the case that theology is a science founded on faith, revealed through the Holy Spirit, and pertaining to grace, glory, and eternal wisdom.[46] Theology, said Bonaventure, concerns God the First Principle, such that this science resolves all things in God. Bonaventure bases his argument on God the First Principle in order to demonstrate that the truth of Holy Scripture is from God, about God, according to God, and for the sake of God, thereby embracing the efficient, formal, exemplary, and final causes.[47] The progress, or development, of Holy Scripture is not confined by the strictures of human reason in the manner of the other sciences. Rather, it is a matter of supernatural light designed to lead the wayfarer to salvation, disclosing its truths sometimes by way of plain speech and sometimes according to mystical words. As the apostle speaks of the breadth, length, height, and depth (Eph. 3:18), so the breadth pertains to the content of the whole universe that Scripture describes, the length to the course of history, the height to the glory that awaits the saved, and the depth to the divine judgment. This progress, moreover, is designed to accommodate human capacity, which is capable of grasping the created world in both natural and supernatural ways.[48] Attaining the final goal of Scripture—which is eternal life—is a trinitarian

---

45. *De reductione artium ad theologiam*, see Latin with facing English translation in *Reduction of the Arts to Theology*, trans. Zachary Hayes (St. Bonaventure, NY: Franciscan Institute, 1996), 36–61.

46. *Breviloquium*, prologue 3, in *Opera Omnia*, 10 vols. (Quaracchi: Collegii S. Bonaventurae, 1882–1902), 5:205. See also Marianne Schlosser, "Bonaventura: Breviloquium, Prolog," in *Handbuch der Bibel-Hermeneutiken*, 177–89.

47. *Breviloquium*, prologue 6 (*Opera*, 5:208).

48. *Breviloquium*, prologue, intro. (*Opera*, 5:201–2).

matter. We must begin with the Father of lights, coming with a pure faith and bending the knees of our hearts so that he might, through his Son and in the Holy Spirit, grant us the true knowledge of Jesus Christ. As Bonaventure once again insists, we must be rooted in the knowledge and love of Christ if we are to understand Scripture.[49]

Even the senses of Holy Scripture are conformed to the Trinity. As the Trinity is one essence in three persons, so Scripture bears a threefold understanding beneath a single literal sense. The subject matter of Scripture is God, Christ, the works of reparation, and the articles of faith. Here again, though, if the hearers of Scripture are to penetrate beyond the husk of the letter, they must be humble, pure, and faithful, since the mysteries contained therein remain hidden from the proud. Scripture actually resembles Christ the teacher, who is humble in his humanity and exalted in his divinity, just as the teaching of Scripture is both humble in word and profound in meaning. And as Scripture was designed to teach all truth, so it was fitting that in one word there might lie many meanings. The senses of Scripture actually play a vital role in the process of salvation. Scripture leads us to our final end as it instructs by way of allegory, tropology, and anagogy so that we might be cleansed by virtuous operation, illuminated by radiant faith, and perfected by the most ardent charity.[50]

Ultimately, though, Holy Scripture is secured in its perfection by its eternal author. Scripture's authority, authorship, and authenticity are all of a piece. In his *Sentences* commentary, Bonaventure mentions four ways of making a book. On the most basic level is the *scriptor*, that is, the person who writes down material that is not his own (*aliena*), and he neither adds to it nor changes it. Then there is the *compilator*, who adds someone else's material. On the third level is the *commentator*, who is not an *auctor* but does contribute some material of his own in order to clarify (*ad evidentiam*) the material that he is commenting on. And finally there is the one who may be rightfully called the *auctor*; most of what he writes is his own, and the material drawn from others is added in order to confirm (*ad confirmationem*) his own material.[51] In the case of Holy Scripture, therefore, the Holy Spirit is the most perfect author (*auctor perfectissimus*), who teaches only what is true and useful. And we can be confident that God has provided Scripture with certitude of authority (*certitudinem auctoritatis*) such that it can never deceive or be deceived. Handed down through divine revelation rather than

---

49. *Breviloquium*, prologue, intro. (*Opera*, 5:202).
50. *Breviloquium*, prologue 4 (*Opera*, 5:206).
51. *Sententiae*, proemium, q. 4 in *Opera Omnia*, 15 vols. (Paris: Vives, 1864–71), 1:14–15.

by human investigation, Scripture is authentic (*authentica*) and of perfect authority (*perfectae auctoritatis*).[52] Bonaventure's confidence in the absolute and final authority of Holy Scripture is ultimately rooted in Christ the Word.

Peter John Olivi

The Franciscan theologian and prolific biblical exegete Peter John Olivi wrote a series of *principia* for his Scripture lectures, which we will treat as a single whole. In a primary lecture to his students on the nature of study generally, Olivi reminds them that there is nothing higher or more blessed among all the sciences than the contemplation and science of God.[53] If God had not wished us to seek out this knowledge, he would not have passed it down to us in the Holy Scriptures, which speak to the worship of God and the way he governs the world through his providence. For Olivi, the entire text (*tota littera*) of Scripture is contained within four parts: historical, legal, sapiential, and prophetic. In addition to this classification there are also the standard four senses: literal, allegorical, moral, and anagogical. As for the two Testaments, they are like two great lights; like two cherubim they are filled with the knowledge of God (*plena scientia Dei*). That is why Christ admonished the Jews to search the Scriptures that bear testimony to him (John 5:39), and Paul called on Timothy to abide in what he learned from the Holy Scriptures, which are divinely inspired (2 Tim. 3:14–16).[54] Study, therefore, must begin with the articles of faith and the authority of Scripture rather than simple human reason or human authority.[55] Here Olivi sets out his basic principle of authority in matters of faith. Right order begins with "faith and the font of Holy Scripture, and thereafter through the books of the saints which, like rivers, flow immediately from the principal font." Compared with these, the works of the worldly philosophers are no more than a stagnant bog.[56]

When Olivi applies the four Aristotelian causes to Scripture, he concludes that the efficient cause is the right hand of God, which is itself divine power and wisdom. The material cause is the interior and the exterior qualities of all things, namely, their perfect truth. The formal cause is the sevenfold sealing,

---

52. *Breviloquium*, prologue 6 (*Opera*, 5:207).

53. *Principium, De studio*, in *Principium Quinque in Sacram Scripturam* 1.1, in *Peter of John Olivi on the Bible*, ed. David Flood and Gedeon Gál (St. Bonaventure, NY: Franciscan Institute, 1997), 20. See also Johannes Karl Schlageter, "Petrus Johannis Olivi: Hermeneutik der Heiligen Schrift," in *Handbuch der Bibel-Hermeneutiken*, 221–38.

54. *Principium, De studio* 1.9 (Flood and Gál, 22).

55. *Principium, De studio* 1.27 (Flood and Gál, 27).

56. *Principium, De studio* 1.28 (Flood and Gál, 27).

which is the symbolic multiformity of the divine mysteries. And the final cause is contemplation of God and thus the perfected state of conformity to God (*deiformitas*).[57] On account of the loftiness of its origin, Holy Scripture is the principle of every wisdom and science, the integral totality of every salvific truth, the exemplar and mirror of all wisdom, indeed the exemplar and final end of every science.[58] Scripture goes out from God as though from an artisan of the highest skill; as from an emperor of the highest authority, it is the most imperial of edicts; as from a teacher of the greatest wisdom and truth, it is the most wise and certain document; as from a priest of the highest sanctity and piety, it is the most salubrious remedy; and as from a judge of the greatest equity, it is the most righteous judgment.[59] With its charity, Scripture surpasses all other laws and mandates.[60] It is the supreme artifact to which all others are subservient,[61] the highest gift to which all others must yield.[62] Scripture is the queen that sits at the right hand of Christ, wearing the vestments of charity (Ps. 44:10 Vulg. [45:9 Eng.]).[63] Scripture assumes unto itself all the natural sciences, mathematics, logical inferences, and rhetorical and grammatical figures.[64] It stands above all other laws, such that human cases and judgments must always submit to it.[65] The abyss and ocean of Scripture reveal themselves to those who investigate it under three forms: the indubitable radiance of truth, the flawless inflaming and intoxication of love, and the blameless judge of fairness.[66] And so it is that Holy Scripture presents itself as the mirror of divine truth. "She is the dazzling brightness of eternal light and an unblemished mirror of God's majesty" (Wis. 7:26).[67] The notion of Scripture personified as Wisdom found here with Olivi extends across the medieval exegetical tradition, from secular theologians such as Henry of Ghent all the way to John Wyclif.

Olivi continues: the christological aspect of Scripture becomes clearer as we see that the person of Christ forms the very center of Holy Scripture. Olivi informs us that Scripture has a center and circumference. Just as infinite lines proceed from the one most simple center, so from one word of Scripture

57. *Principium, De causis Scripturae* 2.2–3 (Flood and Gál, 43).
58. *Principium, De causis Scripturae* 2.4 (Flood and Gál, 44).
59. *Principium, De causis Scripturae* 2.5 (Flood and Gál, 44).
60. *Principium, De causis Scripturae* 2.6 (Flood and Gál, 44).
61. *Principium, De causis Scripturae* 2.7 (Flood and Gál, 44).
62. *Principium, De causis Scripturae* 2.8 (Flood and Gál, 45).
63. *Principium, De causis Scripturae* 2.10 (Flood and Gál, 46–47).
64. *Principium, De causis Scripturae* 2.11 (Flood and Gál, 47).
65. *Principium, De causis Scripturae* 2.13 (Flood and Gál, 47).
66. *Principium, De Christo, medio Scripturae* 4.1 (Flood and Gál, 127).
67. *Principium, De Christo, medio Scripturae* 4.3 (Flood and Gál, 180).

there is an infinite mystery of spiritual senses. Scripture turns around its center, which is the one precept of charity, the very center around which all other precepts and counsels must rotate. More specifically, Scripture turns around the one redeemer Christ and around the Triune God.[68] If Christ and his love are at the center of Scripture, there to be contemplated in devotion, then biblical exegesis will have to proceed in a manner exceeding merely dispassionate critical analysis. To seek this center, Olivi says, one must proceed more by way of affection (*affectualiter*) than intellect (*intellectualiter*), more through sensual tasting (*sensualem gustum*) than visual apprehension (*visualem aspectum*).[69] Only in the excess of love (*in solo excessu amoris*) can this center be discerned.[70]

At the center of Holy Scripture is a person. Jesus Christ himself is the middle, or axis, of Scripture; hence Paul's admission that "I have decided to know nothing else among you except for Jesus Christ and him crucified" (1 Cor. 2:2), the one in whom "are found all the treasures of wisdom and the knowledge of the hidden God" (Col. 2:3), "the Word of God in heaven is the source of wisdom" (Sir./Ecclus. 1:5).[71] As the middle of Scripture, like the axis of the wheels (Ezek. 10:2), Christ possesses an indivisible simplicity, immovable solidity, an entirely enclosed depth and profundity.[72] Christ is the beginning and end of all things, the connection of all, the rule and measure of all things, the Alpha and Omega (Rev. 1:8).[73] The wisdom of Christ illuminates all things, and through contemplation of the divine works, leads all back to the Sabbath of spiritual rest. The grace of Christ irrigates and revives all, and the justice of Christ renders judgment on all sins.[74] Thus we should drink in the divine love and sweetness found within the Scriptures, all of which Christ administers to us, for he is the font of truth, equity, and love.[75] The study of Scripture, therefore, is a process of entering into Christ. Evangelical teaching is, for Olivi, what he deems "a super-intellectual and super-affectual expression and proclamation of divine praises." And in order to attain this end, one must taste of super-ineffable love and friendship.[76] The gospel writers had themselves excelled in this regard: "They were unsurpassed in their taste of the most blessed Trinity, in their worship of the highest divine majesty, and

68. *Principium, De causis Scripturae* 2.29 (Flood and Gál, 51).
69. *Principium, De doctrina Scripturae* 3.7 (Flood and Gál, 80).
70. *Principium, De doctrina Scripturae* 3.8 (Flood and Gál, 80).
71. *Principium, De Christo, medio Scripturae* 4.6 (Flood and Gál, 128).
72. *Principium, De Christo, medio Scripturae* 4.7 (Flood and Gál, 128).
73. *Principium, De Christo, medio Scripturae* 4.8 (Flood and Gál, 129).
74. *Principium, De Christo, medio Scripturae* 4.9 (Flood and Gál, 130).
75. *Principium, De Christo, medio Scripturae* 4.43 (Flood and Gál, 138).
76. *Principium, De evangeliis* 5.14 (Flood and Gál, 148).

in their vision of the highest splendor and truth. From them alone, therefore, was it possible and fitting that the Gospel of Christ be handed down to the Universal Church of Christ."[77]

Olivi produced important, and controversial, commentaries on Matthew and Revelation among other books.[78] Here, though, we will examine a small portion of an uncontroversial commentary on the prophet Isaiah, which is nevertheless quite interesting. Part of this work includes a sophisticated discussion of the nature of prophecy in response to a series of questions. It is only natural that, in the course of lectures, the master and his students would have to grapple with all the issues attendant upon a human being speaking on behalf of God about future events. Thus the first question asks whether Isaiah looked upon with certitude, and as though present, the things that he predicted, such that his prophecy could rightly be called a vision. It would seem that he did not, for these things were future contingents, the truth of which cannot be seen in themselves since they do not yet exist whether in their proximate or remote causes. Indeed, these things were as yet no more determined than were their opposites, which also could have happened. Nor could the prophet have seen these things in their divine exemplars, since these can be seen only by the blessed. The arguments against mount up to the effect that Isaiah could not have infallibly known what he prophesied, let alone could he have seen such things in a present fashion.[79]

The next question speaks to the type of vision Isaiah may have had: Was it only intellectual, or imaginary, or perhaps corporeal, or perhaps all of the above? Olivi recounts various opinions, the first of which holds that Isaiah saw what he did by way of uncreated light (*de luce increata*). This, then, is the divine illumination theory whereby, as Olivi explains, all people know whatever they know, albeit to varying degrees, by way of the divine light. In the case of the prophets, they see the secrets of God, which are beyond the general understanding even of the wise. This is not to say that they see as the blessed see, nor do they attain to the divine light in such copious amounts as to dispel all of their present misery. They do not gaze immediately on the essence of uncreated light, but rather they see the representative principles of things. Still others say that the prophets see by way of a created light that has been poured into them by God; hence they do not see these things immediately in God or in their eternal exemplars. Olivi says that he favors the

77. *Principium, De evangeliis* 5.15 (Flood and Gál, 148).
78. See Kevin Madigan, *Olivi and the Interpretation of Matthew in the High Middle Ages* (Notre Dame, IN: University of Nore Dame Press, 2003); and David Burr, *Olivi's Peaceable Kingdom* (Philadelphia: University of Pennsylvania Press, 2003).
79. *Postilla in Isaiah, super titulum* (Flood and Gál, 192–93).

second opinion as more likely, but confesses that some problems still remain that he cannot easily reconcile.[80]

For his part Olivi preferred to speak of a prophetic certitude (*certitudo prophetalis*) whereby the prophet's mind is raised up by God to such heights of immutability that it cannot doubt its divine source, with the result that the things he is shown, and all that is spoken to him, he grasps with such supreme certainty that he knows it is from God. And by that very fact, he is supremely confident that such things are infallibly true. As Olivi describes it, the conviction of the prophet is so certain that he can be said not merely to know but even to taste; there is a sort of savoring of truth and divinity (*quendam gustum veritatis et divinitatis*) in which the prophet recognizes in some ineffable way that what he encounters is something of divine wisdom, dispelling all doubt that it is most true and divine. God himself and his truth are then found to be sweet to the taste (*suavitas gustetur*). And yet the prophet also recognizes that what he sees so clearly could never be proved by human reason.[81]

When Olivi reaches the crucial verse, "Behold a virgin shall conceive and bear a son" (Isa. 7:14), he rehearses the arguments made by Andrew of St. Victor, who, he says, was "speaking in the person of the Jews" (*in persona Iudaeorum loquatur*). Olivi states Andrew's case while turning to Richard's rebuttal as well as Jerome's exposition. Olivi offers a sustained treatment, which shows that he took this question very seriously. While we cannot recount the discussion here at length, a few exegetical points are worth mentioning. First, Olivi does not automatically discount the historical context of the prophecy, even though he does not limit its extent to the time of Isaiah himself. Olivi asserts that just because the prophecy had been fulfilled in a shadowy way (*umbratiliter*) in some son of Isaiah, that does not discount its application to Christ, for there are many things prophesied of Christ that were nonetheless fulfilled to some degree (*semiplene*) before being wholly fulfilled in Christ himself. There are, Olivi says, innumerable examples from the Old Testament, notably the many things said of Christ under the type of Solomon (*sub typo Salomonis*). Thus there are some things said by the prophets that, although fulfilled to some extent in their own time, the very force of their words (*ipsa vis verborum*), as well as the mind of the author and manner of speaking (*mens auctoris modusque dicendi*), surely demand another form of fulfillment that is more excellent and more spiritual than the first. And it is in this way that so many authoritative texts are drawn from the Old Testament into the New by the apostles and evangelists. In the case of Isaiah's prophecy of

80. *Postilla in Isaiah, super titulum* (Flood and Gál, 193–94).
81. *Postilla in Isaiah, super titulum* (Flood and Gál, 195).

Immanuel, therefore, the force of his words and indeed his entire prophecy require that they be fulfilled in Christ according to the spiritual mode (*iuxta modum spiritualem*), which we understand of Christ.[82]

Henry of Ghent

We take our leave of the mendicant commentators for a moment to examine an influential secular theologian, Henry of Ghent, who was a regent master at the University of Paris from about 1276 to 1293. In his *principium* (titled *Lectura ordinaria super sacram scripturam*), Henry broke down Scripture in standard fashion according to the four Aristotelian causes. The efficient cause refers to Scripture's sublime authority, since it is the book of God's commandments. The material cause corresponds to the depth of its truth, inasmuch as it is the law that abides for eternity. The final cause is Scripture's fruitful use, which leads to eternal life. And last, there is the formal cause pertaining to the variety of its means.[83] What is more, Henry says, Scripture is worthy of greater credence than any human authority since it surpasses all human reason; its authority is rooted in its eternal author.[84] When Henry speaks here of authors and authority, he is invoking quite specific concepts, for as Mariken Teu ween writes: "The terms *auctor* and *auctoritas* had strong connotations of 'veracity' and 'sagacity.' An *auctor* was the author of not just any literary work but a work with officially acknowledged authority, worthy of study and imitation. *Auctoritas*, on the other hand, was used not only for the abstract notion of 'authority,' 'prestige,' or 'esteem' but also for the authoritative texts themselves or for quotations or extracts from the works of *auctores*." Holy Scripture first, and also the works of the fathers, possessed genuine *auctoritas*, whereas recent writers were rarely referred to as *auctores*, and their works did not achieve *auctoritas*.[85]

When he turns to address the truth of Holy Scripture, Henry appeals to what was becoming a locus classicus throughout the Middle Ages: Wisdom 7:26, "For she is a radiance of eternal light, a spotless mirror of the working

---

82. *Postilla in Isaiah, prima pars* (Flood and Gál, 240–42).

83. *Lectura ordinaria super sacram scripturam*, ed. R. Macken (Leiden: Brill, 1980), 5. See also Gilbert Dahan, "Henri de Gand: L'Introductio generalis ad Sacram Scripturam," in *Handbuch der Bibel-Hermeneutiken*, 207–19.

84. *Lectura Ordinaria* (Macken, 6).

85. Teeuwen, *Vocabulary of Intellectual Life in the Middle Ages*, 222–23. For substantial analysis of medieval discussions of authorship, see Alastair Minnis, A. B. Scott, and David Wallace, *Medieval Literary Theory and Criticism c. 1100–c. 1375: The Commentary Tradition*, rev. ed. (Oxford: Clarendon, 1992); Alastair Minnis, *Medieval Theory of Authorship: Scholastic Attitudes in the Later Middle Ages*, 2nd ed. (Philadelphia: University of Pennsylvania Press, 2009).

of God, and an image of his goodness." Generations of medieval theologians embraced Scripture as the *speculum sine macula*, the eternal standard of all truth. Henry describes Scripture as untainted by any falsehood, certain and thus without doubt, and free from all error. As this divine radiance, Scripture contains the eternal truths that have been transcribed by the rules of the eternal light. It is the truth of divine law and thus of eternal righteousness. Scripture is clear enough to refute all error. By its irrefragable truth, it stands in judgment of, and reigns over, every other doctrine and discipline.[86] Scripture transcends all other sciences of discourse, endowed as it is with literal and spiritual senses. It will always yield the truth. Hence when read by way of a double exposition—historical and mystical/spiritual—whatever seems absurd according to the letter must immediately be referred to the spiritual sense.[87]

Generally following Augustine, Henry argues that the division of Scripture into Old and New is not on account of a diversity of things, but rather owing to the different ways of treating one and the same thing. There is a distinction of different parts within one science, he states, just as there is a distinction between different sciences themselves. This is not only on account of the diversity of things that the sciences treat, as for instance arithmetic deals with number and geometry with magnitude. It is also on account of the diverse means of treating the same thing; for example, arithmetic treats number simply as number, whereas music deals with number as it is reduced to sound.[88]

Henry proceeds to observe that the Old Testament is divided up into the law, prophets, and psalms, which in turn correspond to the tropological, allegorical, and anagogical senses. The law describes what one is to do; the prophets reveal what is to be believed; and the psalms make known what is to be hoped for. That they correspond to the three mystical senses is fitting, Henry says, because we primarily read the Old Testament by the mystical sense and the New Testament by the literal.[89] As for the new law, it is divided, like the Old, into precepts and directives. The precepts are contained in the evangelical doctrine that Christ himself fashioned per se, while the directives are contained in the apostolic doctrine that Christ fashioned through the apostles and their disciples.[90] Henry then addresses apostolic law, which is divided into the examples of righteous behavior handed down in the Acts of the Apostles and the directive words handed down in the letters of the apostles. The latter are then divided again into

86. *Lectura Ordinaria* (Macken, 6–8).
87. *Lectura Ordinaria* (Macken, 9–10).
88. *Lectura Ordinaria* (Macken, 13).
89. *Lectura Ordinaria* (Macken, 17).
90. *Lectura Ordinaria* (Macken, 25).

precepts for forming the faithful in time of prosperity and consoling the afflicted in time of adversity.[91]

As we have seen here in his *Lectura*, Henry grounds the authority of Scripture in its eternal author. Then, in his *Summa*, he specifically takes up the question of "whether God is the author of Holy Scripture." Here Henry begins by explaining what it means to be an author (*auctor*) in the most correct sense of the term. He mentions that in the creation of an object where there is one artisan (*artifiex*) who directs the work and another who works by hand according to the rules established by this artisan, then the true *auctor* is the directing artisan, not the laborer.[92] In this vein, following Aristotle's *Metaphysics* (1.1.981b), Henry states that the one who possesses an inherent knowledge of the principles and the rules of the art should be called the principal author of the science, rather than the one to whom he describes these principles and rules. When it comes to Scripture, therefore, it is God alone who by his very nature knows the rules of this science. These are the rules that creatures cannot attain by their own natural faculties (*ex puris naturalibus*) but can know only when inspired by God. Hence God alone is properly called the author of this science. Yet Henry does take seriously the role of human beings in this process. It is through men that the Scriptures are ministered, for they have conscribed these Scriptures and have contemplated this wisdom to the extent that is possible for the human heart. They perfectly understood the rules of this art, which they wrote down, and thus were not mere organs or channels. They were genuine, albeit secondary, authors who described what was infused into them from the great treasury of this art.[93] Thus Henry agrees that human testimony should be believed in this science, not of itself, but rather on account of the divine authority that manifests itself through human beings in signs and miracles.[94]

As Henry delves more deeply into the question of authorship with greater specificity, he observes that the Holy Trinity is the principal author of this science. First, he points out that the act of revelation, or inspiration, is common to the whole Trinity. Henry bases this on the long-established principle that there is only one divine energy in the Trinity, even as there is a distinction among the three persons. The Son and Spirit do fully act, yet they still derive their eternal existence from the Father, who is the eternal source of the Godhead. In that sense, Henry says, this science's principal authority resides

91. *Lectura Ordinaria* (Macken, 26).

92. Art. 9, q. 2, in *Summa quaestionum ordinarium* (Paris: Badii Ascensii, 1520; repr., St. Bonaventure, NY: Franciscan Institute, 1953), f. 71r.

93. Art. 9, q. 2, *Summa quaestionum ordinarium*, f. 71v.

94. Art. 9, q. 2, *Summa quaestionum ordinarium*, f. 71v.

with the Father, since all divine action ultimately derives from the Father as First Person of the Trinity. Henry insists, however, that this should not be seen as diminishing the roles of the Son and Spirit. Principal authority can be attributed to the Son when considered in terms of the act of revelation. And revelation, because it proceeds only from a gift that is appropriated to the Holy Spirit, will allow authority to be attributed also to the Spirit. In these various ways, therefore, the authority of this science must ultimately be attributed to the one God, who is Trinity.[95]

When it comes to perfect knowledge of Holy Scripture, three things happen concurrently. First, one must thoroughly understand the most basic literal sense of the text, the meaning of the letter (*mentem literae*). Second, one needs to know how to explicate those things that lie hidden in potency (*in potentia*) underneath the things that are primarily understandable; these are things that the letter itself does not explain. This can be accomplished through a process of rational deduction. Third, one believes things from the beginning by faith alone and then later comes to understand by reason. Now, Henry says, apart from the special grace of divine revelation, one cannot really know (*scire*) Holy Scripture without the assistance of a teacher. Where other sciences employ words as signs, Scripture also utilizes things as signs. Things signify according to their properties. Yet because the same thing can have various properties, some of which may signify in contradictory ways, and Scripture makes known its intention under these figures, one cannot immediately grasp their precise signification within Scripture. Thus when one reads Scripture one will not be able to understand it so long as one remains uncertain of the various figurative significations. Indeed, Henry says, this is precisely why Augustine wrote *De doctrina christiana*—to help Christians make sense of all the ambiguous signs. Henry thus appealed to the story of Philip and the eunuch (Acts 8:27–38) to make the point that Philip had declared the truth about Christ, who to that point remained hidden within the letter of the prophet Isaiah.[96]

In the next question, Henry addresses the charge that the writers of Holy Scripture did not perfectly understand what they had written. The first example is that of Jonah, who predicted the demise of Nineveh after forty days (Jon. 3:4). Now, according to the *Glossa Ordinaria*, this was not a prophecy based on divine foreknowledge but merely a threat issued for the sake of correction. Nevertheless, apparently Jonah did not know this; he believed his own prophecy in its literal sense (*ad litteram*). Thus he was ignorant of the mysteries and figures that the Lord had revealed through the text that

95. Art. 9, q. 2, *Summa quaestionum ordinarium*, f. 71v.
96. Art. 13, q. 8, *Summa quaestionum ordinarium*, f. 98r.

the prophet had written. And there is the case of Jeremiah: "Ah, Lord GOD, how utterly you have deceived this people and Jerusalem, saying, 'It shall be well with you,' even while the sword is at the throat!" (Jer. 4:10). According to the Gloss, Jeremiah was distressed and thought that God had lied, but that is because he did not realize that the good times were to arrive far in the future. Yet that does not change the fact that Jeremiah did not understand what he wrote. In response, Henry turns to the apostle Paul's words, "The Spirit we have received is not the spirit of the world, but God's own Spirit, so that we may understand the lavish gifts that God has given us. And these are what we speak of" (1 Cor. 2:12–13). Hence they knew of what they spoke, and these things they wrote down. Henry also looks to the Gloss on 2 Peter 1:21 so as to argue that the men of God spoke under the inspiration of the Holy Spirit and thus were not only inspired with respect to the words they wrote but also understood their full meaning (*ad intellectum sententiarum*).[97]

Henry is aware that his question asks not simply whether the biblical writers understood what they wrote but whether they perfectly understood it (*perfecte intellexerunt*). Yet he notes that perfect understanding can be taken in two ways. It can be simply and absolutely perfect without any qualification, or it can be perfect only to the extent necessary for one's understanding under one's specific circumstances (*pro loco et tempore*). This second category generally pertains to the holy doctors who spoke under the inspiration of the Holy Spirit and thus perfectly understood what they wrote. Perfect understanding of the first sort, under the highest and most perfect inspiration, was the case with Moses, who perfectly understood every possible exposition according to all of its conditions.[98] As for the prophets, Henry claims that Jonah well understood (*bene intellexit*) the mystical sense of the threat in the words that he wrote, although he might not have known some other aspects of the literal sense, namely, whether God meant literally (*literaliter intellexit*) that Nineveh would be destroyed after forty days. Therefore, Jonah sat outside the city waiting for events to unfold. Similarly, Jeremiah understood the good things that God promised through his words, even though he did not know the time when the promise would be fulfilled. God delayed revealing all of this to his prophet, since it was not expedient to do so at the time.[99] Hence these

---

97. Art. 13, q. 9, *Summa quaestionum ordinarium*, f. 98v–99r. For these glosses on Jonah, Jeremiah, and 2 Peter, see respectively *Biblia Latina cum Glossa Ordinaria*, ed. Karlfried Froehlich and Margaret T. Gibson, 4 vols. (Strassburg, 1480/81; repr., Turnhout: Brepols, 1992), 3:402; 3:107; 4:530.

98. Art. 13, q. 9, *Summa quaestionum ordinarium*, f. 99r. See Augustine, *Confessiones* 12.42 (CCSL 27:240–41).

99. Art. 13, q. 9, *Summa quaestionum ordinarium*, f. 99v.

prophets were not wrong in what they said, even as they did not know everything. In that sense, therefore, the text is preserved from any charge of error.

Henry devotes a good amount of space to the method of exposition (*modus exponendi*) suitable for the science of theology. He sets himself to answer the question of whether exposition of the depths (*expositio profunda*) is a suitable means of investigation. Some say it is not, because man should not investigate what he cannot find; he will labor in vain. The profundity of Christian letters is just too great. However, a great thing is worthy of diligent inquiry, and Scripture is the greatest of all.[100] Henry begins by pointing out that, in the exposition of Scripture, two things must be considered: the evidence of the truth that is sought and the capacity of the learner who intends to be informed by that truth. With regard to the first, Henry says that one must not give up until one has arrived at the clear truth (*ad liquidam veritatem*). Of course, on the one hand, there are many passages that need to be read allegorically, such that the expositor who relies on the historical sense alone will miss the meaning. As a general rule, therefore, if the clear truth is located in the simple literal sense of the text, there is no need to investigate any more deeply. If, on the other hand, the letter obscures the truth, then one must keep on looking until the truth becomes apparent. Henry appeals to Christ's admonition to build one's house on the solid rock (Matt. 7:24). Let us think of Scripture as field where we wish to build. We must not be lazy or content with the superficial. Instead, we must dig deep until we reach the rock, the very rock who is Christ (1 Cor. 10:4). This is where all the treasures of knowledge and wisdom are hidden. Immediately, though, Henry warns that this task must be approached cautiously lest we rashly affirm things that are still in doubt. Yet what can be shown to agree with the most certain authority of Scripture may then be asserted without compunction.[101]

Here, though, Henry warns that this sort of exposition should be carried out with the utmost reverence and caution. One must never dare to assert anything on the basis of such exposition that cannot be supported with certainty by the rule of faith (*regula fidei*), for it is precisely the lack of due caution that gives rise to heresy. Heresies are born when the good things of Scripture are not rightly understood (*scripturae bonae intelliguntur non bene*). Expositors, therefore, must proceed with a pious heart, imbued with the very faith that will enable them to understand. There will be some things

100. Art. 16, q. 1, *Summa quaestionum ordinarium*, f. 104r.
101. Art. 16, q. 1, *Summa quaestionum ordinarium*, f. 104r. See Augustine, *Tract. in Ioh.* 23.1 (CCSL 36:232).

that the expositor might not yet be able to comprehend, but this must not give way to doubt. Where our understanding reaches its limits, remember that "faith is the measure of knowledge." To the extent that one can investigate the profound things of this science, moreover, one will need the assistance of divine grace (*per gratiam Dei*), since there are many things here that exceed the investigation of natural reason. When profound investigation exceeds the control of the investigator's intellect, one must turn to the rule of faith. If the investigation is within the capacity of the investigator's intellect, then one can proceed under the guidance of right reason; yet even here reason will be guided by the rule of faith. Thus, on the one hand, it would be presumptuous to investigate profound matters when they clearly surpass the capacity of the human intellect. That is rashness and creates heretics who seek lofty things (cf. 1 Cor. 2:9). On the other hand, though, profound investigation of things that do fall within the intellect's capacity can be approached with charity and diligence to the extent that it remains within sensible bounds. Henry then wraps up the discussion: "Profound investigation is only suitable for the spiritual and the perfect; for the rest it is dangerous."[102]

The objection is then raised that Holy Scripture should not be explained in multiple ways. After all, what is maximally a science of truth ought to use simple forms of discourse (*simplices sermones*). The simplicity of discourse is greater when there is only one sense and one exposition rather than many. In fact, multifold discourse that yields many apparently true meanings is really the mark of sophistical discourse. This would mean, in turn, that theology is a chiefly sophistical science. Henry concedes that the exposition of Scripture must indeed be multiple, because Scripture has been written by the Holy Spirit in such a way that there is not only a manifest sense but also many hidden senses as well. Different meanings are there to be discovered beneath the same letter. Hence these different senses and mysteries will become apparent only through a variety of explanations. In the case of Holy Scripture we are not dealing merely with words. Here one moves from the signification of words (*vocum*) on the historical level to the signification of things (*rerum*) on the mystical level. In fact, the mystical sense based on the *significatio rerum* will allow for different meanings attached to the same thing according to its various properties. None of this diversity renders the discourse either sophistical or multiple. The simplicity of the word is not compromised for Henry, because the word does indeed point to only one thing. The multiplicity of senses begins on the level of the thing that is signified. Theology is unique among the sciences in this way. In all the others there

102. Art. 16, q. 1, *Summa quaestionum ordinarium*, f. 104v.

can be only one sense contained under the simplicity of the word, whereas in theology there can be many senses, all of which points to the great efficacy and virtue of this science.[103]

We can conclude this section with a look at Henry's response to the question of whether the truth subsists in every exposition and sense of Scripture. It does not appear to be the case when one considers Judges 9:7–15, as the trees went out to anoint a king, which is just absurd. Then there is Jacob deceiving his father, Isaac, by pretending to be Esau (Gen. 27:19). This seems to be a clear lie that Scripture maintains as though it were true. The Lord said to Abimelech (Gen. 20:3) that he would die because he had taken Sarah, but he did not die; thus Scripture lied here. Henry lists six such cases. Then he issues his rejoinder: "Insofar as every explanation of Holy Scripture proceeds according to the rule of faith, no falsehood can subsist within it, because it imitates the First Truth."[104]

Henry elaborates that "the sayings of Holy Scripture are nothing other than divine oracles and testimonies of eternal truth." What is more, Scripture's veracity is ensured by none other than Christ himself: "Christ has said that he is the author and principal expositor of Scripture." He came into the world to bear witness to the eternal truth that is free from all falsehood. Hence all exposition and every sense must be subject to the truth. Appealing to Augustine, Henry urges that the reader who sets out to explain Scripture must hold with an unshakable faith that the truth is never lacking, no matter how difficult it may be to find on account of its lofty subject matter.[105] Now in the instance of the talking trees, Henry falls back on Augustine's rule that in those cases when the letter cannot have a true historical sense, one must turn to the mystical sense and explain the passage figuratively. According to the *Glossa Ordinaria*, the trees signify men in the allegorical sense. Hence there is truth to be found in parables and metaphors with regard to the signification of things (*rerum*), just as the truth in histories is expressed according to the signification of words (*vocum*). Like Aquinas (*ST* 1, q. 1, a. 10), therefore, Henry teaches that in this science words not only signify things, but things also signify yet other things. As for Jacob and Esau, even though this event may well have occurred, that is not the important point. The truth in this passage is its prophetic sense: the two brothers signify the church and synagogue. And finally, the Lord's words to Abimelech must be understood conditionally (*sub conditione*): he will die

103. Art. 16, q. 2, *Summa quaestionum ordinarium*, f. 104v–5r.
104. Art. 16, q. 5, *Summa quaestionum ordinarium*, f. 107v.
105. Art. 16, q. 5, *Summa quaestionum ordinarium*, f. 107v. See Augustine, *De praedestinatione et gratia* 1 (PL 45:1665).

unless he returns Sarah to her husband. In sum, any apparent lies found in Scripture are neither asserted nor commended; they are recited only for the sake of our instruction.[106]

Nicholas of Lyra

Now we return to the mendicants, specifically Nicholas of Lyra, who was perhaps the single most influential biblical commentator in the Middle Ages.[107] Entering the Franciscan Order in 1300, he was a master of theology at Paris by 1309. Nicholas is best remembered for his commentary on the entire Bible known as the *Postilla Litteralis*, begun in 1322 and completed by 1331, the groundwork for which was probably laid when he delivered his cursory lectures on Scripture decades before as a bachelor of theology.[108] He wrote three general prologues for the Bible, the first of which had originally served as his magisterial *principium*.[109] It is in this first prologue that Nicholas of Lyra elucidates his broader vision of Holy Scripture as a sacred repository of divine wisdom, thereby revealing the foundation of his hermeneutics. He adopted Sirach/Ecclesiasticus 24:32 Vulg. as his lead text: "All these things are the book of life." Scripture is the book of life (*liber vitae*), the key to true life for all who believe. To this end Nicholas cites Gregory the Great's remark that "temporal life as compared to eternal life is more fittingly called death than life."[110] Nicholas the theologian observes that the science of the philosophers is ordered to mundane ends, concerned as it is with this present life alone. Yet Holy Scripture, the principal text of theology, is a unique book ordered toward happiness in the life to come, thereby surpassing the merely human knowledge acquired by philosophers. In comparison with the books of Holy Scripture, therefore, philosophical texts are more fittingly designated books of death. "The book containing Holy Scripture—although divided into many partial books and yet contained under one book—which

---

106. Art. 16, q. 5, *Summa quaestionum ordinarium*, f. 107v–8r, see f. 108r. For the gloss on Judges, see *Biblia Latina cum Glossa Ordinaria*, ed. Froehlich and Gibson, 1:487.

107. Some of this material on Nicholas of Lyra has been adapted from my essay "Nicholas of Lyra: The Biblical Prologues," in *Handbuch der Bibelhermeneutiken*, 239–53.

108. For an overview of Nicholas of Lyra's life and career, see the introduction to *Nicholas of Lyra: The Senses of Scripture*, ed. Philip Krey and Lesley Smith (Leiden: Brill, 2000), 1–18; and S. Delmas, "Nicolas de Lyre: Franciscain," in *Nicolas de Lyre: Franciscain du XIVᵉ siècle exégète et théologien*, ed. Gilbert Dahan (Turnhout: Brepols, 2011), 17–27.

109. I have followed the edition of the three prologues found in PL 113 but have also consulted the 1603 Venice *Biblia Sacra cum Glossa Ordinaria novisque additionibus*, which contains Nicholas of Lyra's *Postilla Literalis* and *Postilla Moralis*.

110. *Hom. in Evang.* 37 (PL 76:1275b).

is designated under the general name of the Bible, is properly called the Book of Life."[111]

Like his Franciscans predecessors Bonaventure and Peter John Olivi, Nicholas directly equated Holy Scripture with the science of theology itself. Scripture is properly called theology, he says, precisely because it is the sole text of this science. God himself is its subject matter; indeed, it is a discourse about God (*sermo de Deo*). Holy Scripture, and thus theology, proceeds in the most certain manner, excelling all human sciences, which are confined by the limits of human reason. The problem with philosophy, according to Nicholas, is that even when there is no error in the cognition of first principles, which are known per se, error is still possible in the deduction of conclusions from those principles. That is why philosophers who rely solely on human methods of investigation have often lapsed into error.[112]

As Nicholas continues, he appeals to Deuteronomy 4:6: "That will be your wisdom and your understanding in the sight of the peoples." No matter his occasional disparaging of philosophy, Nicholas actually incorporates a great deal of Aristotle into his own work. He appeals directly to the *Metaphysics* (1.1.981b) when pointing out that wisdom (*sapientia*) properly refers to the science that treats the highest causes. Thus as Holy Scripture has God for its subject, who is himself the first cause of all things, so it must be designated as wisdom. This is the wisdom of the saints, the very wisdom that is Holy Scripture. The point that Nicholas wishes to make is not that philosophical investigation is useless but that it is limited because it does not operate under the grace of divine illumination. Although it is true that philosophers have some knowledge of God, that knowledge remains confined to the properties that can be known by reason through the observation of created things. However, the prophets and apostles, who have handed down Holy Scripture through the revelation of the Holy Spirit, have a knowledge of transcendent divine properties that exceeds the investigations of human reason. The Trinity, according to Nicholas, is a prime example of a truth that could not be reached by the efforts of unaided human reason, that is to say, reason unilluminated by grace. And if the Trinity is the goal of all human longing, then the study of Holy Scripture is no mere academic exercise. The person contemplating Holy Scripture is borne along into the love of the very object of his cognition, who is God himself, and comes to love God above all else.[113] More than wisdom (*sapientia*), Scripture is also understanding (*intellectus*),

---

111. *Prologus . . . De commendatione Sacrae Scripturae in generali* (PL 113:25c–d).
112. *Prologus . . . De commendatione Sacrae Scripturae in generali* (PL 113:25d–26d).
113. *Prologus . . . De commendatione Sacrae Scripturae in generali* (PL 113:26d–27a).

since understanding is the unerring grasp of principles, and it is on account of such principles that one can render judgment as to the truth or falsity of things. So it is, then, that whatever accords with Holy Scripture is reckoned true, while whatever contradicts it must be false.[114] Scripture, comprising as it does the full and perfectly articulated contents of divine revelation, presents the science of theology with the data from which it commences its reflections and the criteria by which all of its subsequent determinations must be judged.

Turning to Wisdom 1:7, "That which contains all things has knowledge [*scientiam*] of the voice," Nicholas of Lyra finds that Holy Scripture contains all things, since it is a science that brings all things under its consideration. The christological aspect of Scripture comes to the fore here, since what is proper to Holy Scripture is that which is expressed by the divine Word himself. It is through the Word that all things were made (John 1:3), which means that all things must fall under the consideration of this science, namely, under the consideration of Scripture. Nicholas is clear, however, that this foundational claim extends not to the knowledge of all particular things that may be discovered through human reason but rather to the larger created order, by which we are led into the knowledge and love of God through a true faith that has been formed by charity (*per veram fidem caritate formatam*). Having appealed to Augustine's proviso that Scripture addresses not everything whatsoever that can be known by man but only that which strengthens faith and leads to true blessedness,[115] Nicholas explicitly turns to the Gloss clarifying Christ's promise to the apostles that the Spirit "will instruct you in all truth" (John 16:13): Christ meant the truth that is "necessary for salvation."[116]

Like Henry of Ghent before him, Nicholas of Lyra compares the book (*liber*) of Scripture to a mirror (*speculum*), drawing on the classic text of Wisdom 7:26, "For she is a radiance of eternal light, a spotless mirror of the working of God, and an image of his goodness." Just as sensible forms are apparent in a mirror, so in this book the intelligible truths shine forth. This is the book of divine foreknowledge from which the apostles and prophets read, those who handed down this science.[117] Nicholas once more cites the Gloss, this time where the prophet Isaiah said to Hezekiah, "Thus says the LORD: Set your house in order, for you shall die" (Isa. 38:1). According to the Gloss, "The prophets are able to read from the book of divine foreknowledge, where all things are written [although they did not perceive all things, but

---

114. *Prologus . . . De commendatione Sacrae Scripturae in generali* (PL 113:27b).

115. Augustine, *De trinitate* 14.1 (CCSL 50A:421–24).

116. *Prologus . . . De commendatione Sacrae Scripturae in generali* (PL 113:27d–28a). See *Biblia Sacra cum Glossa Ordinaria*, 5:1273–74.

117. *Prologus . . . De commendatione Sacrae Scripturae in generali* (PL 113:28a).

only certain things and in the manner that God permitted]." Nicholas clarifies this comment, declaring that the prophets did not actually see the divine essence, which is itself identical with God's foreknowledge, since even prophetic cognition remains obscure at that point (cf. 1 Cor. 13:12). Nevertheless, they have seen the truth through a prophetic light insofar as God's knowledge has been revealed to them. Here he also makes the point that the exegete and the prophet operate on very different levels. The exegete has no such knowledge, since he is not illuminated by the prophetic light and thus cannot read from this book of divine foreknowledge. The exegete is at a further remove from the truth, therefore, as he reads from the book of Holy Scripture that has been handed down to us by the prophets.[118]

Shortly before bringing this first prologue to a close, Nicholas of Lyra touches on the senses of Scripture, a topic given greater attention in the second and third prologues. Directly echoing Thomas Aquinas (*ST* 1.1.10), he finds that one letter in Scripture may contain many senses (*una littera continet plures sensus*). This is because God himself is the principal author (*principalis auctor*) of Scripture, hence its principal efficient cause. He furthermore declares that God has the power not only to make words (*voces*) signify things (*res*), which even human beings can do, but also to have those things signify still other things. Hence the first level of signification in Scripture pertains to what is communicated through the words, and this is accepted as the literal or historical sense. The second level of signification takes place on the level of the things themselves, which Nicholas refers to as the mystical or spiritual sense, itself threefold. The literal sense can thus be reckoned the exterior of Scripture; it is clearer (*patentior*), because it is immediately signified through the words. The interior is the mystical or spiritual sense; it is more obscure (*latentior*) and is revealed only through things that are designated by words.[119]

In his concluding remarks, Nicholas of Lyra returns to a grander plane as he cements the connection between Holy Scripture's life-giving properties and the moral disposition of the reader. Reminding us that only Scripture leads immediately to the true and blessed life that knows no death, he invokes Christ's words to the Jews: "You search the Scriptures because you think that in them you have eternal life" (John 5:39). Nicholas fastens on the words "you think" (*putatis*), which refer to false opinion, or at least to doubt, regarding the truth. Neither can impugn the veracity of Holy Scripture itself, which contains neither falsehood nor doubt, for it remains an instrument that

118. *Prologus . . . De commendatione Sacrae Scripturae in generali* (PL 113:28b). See *Biblia Sacra cum Glossa Ordinaria*, 4:335–36.

119. *Prologus . . . De commendatione Sacrae Scripturae in generali* (PL 113:28c–29a).

leads to eternal happiness. Rather, the error arises on the part of malicious interpreters (*male exponentes*) and those of vicious manners (*male viventes*), who are rightly deprived of the perfect felicity that is the end (*finis*)—one might say final cause—of this science. Such rewards are reserved for those of upright understanding (*sane intelligentes*) and devout living (*pie viventes*): "Those who elucidate me will have eternal life" (Sir./Ecclus. 24:31 Vulg.). Holy Scripture, therefore, is brought to light through accurate exposition (*vera expositione*) and holy conduct (*sancta operatione*). Containing as it does the most perfect practical and speculative sciences, Holy Scripture demands of us both good behavior and genuine comprehension.[120] For Nicholas there is a deeply affective component to biblical exegesis; this sacred text discloses its sublime wisdom only to hearts that are conformed to Christ. We might call this a "hermeneutic of sanctity."

Although Nicholas touches on the relationship between the different senses of Scripture in his *principium*, it is in the second prologue that he more concretely explains the exegetical method that will inform his great *Postilla Litteralis*. Here he turns to Revelation 5:1, "And I saw in the right hand of him who sat on the throne a book written within [*intus*] and without [*foris*], sealed with seven seals." Thus with respect to the book "written within and without," Nicholas again acknowledges that Scripture possesses an exterior literal sense and an interior mystical sense. He insists from the outset, however, that the literal sense must ground the others. As a building that falls away from its foundation will collapse into ruin, so it is with mystical exposition that is not founded on the literal sense. In this regard, Nicholas is sounding a theme that we can trace back to Hugh of St. Victor in the twelfth century. Like Aquinas before him (*ST* 1.1.10, ad. 1), Nicholas also cites Augustine's admonition that arguments in matters of faith must proceed from the literal sense rather than the mystical sense.[121]

Yet even as one needs to begin with the literal sense, Nicholas laments that it is very often obscured in these modern days. First, he says, there are the mistakes of copyists who, on account of the similarity of letters in many places, do not properly transcribe words as they appear in keeping with the true version of the text (*veritas textus*). Then there is the ineptitude of the correctors who place periods where there ought not to be any or begin and end verses in the wrong places, thus altering the meaning of the text (*sententia litterae*). What is more, the literal sense is often obscured in the translation,

---

120. *Prologus . . . De commendatione Sacrae Scripturae in generali* (PL 113:29a–30a).
121. *Prologus Secundus: De intentione auctoris et modo procendi* (PL 113:29c). See Augustine, *Epistula* 93.8 (PL 33:333–35).

which frequently differs from what one finds in the Hebrew books (*libri Hebraici*). Following Jerome's advice on this front, Nicholas finds that when attempting to establish the true Old Testament text (*pro veritate litterae*), it is best to refer to the Hebrew codices. He warns, however, that one should be careful in such instances, because he believes that Jewish scholars have purposely distorted those passages that attest to the divinity of Christ. Thus he assures us that he will alert the reader when such instances arise. But in those cases where it is unlikely that the text has been tampered with, he thinks one is safe in recurring to the Hebrew original so as to reach the true text.[122] One will notice that Nicholas of Lyra, no less than most of his contemporaries, blithely assumes that there is some genuine, or authentic, text that underlies the various Latin editions in circulation. That the conscientious scholar can get at "the truth of the text" (*veritas textus*) and thereby reveal its intended meaning is not only taken for granted but also considered essential for the exegetical task.

At all events, having addressed such textual-critical concerns, Nicholas further complains that the literal sense can be obscured through the manner of exposition (*modus exponendi*) commonly handed down by some who, although they have said many worthwhile things, nevertheless hardly touch on the literal sense. These interpreters multiply the mystical senses to such an extent that the literal sense is obstructed and even suffocated beneath them, resulting in a jumble that divides and confuses the text, making it very difficult to grasp the literal sense. For this reason, as Nicholas informs the reader, he intends to devote the great bulk of his attention to the literal sense and to keep mystical expositions at a bare minimum. To that end he invokes the help of not only the catholic doctors but also the Hebrews, chief among them Rashi of Troyes.[123] Rashi was the Jewish exegete to whom Nicholas principally turned, and it was Rashi who would have mediated to him the earlier rabbinic material. Where Nicholas first acquired his proficiency in the Hebrew language remains a mystery, although it is possible that while still in Normandy he made contact with the Jewish community at Évreux. The Jews were expelled from France in 1306, however, so Nicholas may have learned what he did about rabbinical exegesis in Paris from converted Jews.[124] At any rate, he did not adhere to the rabbis unquestioningly, for he acknowledges

122. *Prologus Secundus: De intentione auctoris et modo procendi* (PL 113:29d–30c).

123. *Prologus Secundus: De intentione auctoris et modo procendi* (PL 113:30c–d).

124. A. Geiger, "A Student and an Opponent: Nicholas and His Jewish Sources," in *Nicolas de Lyre*, ed. Dahan, 167–203; C. Soussen-Max, "La polémique anti-juive de Nicolas de Lyre," in *Nicolas de Lyre*, ed. Dahan, 51–73; D. Klepper, "Nicholas of Lyra and Franciscan Interest in Hebrew Scholarship," in *Nicholas of Lyra: The Senses of Scripture*, 289–311.

that on rare occasions their explanations were untenable, in which case he set them aside. A bit defensively perhaps, he insists that he will follow the Jewish exegetes only to the extent that their guidance is in keeping with reason and the truth of the text. Late medieval schoolmen were anxious that their remarks not be misconstrued, lest they find themselves charged with error or heresy. Not surprisingly, therefore, Nicholas makes clear that he has no intention of speaking assertively (*dicere assertive*) in his postil except in matters that have already been determined through Holy Scripture and the authority of the church. The rest of his comments are to be taken as though spoken in the ways of scholastic disputation (*scholastice et per modum exercitii dicta*), which is to say that they are presented for the purpose of generating discussion. He subjects everything he says to the correction of holy mother church, which means that he stands ready to revoke anything that causes offense.[125] Therefore Gilbert Dahan has speculated that Nicholas's vigorous, if not anachronistic, defense of the literal sense may have been an attempt to forestall criticism of his extensive use of Jewish exegesis.[126]

Nicholas's aforementioned willingness to reject a rabbinic interpretation is evinced in his discussion of Isaiah's prophecy to Ahaz, "Behold a virgin shall conceive and bear a son, and his name shall be called Immanuel" (Isa. 7:14). As we have seen with previous Christian exegetes, this passage was regarded as fulfilled in the angel Gabriel's announcement to the Virgin Mary (Matt. 1:23). Nicholas was uncompromising in his treatment of this text, contending that it has often been "distorted by the Jews" (*scriptura ista multipliciter pervertitur a Iudaeis*). He therefore feels compelled (so he tells us) to offer a meticulous refutation of their objections in order to prove that the passage cannot possibly refer to anyone but Jesus Christ. We cannot here trace the breadth of Nicholas's discussion, but it displays a solid knowledge of Jewish exegetical sources. He even occasionally appeals to Rashi's interpretation in order to refute other Jewish expositors who claim that Isaiah's prophecy referred to Ahaz's son Hezekiah. However, Nicholas also rejects Rashi's claim that the prophecy applied instead to Isaiah's own son conceived by the young woman (*almah*) he had taken as his wife. According to Nicholas, this does not hold up (*sed ista expositio non potest stare*) because Isaiah's son never fulfilled all that was prophesied of this child. One must turn to the New Testament for a clear exposition: Matthew the evangelist was filled with the Holy Spirit to a greater degree than the Old Testament prophet and so was able to recognize

125. *Prologus Secundus: De intentione auctoris et modo procendi* (PL 113:30d–31a).
126. G. Dahan, "Nicolas de Lyre: Herméneutique et méthodes d'exégèse," in *Nicolas de Lyre*, ed. Dahan, 101–24.

the prophecy's true fulfillment in Jesus Christ. Only this person, comprising a divine and a human nature, is the true Immanuel, "God with us."[127]

The remainder of this prologue is devoted to explaining the seven exegetical rules of Tyconius that Augustine had recounted in his *De doctrina christiana* (3.31–37). Forming a basic guide to typological interpretation, Nicholas treats it under the larger umbrella of the literal sense. His discussion of the third rule is especially important, for here he asserts that beneath the same letter, there may be contained both a historical and a mystical sense. Even as the historical truth (*veritas historiae*) is maintained, there may still be a spiritual understanding (*spiritualem intellectum*) to which it refers. This is where Nicholas speaks of the double literal sense (*duplex sensus litteralis*) that applies when there is both a historical and a mystical sense under the same letter. In these instances the historical truth recorded in the text must be preserved even as that truth points to a further spiritual understanding. The example Nicholas gives here is taken from 1 Chronicles 22:10, where the Lord is presented as a father to Solomon. Read literally (*ad litteram*), Solomon was indeed God's son by adoption and thus by grace. Yet the apostle Paul had cited this text in Hebrews 1:5 when speaking of Christ, and he also did so *ad litteram* so that he might prove that Christ was higher than the angels. Paul's point of doctrine, however, cannot be based on the mystical sense, since that would violate Augustine's rule that the literal sense alone is the foundation of doctrine. Here, then, the same text is speaking literally about Solomon, God's son by grace, even as it is speaking about Christ, God's Son by nature. The same text is fulfilled by both Solomon and Christ, although less perfectly by the former and more perfectly by the latter. Nicholas admits, however, that while each exposition belongs to the literal sense unqualifiedly (*simpliciter*), the second interpretation—referring to Christ—is itself mystical or spiritual in a certain respect (*secundum quid*) inasmuch as Solomon functions here as a figure of Christ (*figura Christi*).[128]

In his third general prologue, Nicholas informs readers of his shorter *Postilla Moralis* that, having explained Holy Scripture according to the literal sense (*secundum litteralem sensum*), he will now explicate it according to the mystical sense (*mystice exponenda*), although only in those places where such mystical readings are warranted. Here again we see his characteristic reserve; recourse to the spiritual senses, while suitable at times, must still be carefully measured. Nicholas makes clear, moreover, that he does not intend to address all the possible mystical senses or to cover every single verse. Rather, he plans

---

127. *Biblia Sacra cum Glossa Ordinaria*, 4:93–94. Cf. his much briefer treatment in his Matthew postil, *Biblia Sacra cum Glossa Ordinaria*, 5:45–47.

128. *Prologus Secundus: De intentione auctoris et modo procendi* (PL 113:31d–32a).

to compile a brief work that may be of use to readers of the biblical books and preachers of God's Word. Do not be surprised that he bypassed a lot of material for the sake of brevity, Nicholas cautions, for even Christ himself left parts of his parables unexplained.[129]

Revelation 5:1 is invoked at the outset here as it had been in the second general prologue. Nicholas declares that this is the glorious God in whose right hand Holy Scripture has been divinely given, thereby in keeping with Deuteronomy 33:2 Vulg., "In his right hand is a fiery law." Both the Old and the New Testaments are rightly called "fiery," since they have been inspired by the revelation of the Holy Spirit, who is himself the divine fire. And again we see the delineation of the outer literal and inner mystical senses. Proceeding to break down the mystical senses into the traditional categories of allegory, tropology, and anagogy, Nicholas recites the famous verse *"Littera gesta docet . . ."* and recounts John Cassian's Jerusalem example of the four senses belonging to one word.[130] Nicholas points out, however, that while it is true that Scripture as a whole does possess four senses, not every part of Scripture will necessarily bear all four. Sometimes the text is so straightforward that no mystical sense is required, such as the command to love God with one's whole heart (Deut. 6:5). Yet there are other times when there is no literal sense, as with the parable of the talking trees (Judg. 9:8–15) or Christ's advice that we cut off our hand if it causes scandal (Matt. 5:29–30). If the literal sense is that which is properly signified, then there can be no such sense in these cases. In fact, the meaning would be false if one had to read these texts according to the dictates of proper signification. As such, these passages must be understood by the mystical sense alone: the trees referring to the inhabitants of Shechem and the hand referring to the severance of a destructive relationship. No doubt with Aquinas in mind once again (*ST* 1.1.10, ad. 3), Nicholas reports that some doctors are willing to speak broadly on occasion so as to allow that the parabolic sense can be contained under the literal, for in those cases where there is no literal-historical sense signified by the words, the parabolic sense functions as the primary sense. In that way it can be called the literal, inasmuch as the literal sense is the first sense when no other sense is present. In fact, Nicholas admits that he too has equated the parabolic and literal senses within his own commentaries.[131] Hence the capaciousness of the literal sense can be extended to accommodate the author's intended meaning, thereby preserving Scripture from any charge of falsehood.

129. *Prologus in moralitates Bibliorum* (PL 113:35a–36a).
130. *Prologus in moralitates Bibliorum* (PL 113:33c–d).
131. *Prologus in moralitates Bibliorum* (PL 113:33d–34c).

Last, there are those instances where Scripture has both a literal and a mystical sense, as in the account of Abraham and his two sons, Isaac and Ishmael (Gen. 21:1–14). While this is true according the literal sense, it is also true in the mystical sense, evinced by the apostle Paul's allegorical reading in which the two sons signify the two Testaments (Gal. 4:24). Even here, though, they are not limited to the allegorical but can signify on the moral and anagogical levels as well. There are even instances when one thing displays many different properties, leading to multiple mystical readings. Thus a lion may be Christ the lion of Judah (Rev. 5:5) as well as the devil (1 Pet. 5:8), the first representing constancy and the second voraciousness.[132] For all of his attention to historical circumstance and Hebrew syntax, therefore, Nicholas still allows for the full range of mystical senses, although with less exuberance than some of his predecessors.

We have already seen how Nicholas had implicitly utilized the Aristotelian prologue in his *principium* when considering the subject matter, style, authorship, and purpose of Scripture. Here it will be instructive to see how he set this to work explicitly in prologues that he wrote for certain sets of books, in this case the Psalms and sapiential books. In his prologue to the Psalms, Nicholas takes as his lead text "A great prophet has risen among us" (Luke 7:16). At the outset appealing to the four causes, he begins with the efficient cause, which is itself twofold (*causa efficiens duplex*): principal and instrumental. The principal efficient cause is God revealing his mysteries that are described in this book. David, therefore, is the instrumental cause since, according to Augustine, all the things contained in the Psalter were revealed to, and described by, David. Yet Nicholas is aware that Jerome and Hilary, in addition to all the Hebrew doctors, contend that David may have composed the bulk of the Psalms but not all. Moses and Solomon, among others, were also responsible for some. Then at a later date Ezra, and perhaps another holy prophet, compiled them all into one book. Despite such efforts on Ezra's part, however, he cannot be counted as the author (*auctor*), or even the efficient instrumental cause (*causa efficiens instrumentalis*); that title still belongs to David for having composed the greater part of the Psalter. David can also be reckoned a prophet, for the prophet is one whose mind has been illuminated and elevated by God to supernatural cognition; hidden things have been revealed to him. Proceeding now to the material cause (*causa materialis*), Nicholas finds that the prophet and his prophecy can be called great in two ways. First, this great prophet David possessed a clarity of cognition surpassing the others who had relied on exterior images and conveyed their message through veiled words. David

---

132. *Prologus in moralitates Bibliorum* (PL 113:34d).

customarily eschewed the assistance of external images as he relayed his pro-phetic message under the inspiration of the Holy Spirit. As for the prophecy itself that is contained in this book, it too can be reckoned great inasmuch as it extends itself to all things touched on in Holy Scripture. According to Cassiodorus, as Nicholas explains, the whole Christ—head and members—is the subject matter throughout all of Scripture. And so too the whole Christ is the subject of the Psalter, although in a different manner from the rest of Scripture, for here he is the subject matter treated by way of praise. Turning now to the formal cause, it can also be broken down into two components: the *forma tractatus* and the *forma tractandi*. The first refers to the division of the book, which Nicholas lays out as he proceeds in his commentary. The *forma tractandi*, also known as the *modus agendi*, is the literary style under which this material is treated—in this case in the manner of divine praise. As for the final cause, that is what pertains to our benefit and salvation. In this vein, Nicholas returns to a theme that we have encountered above, namely, the divide between what humankind can attain by unaided natural reason and what must be revealed under the light of grace. In ourselves, we are not capable of knowing and loving God as befits the supernatural end (*finem supernaturalem*) to which we have been ordered. And because we cannot direct ourselves to an end that is totally unknown to us, it is necessary that such things be divinely revealed in Holy Scripture. The Psalter can fulfill this task, since it contains the entirety of Holy Scripture, under the form of praise, thereby providing to the whole church what is beneficial for hope and the attainment of eternal beatitude.[133]

Turning to Nicholas's prologue for the books of Solomon, we will focus specifically on the Song of Songs. In the sapiential books, not unlike the Psalter, God is the principal efficient cause revealing the wisdom contained therein, while Solomon is the instrumental cause, who possesses this wisdom that has been divinely infused. Here Nicholas makes a point similar to what we have seen in his first general prologue but with a greater specificity that reveals his fundamental reliance on an Aristotelian organization of knowledge. He begins by pointing out that a mobile body is, under an absolute principle, the subject matter of the whole of natural philosophy, and yet it can also be treated under more restrictive parameters as one finds in Aristotle's *On the Heavens*. In this vein, therefore, God is the subject throughout the whole of Scripture under the principle of absolute divinity, and for that reason theology is called *sermo de deo*. Yet, just as in the natural sciences, so it is that in the

---

133. Nicholas of Lyra's postils and prologues circulated in early printed editions of the Gloss. Here see *Biblia Sacra cum Glossa Ordinaria*, 3:415–20.

different books of Scripture the subject is more precisely delineated. In the Old Testament, the subject is God as creator, whereas in the New it is God as redeemer. And then, furthermore, in the sapiential books the subject is God as the giver of wisdom. In the whole of Scripture, Nicholas says, God is the efficient and material cause: efficient because founded and regulated by God; material because God is known by men through what he has infused. The final cause is the good of the whole church inasmuch as the teaching contained therein leads to grace at present and glory in the future. The formal cause is (as we have seen) the twofold *forma tractandi* and *forma tractatus*. Here in the sapiential books the *forma tractandi* is itself threefold: coming down as warning, threat, and promise. One who does not acquiesce to warning is compelled by threats or attracted by promises. The *forma tractatus* is noteworthy here for its canonical implications, since it constitutes a division into the three books of Proverbs, Ecclesiastes, and Song of Songs, thereby leaving out Wisdom and Ecclesiasticus (Sirach). Here Nicholas contends that these latter two books are not part of the canon, thus in keeping with Jerome's recommendation, as we saw in his Kings prologue (the so-called *Prologus Galeatus*). Nor, as Nicholas points out, are these two books contained in the Hebrew canon; hence he does not propose to deal with them in this prologue. What Nicholas has to say here about the Song of Songs specifically proves to be a direct application of the principle enunciated in the third general prologue regarding the relationship between the mystical and literal senses. According to Nicholas, the Song of Songs is all about the desire for heavenly felicity as Solomon speaks in the person of the church (*in persona ecclesiae*), "Let him kiss me with the kiss of his mouth" (Song 1:1 Vulg. [1:2 Eng.]).[134] In the prologue to the Song, Nicholas continues in this vein when he declares the book to be a bridal song in which Solomon sings mystically (*mystice canit*) of the union between Christ and the church. Transcending the visible order, Solomon contemplates heavenly things as he proclaims this union under the appearance (*sub specie*) of husband and wife. The subject matter is indeed the bridegroom and his bride, but its direct reference is Christ the head and his bride the church. Here is an instance, therefore, in which the parabolic sense is the literal sense; this is not, for Nicholas, a love song of carnal desire.[135]

Finally, we will address Nicholas's analysis of how the Bible as a whole is structured. In his prologue to the book of Genesis, Nicholas offers a general overview of the Bible's structure, first pointing out that Scripture is divided

---

134. *Biblia Sacra cum Glossa Ordinaria*, 3:1597–98.
135. *Biblia Sacra cum Glossa Ordinaria*, 3:1815–16. For a thorough analysis, see Mary Dove, "Literal Sense in the Song of Songs," in *Nicholas of Lyra: The Senses of Scripture*, 129–46.

into two parts: the Old and the New Testaments. While it is true, Nicholas says, that the whole of sacred Scripture has God for its subject matter, the first part deals with God principally as creator and governor, while the second treats God as the redeemer and glorifier. The two Testaments are themselves then subdivided into distinct categories. The Old Testament consists of four parts: the legal books, histories, wisdom literature, and prophets. Not only is the New Testament likewise divided into four parts, but these parts neatly complement those of the Old Testament. Thus the legal books of the Old correspond to the gospels, the wisdom literature to the epistles, the histories to Acts of the Apostles, and finally the prophets to the Apocalypse. What emerges from this arrangement of books is the essential harmony that extends throughout God's revelation. Here Nicholas has recourse to Gregory the Great's classic reckoning of the Old and New Testaments forming the wheels within wheels of the prophet Ezekiel's vision (Ezek. 1:16).[136]

Then, in the prologue to his Revelation commentary, Nicholas reminds the reader of his opening remarks in the Genesis prologue in which he outlines the symmetry of the two Testaments. Nicholas thus ties together the whole of Scripture, its first and its last book. He also wants to show how Revelation fulfills its relationship to the Old Testament prophetic books to which it corresponds. Nicholas adopts as his theme the words of Revelation 10:11, "You must prophesy again to many peoples and nations" (*Oportet te iterum prophetare populis et gentibus*). Nicholas works through this verse word by word, noting that "again" (*iterum*) is used here to signal that this final prophecy comes after the Old Testament prophets. There are, moreover, four foundations of this book: necessity, which is signaled by "you must" (*oportet*); truth, insofar as "you must prophesy [what is divinely revealed]" (*te prophetare*); the quality of order, as he prophesies "again [following previous prophecies]" (*iterum*); and universality, by proclaiming his message to "many peoples and nations" (*populis et gentibus*). Whereas the Old Testament prophecies may have come to pass, in this New Testament prophetic book John is describing the tribulations yet to come, those that will continuously beset the church until the end of the world. Revealing these events will better enable Christians to fortify themselves with the patience needed to endure this suffering. Hence the necessity of this book, Nicholas says, so that the church might be prepared. With respect to the truth of what John prophesies, Nicholas sounds a chord that we have already encountered in his *principium*, namely, that whereas human cognition is prone to error even when beginning from first principles, divine revelation excludes all possibility of error inasmuch as it constitutes the very

136. *Biblia Sacra cum Glossa Ordinaria*, 1:1.

"measure of truth" (*regula veritatis*). The prophetic revelation contained in the Apocalypse does not proceed from human investigation, therefore, but from divine revelation that guarantees its veracity.[137]

The aforementioned quality of order actually raises an interesting canonical question. Nicholas observes that the prophetic books are last according to the order commonly found in "our Bibles," although among the Jews this is not the case. Nicholas concedes that the books of Maccabees are placed in Christian Bibles after the prophets, but this does not impede the desired symmetry because they do not belong to the canon; he states this on the authority of Jerome's prologue to the book of Kings (the *Prologus Galeatus*). And so it is, Nicholas says, that among the canonical books (*inter libros canonicos*) of the Old Testament, the prophetic books are indeed last, thereby securing the correlation with the New Testament. Finally, one observes that whereas the Old Testament prophets may have spoken about many peoples and nations, they addressed themselves to only one, their fellow Jews (Jonah's mission to the Ninevites being the sole exception). John, on the other hand, prophesies to all peoples and nations because he addresses the universal church, which comprises the multitude of peoples and languages across the earth.[138]

As mentioned, Nicholas's fourfold arrangement of the Testaments aligns the legal books of the Old Testament with the gospels in the New. Nicholas makes clear that the gospels, taken together, constitute a unique and perfect law bestowed by the only begotten Son of God and ordered to a single end. By virtue of its fourfold knowledge, it exceeds not only human law but also the divine law given to Moses. Content to treat the gospel as law (*lex*), therefore, Nicholas proceeds to compare it to these other laws with respect to four basic functions: extirpation of vice, establishing principles of human conduct, leading people to happiness, and conveying truth clearly. Evangelical law is alone capable of genuinely fulfilling these functions.[139] Nicholas's extensive argument to that effect is designed to illustrate the perfection of the gospel as it is contained in the books of the New Testament. More to the point, however, is the emphasis that is placed on Jesus Christ as the one who reveals to humans this ultimate and enduring expression of the divine will.

Nicholas begins by observing that no human law is capable of removing all vice, precisely because none is able to prohibit every sort of evil. In fact, some evils in human society are inevitably tolerated for the sake of the greater common good. Neither, however, could the Mosaic law eradicate vice entirely, a

---

137. *Biblia Sacra cum Glossa Ordinaria*, 6:1445–46.
138. *Biblia Sacra cum Glossa Ordinaria*, 6:1446. For Jerome's prologue, see *Biblia Sacra iuxta Vulgatam Versionem*, ed. Robert Weber (Stuttgart: Deutsche Bibelgesellschaft, 1969), 364–66.
139. *Biblia Sacra cum Glossa Ordinaria*, 5:5.

case in point being the allowance of divorce (Deut. 24:1), which Christ himself said was permitted to the Israelites on the grounds that they were an obdurate people (Matt. 19:8). Only the most perfect law of the gospel has the capacity to eradicate evil and even foretells punishment for transgressors. Jesus, here designated the "evangelical lawgiver," warns that "on the day of judgment you will have to give an account for every careless word you utter" (Matt. 12:36).[140]

Drawing on Aristotle's principle that the intention of every lawgiver is to make people good citizens (*Ethics* 2.1.1103b), Nicholas next addresses human conduct. Here again human law is found to be deficient because it can regulate only exterior actions. The Mosaic law also falls short on this score; hence the comment that it "constrained the hand but not the will" (*prohibebat manum non animum*). In this instance, Nicholas appealed to the *Glossa Ordinaria*, pointing to a marginal gloss that appears at Philippians 3:6, "*secundum iustitiam quae in lege. . . .*" A subtle analysis follows, in which Nicholas explores the Mosaic law's capacity to prevent evil. The Jewish teachers (*doctores iudaeorum*) fail to understand the matter, according to Nicholas, when they say that an evil will is no sin unless it is somehow put into action—here citing Josephus to that effect.[141] And when one argues against them on the basis of the commandment that "you shall not covet your neighbor's wife" (Exod. 20:17), they respond that this commandment does not actually prohibit interior desire but instead forbids its exterior manifestation. Hence "Do not covet" means you are not to perform actions that are indications of desire (*signa concupiscentiae*), such as embraces and kisses. Nicholas regards this reading of the text as patently false. This is because an exterior action in itself is morally neutral, neither good nor evil; its moral status is determined by the interior act that prompts it. It is the voluntary character of the action, as an act of the will, that gives an action its moral force. Better to say, therefore, that the old law did in fact prohibit a few thoughts and desires, such as adultery and avarice. It did not, however, inflict any punishment on those interior acts; in that sense it was imperfect. Only the most perfect law of the gospel universally prohibits evil desires and lays out the punishment for them, as the Savior says in his Sermon on the Mount, "You have heard it said to those of ancient times, You shall not kill. . . . But I say to you that if you are angry . . ." (Matt. 5:21–22). Thus the gospel law alone establishes an order not only for exterior acts but also for interior, thus comprising the entirety of the human person.[142]

140. *Biblia Sacra cum Glossa Ordinaria*, 5:5.
141. *Antiquities* 12.9.1.
142. *Biblia Sacra cum Glossa Ordinaria*, 5:5–6. Cf. Nicholas's postil on Matthew where, when commenting on the Sermon on the Mount, he also references Josephus on this point

For leading people to happiness, Nicholas finds that human law is capable only of creating conditions of political happiness, the peacefulness and tranquility of the state in this mortal life. Yet the human person considered with respect to the intellect, the chief component of man, is immortal, so it is fitting that we should affirm the existence of some other happiness beyond this mortal life.[143] It is only the divine law that orders humans to this end, something that human law cannot achieve. Insofar as humans are ordered to a certain beatitude beyond natural happiness, an appropriate law would have to be divinely revealed that could direct them to that end. Even the Mosaic law could not fulfill this role, since the achievement of happiness beyond the natural order is impossible apart from grace: "The free gift of God is eternal life" (Rom. 6:23). In keeping with its preparatory role, therefore, the Mosaic law could only dispose us to this grace; it could not actually confer it. For this one must look to the Savior: "The law indeed was given through Moses; grace and truth came through Jesus Christ" (John 1:17).[144]

Turning to the final purpose of law, to hand down the truth clearly and openly, Nicholas determined that human law, comprising both civil and canon law, is defective. All manner of obscurities are found therein, Nicholas observes, not to mention the inevitable changes and variations. Although the Mosaic law does hand down the truth, it does so under veils and figures, illustrated by the veiling of Moses's own face when he came down from Mount Sinai (Exod. 34:33). Appealing to the classic assessment of the relationship between the Testaments, Nicholas recounts how the truth that remained veiled in the Old Testament, hidden within symbols, was then made manifest in the New Testament. This is in keeping with Christ's words, "The hour is coming and now is when I will no longer speak to you in figures" (John 16:25).[145]

John Wyclif

The English theologian John Wyclif was the first man since Nicholas of Lyra to produce a commentary on the entire Bible, and this work was itself heavily indebted to that of the Franciscan scholar whom Wyclif so admired.[146] When

---

(*Biblia Sacra cum Glossa Ordinaria*, 5:106, 110). See also Nicholas's similar comments on the Decalogue in his Exodus postil (*Biblia Sacra cum Glossa Ordinaria*, 1:676). For the gloss of Phil. 3:6, see *Biblia Sacra cum Glossa Ordinaria*, 6:594.

143. Cf. Aristotle, *Ethics* 1.10.1101a.

144. *Biblia Sacra cum Glossa Ordinaria*, 5:6.

145. *Biblia Sacra cum Glossa Ordinaria*, 5:6.

146. Some of this material on Wyclif has been adapted from my essay, "John Wyclif: The Hermeneutics," in *Handbuch der Bibelhermeneutiken*, 255–70.

Wyclif incepted as a master of theology about 1372, he was in the midst of delivering the biblical lectures that would eventually form his *Postilla super totam bibliam*, which he completed by 1379. Wyclif's own *principium* had also served as his second prologue to the Song of Songs.[147] While adhering to the basic formula of the genre, whereby the new master extols the sublimity of Holy Scripture, there are two prominent features in Wyclif's *principium*: his emphasis on the moral state of the exegete and a deep appreciation for the role of philosophy in the exegetical task. Here Wyclif locates three essential criteria for the study of Holy Scripture, which he equates with the science of theology itself. There is the moral disposition that informs one's affections (*moralis dispositio affectum*), experience in the three main branches of philosophy, and finally the virtuous way of life that results from these habits. According to Wyclif, it is the rightly ordered will that makes possible genuine comprehension of theological truths. Infidels, heretics, and those in a state of mortal sin are mistaken, therefore, when they imagine that they can comprehend the wisdom of the Scriptures. This is because theology itself is a wisdom (*sapientia*) that cannot be genuinely experienced (*sapit*) by those with a disordered will. Wyclif's treatment of theology as wisdom—and thus his play on *sapientia*, *sapere*, *sapor*—runs close to thirteenth-century Franciscan treatments that emphasized the experiential component of theological inquiry. Wyclif likewise prioritized the will as the highest power of the soul and so contends that rectitude of the will—properly ordered to justice—is essential to the study of Scripture because the author of the book of life is the Holy Spirit, to whose will this eternal book personally corresponds. This emphasis on the ordering of one's affections so as to be brought into conformity with Christ and the Spirit stands at the heart of Wyclif's biblical hermeneutics across the span of his career.[148]

Yet even the exegete whose will is properly disposed to plumb Scripture's depths must be academically equipped for this task. Wyclif's debt to Augustine's *De doctrina christiana* becomes evident as he proceeds to break down the three main aspects of philosophy that are useful for the study of Scripture. Wyclif begins with the trivium. Grammar instructs one in the identification

147. Oxford, St. John's College MS 171, fols. 323v–326v. The text is transcribed in Gustav Benrath, *Wyclifs Bibelkommentar* (Berlin: de Gruyter, 1966), 338–46. See also Beryl Smalley, "Wyclif's *Postilla* on the Old Testament and His *Principium*," in *Oxford Studies Presented to Daniel Callus* (Oxford: Clarendon, 1964), 253–96; Smalley, "John Wyclif's *Postilla super Totam Bibliam*," *Bodleian Library Record* 4, no. 4 (1953): 186–205.

148. Benrath, *Wyclifs Bibelkommentar*, 338–41. Cf. Alexander of Hales, *Summa Theologica* 1.1, ed. B. Klumper, 4 vols (Quaracchi: Collegii S. Bonaventurae, 1924–48), 1:1–2. For Wyclif's treatment of the upright will ordered to justice, see Anselm of Canterbury, *De veritate* 12, *Opera Omnia*, ed. F. S. Schmitt, 6 vols. (Edinburgh: Nelson, 1946), 1:191–96.

of terms that are necessary when determining the literal sense of the text, but also helps one with the figures and tropes employed by the mystical senses: allegory, tropology, and anagogy. Happy is the person who knows these perfectly, Wyclif says, but happier still the one who can trace Latin terms back to the original Greek and Hebrew so as to understand the properties of things and the reason behind their names (although Wyclif himself possessed no such language skills and thus relied on earlier commentators). Yet happiest of all is the person who perfectly grasps dialectic: the art of syllogizing that allows one to uncover hidden metaphysical truths within the sacred text. As for rhetoric, it is essential for communicating this wisdom effectively to different audiences. The purpose of all Christian eloquence is to render the doctrine necessary for salvation more intelligible so that it might be more readily received. Nothing is worse than florid and grandiose discourse that serves only to obscure the truth. The theologian, moreover, must be acquainted with natural science so that he can comprehend the mystical and parabolic expressions in Scripture. The author of Scripture has drawn on a great multitude of things in the created order whose various properties are replete with mysteries. Holy Scripture is also filled with moral philosophy, conveyed both explicitly and implicitly, which readers will scarcely be able to grasp if they have not already studied such works as Aristotle's *Ethics*. Like Augustine, therefore, Wyclif maintains that while Scripture contains all truth, the exegete will need solid training in the liberal arts to bring that truth to light. More than that, however, Wyclif consistently follows Augustine's foundational principle that the mysteries of Scripture are revealed to the humble of heart who are subject to Christ and rooted in love. Wyclif then comes full circle at the conclusion of his *principium*, as he highlights these themes of humility and charity, reminding his university audience that the purpose of their scriptural studies must always be to put the gift of this knowledge at the service of the church. The theologian fulfills his duty by illuminating others, whether through holy preaching, scholastic instruction, or at least sanctified conduct, never seeking his own glory but always working to the praise of God.[149]

A few years later, around 1377–78, Wyclif produced a grand defense of Holy Scripture. This is a wide-ranging work that seeks first to secure the logical coherence of biblical propositions before making the case for the principal role of Holy Scripture in the formation of a properly ordered Christian society. Wyclif says that he felt compelled to act, because errors regarding the meaning of Scripture (*sensus scripturae*) were being disseminated at an alarming

---

149. Benrath, *Wyclifs Bibelkommentar*, 341–46. Cf. *De doctrina christiana* 2.42.63 (CCSL 32:76–77). Cf. also Matt. 11:29; Eph. 3:17.

rate in his own day. As a master of the sacred page, Wyclif was duty-bound to defend the text that was not only the very basis of his discipline but also the lifeblood of the church. In the first part of this work, his principal opponents are members of the arts faculty, commonly known as the "sophists," who had located apparent logical contradictions within the sacred text. What the sophists may have reckoned merely an academic exercise designed to expose false constructions, Wyclif regards as a reckless and destructive practice that ultimately betrays the mission of the university.

In tones reminiscent of Nicholas of Lyra, Wyclif proceeds to describe Scripture as the eternal exemplar that will establish orthodoxy and root out heresy. Here is the "radiance of eternal light and spotless mirror" (Wis. 7:26) wherein the truth has been indelibly inscribed. In fact, Wyclif speaks of an identity between the book, the truths it contains, and its author—even as the three remain formally distinct—such that Scripture may even be called a mirror of the will of God, the perfect author who cannot deceive.[150] Scripture will form the absolute standard by which to judge matters of orthodoxy and heresy. And this means that theologians, precisely as masters of the sacred page, will lead the way forward, since they are best equipped to grasp Holy Scripture's unique manner of speaking (modus loquendi) and thus can determine which practices are in keeping with this perfect law. By asserting the special prerogatives of the theologian, Wyclif stakes out ground against the canon lawyers, whose influence was steadily growing throughout the fourteenth century. Following in a long line of medieval theologians, Wyclif contends that the role of the canonists in the determination of orthodoxy and heresy would always remain secondary. Theirs is a subaltern science that reaches its conclusions on the basis of what has first been established by the theologians through their study of Scripture.[151]

Wyclif's defense of Holy Scripture, and thus the hermeneutics that facilitated it, is founded on the principle of divine authorship. This means that the many terms and propositions embedded within Scripture maintain their logical veracity so long as they are read as originally intended by their divine author, for the literal sense is coterminous with the author's intention.[152] Wyclif observes that an author (auctor) is formally constituted by the authority (auctoritas) that he possesses, which in turn renders the text that the author

---

150. *De veritate sacrae scripturae* 1, ed. R. Buddensieg, 3 vols. (London: Trübner, 1905–7), 1:1–2; *De veritate* 6 (Buddensieg, 1:111–12); *De veritate* 15 (Buddensieg, 1:377). Cf. Nicholas of Lyra, *Prologus . . . De commendatione Sacrae Scripturae in generali* (PL 113:28a); and Henry of Ghent, *Lectura Ordinaria super sacram scripturam*, 5–8.

151. *De veritate* 27 (Buddensieg, 3:63).

152. *De veritate* 1 (Buddensieg, 1:3–5).

produces authoritative. Although Wyclif does not explicitly apply the Aristotelian principles of efficient causation to this issue, he lays out a division of authorial responsibility along those general lines. In the case of Holy Scripture, God is an author in the fullest sense of the word, whereas the biblical writers are authors in a derivative sense; they participate in divine authorial power for the greater good of the church. It is God, the Holy Trinity, who alone possesses a supreme and pure authority, thereby rendering every truth that he speaks of equal authority. If truth is the definitive adequation of a thing with the divine intellect, it cannot be susceptible to degrees of truthfulness. From this it follows that the entirety of Scripture possesses the same authority with respect to every single one of its parts. Establishing the integrity of Scripture means focusing one's attention on the person of the eternal Word. Thus in attempting to discern the truth, one gives heed principally to the authority of the one who is speaking; the personal veracity of the speaker is what ultimately secures the truth of what is spoken.[153] We place our trust primarily in a person, therefore, and only subsequently—on the strength of our confidence in that person—in what has been said.

Even though Wyclif is willing to concede that the human author functions as a sort of secondary efficient cause, it must be admitted that his autonomy, for Wyclif, remains fairly restricted. There is not the same latitude afforded the human author that one finds in Nicholas of Lyra, although Wyclif is not opposed to such authorial classifications in principle. His anxiety was doubtless exacerbated by the polemical quality of the hermeneutical exchanges; too many concessions to human authorship might bolster the efforts of those seeking to undermine Scripture's veracity and thus its inherent authority. There are some, according to Wyclif, who are attempting to refute the truth of Scripture when they assert that the Old and New Testaments contain parables that are patently false. This charge prompts Wyclif to examine the different sorts of figurative locutions employed by Scripture, all of which can be proved true when assessed within their proper categories. To make his case Wyclif turns to Thomas Aquinas, who had observed that figurative locutions, if read metaphorically, are not false. Wyclif proceeds to break down Scripture's figurative locutions into metaphors or similitudes, some of which are allegorical, some parabolic, and others fictive.[154]

Discourse is allegorical, Wyclif says, whenever the history recorded in Scripture according to its literal-historical sense (*ad litteram*) serves to signify what

153. *De veritate* 15 (Buddensieg, 1:391–92).
154. *De veritate* 4 (Buddensieg, 1:63–65). See Aquinas, *De Potentia* 7.5, in *Opera Omnia*, 34 vols. (Paris, 1871–80), 13:225–29.

the future church ought to believe. For instance, Christ was signified in the killing of the paschal lamb in the Old Testament (Exod. 12:3–6) and thus may truly be called the Lamb of God (John 1:36). This is the sort of allegorical locution that Paul had in mind when he recounted the fact—as recorded in Genesis—that Abraham had two sons, who further signify the two Testaments (Gal. 4:22–31). Allegory, therefore, always requires some figure in Scripture that has its basis in an event that actually took place according to the literal-historical sense.[155] A locution is parabolic, however, when some similitude is employed by Scripture to convey a particular meaning, even though the thing itself is not recorded as a historical event (*historizata*) in Scripture. Such discourse is often found in the gospels where Jesus speaks in parables. And then there is fictive similitude when the thing depicted, although not literally true (*ad litteram*), does signify the truth in a mystical way; consider the talking trees of Judges 9:8–15. As it turns out, Wyclif was willing to pursue this passage's mystical implications for the reform of the universal church. Here the three fruit-bearing trees represent those persons in the three states of the church—before, under, and after the law—who had rejected the civil dominion of the clergy.[156]

Wyclif wished not only to secure the truth of these allegories and parables from any charge of falsehood but to bring them all within the orbit of the literal sense. He specifically follows Aquinas, therefore, in his affirmation that the parabolic sense of Scripture is contained under the literal, for the literal sense is not the figure itself but rather that which is symbolized.[157] On this basis Wyclif concludes that all parabolic expressions in the gospel are true according to the meaning that they were intended to relate. When Christ recounts a parable, therefore, the parabolic sense is the literal, or authentic, sense even if not the historical. As it stands, then, the literal sense (*sensus litteralis*) proves to be quite expansive and is by no means confined to a bare reading of the letter (*ad litteram*).[158]

This expansion of the literal sense to include parables and metaphors did not, however, resolve such exegetical difficulties once and for all. By the middle of the fourteenth century, these matters were at the forefront of logical debates within the arts faculty at Paris regarding proper and improper supposition. Some wished to constrict the range of the literal sense such that the "force of the word" (*virtus sermonis*) encompassed a term's proper grammatical signification within a proposition. It was thus distinct from the more expansive usages of improper supposition: the common parlance (*usus loquendi*)

---

155. *De veritate* 4 and 6 (Buddensieg, 1:65–66, 121–23).
156. *De veritate* 4 (Buddensieg, 1:66–69).
157. *De veritate* 4 (Buddensieg, 1:73). See Aquinas, *Summa Theologiae* 1.1, 10.
158. *De veritate* 4 (Buddensieg, 1:82–83).

that permits metaphors and tropes in keeping with the author's intended meaning.[159] At its heart the debate turned on whether the truth-value of a proposition could be evaluated independently of the intentions of its author. Did the proposition have a life of its own separate from the person who spoke it and irrespective of any conditions under which it was spoken? The means to evaluate propositions was no mere logical game; statements culled from university lectures could be censured as erroneous, or even heretical, simply on the basis of how they sounded (*prout sonant*), or just as they lay (*prout iacent*), no matter the intended meaning of the master.[160]

When Wyclif waded into this debate, he faced some stiff opposition even from the ranks of his fellow theologians. The Oxford Carmelite John Kynyngham was among those who restricted the range of proper supposition; the intention of Scripture may be clear, Kynyngham said, even as what the bare words signify is erroneous.[161] It seems that others too were of the opinion that "any number of propositions found in Holy Scripture, when taken according to the primary signification of the terms, cannot be excused from falsehood *de virtute sermonis*."[162] Wyclif, however, refused to concede the ground of *virtus sermonis* and proceeded to argue that every proposition contained in Scripture is properly, or literally, true even when using figurative language. To that end Wyclif consistently appealed to the general principle that "in cases of equivocation there is no contradiction," by which he meant that the same word can signify in multiple, noncontradictory ways depending on the context in which it is employed.[163] Wyclif regarded this principle as fundamental to a sound education, taking his opponents to task for their ignorance of Aristotle, who often spoke in accord with the logic of Scripture and thus recognized the subtleties of equivocal construction.[164]

One quickly realizes that recourse to equivocation in these matters means more than brushing up on logical methods. It requires a conversion of the

159. For the most comprehensive analysis, see Zénon Kaluza, "Les Sciences et Leurs Langages," in *Filosofia e Teologia nel Trecento: Studi in ricordo Eugenio Randi*, ed. Luca Bianchi (Louvain-la-Neuve: Fédération internationale des Instituts d'Etudes Médiévales, 1994), 197–258.

160. See J. M. M. H. Thijssen, *Censure and Heresy at the University of Paris: 1200–1400* (Philadelphia: University of Pennsylvania Press, 1998), 1–39.

161. *Fasciculi Zizaniorum Magistri Johannis Wyclif cum Tritico*, ed. W. W. Shirley (London: Longman, Brown, Green, and Longmans, 1858), 26–42. See also my article, "Defining the Responsibilities of the Late Medieval Theologian: The Debate between John Kynyngham and John Wyclif," *Carmelus* 49 (2002): 5–29.

162. *De veritate* 5 (Buddensieg, 1:101).

163. *De veritate* 1 (Buddensieg, 1:9–10). See the substantial treatment of this topic by Alexander Brungs and Frédéric Goubier, "On Biblical Logicism: Wyclif, *Virtus Sermonis* and Equivocation," *Recherches de théologie et philosophie médiévales* 76 (2009): 199–244.

164. *De veritate* 1 and 3 (Buddensieg, 1:14, 47–48).

heart and will, since the Lord instructs the faithful in his own logic and grammar, which remain hidden to unbelievers.[165] The sophist, according to Wyclif, is primarily interested in burnishing his lecture-hall reputation, whereas the gospel-attuned logician sets aside worldly fame; better to be reckoned a fool in the eyes of the world for Christ's sake so as to be counted wise before God.[166] Exegesis must be carried out in a state of humility. The pious Christian teaches and disputes solely for the sake of God's honor and the benefit of the church.[167] He thereby places himself under the authority of Christ the master, since it is only by adopting his way of speaking that one can be reckoned his beloved child and dear disciple. The virtuous student imitates his master's discourse, just as a dutiful son imitates his father.[168]

As touched on above, the principle of equivocation often emerges in instances of figurative discourse, which for Wyclif's sophist opponents cannot be counted as proper supposition; tropes (they say) belong to improper speech and thus must be counted false *de virtute sermonis*. In this vein, Wyclif takes up the question as to whether Christ could properly be called a lion as he is in the Apocalypse (see Rev. 5:5). Here Wyclif observes that propriety and impropriety are twofold, pertaining to the figure and to the thing that is symbolized. On the one hand, Christ is not properly a lion according to those properties belonging to a roaring four-legged beast; however, it is conceded that he is a lion by way of improper speech owing to the impropriety of the figure. On the other hand, Christ is properly a lion when speaking by way of the analogous propriety of the thing that is symbolized, in this case the lion of Judah (Rev. 5:5; cf. Gen. 49:9–10). For even as the predication is metaphorical, it is still proper, since the analogy uniquely refers to Christ, the sole lion of Judah, who opens the book and breaks the seven seals. By means of equivocation, therefore, the proper significate is the metaphorical lion rather than the actual lion.[169]

Thus, according to Wyclif, whenever the exegete encounters what appears to be a contradiction in Scripture, he must recognize this as a lesson in the ways of equivocation, requiring that we accommodate our speech to the temporal and spatial context of the proposition. And here again there is an abiding moral component underlying a basic grammatical principle: we are called on to set aside duplicity and adapt our way of speaking to the common understanding of those with whom we are communicating. The rules of sophistical

165. *De veritate* 1 (Buddensieg, 1:10–11).
166. *De veritate* 2 (Buddensieg, 1:23).
167. *De veritate* 2 (Buddensieg, 1:28–29).
168. *De veritate* 3 (Buddensieg, 1:55).
169. *De veritate* 3 (Buddensieg, 1:40).

refutation that otherwise reign in the lecture hall must ultimately yield to the demands of Christian charity. Only then, by preserving this sacred logic, can we avoid lapsing into the sort of vainglorious verbal sparring that is so unbecoming in God's sight. A sober use of equivocation might then salvage the truth of Christ's own discourse. For instance, it is recorded in the Gospel of John that Jesus said to his brothers, "'I am not going to this festival.' . . . But after his brothers had gone to the festival, then he also went, not publicly, but as it were in secret" (John 7:8–10). Had Christ therefore lied to his brothers? No, for when Christ was asked at what hour he would go up to Jerusalem, he responded truthfully, provided that one grasps his unstated implication: that he was not planning to go up publicly at that time, which was both true and directly pertinent to the question that he was asked. The context in which the proposition is uttered is of the utmost importance, since the truth-value depends on the application of additional facts that are understood to be implied even if not precisely stated. Wyclif offers the following example: It is as though someone were to ask me whether I have celebrated Mass and I were to respond pertinently to what I suppose to be the questioner's intention, the answer to which is no. By answering no, I am not thereby stating that I have never celebrated Mass, even as I am saying that I have not celebrated today. I am specifically supplying in thought a particular time frame that is understood by my interlocutors. Likewise, in the case of Christ's statement to his apostles, contradiction is avoided through equivocation, since the proposition "I am not going up" is existentially quantified and thus does not contradict the fact that Christ later went up to the festival privately. There is, moreover, a deeper significance in Christ's answer that is borne out by the fourfold sense of Scripture. Wyclif finds that on the moral level Christ went up to the Feast of the Tabernacles in secret so as to teach us not to desire worldly glory; allegorically so that we might realize that Christians "have no lasting city here" (Heb. 13:14); and anagogically so that we would see how the festival day prefigures Christ's ascension to the eternal feast, for "we know this, however, when he has appeared we will be like him" (1 John 3:2). Thus what appeared to be contradictory at first glance actually manifests the wisdom of Scripture's unique manner of speaking that is rich in levels of meaning.[170]

Jean Gerson

The Parisian master of theology and university chancellor Jean Gerson addressed questions of biblical hermeneutics in various, often contentious,

---

170. *De veritate* 2 (Buddensieg, 1:23–27).

contexts. In the early fifteenth century Gerson and his colleagues at Paris were routinely called on to render determinations on important matters of state. One such case required that Gerson pen a rejoinder to fellow master Jean Petit, who had defended the murder of the Duke of Orléans at the order of the Duke of Burgundy in 1407. In doing so, Gerson presented a detailed account of his own exegetical methodology. Petit had argued that this was a case of legitimate tyrannicide, which meant that the commandment "Thou shalt not kill" could not be strictly applied. Instead, he claimed, it had to be read through the Aristotelian principle of equity (*epikeia*), which allowed for the spirit of the law to be fulfilled rather than slavishly adhering to the letter. Basing his argument on 2 Corinthians 3:6, "The letter kills, but the spirit brings life," Petit concluded that "it is dangerous to one's soul to always abide by the literal sense [*le sens litéral*] of Holy Scripture." This matter was brought for examination to the Council of Constance, with seventy-five masters rendering opinions on Petit's exegesis. Much of the support for his exegesis rested on the fathers, especially Gregory the Great's remark that not all passages of Scripture ought to be read literally (*iuxta litteram*), since a mere surface reading might lead to error rather than edification (*Moralia* 1.3). Petit, for his part, equated the literal sense of Scripture with the bare grammatical meaning, which he then felt free to dismiss. Yet Gerson in his response argued that this means of bypassing the so-called literal sense—on the grounds that it is absurd—could quickly become a license to make a text say whatever the reader wants it to say. When the words of the biblical text are no longer trusted to reveal the true meaning, there will be no end to capricious interpretations. Indeed, if the literal sense were no longer considered reliable, then the very authority of Scripture would be at stake.[171]

Now according to Gerson, the literal sense of the text is identical to the intention of the author. He writes, "The literal sense of any discourse is the sense which the speaker himself principally and directly intends. Hence it is the same thing to say that one should not hold to the literal sense as to say that one should not grasp the intention of the speaker. Yet since the Holy Spirit is the one who speaks in Holy Scripture, it is erroneous to say that the literal sense is not true sometimes and thus should not always be held."[172] The key here, for Gerson, is that the letter (*littera*) and the literal sense (*sensus*

---

171. See the excellent analysis by Karlfried Froehlich, "'Always to Keep to the Literal Sense in Holy Scripture Means to Kill One's Soul': The State of Biblical Hermeneutics at the Beginning of the Fifteenth Century," in *Literary Uses of Typology from the Late Middle Ages to the Present*, ed. Earl Miner (Princeton: Princeton University Press, 1977), 20–48.

172. *Circa damnationem propositiorum Johannes Parvi*, in *Joannes Gersonii Opera Omnia*, ed. Ellies Dupin, 5 vols (Antwerp, 1706), 5:926c.

litteralis) are not always the same, since one thing is signified through the terms of the letter (*per terminos litterae*) and another through the things signified (*res significatas*). Because the Holy Spirit speaks in the latter way at times, it is simply false to equate the grammatical sense of the text with the literal sense, since the sacred letter expresses the intention of the speaker by way of things, not terms.[173]

Like Nicholas of Lyra before him, Gerson allowed for a *duplex sensus litteralis*. Thus in the case of David and Solomon, these kings not only symbolize Christ, but accounts of their lives may also offer moral instruction when read as simple narratives. Yet there are also instances when a text might reduce from a double literal to a single literal sense over time. This is the case with Genesis 17:14, where the uncircumcised boy will be removed from the people of God. At one time it both taught the intellect insofar as it was figurative, and induced right action insofar as it was preceptive. Considered from the perspective of the new law, however, this verse has only one literal sense: the figurative. For with the advent of baptism, the Holy Spirit does not intend for Christians to practice circumcision. Hence a proposition that once had a double literal sense now has only one sense in the age of grace.[174]

Not unlike John Wyclif some four decades earlier, Gerson was unnerved by the logicians of the arts faculty who claimed to have located errors in the narratives of the biblical authors. Gerson set himself to respond to the sophists who had reproached Mark the evangelist for having said that "people from the *whole region* of Judea and *all the people* of Jerusalem were going out to [John the Baptist]" (Mark 1:5–6). Apparently the *tractatores logicae* were scandalized by this statement and found fault in such a form of speech, for by the "force of logic and the propriety of speech," this statement appears to be false, inasmuch as Mark chose to employ "universal discourse" in this instance.[175] Here Gerson contends that one must distinguish between two sorts of logic: that which is employed by the natural and speculative sciences, which may simply be called logic, and another logic that Gerson calls rhetoric. Both sorts have their own rules of discourse. The first demands proper speech (*sermonis proprietatem*) and thus rejects the use of metaphor and figurative language in its attempt to be as precise as possible. Yet the other form of logic, which is called rhetoric, fittingly employs figures and tropes, which are helpful to the moral sciences. There is no need, therefore, for prophetic texts, historical narratives, and moral discourse to abide by "the strict rules of the first logic;

173. *Circa damnationem* (Dupin, 5:927a–b).
174. *Circa damnationem* (Dupin, 5:927c).
175. *De duplici logica*, in *Oeuvres complétes*, ed. P. Glorieux, 10 vols. (Paris: Desclée, 1960–73), 3:58.

it is enough that it follows the common manner of speaking [*modus loquendi communis*]."[176] Gerson insists that theological texts should not be bound to the rules of the first sort of logic. Theology has its own manner of speaking and thus could never be false *de virtute sermonis*. Indeed, to claim otherwise would rightly be rejected as blasphemous by faithful catholics.[177] For Gerson, it is nothing less than heresy to assert that the literal sense of Scripture might ever be false. This turns on Gerson's distinction between the letter (*littera*) and the literal sense (*sensus litteralis*). As touched on above, the literal sense, according to Gerson, is what the Holy Spirit principally intended, and it can be elicited from the context of the letter of Scripture.[178] That is why he insists that the literal sense of Scripture must not be taken according to the force of logic or dialectic, but more fittingly according to common usage of speech found in rhetoric, which allows for tropes and figures of speech. Again, therefore, we are reminded that Scripture possesses its own form of logic that is not beholden to human determinations.[179]

Gerson also discussed his hermeneutical methods amid debates with the Bohemian Hussites. In a battle over the correct interpretation of texts, Gerson cautioned that all the parts of Scripture are interconnected and should be read comprehensively. Only then can one begin to understand the intention of its divine author, the Holy Spirit. Exegetes need to compare one passage with another to weigh up the totality; they cannot isolate certain passages to make their case. Yet biblical exegesis is not simply a matter of harnessing a set of linguistic skills. There is a subjective, if not an individualistic, component to the exegetical process. Exposition of Holy Scripture relies on learned people who are operating not merely by the strength of their own wits but under the inspiration of the Holy Spirit. Thus when comparing the various expositions of the doctors, we must pay close attention to those that appear to exhibit certain spiritual gifts. It is not enough to cite any given doctor of the church in support of one's case; one must cite the right doctors. Beyond this, one must have respect for the interpretive authority of those expositions embodied in the glosses, the canons, and the decrees—all of which will assist us in making sense of the biblical text. Indeed, Holy Scripture receives its interpretation not only in the examination of the original words but also as its meaning comes to light in later expositions. Where then does this layered interpretation reach its conclusion? Authentic reception and exposition, says Gerson, is finally resolved in the authority, reception, and approbation

176. *De duplici logica* (Glorieux, 3:58–59).
177. *De duplici logica* (Glorieux, 3:59–60).
178. *Quae veritates* (Dupin, 1:24c–d). See also Glorieux, 6:185.
179. *De sensu litterali sacrae scripturae* (Dupin, 1:3a). See also Glorieux, 3:334.

of the universal church, especially that of the primitive church (*praesertim primitivae*), which received this interpretive acuity directly from Christ by the revelation of the Holy Spirit.[180]

Paul of Sainte-Marie

We conclude this lengthy section with Paul of Sainte-Marie, a convert from Judaism and later bishop of Burgos, who produced a substantial and sometimes critical commentary on Nicholas of Lyra's postil. Of special interest, though, is Paul's preliminary discussion of the parameters of the literal sense. Here in his commentary on Nicholas's postil, Paul notes an objection raised against claims for the superiority of the literal sense. If the literal sense (*sensus litteralis*) is taken to be the first signification of the letter by which the words signify things, there appear to be many falsehoods in Scripture, especially in cases where God is assigned corporeal qualities.[181] Now there is no doubt that when Scripture employs parables, there will be apparent falsehoods of this sort. But, Paul says, the aforementioned definition of the literal sense is clearly too narrow. Rather, it should be understood to refer to the sense intended by the author of Holy Scripture, who is God. Paul's reasoning is as follows:

> The literal sense of any writing is that which the author intends, since the words which are in his mind are signs of his feelings, as we read in [Aristotle's] first book of *On Interpretation* (1.16a). Yet it is certain that the author of Holy Scripture is God, and so it is clear that the literal sense of the text under discussion is that [sense] which is intended by God. And it is through the words [*voces*] contained in the letter that [his intention] is signified. It follows from this that one should not call the literal sense of Holy Scripture the sense that in some way contradicts the authority or determination of the Church, however much such a sense might be in conformity with the signification of the letter. For such a sense is not intended by the author, but rather is heretical.

Here Paul appeals to Jerome's classic definition of heresy recorded in Gratian's *Decretum* (C. 24, q. 3, c. 27): it is an understanding of Scripture that runs contrary to what the Holy Spirit requires.[182] Nor should one accept as the literal sense anything that is contrary to reason, for neither can that be

---

180. *De necessaria communione* (Glorieux, 10:55–59).

181. *Additiones ad postillam magistri Nicolai de Lira . . .* (PL 113:38c).

182. *Additiones ad postillam magistri Nicolai de Lira . . .* (PL 113:39d–40a). See C. 24, q. 3, c. 27 in *Corpus iuris canonici*, ed. Emil Friedberg, 2 vols. (Graz: Akademische Druck- u. Verlagsanstalt, 1959), 1:997–98. Cf. Jerome, *Comm. in Epist. ad Galatas* (PL 26:417a).

intended by the divine author, who is himself the first truth from which all truth is derived.[183]

Paul then takes up the question as to whether there can be only one literal sense in any given passage of Scripture. He looks to Augustine's discussion in the *De utilitate credendi* of the four senses: historical, etiological, analogical, and allegorical.[184] Paul draws on the first three of these in order to provide a fuller explanation of the literal sense. First, he says, there is the letter simply explained: this is the historical sense. The second is the cause of that which is contained within the letter: the etiological sense. And the third is the truth of the letter that is shown not to be contrary to some other part of Scripture: the analogical sense. These categories can then be applied to Genesis 2:22, where the historical sense is simply what is contained within the letter: that God created woman from the rib of Adam. The etiological sense offers the cause why woman was taken from the side of man rather than some other part. And finally, the analogical sense demonstrates that this account does not contradict Genesis 1:27, where the text appears to state that God created male and female at the same time rather than successively as in Genesis 2:22. Yet, Paul says, this does not mean that there are three sorts of exposition contained under the category of the literal sense, such that any one of them is properly the literal sense. Rather, it is the first exposition alone that is the literal sense, whereas the second renders the cause of the literal sense, and the third resolves the apparent contradictions. Hence, while it is true that the second and third expositions pertain to the literal sense, inasmuch as they perfect and elucidate it, they are nevertheless not literal senses properly speaking.[185]

The etiological and analogical senses may not be the literal sense, properly speaking, but that is not to say that there cannot be more than one literal sense of a given text. In fact, Paul contends that when it comes to the simple exposition of Scripture, which arises from the primary signification of the word, it is clear that many literal senses (*plures sensus litterales*) are handed down, not only by the expositors and writers generally, but also by the holy doctors. It is clear, Paul says, that "not every text of Scripture has only one literal sense." Yet it can be objected that, although different senses may be attributed to the same sacred letter, that does not mean that the letter actually possesses many senses. After all (the objection runs), the literal sense is limited to the sense that the author intends. Paul meets this objection by

183. *Additiones ad postillam magistri Nicolai de Lira* . . . (PL 113:40b).
184. See Augustine, *De utilitate credendi* 3.5–9 (PL 42:68–71). Paul's text reads *etymologicus* for Augustine's *aetiologia*, and *anagogicus* for Augustine's *analogia*. I am following Augustine's original, since it makes more sense for Paul's arguments.
185. *Additiones ad postillam magistri Nicolai de Lira* . . . (PL 113: 41c–d).

turning to Aquinas's remark that God is the author of Scripture and can simultaneously comprehend all things by his act of simple understanding (*ST*
1, q. 1, a. 10). Along these lines, Paul also appeals to Augustine's belief that
if the literal sense of Scripture provides many senses that seem to conform to
the letter and are not contrary to the determination of the church and right
reason, they can be accepted so long as they do not contradict one another.
If, however, two literal senses are at odds with each other, then only one can
be the literal sense.[186]

According to Paul, the literal sense of Scripture is of such great capacity
and virtue that all things pertaining to faith and good morals are contained
within it. The testimonies of the truth are established for eternity; these are
the testimonies of Holy Scripture grasped according to the literal sense, from
which sense alone testimony can be accepted. Having said that, it must be
recognized that not all things that might be grasped according to the literal
sense are immediately at hand so that they could all be understood from the
primary signification of the letter. The addition of some other truth may be
required, and from that added truth another truth might then be deduced.
For example, in Luke 20:37–38, Christ appealed to the letter of Exodus 3:6
when responding to the Sadducees, who denied the resurrection. From the
literal sense of the words "I am the God of Abraham, the God of Isaac, and
the God of Jacob," Christ concluded that God is the God of the living, not
of the dead. Here the literal sense tells us something about God, namely, that
he is the God of Abraham, Isaac, and Jacob. Now reason dictates that God
is said to be God with respect to something that really exists, from which it
follows that Abraham and Isaac must really exist. Yet such a conclusion could
not have been deduced from the literal sense of Exodus 3:6 unless another
true proposition were added to it. Conclusions such as these, therefore, can
be gleaned from the sacred letter, sometimes by one deduction and at other
times through a series of deductions. This process is similar to the sciences
or liberal arts, where some conclusions are deduced immediately from first
principles that are naturally known, whereas others must proceed through
various intermediary steps. Hence the literal sense that arises from the primary
signification of the text should be called the first literal sense (*primus sensus
litteralis*), whereas subsequent senses ought to be designated secondary senses
(*sensus secondarii*). The certitude of these secondary senses depends on the

---

186. *Additiones ad postillam magistri Nicolai de Lira* . . . (PL 113:42b–c). See Augustine,
Confessiones 12.42 (CCSL 27:240–41); and *De doctrina christiana* 3.27.38 (CCSL 32:99–100).
Paul is also referring here to Peter Lombard's survey of patristic interpretations of the open-
ing verses of Genesis in his *Sententiae in IV Libris Distinctae* 2.13, ed. Ignatius Brady, 2 vols.
(Grottaferrata: Quaracchi, 1971–81), 1:389–95.

certitude of the first sense, which is itself more certain than the secondary senses. The first principles that are naturally known are always going to be more certain than those that are deduced from them.[187] Inasmuch as there are many literal senses, various criteria have to be established for discerning which one is preferable. We should look for the literal sense that rests more on reason, is more consonant with the letter, and is favored by the holy doctors. Now if there are two literal senses and neither is contrary to ecclesiastical authority or right reason, but one is handed down by catholics and the other by infidels, then the former should be preferred. Those people who are within the bosom of the church—to which Christ promised the Holy Spirit—are going to have the true understanding of Scripture. Paul admits, however, that it rarely happens that where there is a plurality of senses, one of them will exceed the rest in all of these categories. More often than not, one will excel in this way and another in that.[188]

Paul points out that, while it is true that an effective argument can be made only from the literal sense of Scripture, that is not to say that such an argument can be made from just any passage of Scripture read literally. There are many texts in Holy Scripture that have been expounded on by the holy doctors in a variety of ways. One could not, therefore, mount an effective argument from such senses given this level of variation. Although the literal sense of Scripture is not always the same for all readers, one could still find a valid argument within some literal sense that would hold up against people who accept the same literal sense. But one could not use the same argument against those who have a different exposition, or literal sense, of that same passage. There are some texts of Scripture whose literal sense is held to be true among catholics, therefore, even though it will not serve as an effective argument among infidels and heretics. That does not make the sense held by catholics any less true or literal, however. For example, the psalmist says, "By the Word of the Lord the heavens were made" (Ps. 32:6 Vulg. [33:6 Eng.]). For catholics, the true and literal sense of this text refers to the Son of God, which is in keeping with John 1:3, "All things were made through the Word." Yet this will not be an effective argument against infidels who have not accepted the gospel, since they do not concede that there is any real distinction within God that would allow one divine person to proceed from another in the manner of a mental word. As it is, then, the catholic ought to explicate this passage in a catholic way and not worry about the fact that it will be rejected by the infidels who deny the Trinity, for it is not

187. *Additiones ad postillam magistri Nicolai de Lira* . . . (PL 113:42d–43b).
188. *Additiones ad postillam magistri Nicolai de Lira* . . . (PL 113:43c–44a).

necessary to muster an argument from every single literal sense against all potential adversaries.[189]

All the while, though, Paul affirms that everything necessary for salvation is handed down under the literal sense. Indeed, the mystery of the Trinity is founded on the literal sense; only in that way could one render an effective argument on its behalf. Nowhere does Christ ever cite an authoritative passage of Holy Scripture, whether to instruct his disciples or contradict his Jewish opponents, unless it can be understood under the literal sense. Here Paul reports that when Nicholas of Lyra, in his Old Testament postil, comes across an authoritative passage that is cited in the New Testament by Christ and his disciples, he always expounds it according to the literal sense. Thus Nicholas believes that Psalm 117:22 Vulg. (118:22 Eng.), "The stone that the builders have rejected has become the chief cornerstone," should be taken literally as referring to Christ, since Christ had cited this very text about himself (Matt. 21:42).[190] Christ has the authority, therefore, to determine the true literal sense of the Old Testament. This authority with respect to the Old Testament actually extends to all the New Testament authors, as when the apostle Paul cites texts such as Psalm 2:7 to prove the divinity of Christ in the Epistle to the Hebrews (1:5). All the mysteries of Christ are clearly set forth (*expressa*) in the Old Testament and are completed in Christ. It is certain, therefore, that all the authoritative scriptural passages cited by Lyra according to the literal sense signify such mysteries. Thus when Christ spoke of searching the Scriptures, which bear witness to him (John 5:39), this refers to the literal sense, which is to say, the intended sense (*ad sensum litteralem, quod est intentum*).[191]

We see now that, for Paul of Sainte-Marie, the literal sense—understood as the divinely intended sense—is ultimately discernable only to those who are predisposed by grace to recognize the truth. It had been objected that the literal sense has no need of all this intense scrutiny, since it is taken from what is signified through words, that which presents itself immediately to the intellect. In response to this claim, however, Paul points out that many people still manage to err in determining the literal sense of both the Old and the New Testaments: "The ways of the Lord are right and the just walk in them, but transgressors stumble in them" (Hosea 14:9). Paul insists that the spiritual disposition of the exegete is essential if one is to discern the true sense of the text. Although the literal sense is always right, it will be clearer

189. *Additiones ad postillam magistri Nicolai de Lira* . . . (PL 113:44b–d).
190. *Biblia Sacra cum Glossa Ordinaria*, 3:1335.
191. *Additiones ad postillam magistri Nicolai de Lira* . . . (PL 113:52d–54d).

to the just, who possess the light of faith. Those who walk in the ways of the Lord adhere to what was intended through the literal sense of faith, whereas transgressors lack that very light of faith (*lumen fidei*) and consequently stumble. Hence the blindness for which Christ rebukes the Jews is their own false understanding of the literal sense. There are certain Old Testament passages that signify the mysteries of Christ by way of the literal sense, the very literal sense that Jews distort when they deny that the true faith is expressed in these texts. Again, "to search the Scriptures" is to attend to the "true literal sense that is contained within them." The key here, for Paul, is the *verus sensus litteralis*, since a false conception of the literal sense opens up the door to heresy. If Arius had possessed the true literal sense, he would have seen that "The Father and I are one" (John 10:30) speaks to the unity of the divine nature, while the genuine understanding of "The Father is greater than I" (John 14:28) refers to the Father's superiority with respect to Christ's assumed human nature. Heresy inevitably results when texts are understood *ad litteram* apart from the light of the Holy Spirit. So it is that one must abide by the "true literal understanding of the gospel" (*verum intellectum litteralem evangelii*) revealed by the Spirit.[192]

192. *Additiones ad postillam magistri Nicolai de Lira* . . . (PL 113:55a–d).

8

Applied Exegesis

The New Testament and the Medieval Papacy

If Holy Scripture formed the basis for Christian doctrine in the Middle Ages, then it would need to be interpreted by the theologians in its application to central questions facing the church. Biblical exegesis had to be brought to bear on a range of issues, from sacraments to soteriology and ecclesiology. Were not the great battles over the Eucharist and predestination, to name just two, ultimately debates over the proper interpretation of biblical texts? Across the centuries each side marshaled a raft of passages that, when properly aligned, were meant to cement the argument its proponents wished to make. Central to this process was the principle of intertextuality, whereby different texts were compared to one another in an effort to achieve greater elucidation. The purpose of this chapter is to examine one such example of "applied exegesis," in this case determining the scope of papal authority in the later Middle Ages. Along the way we will encounter a number of exegetes, especially from the later medieval period, whom we have already visited during the course of this study.[1]

According to Pope Innocent III, writing in the first decades of the thirteenth century, Christ committed the church to Peter on three different occasions: in

1. This chapter has been adapted from my essay, "The Gospels and the Papacy in the Late Middle Ages," in *Producing Christian Culture from Augustine to 1500s: Medieval Exegesis and Its Interpretative Genres*, ed. Giles E. M. Gasper, Francis Watson, and Matthew R. Crawford (London: Routledge, 2017), 192–210, and is used by permission of the publisher.

the midst of his earthly ministry (*ante passionem*), when he named Peter "the rock" and granted him the keys (Matt. 16:18–19); at the time of his arrest and trial (*circa passionem*), when he prayed that Peter's faith would not fail (Luke 22:32); and then in his resurrected state (*post passionem*), when he told Peter to feed his sheep (John 21:15–17).[2] Writing to Alexius of Constantinople, Innocent invokes two of these passages in quick succession, reminding the emperor that when Christ committed his sheep to Peter, he did not distinguish between "these" or "those" sheep, as if there were different flocks. Rather, he plainly stated that anyone who fails to recognize Peter and his successors as teacher and shepherd is thereby estranged from the sheepfold of Christ. Making clear how far Petrine jurisdiction extended, Innocent points out that Christ chose his words carefully when he promised Peter that "whatsoever you bind on earth will be bound in heaven" (Matt. 16:19); "whatsoever" (*quodcunque*) admits of no exception.[3]

Pope Innocent's exultant rhetoric aside, his identification of these three New Testament passages as the foundation of medieval papal authority was certainly accurate. This is not to say, however, that there was uniformity of interpretation. In fact, critics and supporters of the papacy alike emphasized different aspects of these texts, often read in conjunction with other New Testament passages, as they sought to define more precisely the rights and duties of the Petrine office. As we have observed throughout this book, such a balancing of texts, which allowed for alternative readings, was in keeping with a fundamental aspect of medieval biblical exegesis, namely, that Holy Scripture is its own interpreter.

Of the three aforementioned passages, it was Matthew 16:18–19 that received the most attention, as evinced already among the church fathers who established the basic parameters that would guide later medieval exegetes. Augustine had pointed out that Christ did not say, "You are the rock [*petra*]," but rather "You are Peter [*petrus*]," inasmuch as Christ himself was the rock whom Simon had confessed. Thus when declaring Christ to be the Son of the living God, Peter was speaking on behalf of the whole church, which is built on Christ the rock.[4] Already in the third century, Origen—who was then followed by John Chrysostom and Jerome—maintained that Peter had been rewarded for his correct confession and that this title was actually bestowed

<hr>

2. PL 215:28a–b; 217:658d, 778b. See also the comprehensive essay by Karlfried Froehlich, "Saint Peter, Papal Primacy and the Exegetical Tradition, 1150–1300," in *The Religious Roles of the Papacy: Ideals and Realities, 1150–1300*, ed. Christopher Ryan (Toronto: Pontifical Institute for Mediaeval Studies, 1989), 3–44.

3. PL 216:1185.

4. *Retractationes* 1.21, ed. A. Mutzenbecher, CCSL 57 (Turnhout: Brepols, 1984), 62.

on all believers. In light of Peter's later denial of Christ, the name "rock" must have been derived from Christ the true rock, so designated by Paul (1 Cor. 10:4). The foundation image was connected to 1 Corinthians 3:11 (where Paul calls Christ the church's sole foundation) and Matthew 7:24 (where Christ speaks of the house built on the rock).[5] One finds among the patristic authors, therefore, a consistent christological emphasis that tempered subsequent Petrine determinations of these texts.

This same stress on Christ as the church's foundation, along with a distribution of authority among all the apostles, can also be found among early medieval exegetes. Bede identified the rock as the Savior on whom the church is built, the very one Peter had just confessed. The power of binding and loosing, according to Bede, was without doubt (*sine dubio*) granted to all the apostles whom Christ had addressed following his resurrection, when he said "Receive the Holy Spirit" (John 20:22).[6] Paschasius Radbertus also explained that Peter's name is derived from *petra*, which refers to Christ, the one on whom the church is built. It is not, as some people wrongly think (*male putant*), that Peter is the foundation of the whole church. Here Paschasius had recourse to 1 Corinthians 3:11 to affirm that Christ himself is the church's sole foundation. Peter thus confessed on behalf of all the faithful, and the very faith that he confessed could come only through the revelation of God the Father and the inspiration of the Holy Spirit. In fact, Paschasius says, anyone who possesses this same faith is said to be built on the solidity of this rock.[7]

Much of this patristic and early medieval material then found its way into the *Glossa Ordinaria*. According to the interlinear gloss on Matthew 16:18–19, the rock is Christ himself, in whom Peter believes, or, as one marginal gloss has it, the rock is the confession of faith on which the church is built. And as *Petrus* is derived from *Petra*, so then Peter symbolizes the person of the church (*persona ecclesiae*), which is built on this rock, namely, Jesus Christ himself. The Gloss does accord a certain primacy to Peter. He was the first of the apostles to confess Christ and so is given the keys before the rest; these are the penitential keys of knowledge (*scientia*) and power (*potestas*). Yet the other apostles possess the same judicial power, for Christ had said to them following the resurrection, "Receive the Holy Spirit. If you forgive the sins of any, they are forgiven them" (John 20:22–23). But even as all bishops and presbyters have this same power, Peter still received it in a special manner. This was in order that everyone might understand that whoever separates himself

---

5. See Froehlich, "Saint Peter, Papal Primacy and the Exegetical Tradition," 8–10.
6. *Expositio in Matthaei Evangelium* (PL 92:78d, 79a).
7. *Expositio in Matheo*, V–VIII, ed. B. Paulus, CCCM 56a (Turnhout: Brepols, 1984), 803–5.

from Peter's faith and fellowship can neither be absolved of his sins nor enter into heaven.[8] According to the Gloss, therefore, Peter was established as the principle of unity within the church, although with no greater jurisdictional authority than his fellow apostles.

Some of the staunchest defenders of Petrine primacy in the Late Middle Ages could be found within the mendicant orders, whose many rights and privileges were guaranteed by the papacy, often to the consternation of the secular clergy. When the Dominican theologian Albert the Great commented on Matthew 16:18–19, he was in dialogue with the Gloss. Albert followed along closely as he states that the rock on which the church is founded is Peter's steadfast confession.[9] It is in the reception of the keys, however, that Albert amplifies Peter's position, stressing his unique authority. Peter is not the only one who received the keys, that is true, but he is the one who received them in the fullness of power (*plenitudine potestatis*); so it is for Peter's successors. Other churchmen have only a share in that power (*in parte potestatis*) insofar as they are called into a portion of the Petrine responsibility. Albert proceeds to gloss the Gloss's invocation of John 20:22–23 to bolster Peter's role at the expense of his fellow apostles. It is only in such a derivative sense, Albert says, that Christ spoke in the plural when granting to all the apostles the authority to forgive sins.[10]

Thomas Aquinas, for his part, contended that Peter had received his name as a reward for his confession. Following a traditional line, Thomas declares that Christ himself is the rock, as determined by 1 Corinthians 10:4, and also the foundation, in keeping with 1 Corinthians 3:11. Yet even as Christ is the church's foundation in himself (*secundum se*), and Peter only insofar as he confessed Christ, Peter has still been uniquely appointed vicar of Christ. Thus while it is true that the apostles as a whole form the foundation of the church, according to Ephesians 2:20, Peter still enjoys some measure of primacy, inasmuch as the house of Peter is specifically founded on the rock of Christ and will never be destroyed.[11] The role of Peter, and that of the Roman church, is then strengthened by Christ's promise of protection against the gates of hell in Matthew 16:19, since Rome alone—as opposed to Constantinople, Thomas says—has remained unsullied from heretical depravity. Only in the

8. *Biblia Latina cum Glossa Ordinaria*, ed. Karlfried Froehlich and Margaret T. Gibson, 4 vols. (Strassburg, 1480; repr., Turnhout: Brepols, 1992), 4:55–56.

9. *Expositio in Evangelium Matthaei* 16, in *Opera Omnia*, ed. E. Borgnet, 38 vols. (Paris: Vivès, 1890–99), 20:640.

10. *Expositio in Evangelium Matthaei* 16 (Borgnet, 20:642).

11. *Expositio in Evangelium Matthaei* 16, in *Opera Omnia*, ed. E. Fretté and P. Maré, 34 vols. (Paris: Vivès, 1872–80), 19:473–74.

church of Peter has the faith remained inviolate, thereby in keeping with Luke 22:32, "I have prayed for you that your faith may not fail." And this refers not only to the church of Peter but also to the faith of Peter and the whole Western church.[12] Yet a question then arises: for all that Thomas has just said here, how does one account for John 20:22–23, where all the apostles received the power to forgive sins? Thomas responds that Peter stands above his fellow apostles, since the keys were given to him immediately, while the others received them secondarily from Peter. For although the other apostles do possess the power to forgive sins, it is the pope who, in the place of Peter, maintains the plenary power (*plenaria potestas*) from which the other bishops draw their own.[13]

Not all mendicant authors were so eager to extol the unique prerogatives of the papacy. When Nicholas of Lyra comments on Matthew 16:18–19 in his *Postilla Litteralis*, he adopts a moderate, even cautious, tone. That Christ says "You are Peter" meant that Peter is the confessor of the true rock, who is Christ himself. Yet, for Nicholas, the church to which Christ is referring here does not consist merely of those with pretensions to ecclesiastical or secular power; after all, many princes and high priests have forsaken the faith. The church in reality comprises those in whom there is genuine knowledge and a true confession of faith. And when it comes to the granting of the keys, Nicholas appears to sidestep the Petrine fullness of power that Albert and Thomas emphasize. He points out that the keys were meant not for Peter alone but for the other apostles as well. Just as Peter confessed on behalf of his fellow apostles, so the power that he received was intended for all the apostles. Nicholas qualifies this observation simply by remarking that the power was bestowed on Peter "more chiefly" (*principalius*), inasmuch as he was the "captain" (*caput*) of the other apostles. Nicholas did not elaborate on the nature of this hierarchy, however, and there is nothing here about the pope as the source of episcopal authority.[14]

Marsilius of Padua: The Rejection of Papal Supremacy

One of the keenest critics of a monarchical papacy, the fourteenth-century political theorist Marsilius of Padua, denied outright that the New Testament contained any doctrine of Petrine primacy, thereby attempting to demolish the very foundation on which the late medieval papacy had constructed the

12. *Expositio in Evangelium Matthaei* 16 (Fretté and Maré, 19:474).
13. *Expositio in Evangelium Matthaei* 16 (Fretté and Maré, 19:475).
14. *Biblia Sacra cum Glossa Ordinaria*, 6 vols. (Venice, 1603), 5:280.

edifice of its authority. Marsilius exhibited a genuine facility with Scripture and the interpretative tradition as he painstakingly made the case for the fundamental equality of the apostles. Preparing his response to the pro-papal arguments, Marsilius laid out his basic exegetical method. Those scriptural texts that do not require mystical exposition will be read according to their clear literal sense (*sensus literalis manifestus*). In those instances when a mystical interpretation is needed, he will adhere to the more probable reading of the saints, recognizing that even they can disagree at times. In fact, though, Marsilius generally sticks to the literal sense of the text, which can be clarified through comparison with other New Testament passages and further bolstered by the Gloss, which itself belongs to authoritative exegetical tradition.[15] Thus when his opponents evoked Luke 22:32 to claim that the Roman church's adherence to the faith depends on Peter and his successors or that Christ had exalted Peter beyond his fellow apostles, Marsilius flatly states that neither of these interpretations follows from the words of Christ literally understood (*per virtutem sermonis*). They are belied, among other reasons, by Christ's promising the whole company of apostles that he would be with them until the end of the age (Matt. 28:19–20), thus showing that he had in mind all of their successors.[16]

So it was that in his reading of Matthew 16:18–19 Marsilius finds no warrant for special jurisdictional authority having been granted to Peter—and thus to the papacy—over all Christians. Explicitly in keeping with the patristic reading (notably Augustine) and what came down through the Gloss, Marsilius maintains that the sole foundation of the church is Jesus Christ, who is himself "the rock." Peter the wayfarer erred and sinned by his own free will to the point of denying Christ and not walking by the truth of the gospel (Matt. 26:69–75; Gal. 2:14). Christ alone, therefore, is the foundation (1 Cor. 3:11) who could not err, since he was confirmed in impeccability from the moment of his conception.[17] Marsilius likewise rejects the reading of John 21:17 that gave to the bishops of Rome charge over all the faithful sheep. Rather, as Marsilius writes, the power granted to Peter was bestowed on all the apostles equally, just as Christ's words at the Last Supper were spoken to them in the plural: "Do this" (*facite*). Likewise, "Receive the Holy Spirit" (John 20:22–23) and "Go therefore . . . teach the nations" (Matt. 28:19–20) were spoken to the apostles generally. Paul, moreover, made clear that he had not received his office from Peter (Gal. 2:6). Many such examples are amassed, all to the

15. *Defensor Pacis* 2.28, ed. Richard Scholz (Hannover: Hahn, 1932), 528–29.
16. *Defensor Pacis* 2.28 (Scholz, 535–36).
17. *Defensor Pacis* 2.28 (Scholz, 532–34).

point, according to Marsilius, that the "words of Scripture" cannot support the notion that Peter exercised jurisdiction over his fellow apostles.[18] More than merely diminishing papal authority as such, therefore, Marsilius tries to instill a greater sense of apostolic fraternity that would translate into an episcopal college wherein the bishop of Rome takes his place among equals. This stance served, in turn, Marsilius's conciliarist goals and his larger vision of a politically reordered Christendom.

William of Ockham: Defining the Office of the Papacy

Some years later the English Franciscan William of Ockham set out to correct Marsilius's reading of Matthew 16:18–19 in order to establish Petrine primacy based on this same text.[19] Although Ockham could be a fierce critic of individual popes (e.g., John XXII), he had a high view of the papal office itself. Ockham maintained that Christ had indeed established the unique authority of the papacy in Peter; whether every man who sat in Peter's chair exercised that authority properly was another matter. Yet even as Ockham held that this Matthean passage supports Petrine primacy, he admitted that this doctrine does not proceed from the plain literal sense of the text, as Marsilius had required. That does not mean that these verses lack the primacy doctrine outright, only that the unaided intellect will not grasp it straightaway. One will require assistance in order to understand the full meaning of the text. For that assistance, Ockham turned to other passages of canonical Scripture as well as the expositions of those whom he considered reliable sources, such as the earliest fathers. In that vein, Ockham appeals to Clement of Rome (d. 99), who said that we must acquire the true meaning of Scripture from the one who preserves it according to the truth handed down to him from his predecessors. Ockham maintains that we should read "You are Peter" as it was understood by those reliable sources who gathered the full import of this statement from the apostles themselves.[20]

Correct exegesis of Matthew 16:18–19 is secured precisely because the early fathers were able to report what they had received from people in a position to know. Ockham cites the famous canon in Gratian's *Decretum*

18. *Defensor Pacis* 2.16 (Scholz, 337–55).

19. See also I. C. Levy, "Flexible Conceptions of Scriptural and Extra-scriptural Authority among Franciscan Theologians around the Time of Ockham," *Franciscan Studies* 69 (2011): 285–342.

20. *Dialogus* 3.1.4.13, in *Monarchia S. Romani Imperii*, ed. M. Goldast, 3 vols. (1614; repr., Graz: Akademische Druck, 1960), 2:859. See *Relatum nobis est quod*, D. 37, c. 14; *Corpus iuris canonici*, ed. Emil Friedberg, 2 vols. (Leipzig: Bernhard Tauchnitz, 1879), 1:139.

supporting Petrine primacy, *Sacrosancta Romana* (D. 22, c. 2), attributed to the first-century Pope Anacletus (d. 91). Here the pope had allegedly asserted that Peter obtained his primacy directly from Christ himself. Ockham insists that while Anacletus could err in matters of knowledge or reason, he would never have lied about what he had been taught by the apostles.[21] And although Pope Marcellus (d. 308) and Cyprian of Carthage (d. 258) are quite a bit later than Anacletus, they too are cited as close to the apostolic era. These trustworthy men would have received the true meaning of Christ's address to Peter either from the sayings (*dicta*) or the writings (*scripta*) of the apostles or their disciples.[22] The authentic exegetical tradition, therefore, can be counted on to explicate the doctrine of Petrine primacy implicitly conveyed by Matthew 16:18–19.

Although Ockham believed that Christ had established the primacy of Peter and his successors in Matthew 16:18–19, he did not think that such primacy entailed coercive power. Thus in order to delineate the precise nature of Petrine authority, Ockham appeals to another passage in the Gospel of Matthew, where Christ says "You know that the rulers of the peoples lord it over them and the great men exercise power over them; it will not be so among you" (20:25–26). For Ockham, the optimal form of rule is organized for the common good (*bonum commune*) rather than the ruler's personal advantage. Yes, in Matthew 16:18–19 Christ did place Peter over the rest of the apostles, but it was for building up the church, not for the sake of domination. Peter received power from Christ only insofar as it would serve the good of the whole church. What is more, the authority granted to Peter could not infringe the rights and liberties of the faithful (*iura et libertates fidelium*) that were conceded to them by God and by nature. Thus any judgment of Peter that sought to curtail those divinely bestowed rights would have no force (*iure nulla*), because these rights remain exempt from his jurisdiction. That Christ located rulership (*principatum*) in the church in Peter and his successors is a principle that Ockham confirms, therefore, but only for the sake of humble service, not for domination and glory. Here, then, is a prime example of Scripture interpreting Scripture. Matthew 20:25–26 explicates the fuller meaning—the *sensus plenior*—of Matthew 16:18–19. The genuine exercise of papal primacy does not entail being served, but rather serving others.[23]

21. *Dialogus* 3.1.4.15 (Goldast, 2:860). See *Sacrosancta Romana*, D. 22, c. 2 (Friedberg, 1:73–74).

22. *Dialogus* 3.1.4.16 (Goldast, 2:861). For Marcellus, see *Rogamus vos*, C. 24, q. 1, c. 15 (Friedberg, 1:970); and for Cyprian, see *Loquitur Dominus*, C. 24, q. 1, c. 18 (Friedberg, 1:971).

23. *Octo quaestiones de potestate papae* 4, in *Guillelmi de Ockham Opera Politica*, ed. H. S. Offler, 3 vols. (Manchester: Manchester University Press, 1956), 1:103–6.

Peter John Olivi on Papal Infallibility

When we earlier encountered the Franciscan theologian Peter John Olivi, we contented ourselves with his broader theories of the nature and structure of Holy Scripture. Yet Olivi, hero to the "spirituals" in his order, was perhaps the earliest advocate for the doctrine of papal infallibility, and in support of that rather controversial position, he most assuredly turned to Scripture to prove his point. We will soon look at the work in which he most clearly enunciates his position, but we can begin with his commentary on the Gospel of Matthew. Although there is no discussion of infallibility here, Olivi does contend that Peter's preeminence among the apostles becomes clear during his exchange with Christ at Caesarea Philippi (Matt. 16:16–19), noting Peter's particular authority and constancy along with his ardent faith and love for Christ. And so, in turn, Christ treated Peter as though he were the leader (*quasi ad principalem*) answering on behalf of all the apostles. This was on account of not only Peter's greater zeal but also a certain bearing of authority (*imago auctoritatis*) that he maintained among the rest. Olivi was well aware of the patristic interpretation of these verses and duly recounts the positions of Chrysostom and Augustine whereby Simon is called the rock on account of his solid confession of faith or because he bore witness to Christ, who is himself the rock. For Olivi, these are not competing readings; either one is acceptable. Nevertheless, when it comes to the granting of the keys, Olivi is sure that Peter was given "full authority over the church." That Christ committed the keys of power to Peter singularly was intended to demonstrate that this unique and highest authority had been committed to Peter and to his successors.[24]

In his commentary on the Gospel of Luke, Olivi addresses Christ's words to Peter, "I have prayed for you that your faith may not fail" (Luke 22:32). He explains that in making sense of this passage, one must supply Christ's implication that Peter's faith would finally (*finaliter*) prevail, even though Peter would deny him on that night. According to Olivi, Christ's words to Peter may be taken in three ways. First, they apply to Peter personally insofar as Christ had chosen him to be the head and foundation of the church. Thus, in his human nature, Christ is here calling on the whole Trinity to secure Peter's unfailing faith (*fides indefectibilis*) throughout his prelacy so that he

---

24. Chapter 16 of Olivi's *Lectura super Mattheum* has been edited by Sarah Pucciarelli. An unpublished copy of this text is avaliable on David Burr's webpage via the history department at Virginia Polytechnic: www.history.vt.edu/Burr/OliviPage/OliviSources. See also the study by Kevin Madigan, *Olivi and the Interpretation of Matthew in the High Middle Ages* (Notre Dame, IN: University of Notre Dame Press, 2003), 79–128.

might in turn be able to support the rest of the apostles in their moment of weakness. In a second way, these words could apply to all of Peter's successors in the papal office so that the apostolic see of Peter, as the heart of the church, would be confirmed in this same unfailing faith in order to bolster the suffragan churches when their faith wavers. Last, though, Christ's words were directed to the twelve apostles in their entirety and to all the elect, that they would receive not only the first grace but also the increase of grace and the gift of final perseverance.[25]

Then, in a work devoted specifically to the question of papal infallibility, Olivi constructs a theory based largely on Christ's aforementioned prayer for Peter (Luke 22:32).[26] At stake here was the preservation of the papal bull *Exiit qui seminat*, issued by Nicholas III in 1279, wherein the pope had confirmed Franciscan poverty as the most perfect form of adherence to the life of Christ and his apostles. Any future attempt to overturn this bull would therefore amount to an assault on the gospel itself. Olivi begins with the traditional line that the church could never err, since that possibility would deprive her of any legitimate claim to authority, and she could not be believed.[27] Yet Olivi takes things further as he proceeds to argue that God would never have given someone full authority to decide matters of faith and divine law while yet permitting that same person to err. According to Olivi, God has in fact given this power to the Roman pontiff as revealed in the New Testament. Not only was Peter granted the keys in the Gospel of Matthew (16:18–19), but Christ also prayed that Peter's faith would not fail in the Gospel of Luke (22:32). In the event that the antichrist were to take control of the papacy, one would then have to distinguish between the Roman see in appearance and in reality, and likewise between those who hold the see in name and those who hold it in truth, for the universal church, which can never err, will never be united to an errant head. Hence any pope who errs in general matters of the faith—as opposed to erring personally (*quoad se*)—could not be the true pope or head of the church.[28] Olivi therefore adds a new dimension to the Petrine power of the keys granted in Matthew 16:19 by imbuing this unique grant of jurisdiction with a special gift of inerrancy in its application as determined by Luke 22:32.

---

25. *Lectura super Lucam et Lectura super Marcum*, ed. Fortunato Iozeilli (Grottaferrata: Collegii S. Bonaventurae ad Claras Aquas, 2010), 607–8.

26. *Quaestio de infallibilitate Romani pontificis*, ed. Michele Maccarrone, in "Una questione inedita dell'Olivi sull' infallibilità del papa," *Rivista di storia della chiesa in Italia* 3 (1949): 309–43. See also Brian Tierney, *Origins of Papal Infallibility* (Leiden: Brill, 1988), 93–130.

27. *Quaestio de infallibilitate Romani pontificis*, 338–40.

28. *Quaestio de infallibilitate Romani pontificis*, 342–43.

Guido Terreni: A Proponent of Papal Infallibility

Olivi died in 1298, but in the opening decades of the fourteenth century the Carmelite friar Guido Terreni took it upon himself to write a short work in defense of papal infallibility designed to bolster the authority of Pope John XXII against the attacks of Franciscans, who were outraged by his assertion that Christ and the apostles had possessed private property.[29] Before turning directly to Terreni's treatise on papal infallibility, however, we should look at his commentary on the gospels. Addressing John 21:17, where Christ tells Peter "Feed my sheep," Terreni explains that this passage condemns "the heresy of Marsilius," who opposed the plain meaning of the text (*contra apertam sententiam*) when he claimed that Christ left behind no vicar or head of the church. Terreni, for his part, saw Christ establishing Peter as "vicar, prelate, and pastor of the Lord's entire flock." Peter is clearly the head of all the apostles and supreme pontiff over the whole church. So too, then, is the Roman pontiff the successor of Peter, since he has his authority from Christ through Peter.[30] Turning to Matthew 16:18, Terreni places Christ squarely at the center of the church and so viewed Peter from that perspective. He maintains that just as Christ is "the shepherd of the shepherds," and then after him Peter shepherd of the church, so Christ is the "foundation of the foundations," followed by Peter the foundation of the church founded on Christ.[31] Commenting on Luke 22:32, Terreni admits that Peter did indeed sin when he denied Christ, yet he observed that Christ had prayed not that Peter would not deny him but rather that his faith would not fail. Peter retained the seed of the faith within his heart even when he did not confess it with his mouth. Nevertheless, Christ prayed for the faith of his vicar so that he might then care for the faith of the whole church.[32] As with Olivi before him—even if for different reasons—this verse from the Gospel of Luke became a mainstay in Terreni's defense of papal infallibility, and he devotes a considerable amount of space to this passage in his commentary.[33]

When Terreni specifically addresses the question of papal infallibility, he begins by asking whether a papal successor (with the counsel of his cardinals) can revoke, or even establish the opposite of, what his predecessor had established as a matter of faith, such that it must be firmly believed and its opposite deemed heretical. It would seem that he can, since what has been established

29. See also my essay, "Guido Terreni: Reading Holy Scripture within the Sacred Tradition," *Carmelus* 56 (2009): 73–106.

30. *Quatuor Euangelistarum quasi in vnum ordinem redactorum concordia*, ed. J. Seiner (Cologne, 1631), 1038.

31. *Quatuor Euangelistarum*, 560.

32. *Quatuor Euangelistarum*, 895.

33. *Quatuor Euangelistarum*, 895–901.

by human beings can be erroneous, and error must always be corrected. Thus the erroneous ruling by a former pope will have to be corrected by his successor. Furthermore, the pope can surely err in matters of faith as Peter did when he denied Christ (Matt. 26:69–75) and then later when rebuked by Paul at Antioch (Gal. 2:11–14). There was also the case of Pope Anastasius, who had aligned himself with the heretical Photinus.[34]

Terreni responds to these objections by first appealing to Christ's prayer that Peter's faith would not fail (Luke 22:32). It is clear that, for Terreni, the notion of papal infallibility was to be regarded as a bulwark established for the security of the catholic faith. The papal infallibility question is always handled, therefore, within a larger ecclesial context. Indeed, Terreni contends that Christ's prayer in Luke 22:32 was for the faith of the church. The church is herself founded on the solid rock of the true faith, from which she will never fall away. The church does not err with respect to the truth of the faith, or Holy Scripture, when she renders a determination concerning the catholic faith, precisely because the church in these instances is guided by the Holy Spirit, who teaches all truth and repels all falsehood.[35]

Because Terreni insisted on drawing a distinction between the man and the office, he was prepared to address the inevitability of human weakness. The high priest Caiaphas, for instance, was able to prophesy correctly about Christ on account of the dignity of his office even though he was personally heretical (John 11:51). Hence, even if there were a heretical pope, God would never permit him to determine a heresy, or anything contrary to the faith, since the truth of God must always remain immutable within the church. God would prohibit such an event in some way, whether through the pope's death, the resistance of the faithful, instruction from others, or internal inspiration. There are many ways that God will provide for the faith of his church.[36] Yet here again it is the faith of the whole church that is always at issue: that is the faith that cannot fail. The pope who personally lapses into heresy will never be allowed to exercise the powers belonging to the office in such a way that would imperil the faith of the church. Indeed, the office itself is protected from just such an eventuality since it always remains under aegis of the Holy Spirit. Thus even as the pope could err in himself (*in se*)—as Peter may have done—for the sake of the universal church, the Holy Spirit will not permit him to determine anything contrary to the faith.[37] In this sense, therefore,

34. *Guidonis Terreni Quaestio de magisterio infallibili Romani pontificis*, ed. B. M. Xiberta (Münster: Aschendorff, 1926), 9–10.
35. *Quaestio de magisterio infallibili Romani pontificis*, 13.
36. *Quaestio de magisterio infallibili Romani pontificis*, 26.
37. *Quaestio de magisterio infallibili Romani pontificis*, 28–29.

Christ's prayer for Peter in Luke 22:32 will avail: Peter and his successors, precisely when discharging their unique office as upholders of the catholic faith, can never falter.

John Wyclif and the Limits of Papal Power

John Wyclif not only produced works on scriptural exposition but also wrote some very influential tracts on politics and ecclesiology. According to Wyclif, the papacy was in desperate need of reform, and to that end must conform itself to the most rigorous standards of apostolic poverty and humility.[38] Wyclif adopted a traditional interpretation of Matthew 16:18–19, whereby Peter represented the universal church when he made his confession of faith. Christ is the foundational rock of the church, whom Peter confessed with a pure faith, untainted by any worldly affections.[39] Thus when Peter proclaimed Christ to be both God and man, thereby excluding all heresy, Christ the truth spoke those words—"on this rock"—which Paul had determined was Christ himself (1 Cor. 10:4). Christ the rock had built his own church, and Peter then merited to be his nearest successor.[40] Peter may have distinguished himself as he took the lead in expressing the true faith, therefore, but Wyclif was still insistent that Christ addressed Peter *in persona ecclesiae*, with the result that what he said to Peter applies to the entire priesthood. In keeping with the tradition, Wyclif's reading of Ephesians 2:20 tempers Matthew 16:18, such that Christ is the "cornerstone" on whom the whole edifice is constructed.[41] The spiritual house of the church has the faith of Christ for its foundation, hope for its walls, and charity for its roof.[42]

Just as Peter stood in for the whole church militant when he confessed Jesus to be the Messiah (Matt. 16:16), so too when he received the keys (16:19). Wyclif's point is that no single person holds the keys; they belong to all the faithful. What is more, the authority of the keys has nothing to do with worldly power and wisdom; it is a spiritual power and an evangelical knowledge. Wyclif shifts the balance of authority in the church away from the traditional centers of control when he insists that this true knowledge (*scientia*) is not that of

---

38. See also my essays, "John Wyclif and the Primitive Papacy," *Viator* 38 (2007): 159–89; and "John Wyclif on Papal Election, Correction, and Deposition," *Mediaeval Studies* 69 (2007): 141–85.

39. *Sermones* 2.9, in *Sermones*, ed. Johann Loserth, 4 vols. (London: Trübner, 1887–90), 60–61.

40. *De civili dominio* 1.38, ed. R. L. Poole and Johann Loserth, 4 vols. (London: Trübner, 1885, 1900–1904), 1:281.

41. *De civili dominio* 1.39 (Poole and Loserth, 1:286).

42. *De civili dominio* 1.39 (Poole and Loserth, 1:288).

scholastic disputation or speculation, but rather an evangelical inspiration enabling one to teach the way to final blessedness. Such gifts, however, belong solely to those who worthily follow Christ.[43]

Elsewhere Wyclif speaks of the keys of knowledge and power as referring to knowledge of the Decalogue and the power inherent in the office of the priesthood. Either way, he thoroughly rejects the notion that the papacy has a unique prerogative in the power of binding and loosing. All authentic use of the keys occurs in conformity with the head of the church, Jesus Christ. This means, in turn, that Christ's vicar binds or looses only in an "equivocal sense." The real binding and loosing goes on in heaven, while the pope can at best promulgate what has already occurred.[44] This is because the Holy Trinity possesses this "principal authentic power"; clerics have received only an "instrumental power." And Wyclif insists that this last grade of power has in fact been given to all priests by virtue of their orders. The power of the keys is not the sole province of the papacy but instead belongs to the church as a whole, as Matthew 18:18 and John 20:23 make clear in Christ's address to all the apostles. Thus Wyclif refused to reduce the bishops to mere recipients of a share in the pope's unique plenitude of power.[45]

It comes as no surprise that Wyclif was suspicious of the burgeoning arguments advanced on behalf of papal infallibility. He made his case against this doctrine by examining the life of Peter himself as portrayed within the New Testament. As this saint had sinned three times after having been chosen as an apostle, it is all the more likely that his vicar will also lapse into sin. Peter sinned immediately after receiving the keys and thus was rebuked by Christ (Matt. 16:22–23); later he denied Christ, thereby blaspheming his God (Matt. 26:69–75); and then he sinned again out of blind timidity, even after the sending of the Spirit (Gal. 2:11–14). As it was with Peter, so also with his successors; merely being elected pope does not ensure that one has been confirmed in grace. Wyclif, therefore, dismisses as a "sophistical gloss" the notion that the pope cannot err insofar as he is the pope (*quod papa, sub racione qua papa, nec peccare poterit nec errare*). Wyclif did not accept, therefore, the distinction whereby the pope might err personally, but never when defining a matter of faith for the church. He makes the traditional case neatly when he remarks that, simply because the faith of the catholic church cannot fail (cf. Luke 22:32), does not mean that the faith of the curia cannot. Even in the days following the descent of the Holy Spirit, the apostles recognized

43. *Responsiones ad argumenta cuiusdam emuli veritatis* 2, in *Opera Minora*, ed. Johann Loserth (London: Trübner, 1900), 262–63.
44. *Sermones* 4.12 (Loserth, 102).
45. *De civili dominio* 1.38 (Poole and Loserth, 1:282–84).

their own fragility and confessed not only that they were able to sin but also that they were actually sinners themselves: "If we say that we have no sin, we deceive ourselves, and the truth is not in us" (1 John 1:8). Here, Wyclif says, the apostle John sought to destroy such a prideful notion of sinlessness and restore proper humility.[46]

Jean Gerson and the Cause of Conciliarism

When John Wyclif died in 1384, the Great Western Schism (1378–1417) was only six years old. Resolving the schism was left to men such as Jean Gerson. In 1409 Gerson appealed to the New Testament as he urged the rival popes to consider the full ramifications of their claim to be that shepherd to whom Christ had committed his flock (John 21:17). He reminds them that the good shepherd (John 10:7–18) lays down his life for the sheep by uniting and preserving them. This is a principle of divine law, Gerson says, which remains immutable and eternal.[47] If you call yourself a shepherd, you must have the unity and well-being of the church foremost in mind. You have been called to feed the sheep, not desert them.[48]

Later in 1417, the final year of the schism, Gerson addressed the intransigent Avignon pope, Peter de Luna (Benedict XIII). Here Gerson appeals to Christ's words in Matthew 18:15–18 as a matter of the evangelical law that forms the foundation of the church's supernatural power. This text had become a blueprint for the stages of fraternal and judicial correction:

> If another member of the church sins against you, go and point out the fault when the two of you are alone. If the member listens to you, you have regained that one. But if you are not listened to, take one or two others along with you, so that every word may be confirmed by the evidence of two or three witnesses. If the member refuses to listen to them, tell it to the church; and if the offender refuses to listen even to the church, let such a one be to you as a gentile and a tax-collector. Truly I tell you, whatever you bind on earth will be bound in heaven, and whatever you loose on earth will be loosed in heaven.[49]

Peter de Luna had claimed that he was nevertheless not subject to the judicial correction of the church even if the earlier fraternal correction did not suffice.

46. *De civili dominio* 1.43 (Poole and Loserth, 1:370–73).
47. *Tractatus de unitate ecclesiae*, in *Oeuvres complètes de Jean Gerson*, ed. P. Glorieux, 10 vols. (Paris: Desclée, 1960–73), 6:143.
48. *Tractatus de unitate ecclesiae* (Glorieux, 6:138).
49. *Libellus articulorum contra Petrum de Luna* (Glorieux, 6:267).

For Gerson, such reasoning was plainly heretical because it runs contrary to the evangelical law expressed by Christ in the Gospel of Matthew. Every Christian is our brother, even the pope, who also continues to pray the "Our Father." Gerson does not discount the primacy that the pope enjoys among his brethren, but for all that the pope still remains subject to the immutable evangelical law. Thus if the pope sins against his brothers, he must remain open to fraternal correction; if that fails, he is to be treated as a gentile and tax collector and thereby excommunicated. The church is the judge of the pope when he sins publicly and is denounced to the church. Therefore, the church can now proceed to the judicial phase and excommunicate Peter de Luna, since he has proved himself pertinacious through his unwillingness to accept earlier fraternal correction.[50]

The council fathers at Constance did resolve the schism when they elected Pope Martin V on November 11, 1417. Two years earlier, though, it seemed that the very legitimacy of the council itself might be in doubt when news arrived that the Pisan (antipope) John XXIII had fled the city. In an effort to rally flagging spirits and stiffen resolve, Gerson delivered a masterful sermon to the assembly, taking as his text Christ's admonition "Walk while you have the light, lest the darkness overtake you" (John 12:35). This light and grace that the fathers have been promised is God himself, who is glorified in the council of the saints. From the Gospel of John and then on to Matthew, Gerson reminds his audience to trust in Christ's "infallible promise" that "where two or three are gathered together in my name, I am there among them" (Matt. 18:20). The fathers must not let the darkness of schism and heresy overcome them, for God has placed them in the world to be true lights, the very "light of the world" (Matt. 5:14). They are now to fulfill their role so as to illuminate others and make them perfect. As representatives of the universal church, the fathers should trust that Christ is truly with them in this place, believing his most certain pledge spoken at the close of Matthew's Gospel: "I am with you always, until the end of the age" (Matt. 28:20).[51] For Gerson, the emphasis remained on the church as a mystical body that will always remain united to, and sustained by, its principal and essential head, Jesus Christ.[52]

We have only skimmed the surface of a discussion that consumed the medieval body politic for hundreds of years. Indeed, we have limited ourselves to a set of leading theologians, thereby leaving out the canon lawyers, who were certainly adept at marshaling scriptural passages in defense of papal

---

50. *Libellus articulorum contra Petrum de Luna* (Glorieux, 6:273–74).

51. *Ambulate dum lucem habetis* (Glorieux, 5:39–50).

52. *Libellus articulorum contra Petrum de Luna* (Glorieux, 6:267).

prerogatives. Nevertheless, it is instructive to see how the reading of Scripture was brought to bear in efforts to resolve fundamental issues of ecclesiastical governance. Concluding with Gerson as we did, we see how one theologian balanced different biblical passages in order to meet the challenges of a dire situation, one not only in need of immediate resolution but also crucial for charting a new way forward. As it was, Gerson's greater vision did not ultimately take hold, and we could very easily chart the continued explication of these texts into the sixteenth century. And if we did, we might be struck by how familiar such readings would have been to the medieval predecessors of the Reformation-era theologians.

Conclusion

Can Medieval Exegesis Speak to Us Today?

Now we return to the question that we raised in the introduction to this volume: Do medieval exegetical methods have a place in the way we read the Bible today, or have they been eclipsed by the historical-critical method? We have seen that the Pontifical Biblical Commission affirmed the validity of deeper spiritual meanings known to the Holy Spirit even if not to the human author. Now we might also consider an essay penned by Reformation scholar David Steinmetz, "The Superiority of Pre-critical Exegesis." In this thoughtful, even provocative, piece, Steinmetz argues that the historical-critical method, with its singular focus on what the text meant to its original human author, has forfeited the richness of medieval hermeneutics with its openness to multiple meanings. What is more, according to Steinmetz, the medieval exegetes' allowance for a "field of possible meanings created by the story itself" actually places them in the good company of many contemporary literary theorists. If texts really can develop a life of their own, imbued with meanings that their authors had not conceived, then medieval commentators have grasped a vital component of the reader-text relationship that has eluded historical critics.[1]

Steinmetz's points are well taken, although we would hasten to add that the medieval exegetes remained attentive to the foundational quality of the literal-historical sense of the text in ways that some modern literary critics do not, even as this sense did not exhaust the range of meanings for them. As we have seen, Nicholas of Lyra, with his development of the "double-literal sense" (*duplex sensus literalis*), comprising two equally valid levels of meaning—the

---

1. David Steinmetz, "The Superiority of Pre-critical Exegesis," in *Taking the Long View: Christian Theology in Historical Perspective* (Oxford: Oxford University Press, 2011), 3–14.

literal-historical and literal-prophetic—both upheld the historicity of God's interaction with human beings in their own time and affirmed that these same events pointed beyond themselves to some greater spiritual fulfillment. Thus the historical plane on which flesh-and-blood human beings live their lives need not be compromised to accommodate the grander workings of God's saving power. If anything, Lyra's method enhances the significance of lived human existence by firmly establishing its meaning within a larger eternal horizon; it can be fully what it is (literal-historical) and yet be caught up in something greater and everlasting (literal-prophetic).

Of course, what made Holy Scripture unique among all texts for the medieval exegetes was precisely that, beyond the human author, there remained the divine author, who did intend the many spiritual senses of the text to be recovered. One recalls that Augustine maintained that the Holy Spirit, working through human authors, will have foreseen the multiple meanings that later exegetes find in a single passage. Such variety would not be regarded as reason for consternation, as though the present exegete were forced to choose just one "valid" meaning; rather, it testified to the fecundity of the sacred text. Nor, then, is there any reason to think that the heuristic task must be concluded this side of eternity; the search for still more meanings embedded within the text remains open ended.

We have seen that Thomas Aquinas picked up Augustine's mantle when he affirmed that the literal sense of the text ought to be equated with the sense that the author intended. In the case of Holy Scripture, we are dealing with a divine author who comprehends all meaning within his intellect simultaneously. Such confidence in the Holy Spirit, as the principal author of Scripture, serves to liberate human expositors in their efforts to break open the text. Each succeeding generation of exegetes can come to the sacred text anew, confident that their own discoveries may indeed be genuine so long as they cohere with a passage's given context and the larger scope of Scripture itself, which consistently promotes charity.

Here I propose that if we want to make the case for the continuing relevance of medieval hermeneutics for contemporary readers, we will find a trustworthy guide in the twentieth-century philosopher Hans-Georg Gadamer. First, the medieval exegetes would have found that Gadamer correctly grasped the profoundly relational character of their own hermeneutical project. According to Gadamer, readers are active participants in the determination of a text's meaning; they bring to the text their own experiences and expectations, which help to form the meaning of what they are reading. Yet even as readers come to the text in this way, they remain open to the text's effective power to re-form them as readers, to impress itself on the imagination and thereby evoke new understandings and new expectations. According to Gadamer, "A person who is trying to understand a text is always projecting. He projects a meaning for the text as a whole as soon as some initial meaning emerges in the text. . . . Working out this fore-projection, which is constantly revised in terms of what emerges as he penetrates into the meaning, is understanding what is there."[2]

This process bears some striking similarities to what we have seen in the program laid out by Hugh of St. Victor. Hugh advised his students that sacred reading is an engagement with divine wisdom that serves to illuminate readers so that they may in turn come to know themselves. We saw that reading the sacred text was, for Hugh, a vital component in the process of human restoration. Reading was envisioned by Hugh as a cyclical process as re-formed readers return again to the text, their perspective having been shaped by their last encounter, such that they read the text ever anew. Not only is the reader constantly evolving, but one might also say that the text itself does not remain static. The sacred text never says precisely the same thing twice, because its meaning is always being rediscovered, redetermined, by the very reader whom it is transforming with each encounter. For Hugh and his fellow Victorines, the text is alive inasmuch as it is an expression of a living person, the eternal Word, who is constantly revealing further mysteries to readers and thereby changing them in the process.

Gadamer, for his part, was also pushing back against what he regarded as the self-satisfaction of the Enlightenment's sophisticated reader who had been liberated from the burdensome traditions that had constrained previous generations. What the Enlightenment had missed, of course, was its own cultural and historical conditioning; it too operated from a particular perspective that was no freer of prejudices than the ones over which it claimed superiority. This is not merely an ironic situation, however, for a crucial element of hermeneutical methodology is lost when tradition is factored out of the equation. As Gadamer observes, "The fundamental prejudice of the Enlightenment is the prejudice against prejudice itself, which denies tradition its power. The history of ideas shows that not until the Enlightenment does the concept of prejudice acquire the negative connotation familiar today."[3]

As we have seen, by the late second century the church had recognized that there would have to be some basic standard, some measure, by which competing interpretations of Scripture could be judged. Hence the appeal by Irenaeus and Tertullian to the "rule of faith" (*regula fidei*), a concise

---

2. Hans-Georg Gadamer, *Truth and Method*, trans. Joel Weinsheimer and Donald Marshall, rev. ed. (New York: Continuum, 2004), 269.
3. Ibid., 272–73.

summary of orthodox teaching that was grounded in Scripture itself. The rule functioned as a sort of hermeneutical key that laid out a perspective (*skopos*) of the whole divine economy, thereby allowing for the interpretation of individual texts against this larger coherent narrative. To make sense of these texts, therefore, the reader had to first approach Scripture from a particular vantage point; certain parameters had to be already in place. So it is that to think with, and within, the tradition is not a denial of human freedom or a sacrifice of human reason. Rather, the patristic and medieval exegetes recognized that tradition provides the necessary presuppositions that free the reader to make sense of the text.

Hence the modern rallying cry that one must "think for oneself," although laudable insofar as it implies intellectual rigor, seems to overlook the reality that thinking does not take place in the abstract. It is always undertaken by human beings living in, and conditioned by, their own historical situation. Thus, as Gadamer points out, the notion of unfettered reason free to pursue the truth apart from the constraints of culture and tradition is simply untenable.[4] The medieval commentators would have concurred in the main with this assessment. They were at once aware of their own finite grasp of the eternal mysteries that continue to unfold, such that all of their exegetical conclusions remained provisional, and aware that the conclusions they did reach were formed within a coherent narrative that provided the stability necessary to comprehend the texts they were reading.

Along these lines, and certainly in keeping with the medieval vision, was Gadamer's observation that authority, far from functioning as some sort of intellectual prison, can actually serve as a "source of truth." When correctly understood, authority is not primarily a matter of obedience, Gadamer insists, but of knowledge. By acknowledging the legitimacy of authority in one's own determination of meaning, the reader recognizes that another may possess superior insight into some matter and thus is worthy of being heard.[5] Gadamer therefore emphasized tradition's role in forming our anticipatory understanding of the text whose meaning we seek. We are not, however, bound to make of the text whatever previous generations have already laid down. Rather, we ourselves are part of that living tradition, which is by no means static, but constantly evolving.[6] We have seen ample evidence of this attitude across the centuries covered in this book. The most obvious example might be the *Glossa Ordinaria* produced originally at the Laon school but then

4. Ibid., 277.
5. Ibid., 280–81.
6. Ibid., 293.

expanded in succeeding generations. This careful gathering of patristic and early medieval comments, far from narrowing the possibilities of further commentary, actually served as a springboard for still more discovery. The Gloss facilitated active engagement with the biblical text; it was a sort of conversation partner for the exegete. The medieval commentators recognized that the works of the fathers, while certainly authoritative, were not to be taken as the last word on the matter, but rather as guides to facilitate further exploration. Hence these exegetes struck the balance that Gadamer commends, although they did so always cognizant of a yet greater divine authority, who holds the entire tradition in place. They therefore found a certain level of security in their work amid the limitations of their finite circumstances. Their own quest for meaning may indeed remain open ended, and thus provisional, but these masters of the sacred page remained confident that there nevertheless exists some lasting meaning that will not be lost.

Index of Scripture and Other Ancient and Medieval Sources

Index of Modern Authors

Index of Subjects

Abbey of St. Victor, 4
Abimelech, 228
accessus ad auctores, 64, 112, 146, 148, 192, 210
action, 143
affection, 17
affectus, 203
Alan of Lille, 205n24
Albert the Great, 266, 267
Alcuin of York, 55, 73, 165
Alexander of Hales, 206, 213, 245n148
Alexandrian school, 3
Alger of Liège, 117
allegory, 1, 2, 7–8
  in Bede, 44–46
  in Bruno, 92–93
  in Cassian, 33–34
  in Claude of Turin, 64
  in Diodore, 18
  in Gregory, 27–29, 30
  in Haimo, 74–75
  in Henry of Ghent, 226
  in Hugh of St. Victor, 143–44, 146, 147, 149
  in Origen, 10
  in Peter Comestor, 171–72
  in Richard of St. Victor, 157
  in Robert Grosseteste, 204
  in Robert of Melun, 178
  in Stephen Langton, 191–92, 194

  in Theodore, 19
  in Wyclif, 248–49
Ambrose, 51, 56, 152
Ambrosiaster, 82, 97
amor, 131, 133, 135
Anacletus (pope), 270
anagogical sense, 93, 146, 257
  in Bede, 44–45
  in Cassian, 33–34
  in Langton, 194
  in Peter Comestor, 172
analogical sense, 257
Anastasius (pope), 274
Andrew of St. Victor, 153–56, 158, 159, 205, 220
angelic language, 119–20
angel of the Lord, 121
angels, bodies of, 120
Anselm of Canterbury, 81, 98–99, 214, 245n148
Anselm of Laon, 163, 165–68
antichrist, 212
Antiochene tradition, 3, 17–19
Antiochus Epiphanes, 212
apocrypha, 37, 38, 60, 152, 208
Apostles' Creed, 61
apostolic office, 93
Aquila, 35
Arator, 88
Arians, 9, 115
Aristotle, 73, 74, 82–83, 90, 197, 202, 210, 216, 223,

  230, 238, 243, 244, 246, 250, 253
Arius, 261
ark of Noah, 149–52
ark of the Lord, 201
artisan (artifiex), 223
ascent, 127, 143
aspectus, 203
Athanasius, 9
auctor, 221
auctoritas, 221
Augustine, 3, 19–26, 41, 42, 43, 48, 50, 51, 56, 58, 60, 61, 64, 69, 114, 137, 142, 145, 152, 168, 178, 180, 202, 208, 209n36, 214, 224, 225n98, 228, 231, 231n115, 233n121, 238, 245, 246, 257, 258, 268, 271, 282
Augustinians, 204
aula, 196–97, 206
author (auctor), 215, 221, 223, 247
authorial intention, 23, 145, 247
authority as source of truth, 284

bachelors of theology, 195–96
Bacon, Roger, 171
Basilides, 48